SOLUTIONS MANUAL

to accompany

THE ANALYSIS AND USE OF FINANCIAL STATEMENTS

THIRD EDITION

Gerald I. White, CFA
Grace & White, Inc.

Ashwinpaul C. Sondhi, Ph.D.
A.C. Sondhi & Associates, LLC.

Dov Fried, Ph.D.
Stern School of Business
New York University

WILEY

JOHN WILEY & SONS, INC.

To order books or for customer service call 1-800-CALL-WILEY (225-5945).

ISBN 0-471-37593-4

Printed in the United States of America

1 0 9 8 7 6 5

Printed and bound by Courier Kendallville, Inc.

CONTENTS

NOTE: ALL PROBLEMS ARE RATED BY ESTIMATED SOLUTION TIME;
SEE BEGINNING OF EACH SOLUTION SET AS WELL AS EACH SOLUTION:
{S}   LESS THAN 15 MINUTES
{M}   15 TO 40 MINUTES
{L}   LONGER THAN 40 MINUTES

ESTIMATED SOLUTION TIME FOR EACH CASE IS PROVIDED AT THE
BEGINNING OF EACH CASE SOLUTION.

Chapter 1 - Solutions

Overview:

Problem Length	Problem #s
{S}	1 to 23
[M]	24

1.{S}(i) Short-term lenders are concerned primarily with liquidity. Accounting standards would focus primarily on near-term cash flows and might include cash flow forecasting. Performance reporting would likely emphasize cash-based measures.

(ii) Long-term equity investors are primarily concerned with the earning power of the firm. Income measurement would be the focus of standards for such users.

(iii) Tax authorities are concerned with the generation of tax revenue. Accounting standards might limit the ability of firms to shift income from one period to another and place strict controls on the recognition and timing (accrual) of both revenues and deductible expenditures.

(iv) Corporate managers seek to control their reported earnings, to cast the best possible light on their stewardship. Accounting standards set by managers would be highly flexible, with little supplementary information and footnote disclosure.

2.{S} The matching principle states that revenues should be matched with the expenses that generate them. As the revenues and related expenditures may be incurred in different accounting periods, accrual accounting is required to recognize them in the same period.

3.{S} The going concern assumption states that the enterprise will continue operating in a normal fashion. This assumption permits financial statements to record assets and liabilities based on the cash flows that they will generate as the firm operates. If this assumption were absent, all assets and liabilities would have to be evaluated on a liquidation basis. Accrual accounting could not be used, as the assumption that expenditures would produce future revenues could no longer be made.

4.{S}Public companies must provide current investors with detailed financial statements, mandated by the FASB and the SEC. Because of SEC filing requirements, annual and quarterly financial data are publicly available to potential investors as well. Private companies may not prepare audited financial data. When audited financial statements are prepared, they will lack some disclosures (e.g., earnings per share) and certain SEC-mandated data (such as the management discussion and analysis). In addition, these statements may not be made available to potential investors.

5.{S}All public companies in the United States are required to issue financial statements whose form and content are determined by the FASB after much public debate. The SEC oversees this process and supplements these standards with additional disclosure requirements. As U. S. GAAP have an investor and user orientation, they require detailed disclosures. Financial statements issued by non-U.S. firms follow local (in some cases, IASB) accounting standards, with less disclosure. Local standards reflect legal and political requirements and often do not have the same investor protection objective as in the United States. Foreign firms generally do not provide quarterly reports; semi-annual reporting is the norm.

6.{S}The FASB sets accounting standards for all audited financial statements prepared under U.S. GAAP. The SEC has jurisdiction over all public companies. Given the overlapping jurisdiction, the SEC generally relies on the FASB to set standards but supplements those standards with additional disclosure requirements deemed necessary to inform and protect investors in public companies.

7.{S}The balance sheet includes only those economic events that qualify as assets and liabilities. As accounting standards define, in effect, assets and liabilities they determine which economic events are accounted for and which are ignored. Events ignored (such as many contracts) are excluded from the process of preparing financial statements. The recognition rules also influence managers' decisions regarding the form of contractual agreements used to acquire assets and incur liabilities, thereby affecting the preparation of financial statements.

8.{S}Liabilities represent the assets of the firm funded by trade and financial creditors. Equity represents the permanent capital of the firm, and is the residual after all liabilities have been satisfied. Thus the distinction between liabilities and equity is the difference between prior claims and permanent capital. Misclassification will over- or understate the firm's reported debt and the degree of leverage or financial risk.

9.{S}Historical cost is more reliable as it reflects actual past transactions. Market values are less reliable as they may require assumptions and estimates. However, general inflation and specific price changes make historical costs less useful (relevant) as time passes. Market values always have relevance as they represent the current value of the firm's resources. The nature of the markets (liquidity, volatility, and transparency) affects the reliability of the values reported.

10.{S} Contra accounts are deductions from asset or liability accounts that accumulate valuation or other adjustments (such as accumulated depreciation) and reduce the asset or liability account to its "net" amount. Adjunct accounts accumulate certain adjustments outside the historical cost framework (such as fair value adjustments for marketable securities under SFAS 115) and other adjustments (for example, premiums and discounts on debt issues). Adjunct accounts are often reported separately.

11.{S}Revenues and expenses result from the firm's operating activities; gains and losses result from valuation and other non-operating events. The latter are peripheral to the normal activities of the firm and, therefore, should be separated for analytic purposes.

12.{S} Comprehensive income includes all changes in equity other than transactions with stockholders. It encompasses operating earnings, "non-recurring" items, valuation adjustments, and the cumulative effect of accounting changes. As it includes all changes in stockholders' equity (excluding transactions with owners), comprehensive income is more complete than "income from continuing operations" (most useful for earnings forecasting).

13. {S}Recurring income refers to income from continuing operations, the best measure of the operating profits of the firm for that time period, and therefore the best base for forecasting and valuation. Non-recurring items are unusual and/or infrequent in nature, and usually result from non-operating factors.

14. {S}The classification of cash flows into three categories highlights their differing natures. Cash from operations reports the cash generated or used by the firm's operating activities. Cash for investment measures the outflow for investments in capacity, for acquisitions, or for long-term investments. Cash from financing indicates the source (debt or equity) of any financing required by the firm as well as distributions to preferred and common stockholders.

   These classifications should be viewed over time as indicators of the firm's liquidity and solvency. The relationship among these classifications is especially important.

15. {S}Footnotes are an integral part of the financial statements and are audited. They supply details that augment financial statement data (e.g. employee benefit plan data). Supplementary schedules may be included within the financial statements (e.g. oil and gas disclosures) but may not be audited.

16. {S}The Management Discussion and Analysis is intended to explain changes and trends in reported income statement, balance sheet, and cash flow items and therefore help financial statement users to interpret these financial statements. The MD&A should discuss trends, including those expected to continue in the future. This discussion should aid the prediction of future cash flows and earnings.

17. {S} Global accounting standards offer the possibility of comparability, as all companies would be required to prepare financial standards using the same accounting methods.

    There may also be the following disadvantages:
    (i) Lack of comparability if there is no body empowered to enforce uniform application of global standards.
    (ii) Loss of the information provided by reconciliations from one set of accounting standards to another, which sometimes highlight important aspects of a firm's operations.
    (iii) Different economic and social structures may require differing accounting standards. For example, in an environment where financing comes primarily from banks rather than through issuance of shares, accounting standards would be *appropriately* geared to the needs of creditors rather than equityholders.

18. {S} (i) The opinion should report any changes in accounting principles used and may refer to the footnote providing additional information on the change.

    (ii) Changes in accounting estimates are <u>not</u> referred to in the auditor's opinion.

    (iii) The auditor's report must describe uncertainties when they are material to the firm's financial position.

    (iv) While the auditor's opinion provides reasonable assurance that there are no material errors in the financial statements, it is not a guarantee against error or even fraud.

    Statement on Auditing Standards (SAS) 82 (1997), requires auditors to assess the risk of financial statement fraud.

19. {S}a. Without knowledge of the effects of accounting changes, the analyst may draw incorrect conclusions about trends within the enterprise over time. Comparisons with other companies may also be made incorrectly if differences in accounting methods or the effects of accounting changes are ignored.

    b. Changes in accounting methods should be highlighted in the auditor's opinion to inform financial statement users that year-to-year comparability is absent. The accounting changes that Roche adopted in 2000 have significant effects on reported data.

20. {S} The preparer gathers financial data, chooses accounting principles and estimates, and assembles the data into financial statements using those methods and estimates. The auditor examines the financial statements for errors, and checks that the accounting methods and assumptions are permissible under GAAP and whether they have been applied consistently over time.

21. {S} Companies generally prepare financial statements using the accounting principles of their home country. When selling securities in a foreign jurisdiction, they may be required to prepare supplementary financial statements using the accounting standards of that country. The cost and inconvenience of this extra work may dissuade the firm from selling securities in that country, thus depriving that country's investors of the opportunity to invest.

    On the other hand, investors must choose between that firm's securities and those of home country firms using local accounting principles. If the foreign firm uses different accounting principles, investors may make poor investment decisions because of their inability to separate real differences between firms from differences caused by alternative accounting principles.

22. {S}a. Because the probability of loss is so low (less than one in ten thousand), Bonnywill will report no loss. If a fire occurs, the firm will then accrue the estimated loss.

    b. An alternative method would accrue the expected value of the loss, computed by multiplying the number of units sold by the expected loss per unit. The result would be 10,000 x .00009 x $100,000 = $90,000.

23. {S} a. For firm A the probability of loss is remote (.3%) so that no liability should be recognized. If an accident occurs, the firm would recognize a liability equal to the expected loss.

b. Firm B expects to have 10 workers' compensation claims each year (10,000/1,000) with a loss of $10,000 per claim. Thus firm B should accrue $100,000 per year. The difference from firm A is that the employee population is large enough to make the loss predictable.

24. {M} a. Note 5 of the Roche 2000 financial statements states that CHF1,282 million of the charge was paid in 1999. The same amount is shown within cash flows from operating activities.

b. The remaining amount is included in Provisions (see Roche note 26). There is no information as to whether it is in the current or non-current provisions.

c. The remaining provision will be included in cash flows from operating activities when cash is paid.

d. Assuming that the price fixing that led to the settlement was confined to the vitamin business, the settlement can be viewed as a nonoperating item that should reduce the valuation of Roche shares dollar-for-dollar rather than being deducted from the income used to value the shares.

e. However, there are two other arguments. One is that the settlement may have damaged the vitamin business, reducing its value and, therefore, reducing the value of the entire firm. The second argument is that Roche's business reputation may have been harmed, resulting in a lower value for the firm. [*Authors' note*: Roche announced an agreement to sell its vitamin division in September 2002.]

Case 1-1 - Solution

Estimated time to complete this case is one hour.

1. While Bristol-Myers (BMY) did not report any accrual for breast implant litigation in 1992, the footnote did warn investors that a large potential liability might exist. When such disclosures are made, financial statement users must make their own evaluation of the possible outcome.

2. Because BMY retained the primary liability to pay claims, the expected insurance recovery was shown as a long-term asset, rather than as an offset against the liability. However the 1993 and 1998 income statement charges were reduced by the expected insurance recovery.

3. Exhibit 1CS-1 shows the estimated cash flow effects for each year, computed from the change in the balance sheet liability and the change in the balance sheet asset:
   Cash outflow =
   Net charge (pretax) – change in net product liability
   For 1993, cash outflow = $352 [$750 – $398]

4. Exhibit 1CS-1 calculates adjusted net earnings for each year. The adjustment is equal to the actual after-tax cash flow less the income statement charge.

   For 1993, for example, [.65 x $(352)] – ($488) = $259

5. As shown in Exhibit 1CS-1, adjusted earnings increase significantly in 1993 to 1995, as the income statement charges exceeded net cash outflows. In 1996, 1997, and 1999 however, adjusted earnings are significantly reduced as there were substantial cash outflows and no income statement charge. Total earnings over the entire period (1993 – 2000) are virtually unchanged but the growth rate (of adjusted versus reported earnings) is reduced. By taking large charges in the early years, the company established a lower base for future growth.

6. The 1993 to 1995 restatements increase earnings and equity. Without actual stockholders' equity data, the effect on ROE cannot be determined. However the higher equity base, and lower earnings in 1996 and 1997 clearly reduce ROE for those years. The higher equity base would decrease ROE for later years as well.

Exhibit 1CS-1

	1993	1994	1995	1996	1997	1998	1999	2000
Cash flow computation								
Balance sheet:								
Net balance sheet liability	$ 470	$ 868	$1,386	$ 978	$ 417	$ 598	$ 114	$ (76)
Change in net liability	470	398	518	(408)	(561)	181	(712)	38
Cash flows:								
For product liability	(30)	(384)	(441)	(514)	(795)	(715)	(767)	(168)
From insurance recovery	-	32	9	106	234	196	55	206
3. Net cash flow	$ 30)	$(352)	$(432)	$ 408	$(561)	$ 519)	$(712)	$ 38
Income statement adjustment								
Net charge (after-tax)	(310)	(488)	(590)	-	-	(433)	-	-
Net cash flow (after-tax)	(20)	(229)	(281)	(265)	(365)	(337)	(463)	25
Adjustment	$ 291	$ 259	$ 309	$ 265	$(365)	$ 96	$(463)	$ 25
4. Adjusted net earnings	1,987	1,801	1,826	2,219	2,379	2,846	3,326	4,121
5. % change from reported	17%	17%	20%	-11%	-13%	3%	-12%	1%

7. Using the data in Exhibit 1CS-1, the total cash outflow through the year 2000 was approximately $3 billion, or approximately $2 billion after-tax. With the benefit of hindsight, this amount should be the charge against 1992 income as that was the year when the problem surfaced. If that amount had been expensed, BMY would have reported a loss for 1992, but higher earnings in the years (1993, 1994, 1995, 1998) when charges were taken. The 1992 charge would have reduced equity, increasing ROE in subsequent years (even those years without charges).

   Ideally, however, the charge should have been recognized during the years when the product was sold. This treatment would match the cost of product liability with the revenues from that product's sales. Had BMY known about the future liability, and accrued the ultimate payment amounts during the period the product was sold, profitability would have been lower in those years but higher in the years (1993, 1994, 1995, 1998) when charges were taken. The effect on later years would be the same as accrual in 1992.

8. Bristol-Myers probably would have been better off taking the charge of $2 billion (computed in part 7) in 1992, for the following reasons:

   a. Future earnings would have been unaffected and reported ROE would have been higher.

   b. The company would have avoided the loss of management credibility that often accompanies repeated adjustments to loss accruals.

   c. The company would have argued that the charge was a nonoperating event that should be ignored when valuing the firm's shares.

   The disadvantage would be a reported loss for 1992, which might have affected investor confidence in the company. For companies with significant debt, a large reported loss might result in violation of debt covenants (see chapter 10).

Chapter 2 - Solutions

Overview:
Problem Length   *Problem #s*
{S}   1, 2, 4 - 11, 15, 16, and 18 - 20
{M}   3, 12 - 14, 17,   and 21 - 23

1.{S}(i)   When the product is a commodity with a known price and liquid market.

(ii) When collection is assured because the risk of non-payment can be estimated.

(iii)When collection is uncertain because the risk of non-payment cannot be estimated.

2.{S}a.   (All data in $ millions)
Under the completed contract method, neither revenue nor pre-tax income would be reported until the project is completed. When the project has been completed, at the end of 2002, LASI Construction would report revenues of $3.0 and pretax income of $0.6 (revenues of $3.0 minus costs of $2.4).

Under the percentage-of-completion method, revenues and pretax income must be reported each year as follows:

Year	Cumulative % Completion	Cumulative Revenue	Current Period Revenue	Current Period Expense	Pretax Income
2000	0.9/2.4 = 37.5%	$1.125	$1.125	$0.900	$0.225
2001	1.7/2.4 = 70.8%	2.125	1.000	0.800	0.200
2002	2.4/2.4= 100.0%	3.000	0.875	0.700	0.175
Total			$3.000	$2.400	$0.600

b.   Computation of construction in progress and advance billings (in $ millions)

	Percentage -of-Completion	Completed Contract
Costs incurred	$ 0.900	$ 0.900
Profit recognized	0.225	0.000
Construction in progress	$ 1.125	$ 0.900
Advance billings	(1.000)	(1.000)
Net asset (liability)	$ 0.125	$(0.100)

Balance Sheet on December 31, 2000 (in $ millions)

	Percentage-of-Completion	Completed Contract
Assets		
Cash	$ 0.100	$ 0.100
Construction in progress (net)	0.125	0.000
Total assets	$ 0.225	$ 0.100
Liabilities and equity		
Advance billings (net)	$ 0.000	$ 0.100
Retained earnings	0.225	0.000
Total liabilities and equity	$ 0.225	$ 0.100

c.   Effect on 2001 revenue and pretax income of a change in estimated costs to complete

There is no change in 2001 revenues and pretax income (both are $0.000) under the completed contract method because no revenue or income can be recognized prior to completion.

Under the percentage-of-completion method, both revenue and pretax income change and are computed as follows:

Year	Cumulative % Completion	Cumulative Revenue	Current Period Revenue	Current Period Expense	Pretax Income
2001	1.7/**2.5**= **68.0%**	**$2.040**	**$0.915**	$0.800	**$0.115**

Note: All changes are in bold. The change in estimated costs to complete raises the total expected costs to complete to $2.500 from the previous estimate of $2.400. Costs incurred at the end of Year 2001 are $1.700 ($0.900 in 2000 and $0.800 in 2001) because we have assumed that the incremental costs ($0.100) will be incurred in Year 2002. Cumulative revenue of $2.040 must be recognized at the end of 2001; since we recognized $1.125 in revenue in 2000, the difference ($2.040-$1.125) or $0.915 must be recognized in 2001. The effect of the change is recognized in Year 2001 and Year 2000 results are not changed.

3.{M}a. Because of the highly uncertain life of software products, technological obsolescence, and the possibility of refunds or other concessions, software revenue recognition standards include a presumption that extended payment terms render the sales price (fees) not fixed or determinable. Any extended payment terms beyond the normal payment terms may indicate that the fees are not fixed or determinable.

In general, a license fee is not considered fixed or determinable if, at the inception of the transaction, a significant portion of the fee is due more than twelve months after delivery or after the expiration of the license. In practice, 10% or more is considered "significant." When the fee is not fixed or determinable at the outset, revenue must be recognized as payments become due, assuming all other revenue recognition criteria are met.

(i) No revenue can be recognized for the fiscal year ending January 31, 2001 because the fee is not fixed or determinable when the product is delivered.

(ii) $600,000 would be recognized as revenue for the fiscal year ending January 31, 2002 because that amount is due 30 days after delivery on January 30, 2001. The remaining $400,000 would be reported as revenue for the fiscal year ending January 31, 2003 because it is due 13 months after delivery and falls outside the fiscal year ended January 31, 2002.

(iii) No revenue can be recognized in the fiscal year ending January 31, 2001 if the licensing period begins on March 1, 2001. The customer cannot use the product prior to licensing and the seller has not provided any services prior to the onset of the licensing period.

b. Since Jasmine, Inc. is not involved (not at risk) in the financing arrangements, revenue can be recognized on receipt of payments, assuming all other revenue recognition criteria are met.

c. There is no change in Jasmine's ability to recognize revenue if it transfers, without recourse, the rights to receive payments to an unrelated third party because the presumption that the fee is not fixed and determinable is not overcome. The transfer of payments does not change the substance of the transaction between Jasmine and its customer.

(i) If Jasmine's participation in the financing arrangement increases the probability that the customer or the financing party will receive a refund or a concession, the fee is not fixed and determinable.

Where participation indicates that Jasmine (1) does not have the intent or the ability to enforce the original payment terms absent the financing or (2) exhibits a pattern of amending or tailoring payment terms to the financing plan, the fee is not fixed and determinable. In these circumstances, revenue must be recognized as the customer's payments become due and payable to the financing party (and all other revenue recognition criteria are met).

(ii) Payments received from the customer or the financing party in advance of revenue recognition must be recorded as a liability, deferred revenue. Although there is no difference in the cash reported on the balance sheet, the deferred revenue increases the liability. Revenue (and consequently, income) may be recognized later on the income statement.

The presumption that the fee is not fixed or determinable given Jasmine's participation in customer financing may be overcome if Jasmine can demonstrate that such arrangements are part of its standard business practice (similar financing arrangements with substantially similar terms) and that it does not grant refunds or concessions to customers or the financing parties.

4.{S}a. The retailer's policy results in the recognition of revenue prior to delivery, that is, before it has been earned - a violation of the basic revenue recognition criteria. U.S. GAAP does not permit recognition of revenue prior to delivery.

b. Revenue recognition must be delayed until delivery, making reported revenue, cost of goods sold, accrual of tax expense, and income lower than under the previous method (assuming rising sales). Inventory balances will remain on the balance sheet for a longer period and increase the number of days inventory is on hand. In the period the change is first reported, revenue, cost of goods sold, tax expense, income, and retained earnings (and therefore, stockholders' equity) will be lower and ending inventory will be higher than that previously reported by the company. If we assume that the timing of cash receipts and payments for inputs are unchanged, reported cash flow from operations will be unchanged.

c. Monthly sales data based on orders written are a useful indicator of market trends and an important input for forecasting and valuation models. However sales data need to be carefully evaluated to ensure continuing relevance and correlation with future revenue, income, and cash flow.

5.{S}a. Under the completed contract method, reported earnings are more volatile because all recognition is delayed until completion. As a result, net income is reported only in periods when projects are completed, and depends on the number and profitability of projects completed in each period.

b. With many contracts, some averaging occurs so that the volatility of firm results is not as great (although it is still greater than under the percentage of completion method).

c. When a firm has relatively few projects and uses the completed contract method, reported revenues and net income are highly variable. The volatility makes forecasting extremely difficult. With a greater number of contracts, volatility is reduced, and forecasting is easier. The percentage of completion method, by reporting revenues and net income as earned over the life of the project, provides better data regarding the operations of the firm. However, reported cash flows are not affected by the choice of accounting method.

6.{S}(i) Under the completed contract method, no revenues or cost-of-goods-sold are recognized until completion; both are lower during the project but higher in the period when completion takes place. Their trend is highly volatile. Under the percentage of completion method, revenues and COGS are recognized as projects progress; they are higher during the project but lower at completion. The trend will reflect the overall level of activity and will be less volatile.

(ii) Earnings recognition follows the same pattern as revenue recognition, as explained in (i), assuming that estimates of project profitability prove to be accurate. Under the percentage of completion method, revised estimates of profitability increase the volatility of income as the past over- or underaccrual of income must be offset in the period of revision.

(iii) No difference between methods; operating cash flows are not affected by the choice of accounting method.

(iv) Accounts receivable will always be higher under the percentage of completion method, as that method recognizes revenue sooner, creating accounts receivable. Total current assets will also be higher as the higher level of accounts receivable under the percentage of completion method more than offsets the higher level of inventory under the completed contract method. Long-term assets are not affected by the choice of method.

7.{S}

Account	Part a	Part b
Contracts in process	This account reflects the costs actually incurred and the proportionate share of profits on those contracts for which the amount of revenue recognized exceeds payments received from customers	The account is similar to accounts receivable that also reflects the excess of revenue recognized over cash payments received.
Advance billings	This account reflects those contracts for which payments received exceed revenue recognized.	The account is similar to advances from customers.

c. The company most likely uses the percentage-of-completion method. Under that method, the **contracts in process** account includes estimated earnings on uncompleted contracts, making it larger than under the completed contract method. As a result, it is more likely that some or all contracts will have an excess of contracts in process over advance billings, as illustrated in Exhibit 2-1B on page 42.

8.{S}a. (i) and (ii)

2001:   Revenue = 20% x $6 million = $1.2 million

Costs incurred = 20% x $4.5 million = $.9 million.

(Income recognized is $.3 million difference.)

2002:   Revenue = 60% x $6 million = $3.6 - $1.2 = $2.4 million

Costs incurred (cumulative) = 60% x $4.8 million = $2.88 million. As 2001 recognition was $.9 million, 2002 recognition must be $ 1.98 million ($2.88 - $0.9).

(Income recognized is $.42 million difference, making cumulative recognition $.72 million for two years.)

b. There should be no effect; expenditures that do not contribute to the completion of the project do not affect revenue or income under the percentage of completion method.

9.{S}(i) Recognition of revenue earlier than justified by GAAP accelerates the timing of recognition of accounts receivable, overstating the amount of both the current and total assets on the balance sheet.

(ii) Inventories would be understated because cost of goods sold is recognized early. Both current and total assets would be understated. For profitable transactions, the early recognition of accounts receivable will exceed the effect of lower inventories on both current and total assets, resulting in overstated net operating assets or working capital.

(iii) Earlier recognition increases reported revenues.

(iv) Operating profit (assuming profitable sales) would be higher as a result of higher revenues.

(v) Stockholders' equity would be higher because profit is recognized earlier than justified by GAAP.

10.{S}a.

	Able	Baker	Charlie	David
Sales	$ 170,000[1]	$ 160,000[2]	$ 100,000	$ 50,000[3]
COGS	85,000	80,000	50,000	25,000
Net income	$ 85,000	$ 80,000	$ 50,000	$ 25,000

[1] Sales = goods shipped + inventory + backorders, all measured at selling price.
[2] Sales = goods shipped + inventory
[3] Cash collected = sales - accounts receivable

b. & c. CFO and cash balances will be identical; revenue and net income differences reflect only the choice of accounting method, not any economic differences among the companies.

11.{S}a. (i) & (ii)
> The patterns of income and revenue recognition are identical. Therefore, the answers to a(i) and a(ii) are identical.
>
> To maximize the present value of the bonus, you should prefer the method that recognizes revenue (and income) earlier. Thus, you should prefer the percentage of completion method to the completed contract method.
>
> The pattern of recognition is (1/2, 1/4, 1/4) for the percentage of completion method and (1/3, 1/3, 1/3) for the installment method. Since on a cumulative basis, the percentage of completion method (1/2, 3/4, 1) dominates the installment method (1/3, 2/3, 1) it is preferred.

    (iii) All three methods show identical CFO patterns and you would be indifferent under the third bonus criterion.

b. Over the project's life all three methods generate identical total revenue, income, and CFO. Since payment is made at completion, you are indifferent.

12.{M} This problem provides a good opportunity to discuss the subtleties and implications of revenue and expense recognition criteria.

a. Revenue recognition is predicated on the following two criteria:

(1) Collectibility of cash
(2) Provision of service.

Criterion (1) is satisfied as the license fee is paid in advance.

The focus of the question becomes criterion (2) - provision of service. Some readers will argue that the service is only provided when the games are actually played. Does this argument hold only for the revenues from the *season (game) tickets* themselves and *not to the license fee* - as the former is refundable if games aren't played (e.g., players strike) or if the team "folds." The license fee is presumably nonrefundable no matter what happens. Thus, the question is whether it is reasonable to recognize the full amount of the license fee as revenue immediately.

Consider what would happen if the Raptors did not sell the ticket and license fee separately but rather sold lifetime season tickets - i.e. one payment up front entitled the buyer to attend all games forever without additional payment.

The first issue that would have to be addressed is similar to the above; i.e. what is refundable if games are canceled? If we assume that nothing is refundable then should the team recognize the full amount as revenue immediately, even if no games are played? This would lead to the team recognizing revenues without incurring expenditures in performing the service.

If one argues that revenues should be recognized pro-rata, what is the correct number of years? Remember that the tickets are sold as a "lifetime" right. Finally, if one made the pro-rata argument for this latter case, one would have to argue as to why it is different than the license portion in the case where there is a separate license and season ticket fee.

The correct accounting policy depends on the details of the season ticket plan. If the ticket buyer takes all the risk (the team could fail or be moved to another city) then the earnings process is complete and the license fee can be recognized immediately. If the team retains some risk (e.g. the fee is refundable if the team is sold or moved to another city) then the accounting policy must reflect that risk by deferring some (or all) of the license fee and recognizing it over the estimated life of the agreement. SFAC 7 (see Box 1-1 on page 11 of the text) provides a framework for this policy.

b.   A corporation that purchased the license would have an intangible asset (see chapter 14) with an indefinite life. For accounting purposes, therefore, it should not recognize any expense for the license fee. However, the firm should evaluate the asset annually to ensure that its "indefinite life" estimate remains appropriate. The asset should also be evaluated annually for impairment with reference to its fair value. Assuming a market develops for the license, the fair value can be estimated using the current market prices.

As suggested in the answer to part a, if the license agreement suggests that the license is likely to expire, then amortization over the estimated life would be more appropriate.

c.   In analyzing expected earnings, license fees for a given seat sold are a one-time event. Although licenses for other seats may be sold in future years, as capacity is fixed, in the long run revenues from license fees are nonrecurring. *The long-run earnings potential depends on season ticket sales.*

The license fees, however, provide a valuable input in forecasting future season ticket sales. It is reasonable to assume that (relative to a season ticket holder without a license) there is a greater probability that a licensee will either buy season-tickets themselves or (if they are not interested) they will try to find someone to sell their license to who would be willing to buy season tickets.

Thus, the number of licensees acts as a base or threshold level for anticipated season tickets sold each year. The more licenses sold the higher the expected recurring revenues from season ticket sales.

13.{M}a. The settlement with the Internal Revenue Service (IRS) and the reversal of previous year's writeoffs are not related to the company's 1994 performance. The IRS settlement dates back to a 1985 event and the interest earned thereon is related to the 1985 - 1994 period, not 1994 alone. Similarly, the $49 million reversal of pretax income is a correction of an incorrect estimate made in 1992 and 1993 and certainly does not relate to 1994 performance. If we eliminate these amounts, after tax income would be reduced by $51 million:

Elimination of IRS settlement $ 21 million
Elimination of restructuring reversal*   30
                                             $ 51 million
* From the IRS settlement we estimate tax rate of (1 - $21/$33 =) 38% Therefore, $49 million equals $30 million net of tax)

Adjusted Net Income = $622 - $51 = $571

Note: No adjustment is required for equity as these amounts relate to prior years and they should be incorporated in equity in those previous years.

Adjusted ROE = $\dfrac{\$571}{\$2,902}$ = 19.7%

If these adjustments are made then the "annual incentive award of achieving or exceeding a net income goal" would likely be reduced as net income is reduced by 8% or $51 million. Similarly, the stock options should not be issued as the adjusted ROE of 19.7% is less than 20%.

On the other hand, one might argue that the one time (after-tax) charge of $55 million should also be excluded from 1994 income. Even though the charge was taken in 1994, these charges are for staff reductions and closures to be taken in *future* years and do not reflect current operations. Excluding these charges:

Adjusted net income = $571 + $55 = $ 626
Adjusted 1994 equity = $2,948 + $55 = 3,003
Adjusted average equity = .5 x ($2,855+$3,003)= 2,929

Adjusted ROE = $\dfrac{\$626}{\$2,929}$ = 21.4%

After this adjustment, net income would be higher and ROE would be above the threshold level of 20%, entitling the CEO to the various incentives.

b. These non-recurring charges should be excluded when assessing current performance. The charges (often) reflect expenses of past (or future) years. Moreover, as they are subject to management discretion, they can be used to manipulate both reported performance and performance trends.

However, ignoring them totally raises another problem. These are real costs and management must be held accountable for them. Otherwise, management can "warehouse" and bury such recurring costs on a year-to-year basis and then clean the slate in a series of lump sum "nonrecurring" charges.

This suggests that incentives should perhaps be based on both current performance ignoring noncurrent charges as well as nonrecurring charges using a measure of "average" performance taken over a few years.

c. The best estimate of the level of reported "recurring" profits and ROE would start with this year's "recurring" level of $571 and 19.7%. Given the restructuring, one might expect future profits to increase as future employee costs will be lowered.

However, the *reported* "recurring" levels may not paint an accurate picture of Monsanto's profitability. One must not ignore the fact that Monsanto may be "warehousing" costs and periodically charging them off as "nonrecurring". The firm's profit levels should be adjusted downwards to reflect these periodic non-recurring charges perhaps by averaging the nonrecurring costs over a number of years. These adjusted levels should then be used to forecast future "real" profitability rather than future "reported" profitability.

14.{M}a.& b.

ATT's adjusted income before nonrecurring charges is computed by adding back the non-recurring charges to reported income.

	1991	1992	1993	1994	1995
Revenues	$41.8	$43.0	$43.8	$46.0	$48.5
Percent change		2.67%	1.91%	5.07%	5.34%
Operating income					
Reported	$ 2.7	$ 6.2	$ 6.6	$ 7.4	$ 5.2
Special charges	3.5	0.0	0.0	0.0	3.0
Adjusted	$ 6.2	$ 6.2	$ 6.6	$ 7.4	$ 8.2

	1996	1997	1998	1999	2000
Revenues	$50.5	$51.3	$53.2	$ 62.6	$66.0
Percent change	4.32%	1.53%	3.71%	17.62%	5.40%
Operating income					
Reported	$ 8.8	$ 7.0	$ 7.5	$ 10.9	$ 4.3
Special charges	0.0	0.0	2.5	1.5	7.0
Adjusted	$ 8.8	$ 7.0	$ 10.0	$ 12.4	$ 11.3

Comparing the reported and adjusted operating income, we find that with the exception of the year 1997, the adjusted amounts follow a smoother pattern mirroring that of the revenue stream. The reported amounts however are erratic and, although the trend is upwards, the path is volatile and follows no discernible pattern (see graph on page 15).

c.   If our objective is to forecast earnings power, the adjusted data appear to be more relevant. They follow a smooth trend that is consistent with that of revenues. However, the repetitive nature (the firm reported such charges in five of the ten years of data shown) of AT&T's "non-recurring" restructuring charges indicates that the firm is engaging in smoothing/big bath behavior. The firm is storing costs and periodically charging them to earnings in order to make "recurring" operating income look better. Thus, to analyze AT&T's actual economic performance or future earnings power the non-recurring items must be considered and the reported operating income adjusted to better reflect future earnings power. Over the 10-year period, nonrecurring items totaled $17.5 billion. Charging an average of approximately $1.75 billion to each year results in the "smoothed A" line on the second graph (page 16). It is closer to the pattern implied by revenues than the adjusted operating income.

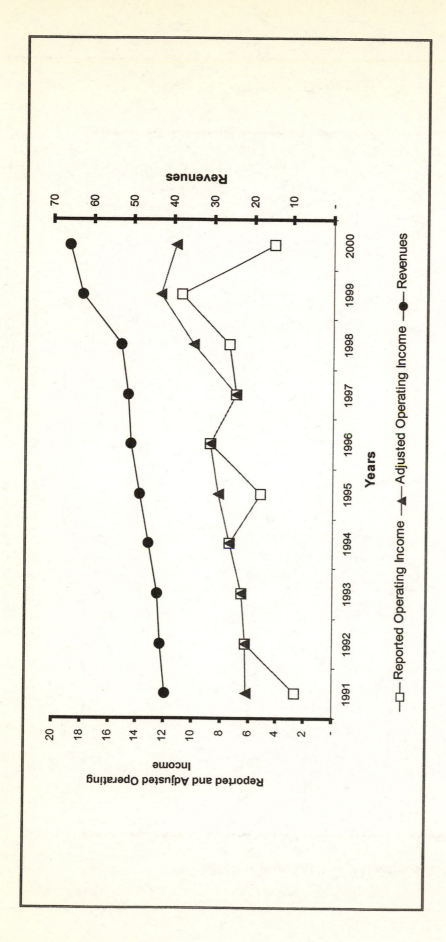

2-15

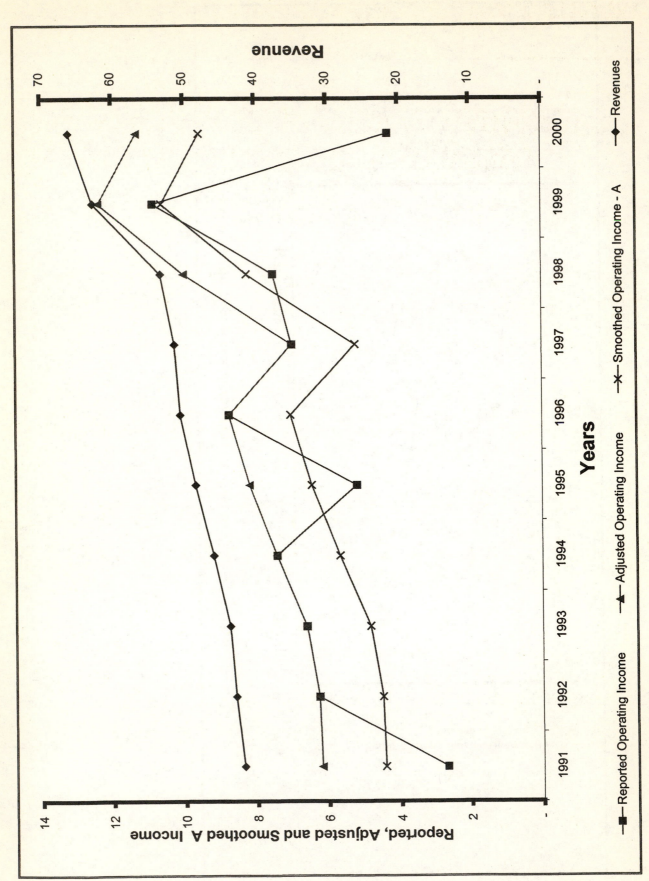

However, in our time series, the first instance of special charges arises in 1991 and the next one occurs in 1995. The analyst should review footnote disclosures and management's discussion of the charges in 1991 and 1995 to determine whether they are related, i.e., do they relate to the same segment, are they similar charges, etc. Assuming that these two announcements are unrelated, we may focus on the 1995 - 2000 period. There we find 4 announcements of special charges (for a total of $14 billion) over the six-year period. When these charges are allocated equally over the six-year period, the revised (smoothed B) data are not highly correlated to the reported revenue data. A glance at the graph below shows that smoothed operating income declined despite an increase in revenue. The analyst should review the financial statements to better understand the operating income reported in 1997 and 2000 in the context of improving revenues.

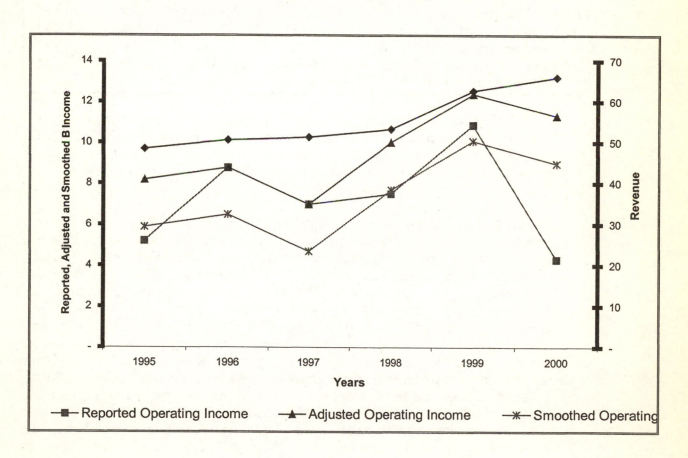

15.{S}a. Amazon.com is an internet retailer of books, music, and other products. The company's description of fulfillment costs shows that these are costs of the primary services it provides to its customers and as such are directly related to and incurred to complete its earnings process. This direct relationship between fulfillment costs and sales strongly suggests that those costs should be treated as a component of cost of sales.

b. Recalculation of Amazon Gross Margin Percentage:

	1997	1998	1999	2000
Net sales	$ 148	$ 610	$1,640	$2,762
Cost of sales	119	476	1,349	2,106
Gross margin	$ 29	$ 134	$ 291	$ 656
Gross margin %	19.6%	22.0%	17.7%	23.8%
Fulfillment costs	$ 12	$ 65	$ 237	$ 415
Adjusted cost of sales*	131	541	1,586	2,521
Adjusted gross margin	17	69	54	241
Adjusted gross margin %	11.5%	11.3%	3.3%	8.7%
* Cost of sales plus fulfillment costs.				

Adjusted gross margins are far lower than those based on reported data. The trend is also different with 2000 adjusted margin well below the level of 1997 and 1998 despite higher reported gross margins.

16.{S} When "pro forma operating loss" excludes some costs, it becomes a misleading indicator of operating performance and future profitability. Some of those costs (e.g., stock-based compensation) are integral and recurring, essential to conducting the continuing operations of the company. The amount and frequency of other excluded costs (amortization of goodwill and other intangibles, impairment-related and other costs) result from acquisitions, technology changes, management decisions and other business or market-related conditions. These costs also result from continuing operations. Their exclusion generates an inflated and misleading measure of the earnings power and cash generating ability of the company and, therefore, its valuation.

17.{M} a.

| In $millions | Years ended June 30 | | | | | |
	1995	1996	1997	1998	1999	2000
Revenues	$5,937	$8,671	$11,936	$15,262	$19,747	$22,956
Unearned revenue deferred during the year	69	983	1,601	3,268	5,877	6,177
Recognition of previously deferred revenue	(54)	(477)	(743)	(1,798)	(4,526)	(5,600)
Revenues assuming no deferral	$5,952	$9,177	$12,794	$16,732	$21,098	$23,533
Growth rates:						
Reported revenue		46.05%	37.65%	27.87%	29.39%	16.25%
Revenues assuming no deferral		54.18%	39.41%	30.78%	26.09%	11.54%

b. (i) 1999 reported revenue (which is reported net of the allowance for returns) was increased by $190 million on adoption of SOP 98-8 and by $250 million due to the change in estimates of returns. By extending the life cycle of Windows, subsequent recognition of previously deferred revenues is delayed, reducing revenue by $90 million. Thus, reported revenue growth is higher than it would have been. Disclosure of the pro forma impact of adoption of SOP 98-9 on prior years would improve our understanding of revenue growth reported in 1999.

The change in estimated returns appears to be the result of a substantive change in the way business is conducted; its impact on future revenue growth will depend on the accuracy of the revised estimates. Because 1999 is the first year of the revision, it may take several years to determine whether the new estimates are a better reflection of the true return rate.

(ii) 2000: The increase in the estimated life cycle of Windows decreased reported revenue in 1999, its impact on 2000 in revenue growth is likely to be small. Future revenue growth will depend more on new sales of Windows (especially of new versions) rather than the recognition of previously deferred sales.

The application of SOP 98-8 and the use of lower estimated return rates will increase revenue growth reported in 2000 as they allow for greater revenue recognition. However, any revision in estimated returns due to unfavorable experience would have reduced reported revenues. The lack of disclosure makes it impossible to determine if this took place.

c. (i) Measurement of revenue growth rates using reported revenue: Microsoft defers revenue for services not yet provided and recognizes this previously deferred revenue over time as those services are provided. When the deferral and subsequent recognition appropriately reflect the earnings process, growth rates based on reported revenue provide reliable and relevant indicators of operating activity and both current and future profitability and are useful inputs to forecasting and valuation models. However, deferral and subsequent recognition rules are management decisions and may reflect smoothing rather than the appropriate recognition of the earnings process. [Note that 2000 revenue growth was higher excluding deferrals.] If management abuses this process, revenue (and profit) may be misleading indicators of firm performance and, ultimately, firm value. Adequate disclosure of the assumptions used would significantly improve the user's ability to evaluate reported growth and improve forecasting and valuation.

(ii) Measurement of revenue growth rates assuming no deferral is equivalent to a cash basis of revenue recognition. When a portion of the sales price will be earned over time, this measure inflates the growth rate. However, rapid technological change and significant competition for products and services provided over time (and after delivery of a base product such as Microsoft's Office Suite of software) may indicate that any deferral is inappropriate.

For example, Microsoft defers a portion of the cash received for the use of Internet browser technology and updates. Because of competition and technological change and the fact that browser technology is freely available, an analyst should question any deferral related to that product. Maintenance and updates are provided over time as well as being sold separately; some portion of the purchase price should be deferred. In this case, however, analysts should regularly evaluate the amounts deferred, period of the deferral, and the subsequent recognition method. Such analysis would require adequate disclosures.

18.{S}a. Although (on completion of training) Gigondas.com incurs no incremental costs to provide service, no revenue should be recognized on completion of the initial setup because the economic substance of the contract calls for payment for services delivered over time. Therefore, revenue should be recognized over the annual term of the contract as services are provided.

b. Refundable membership fees should also be recognized ratably over the term of the contract as services are delivered. In some cases, cancellation and refunds may be a function of the completion of the installation or other services. A portion of the revenue must be allocated to those services and deferred until the expiration of the contingency if the vendor cannot develop reasonable and reliable estimates of cancellations. A vendor's ability to develop reasonable and reliable estimates is a function of the number of homogeneous transactions. When a statistically valid inference can be derived from a large pool of identical transactions, the vendor should, on delivery or completion of service, recognize revenue adjusted for estimated cancellations.

19.{S}a. (i) In fiscal 2000 (the year of the change), a change from revenue recognition on receipt to recording revenue ratably over the 12-month membership term would significantly reduce reported revenue relative to the previous method. If customers join Sam's Clubs evenly throughout the year, ratable recognition accrues approximately 54% of the revenue (from new members) reported under recognition on receipt. The company will report even lower net income because the cost of providing services to the members does not change as Wal-Mart has the same number of customers.

(ii) Subsequent periods will show lower revenue and income up to the period in which the ratable method produces the same amount of revenue as the recognition on receipt method. If membership grows, or the membership fee increases, the revenue reported under the new method will lag the amount that would have been reported by the previous method. If there is a decline in membership, then it is possible that the new method will show higher revenues as the previously deferred revenues are recognized.

b. The membership fee gives customers the right to use Sam's Clubs for 12 months; Wal-Mart must provide services to each of the members during that 12-month period. Therefore, revenue (the fee) is earned by Wal-Mart over the 12-month membership term as it provides contractually negotiated services to the members. Revenue recognition on receipt allowed the firm to recognize revenues prior to providing services, that is, before completion of the earnings process.

c. Wal-Mart justifies its policy of not recording reserves for refunds on the basis of a long history of homogeneous membership sales with de minimis refunds. Although acceptable, management should continue to evaluate trends and should be prepared to record reserves for refunds if their experience changes.

20.{S} a. (i) Fiscal 2001: The change in revenue recognition will significantly lower reported income from layaway sales because the deposit (cash) received is now reported as a liability (deferred revenue) and neither revenue nor income is recognized until all payments are received and the product is delivered to the customer. To determine the effect on WMT of this change, we must know the proportion of sales that layaway transactions represent.

(ii) In subsequent years, the drop in income will be lower as customers (depositors) complete payments and take possession of the products resulting in revenue and income recognition. Fluctuations in the proportion of sale that layaway transactions represent would affect the trend. If such sales grow in importance (perhaps during a recession) the effect would be greater.

21.{M}   Required calculations are shown in the table below.

($millions)	1997	1998	1999	2000
Allowance for doubtful accounts				
Opening balance	$ 14.6	$ 18.0	$ 16.3	$ 21.1
Charged to earnings	4.2	(1.4)	5.3	
Writeoffs (net of recoveries)	(0.8)	(0.3)	(0.5)	
Closing balance	$ 18.0	$ 16.3	$ 21.1	$ 27.6
Accounts receivable (net)	386.4	299.2	393.8	350.2
Sales	4,184.5	4,151.2	4,009.3	4,586.1
Pretax income	460.2	415.3	379.2	478.3
Gross receivables*	404.4	315.5	414.9	377.8
a. (i)Closing balance of reserves to gross receivables (%)	4.45%	5.17%	5.09%	7.31%
(ii)Writeoffs (net of recoveries) to revenues (%)	0.02%	0.01%	0.01%	
b. Adjusted pretax income^	$ 463.6	$ 416.4	$ 384.0	$ 478.3
c. Adjusted pretax income^^	460.2	417.6	379.6	478.3

* Net receivables plus amounts charged to earnings.
^ Reported pretax income plus amounts charged to earnings minus writeoffs (net of recoveries). (No adjustment made for 2000)
^^ See calculations below.

The following calculation is based on the assumption that Nucor maintained its closing balance of bad debt reserves at the 1997 ratio of 4.45% of gross receivables. Annual amounts charged to earnings are determined after calculation of required closing balance of bad debt reserve at 4.45% of gross receivables.

($millions)	1997	1998	1999	2000
Allowance for doubtful accounts				
Opening balance	$14.6	$18.0	$14.0	$18.5
Charged to earnings (plug)	4.2	(3.7)	4.9	
Writeoffs (net of recoveries)	(0.8)	(0.3)	(0.5)	
Closing balance at 4.45% of gross receivables	$18.0	$14.0	$18.5	$16.8
Difference between plug and actual charge	0.0	(2.3)	(0.4)	0.0
Adjusted pretax income	460.2	417.6	379.6	478.3

d. One factor should be the actual loss experience (writeoffs). Yet the accrual varied despite continuing low losses. A second factor should be the reserve level relative to receivables. This percentage may reflect economic conditions and should rise when the risk of customer financial distress increases. Nucor's reserve as a percent of gross receivables rose significantly from 1997 to 2000.

e. The actual writeoffs (through 1999) were immaterial, supporting the CFO's statement. However, as the table above shows, Nucor's accruals do not seem to reflect either the actual loss experience or maintaining a reserve that is a fixed percentage of gross receivables.

f. A CFO would prefer not to disclose the actual charge as it preserves management's ability to make accounting decisions without the risk of misinterpretation by analysts. For managements that use this reserve to manage earnings (see chapter discussion) nondisclosure hides such activity from investors and analysts.

g. From the analyst perspective, disclosure permits the analyst to see the effect of management decisions regarding the appropriate reserve level. It also allows the analyst to see the actual loss experience. Finally, disclosure permits the analyst to decide whether management is using the reserve to manage reported earnings.

22.{M}   Calculations required are in the table below

($000s)	1998	1999	2000
Allowance for doubtful accounts			
Opening balance	$ 400	$ 535	$ 1,332
Charged to income	135	1,249	654
Deductions*	0	(452)	(700)
Ending balance	$ 535	$ 1,332	$ 1,286
*Charged to reserves for accounts written off and credits issued			
Other financial data			
Accounts receivable (net of allowance)	$ 44,394	$ 27,567	$ 42,402
Revenues	164,670	149,448	167,881
Pretax income	15,997	(973)	9,073
Gross receivables*	44,929	28,899	43,688
a.(i) Ending balance of reserves to gross receivables (%)	1.19%	4.61%	2.94%
(ii) Writeoffs (net of recoveries) to revenues (%)	0.00%	0.30%	0.42%
b. Adjusted pretax income^	$ 16,132	$ (176)	$ 9,027
c. Adjusted pretax income^^	$ 15,997	$ 15	$ 8,851

* Net receivables plus amounts charged to earnings
^ Reported pretax income plus amounts charged to earnings minus the excess of the closing balance over 1.19% of gross receivables.
^^ See calculations below.

The following calculation is based on the assumption that Boron LePore maintained its closing balance of bad debt reserves at the 1998 ratio of 1.19% of gross receivables. Annual amounts charged to earnings are determined after calculation of required closing balance of bad debt reserve at 1.19% of gross receivables.

($millions)	1998	1999	2000
Allowance for doubtful accounts			
Opening balance	$ 400	$ 535	$ 344
Charged to earnings (plug)	135	261	876
Writeoffs (net of recoveries)	0	(452)	(700)
Closing balance at 1.19% of gross receivables	$ 535	$ 344	$ 520
Difference between plug and actual charge	0	(988)	222

| Adjusted pretax income | $ 15,997 | $ 15 | $ 8,851 |

d. One reason might be anticipation of higher actual losses in future years, as 1999 losses were significant after no losses in 1998. A second reason may have been that 1999 was a year of poor performance and the company may have wished to accrue large reserves so that future year results would not be burdened by actual losses.

e. While the changes in pretax income for 1999 and 2000 were predominantly caused by operating factors, the accrual for receivables losses did impact the level of pretax income. 1999 would have shown positive pretax income if BLPG had not increased its accrual. The lower accrual in 2000 made the comparison with 1999 look even better than if the company had simply maintained its reserve at the 1998 level for both years.

23.{M}   The required calculations are shown in the table below:

In $millions	As Reported		Adjusted	
	Year 1	Year 2	Year 1	Year 2
Sales	$ 7,103	$ 7,047	$ 7,103	$ 7,047
Cost of goods sold	(4,295)	(4,122)	(4,192)	(4,122)
Selling & administrative expenses	(1,712)	(1,724)	(1,690)	(1,724)
Depreciation	(235)	(260)	(235)	(260)
Interest expense	(146)	(149)	(146)	(149)
Gain on sale of business	0	127	0	0
Net income	$ 715	$ 919	$ 840	$ 792

Common Size Income Statements	As Reported		Adjusted	
	Year 1	Year 2	Year 1	Year 2
Sales	100.00%	100.00%	100.00%	100.00%
Cost of goods sold	-60.47%	-58.49%	-59.02%	-58.49%
Selling & administrative expenses	-24.10%	-24.46%	-23.79%	-24.46%
Depreciation	-3.31%	-3.69%	-3.31%	-3.69%
Interest expense	-2.06%	-2.11%	-2.06%	-2.11%
Gain on sale of business	0.00%	1.80%	0.00%	0.00%
Net income	**10.07%**	**13.04%**	**11.83%**	**11.24%**

On declining sales, Rayna reported a significant increase in income in Year 2 as compared to Year 1, with the net profit margin increasing from 10.07% to 13.04%. However, this reported trend is a function of the amount and timing of restructuring charges. If our analysis of the restructuring charges and the gain on sale of the business indicates that these are nonrecurring charges, we need to evaluate profitability excluding these nonrecurring items. The adjusted income statements show that income actually declined in Year 2 from $840 to $792 and a decline in profit margin from 11.83% of sales to 11.24%.

Alternatively, our analysis may indicate that the restructuring charges are recurring costs of the firm's operations and should be allocated evenly over the two-year period. However, the gain on sale of a business may be truly nonrecurring and we again exclude it from our analysis. The computations shown below depict the same declining trend in income and net profit margin.

In $millions	As Reported		Adjusted	
	Year 1	Year 2	Year 1	Year 2
Sales	$ 7,103	$ 7,047	$ 7,103	$ 7,047
Cost of goods sold	(4,295)	(4,122)	(4,244)	(4,174)
Selling & administrative expenses	(1,712)	(1,724)	(1,701)	(1,735)
Depreciation	(235)	(260)	(235)	(260)
Interest expense	(146)	(149)	(146)	(149)
Gain on sale of business	0	127	0	0
Net income	$ 715	$ 919	$ 778	$ 730

	As Reported		Adjusted	
Common Size Income Statements	Year 1	Year 2	Year 1	Year 2
Sales	100.00%	100.00%	100.00%	100.00%
Cost of goods sold	-60.47%	-58.49%	-59.74%	-59.22%
Selling & administrative expenses	-24.10%	-24.46%	-23.95%	-24.62%
Depreciation	-3.31%	-3.69%	-3.31%	-3.69%
Interest expense	-2.06%	-2.11%	-2.06%	-2.11%
Gain on sale of business	0.00%	1.80%	0.00%	0.00%
Net income	**10.07%**	**13.04%**	**10.95%**	**10.35%**

Case 2-1 - Solution

Estimated time to complete this case is two hours.

1. In a typical contract, the patient receives an initial consultation and preliminary procedures (teeth impressions, x-rays, and the placing of spacers between the teeth for braces). Generally, braces are applied two weeks later and subsequent adjustments to the braces are made every four to eight weeks.

    Because the orthodontists provide orthodontic services, most, if not all, of the initial services are provided *by the orthodontist rather than OCA.* The company is responsible for business operations and marketing; OCA states that revenue is earned from long-term service or consulting agreements with the orthodontists. OCA provides staffing, supplies and inventory, computer and management information services, and scheduling, billing, and accounting services. It is not clear why any of these services would be clustered upfront to the extent necessary to justify recognition of 24% of the revenues during the first month of patient contracts.

    To the extent that OCA supplies equipment, supplies, and administrative support needed for teeth impressions, spacers, and x-rays, the company may be able to justify the recognition of more revenue in the first month of the contract. However, recognition of 24% appears excessive and not supported by the description of the typical arrangement provided in the financial reports.

    The services provided by OCA appear to be those needed throughout the contract with the patient. Absent any compelling argument regarding the amount and timing of their delivery, OCA should recognize revenue on a straight-line basis as time passes.

2. The company reported $369.1 million in initial new patient contract balances and it initiated 126,307 treatments for an average new treatment balance of $2,922.25 ($369.1 million/126,307).

3. and 4.Revenue per contract

Assumptions: initial contract balance	$3,000.00
average length of contract (months)	26
3. Revenue recognized	
Initial month (24% of $3,000)	$ 720.00
Each remaining month [($3,000 - $720)/25]	91.20
First year revenue assuming contract	
(i) Signed January 1 [720 + (11 x $91.20)]	**$1,723.20**
(ii) Signed July 1 [720 + (5 x $91.20)]	**1,176.00**
(iii)Signed December 1	**720.00**
Average of three cases	*1,206.40*
4. Second year revenue (all cases) (12 x $91.20)	**1,094.40**
% change from first year revenue assuming contract	
Signed January 1 of 1st year	-36%
Signed July 1 of 1st year	- 7%
Signed December 1 of 1st year	52%
Average of three cases	*- 9%*

Note: we have computed the average for all three cases as these data are needed in question 7.

5.   The calculations for questions 3 and 4 show that when patients are signed during the first half of the year or evenly throughout the year (average of all cases), OCA's revenue per contract declines in the second year. Thus, to report revenue growth, the company needs to continuously add more patients and/or centers (by starting new centers or purchasing existing orthodontic practices).

6. and 7. Revenue per contract after accounting change

Assumptions: initial contract balance	$ 3,000
average length of contract (months)	26
Revenue recognized	*2000*
Initial month	$ 115.38
Each remaining month	115.38
6. First year revenue assuming contract	
(i) Signed January 1 (12 x $115.38)	**$1,384.62**
(ii) Signed July 1 (6 x $115.38)	**692.31**
(iii) Signed December 1	**115.38**
Average of three cases	730.77
7. Second year revenue (all cases)	**1,384.62**
% change from first year revenue assuming contract	
Signed January 1 of 1st year	0%
Signed July 1 of 1st year	100%
Signed December 1 of 1st year	1,100%
Average of three cases	89%

8. (i) The company reported that 2000 revenues were reduced
   by $26.3 million although the company recognized
   revenue of $57.3 million that was included in the
   cumulative effect adjustment. Thus,
   1. The accounting change reduced 2000 revenue
      recognized from new patients by $83.6 million
      ($57.3 + $26.3).
   2. Revenue of $57.3 million was recognized in 2000
      from patients signed in prior years (as stated).

(ii) To estimate the second effect, we must estimate the revenue effects in the second and third year of patient contracts. Comparing the second year revenues under both accounting methods estimated in questions 4 and 6:

Revenue recognition method	Pre-2000	2000
Second year revenue (all cases)	$1,094.40	$1,384.62
Difference		290.22

We must make a similar calculation for third year revenue:

Revenue recognition method	Pre-2000	2000
Third year revenue		
Signed January 1 of 1st year[1]	$ 182.40	$ 230.77
Signed July 1 of 1st year[2]	729.60	923.08
Signed December 1 of 1st year[3]	1,094.40	1,384.62
Average of three cases	$668.80	$846.15
Difference		177.35

[1] Two months at $91.20 and $115.38 respectively
[2] Eight months at $91.20 and $115.38 respectively
[3] Twelve months at $91.20 and $115.38 respectively

The amount of prior year revenue recognized in 2000 is equal to the sum of the third year effect on 1998 net patients and the second year effect on 1999 patients (amounts in $thousands):

New patients	1998	1999	Total
Number of new patients	95,377	126,307	
Second year effect[1]		$36,656.23	
Third year effect[2]	$16,915.48		
Total effect	$16,915.48	$36,656.23	$53,571.71
Percentage error			6.5%

[1] 126,307 X 290.22
[2] 95,377 X 177.35

The estimated total effect differs by 6.5% from the $57.3 amount provided by the company. The difference most likely relates to the timing of new contracts.

9.

Income Statement	Pro forma 2000	
Amounts in $ thousands	Amount	% Change
Net revenue (actual + $26,300	$ 295,136	30%
Net income (actual + $16,569)	64,291	38%

OCA reported that the accounting change reduced reported revenue by $26.3 million in 2000 (net of the effect of prior year amounts). Applying a 37% tax rate to that amount produces an estimated effect on net income of $16,569. Adding these amounts to reported 2000 data results in the pro forma data in the table above.

Therefore, if OCA had made no accounting change, reported revenues and net income would have increased by 30% and 38% respectively from the amounts originally reported for 1999. These increases are similar to the percentage increases originally reported for 1999 (compared with 1998) but below the increases in the pro forma net income assuming the accounting change. The change in revenue recognition policy effectively shifted prior year growth into the year 2000. 10. OCA's revenue recognition policy has a disproportionate effect on net income because its 1999 revenue recognition method permitted it to recognize revenues earlier and faster than expenses that occurred evenly throughout the year.

10. OCA's revenue recognition policy has a disproportionate effect on net income because its 1999 revenue recognition method permitted it to recognize revenues earlier and faster than expenses that occurred evenly throughout the year.

11. The accounting change results in revenue being recognized evenly over the life of the contract. Consequently, new patients (case starts) have less of an immediate effect on revenue growth. As a result there is less short-term pressure to add new patients. Longer-term, however, revenue growth will continue to depend on new patients, whether acquired at existing centers or from newly established or acquired centers.

12.

Operating Data		Years ended December 31						
	1997	1998	% Δ	1999	% Δ	2000	% Δ
Number of orthodontic centers	360	469	30%	537	14%	592	10%
Total case starts	70,611	95,377	35%	126,307	32%	160,639	27%
Number of patients under treatment	130,000	195,000	50%	267,965	37%	343,373	28%

All three operating criteria show marked declines in growth rates over the 1997 to 2000 period. These declines forecast declines in OCA's revenue and income growth rates Income will still grow but at a slower pace. The company may face limits on its ability to expand because of competition or the lack of orthodontic centers with adequate number of patients needed to be profitable. It is also possible that generating a sufficient number of incremental case starts may be costly.

13. The accounting change should decrease OCA's accounts receivable because revenue is now recognized evenly over the life of the contract; previously 24% of the fee was recognized upfront. Note that there is no change in the timing of actual payments as the contracts have not been changed. However, expected payments are recognized later in the operating cycle, thereby reducing receivables.

14.

($thousands) Per patient under contract	Years ended December 31						
	1997	1998	% Δ	1999	% Δ	2000	% Δ
Revenue	$903	$878	- 3%	$844	-4%	$783	- 7%
Expense	626	600	- 4%	557	-7%	550	- 1%
Operating profit	277	278	1%	287	3%	233	-19%
Per center							
Revenue	326	365	12%	421	15%	454	8%
Expense	226	249	10%	278	11%	319	15%
Operating profit	100	116	16%	143	24%	135	- 6%

Trends in Per Patient Profitability
Revenues per patient declined over the 1997 to 2000 period with the most significant decline occurring in 2000. The 1998 and 1999 declines may have resulted from OCA entering into lower income areas where it could not charge as much or its clinics facing competition, keeping prices lower. However, the greater 2000 decline was largely due to the change in revenue recognition method.

Expenses per patient declined 7% in 1999 compared to 4% in 1998. The decline is most likely due to economies of scale – as more centers and more patients are added, OCA reaps those benefits. However, in 2000, the declining growth rate in number of centers and new cases appears to have caught up with OCA as expenses per patient declined only 1%.

The 1998 and 1999 changes in revenues and expenses explain the trend in operating income for those years. However, the decline in revenue per patient, the change in accounting method and the falloff in expenses per patient all combined to result in a 19% decline in operating profit in 2000.

Trends in Profitability per Center

The 1998 and 1999 increases in revenues per center likely reflect increases in the number of new cases per center, given that 24% of new contract revenue was recognized in the first month). Note that the growth rate of revenue per center was below the growth rate of patient under treatment per center. This may reflect lower pricing. The 2000 decline in revenues per center mainly reflects the impact of the change in the revenue recognition method.

Expenses per center rose each year with the greatest percentage increase in 2000. The increase reflects the higher costs incurred at the beginning, higher amortization costs from acquisitions, and higher cost of newer purchases. Note that expense per center grew more slowly than patients under treatment per center from 1997 to 1999, but almost as rapidly in 2000.

Although operating profits per center rose in 1998 and 1999 (as high upfront revenue recognition resulted in faster growth in per center revenue than expense), the 2000 decline in per center revenue (due in large part to the accounting change) and increase in expense reduced operating profit per center.

15.

Amounts in $thousands	1998	1999 Reported Restated		2000
Gross patient receivables:	$25,519	$32,379		
Allowance for uncollectibles	(5,356)	(6,403)		
Net patient receivables	$20,163	$25,976		
Allowance as % of gross receivables	21.0%	19.8%		
Gross unbilled patient receivables:	$48,523	$69,034		
Allowance for uncollectibles	(2,209)	(3,241)		
Net unbilled patient receivables	$46,314	$65,793		
Allowance as % of gross receivables	4.6%	4.7%		
Gross service fee receivables			$97,207	$37,948
Allowance for uncollectibles			(9,644)	(2,598)
Net service fee receivables			$87,563	$35,350
Allowance as % of gross receivables			9.9%	6.8%

(i)   The allowance for billed versus unbilled receivables
suggests that patients are less likely to pay for
treatment already received than for future
treatments. The higher allowance for billed
receivables appears illogical as we would expect that
some proportion of patients do not return for
treatment after the initial consultation despite
signing a contract. On the other hand, many patients
may pay as they visit and the billed receivables may
be those with significant collection problems. It is
also possible that the reserve for unbilled
receivables is too low. Discussion with management
would be required to resolve these questions.

(ii) OCA lowered the allowance for billed receivables in 1999 relative to 1998, while raising it slightly for unbilled receivables. Absent disclosures about write-offs, it is difficult to evaluate the change. However, the larger decrease in the allowance for billed receivables helped the company report higher net revenues and gross margins. The decrease in the 2000 ratio is difficult to understand without knowing the underlying payment and write-off trends. It is especially hard to justify as the 2000 decrease in gross service fee receivables reflects lower *unbilled* receivables, where the loss ratio has historically been lower. The mix change alone would be expected to increase the allowance.

(iii) The aggregation combined with an absence of data on write-offs for the two categories of receivables makes it more difficult to evaluate the quality of earnings. As there should be different loss patterns on billed versus unbilled receivables, the loss of separate data is meaningful. In addition, patient prepayments presumably result in revenue virtually all of the time while receivables are not always collected. Netting them together obscures trends in each component.

16. Diluted earnings per share

	1997	1998	% Δ	1999	% Δ	2000	% Δ
As reported	$0.50	$0.70	40%	$0.96	37%	$0.96	0%
Pro forma	0.26	0.46	77%	0.66	43%	0.96	45%

The level and trend of originally reported earnings per share through 1999 was a function of OCA's front-end loaded revenue recognition method and its rapid expansion through the development and acquisition of new centers. Earnings per share for 2000 are not comparable to the 1999 level due to the change in revenue recognition method.

The pro forma data report earnings per share assuming that OCA had used the 2000 accounting method for all years presented. Therefore the amounts are comparable and this time series better represents operating results over that time period.

17. While the pro forma time series better represents past operating results, it may not be a reliable basis for forecasting future results.

One reason is that it incorporates growth rates in the number of centers and new patients that may not be sustainable. As discussed in the solutions to questions 12 and 14, underlying trends show that growth is slowing.
The second reason why pro forma data must be used with caution is that it implicitly assumes that management behavior is not affected by accounting methods. As discussed in chapter 5 and elsewhere in the text, accounting often affects management due to incentives such as profit sharing and stock options.

As the solutions to questions 5 and 11 state, the change in revenue recognition method reduced the incentive to obtain new patients. Thus we cannot assume that the pro forma data report what OCA's actual earnings per share would have been if it had used the 2000 revenue recognition method in prior years.

Chapter 3 - Solutions

1.{S}a. **Palomba Pizza Stores**
         Statement of Cash Flows
         Year Ended December 31, 2000

Cash Flows from Operating Activities:		
Cash Collections from Customers	$ 250,000	
Cash Payments to Suppliers	(85,000)	
Cash Payments for Salaries	(45,000)	
Cash Payments for Interest	(10,000)	
Net Cash from Operating Activities		$ 110,000
Cash Flows from Investing Activities:		
Sales of Equipment	38,000	
Purchase of Equipment	(30,000)	
Purchase of Land	(14,000)	
Net Cash for Investing Activities		(6,000)
Cash Flows from Financing Activities:		
Retirement of Common Stock	(25,000)	
Payment of Dividends	(35,000)	
Net Cash for Financing Activities		(60,000)
Net Increase in Cash		$ 44,000
Cash at Beginning of Year		50,000
Cash at End of Year		$ 94,000

b.   Cash Flow from Operations (CFO) measures the cash generating ability of operations, in addition to profitability. If used as a measure of performance, CFO is less subject to distortion than net income. Analysts use the CFO as a check on the quality of reported earnings, although it is not a substitute for net income. Companies with high net income and low CFO may be using overly aggressive income recognition techniques. The ability of a firm to generate cash from operations on a consistent basis is one indication of the financial health of the firm. Analysts search for trends in CFO to indicate future cash conditions and potential liquidity or solvency problems.

Cash Flow from Investing Activities (CFI) reports how the firm is investing its excess cash. The analyst must consider the ability of the firm to continue to grow and CFI is a good indication of the attitude of management in this area. This component of total cash flow includes the capital expenditures made by management to maintain and expand productive capacity. Decreasing CFI may be a forecast of slower future growth.

Cash Flow from Financing (CFF) indicates the sources of financing for the firm. For firms that require external sources of financing (either borrowing or equity financing) it communicates management's preferences regarding financial leverage. Debt financing indicates future cash requirements for principal and interest payments. Equity financing will cause future earnings per share dilution.

For firms whose operating cash flow exceeds investment needs, CFF indicates whether that excess is used to repay debt, pay (or increase) cash dividends, or repurchase outstanding shares.

c. Cash payments for interest should be classified as CFF for purposes of analysis. This classification separates the effect of financial leverage decisions from operating results. It also facilitates the comparison of Palomba with other firms whose financial leverage differs.

d. The change in cash has no analytic significance. The change in cash (and hence, the cash balance at the end of the year) is a product of management decisions regarding financing. For example, the firm can show a large cash balance by drawing on bank lines just prior to year end.

e. and f.
    There are a number of definitions of free cash flows. In the text, free cash flow is defined as cash from operations less the amount of capital expenditures required to maintain the firm's current productive capacity. This definition requires the exclusion of costs of growth and acquisitions. However, few firms provide separate disclosures of expenditures incurred to maintain productive capacity. Capital costs of acquisitions may be obtained from proxy statements and other disclosures of acquisitions (See Chapter 14).

In the finance literature, free cash flows available to equity holders are often measured as cash from operations less capital expenditures. Interest paid is a deduction when computing cash from operations as it is paid to creditors. Palomba's free cash flow available to equity holders is calculated as follows:

Net cash flow from operating activities less net cash for investing activities:

$$\$110,000 - \$6,000 = \mathbf{\$104,000}$$

The investment activities disclosed in the problem do not indicate any acquisitions.

Another definition of free cash flows, which focuses on free cash flow available to all providers of capital, would exclude payments for interest ($10,000 in this case) and debt. Thus, Palomba's free cash flow available to all providers of capital would be $114,000.

2. {M}a.

	1996	1997	1998	1999	2000	2001
Sales	$ ---	$ 140	$150	$165	$175	$195
Bad debt expense	---	7	7	8	10	10
Net receivables	30	40	50	60	75	95
Cash collections[1]	$ ---	**$ 123**	**$133**	**$147**	**$150**	**$165**

[1] Sales - bad debt expense - increase in net receivables

b.

	1997	1998	1999	2000	2001
Bad debt expense/sales	5.0%	4.7%	4.9%	5.7%	5.1%
Net receivables/sales	28.6	33.3	36.4	42.8	48.7
Cash collections/sales	87.9	88.7	89.1	85.7	84.6

c. The bad debt provision does not seem to be adequate. From 1997 - 2001 sales increased by approximately 40%, while net receivables more than doubled, indicating that collections have been lagging. The ratios calculated in part b also indicate the problem. While bad debt expense has remained fairly constant at 5% of sales over the 5 year period, net receivables as a percentage of sales have increased from 29% to 49%; cash collections relative to sales have declined. Other possible explanations for these data are that stated payment terms have lengthened or that Stengel has allowed customers to delay payment for competitive reasons.

3.{S}**Niagara Company**
Statement of Cash Flows 2001

Cash collections	$ 980	[Sales - Δ Accounts Receivable]
Cash inputs	(670)	[COGS + Δ Inventory
Cash expenses	(75)	[Selling & General Expense - Δ Accounts Payable[1]
Cash interest paid	(40)	[Interest Expense - Δ Interest Payable]
Income taxes paid	(30)	[Income Tax Expense - Δ Deferred Tax]
Cash from Operations	$ 165	
Purchase of fixed assets	(150)	[Depreciation Expense + Δ Fixed Assets (net)]
Cash Used for Investing	(150)	
Increase in LT debt	50	
Decrease in notes payable	(25)	
Dividends paid	(30)	[Net Income - Δ Retained earnings]
Cash Used for Financing	(5)	
Net Change in Cash	$ 10	
Cash Balance 12/31/00	50	
Cash Balance 12/31/01	$ 60	

[1] Can also be used to calculate cash inputs, decreasing that outflow to $645 while increasing cash expenses to $100.

4.{L}a.   **G Company**
           Income Statement, 2000 ($ thousands)

Sales	$ 3,841	[receipts from customers + increase in accounts receivable]
COGS + operating expenses[1]	3,651	[payments - increase in inventory + increase in accounts payable]
Depreciation	15	[increase in accumulated depreciation]
Interest	41	[payments]
Taxes	42	[payment + increase in tax payable]
Net income	$ 92	[check = change in retained earnings as there are no dividends]

[1] Note that these two items cannot be calculated separately from the information available.

b.   **M Company**
      Cash Receipts and Disbursements, 2000 ($ thousands)

Cash receipts from:		
Customers	$ 1,807	[Sales - increase in receivables]
Issue of stock	3	[Increase in account]
Short-term debt	62	[Increase in liability]
Long-term debt	96	[Increase in liability]
Total	$ 1,968	
Cash disbursements:		
COGS and operating expenses	$ 1,843	[COGS + operating expense + increase in inventory + decrease in accounts payable]
Taxes	3	[Expense - increase in tax payable]
Interest	51	[Expense]
Dividends	22	[Income + increase in retained earnings]
PP&E purchase	33	[Change in PP&E]
Total	$ 1,952	
Change in cash	$ 16	

Note: This is not a true receipts and disbursements schedule as it shows certain amounts (e.g., debt) on a net basis rather than gross. Such schedules (and cash flow statements) prepared from published data can only show some amounts net, unless supplementary data are available.

c. The cash flow statements are presented with the income statement for comparison purposes in answering Part d.

M Company: Statement of Cash Flows ($ thousands)

	1996	1997	1998	1999	2000
CFO:					
From customers	$1,165	$1,210	$1,327	$1,587	$1,807
Less outlays for:					
COGS/oper. exp.	1,130	1,187	1,326	1,672	1,843
Interest	15	19	16	21	51
Taxes	23	19	9	9	3
	$ (3)	$ (15)	$ (24)	$ (115)	$ (90)
CFI:					
PP&E purchase	(14)	(17)	(37)	(30)	(33)
CFF:					
Issue of stock	5	5	8	3	3
Short-term debt	64	65	--	153	62
Long-term debt	--	--	100	--	96
Dividends	(20)	(21)	(21)	(21)	(22)
Stock repurchase	(22)	(14)	--	(10)	--
LT debt repaid	(2)	(2)	(3)	--	--
ST debt repaid	--	--	(8)	--	--
	$ 25	$ 33	$ 76	$ 125	$ 139
Change in cash	8	1	15	(20)	16

M Company: Income Statement ($ thousands)

	1996	1997	1998	1999	2000
Sales	$ 1,220	$ 1,265	$ 1,384	$ 1,655	$ 1,861
COGS	818	843	931	1,125	1,277
Operating expense	298	320	363	434	504
Depreciation	9	10	11	12	14
Interest	15	19	16	21	51
Taxes	38	33	27	26	6
Total	$ 1,178	$ 1,225	$ 1,348	$ 1,852	$ 1,852
Net Income	42	40	36	37	9

G Company: Statement of Cash Flows ($ thousands)

	1996	1997	1998	1999	2000
CFO:					
From customers	$1,110	$1,659	$2,163	$2,809	$3,679
Disbursements:					
COGS/Oper. exp.	1,214	1,702	1,702	2,895	3,778
Interest	11	13	23	29	41
Taxes	13	15	16	29	35
	$ (128)	$ (71)	$ (93)	$ (144)	$ (175)
CFI:					
PP&E purchase	---	---	(20)	(10)	---
CFF:					
Issue of stock	10	---	5	45	30
Short-term debt	80	52	91	3	60
Long-term debt	40	23	20	125	50
	$ 130	$ 75	$ 116	$ 173	$ 140
Change in cash	$ 2	$ 4	$ 3	$ 19	$ 35

G Company--Income Statement ($ thousands)

	1996	1997	1998	1999	2000
Sales	$ 1,339	$ 1,731	$ 2,261	$ 2,939	$ 3,841
COGS	1,039	1,334	1,743	2,267	} ---
Operating expense	243	312	398	524	}3,651
Depreciation	10	10	12	14	15
Interest	11	13	23	29	41
Taxes	13	20	27	31	42
Total	$ 1,316	$ 1,689	$ 2,203	$ 2,865	$ 3,749
Net income	$ 23	$ 42	$ 58	$ 74	$ 92

Note: 2000 COGS and operating expense are combined as there is insufficient information to separate them.

d.   Both companies are credit risks. Although both are profitable, their CFO is increasingly negative. If current trends continue they face possible insolvency. However, before rejecting both loans outright, it is important to know whether CFO and income differ because the companies are doing poorly or because they are growing too fast.

Both companies increased sales over the 5 year period; Company M by 50%, Company G by more than 300%. Are these sales real (will cash collections materialize)? If they are "growing too fast," it may be advisable to make the loan but also to force the company to curtail its growth until CFO catches up. One way to verify whether the gap is the result of sales to poor credit risks is to check if the growth in receivables is "proportional" to the sales growth. Similar checks can be made for the growth in inventories and payables. In this case, the inventory of M company has doubled from 1996 to 2000 while COGS increased by only 56%. The inventory increase would be one area to investigate further.

There is a significant difference in the investment pattern of the two companies. Company M has made purchases of PPE each year, while Company G has made little net investment in PPE over the period. Yet Company G has grown much faster. Does this reflect the nature of the business (Company G is much less capital intensive) or has Company G used off balance sheet financing techniques?

The cash from financing patterns of the two companies also differ. Both tripled their total debt over the period and increased the ratio of total debt to equity. Given Company M's slower growth (in sales and equity), its debt burden has grown much more rapidly. Despite this, Company M has continued to pay dividends and repurchase stock. Company G has not paid dividends and has issued new equity. These two factors account for its larger increase in equity from 1996 to 2000.

Based only on the financial data provided, G looks like the better credit risk. Its sales and income are growing rapidly, while M's income is stable to declining on modestly growing sales. Unless further investigation changes the insights discussed here, you should prefer to lend to Company G.

5.{L}a. (i)

Statement of Cash Flows - Indirect Method
Cash from operations:

Net income		$1,080
Add noncash expense: depreciation		600
Add/Subtract changes in working capital:		
Accounts receivable	(150)	
Inventory	(200)	
Accruals	80	
Accounts payable	120	(150)
		$1,530

Cash from investing:

Capital expenditures	1,150

Cash from financing:

Short term borrowing	550
Long-term repayment	(398)
Dividends	(432)
	$(280)

Net change in cash	**$ 100**

Worksheet for (Indirect Method) Cash Flow Statement

	Income Statement	Balance Sheet 12/31/00	12/31/01	Change	Cash Effect
Net income	$1,080				$1,080
Depreciation	600				600
Accounts receivable		$1,500	$1,650	$150	(150)
Inventory		2,000	2,200	200	(200)
Accruals		800	880	80	80
Accounts payable		1,200	1,320	120	120
Depreciation	(600)				(600)
Net fixed assets		6,500	7,050	550	(550)
Capital expenditures					**$(1,150)**
Note payable		5,500	6,050	550	550
Short-term borrowing					**$ 550**
Long-term debt		2,000	1,602	(398)	(398)
Long-term debt repayment					**$ (398)**
Net income	(1,080)				(1,080)
Retained earnings		500	1,148	648	648
Dividends paid					**$ (432)**
	0				$ 100

The worksheet to create the cash flow statement is presented above. Each balance sheet change (other than cash) is accounted for and matched with its corresponding activity. As a last check, the net income and the add-backs of non-cash items are balanced and "closed" to their respective accounts (PP&E and retained earnings) providing the amounts of capital expenditures and dividends.

a. (ii) Statement of Cash Flows - Direct Method

Cash from Operations:

Cash collections	$9,850
Cash payments for merchandise	(6,080)
Cash paid for SG&A	(920)
Cash paid for interest	(600)
Cash paid for taxes	(720)
	$1,530

Cash for Investing Activities:

Capital expenditures	(1,150)

Cash for Financing Activities:

Short-term borrowing	550
Long-term debt repayment	(398)
Dividends	(432)
	$(280)

Net Change in Cash	**$ 100**

The worksheet to create the cash flow statement is presented below. Each balance sheet change (other than cash) is accounted for and matched with its corresponding activity. Furthermore the operating account changes are matched to their corresponding income statement item. As a last check, the net income is balanced and "closed" to retained earnings providing the amount of dividends.

Note that there is no difference between the indirect and direct methods in the cash flow statement and in the worksheet for cash for investing and financing activities,

Worksheet for (Direct Method) Cash Flow Statement

	Income Statement	Balance Sheet 12/31/00	12/31/01	Change	Cash Effect
Sales	$10,000				$10,000
Accounts receivable		$ 1,500	$ 1,650	$ 150	(150)
Cash Collections					**$ 9,850**
COGS	(6,000)				(6,000)
Inventory		2,000	2,200	200	(200)
Accounts payable		1,200	1,320	120	120
Cash Paid for Merchandise					**$(6,080)**
SG&A expense	(1,000)				(1,000)
Accruals		800	880	80	80
Cash Paid for SG&A					**$ (920)**
Interest expense	(600)				(600)
Cash Paid for Interest					**$ (600)**
Taxes	(720)				(720)
Cash Paid for Taxes					**$ (720)**
Depreciation	(600)				(600)
Net fixed assets		6,500	7,050	550	(550)
Capital Expenditures					**$(1,150)**
Note payable		5,500	6,050	550	550
Short-term Borrowing					**$ 550**
Long-term debt		2,000	1,602	(398)	(398)
Long-term Debt Repaid					**$ (398)**
Net income	(1,080)				(1,080)
Retained earnings		500	1,148	648	648
Dividends					**$ (432)**
	$ 0				$ 100

6.{L}a.   Exhibit 3P-3 does not provide the (changes in the)
           individual components that make up the changes in
           working capital. As such, to create the direct method
           cash flow statement, we must obtain the information
           directly from the balance sheet. This procedure does
           not necessarily yield the same cash flow components
           using the direct method as those provided by the
           company in its indirect method calculations.
           Differences may arise when

           1.   there are acquisitions/divestments
           2.   there are foreign exchange adjustments
           3.   the firm aggregates or classifies investing
                accruals together with operating ones.

In this case, the differences are minimal as indicated below.
(The calculations required for the direct method cash flow
statement are presented in Exhibit 3S-1 along with the
assumptions used to generate the statement)

Direct Method Cash Flow Statement (Exhibit 3S-1)		Indirect Method (Exhibit 3P-3)	Difference
Cash collections	$348,627		
Cash for suppliers	(246,100)		
Cash expenses	(94,791)		
Interest paid	(5,303)		
Tax paid	(2,127)		
CASH FROM OPERATIONS	$ 4,560	$4,398	$ 162
CASH FROM INVESTMENTS	(4,251)	(4,089)	(162)
CASH FROM FINANCING	215	215	---
CHANGE IN CASH	$ 524	$ 524	---

Exhibit 3S-1: Direct Method Statement of Cash Flows

	Income Statement 2001	Balance Sheet 12/31/00	Balance Sheet 6/30/2001	Change	Cash Effect
Sales	$342,215				$ 342,215
Accounts receivable		91,636	85,224	(6,412)	6,412
Cash collections					**$ 348,627**
Cost of goods sold	(238,799)				(238,799)
Inventories		163,206	158,451	(4,755)	4,755
Accounts payable		84,734	72,678	(12,056)	(12,056)
Cash inputs					**$(246,100)**
Operating expenses	(91,795)				(91,795)
Other current assets		1,426	1,843	417	(417)
Prepaid expenses & other assets		55,566	56,630	1,064	(1,064)
Accrued expenses*		17,679	16,299	(1,380)	(1,380)
Postretirement benefit obligation		2,265	2,130	(135)	(135)
Cash expenses					**$ (94,791)**
Interest expense	(5,128)				(5,128)
Interest payable*		175	0	(175)	(175)
Interest paid					**$ (5,303)**
Tax expense	(831)				(831)
Income tax receivable		4,116	2,889	(1,227)	1,227
Income tax payable		1,130	2,383	1,253	1,253
Deferred income taxes		18,096	18,574	478	478
Tax paid					**$ 2,127**
CASH FLOW FROM OPERATIONS					**4,560**
Depreciation expense	(4,732)				(4,732)
Fixed assets		91,108	90,966	(142)	142
Investments in joint ventures		9,714	9,591	(123)	123
Minority interest		971	1,187	216	216
CASH FLOW FROM INVESTMENTS					**$ (4,251)**
Current portion of long-term debt		3,425	3,425	–	0
Long-term debt		161,135	165,799	4,664	4,664
Dividends paid**					(4,461)
Other – change in stockholders' equity					12
CASH FLOW FROM FINANCING					**$ 215**
Net Income (check)	930				
Net change in cash					**$ 524**

* Assumed change in interest payable to conform to interest paid.
** From the indirect method

b.

	1996	1997	1998	1999	2000	1st 6 Months 2001	Totals
CFO	$34,915	$ 5,165	$(23,528)	$73,597	$(18,606)	$4,560	$ 76,103
CFI	(38,007)	(42,977)	(46,767)	(13,500)	(9,017)	(4,251)	(154,519)
	$(3,092)	$(37,812)	$(70,295)	$60,097	$(27,623)	$ 309	$(78,416)
CFF	4,230	38,782	70,474	(60,473)	27,124	215	80,352

As noted in Box 3-2, from 1996 to 2000, the company generated free cash flow (CFO less net capital expenditures) of $1.5 million, during the first six months the A. M. Castle added another $309 thousand. However, Box 3-2 also showed that over the five-year period, Castle paid nearly $50 million in dividends and borrowed nearly $130 million to finance its investments and acquisitions. This trend continued in the first six months of 2001 during which the firm borrowed an additional $4.664 million to help pay its dividends and meet capital expenditure needs.

Cash generated from operations from 1996 through the end of the first 6 months of 2001 was $76 million but the company spent $154 million to replace productive capacity and for investments and acquisitions. When free cash flows is calculated on this basis (i.e. CFO – CFI) there is a shortfall of $78 million. This shortfall as well as dividend payments were financed by borrowing over the same period.

The inability to meet its capital and dividend needs from operations clearly indicated that either the dividend would have to be reduced or the company would not be able to remain competitive and/or grow as needed.

7.{M}a.

- The Swedish GAAP cash flow statements (CFS) begin with pretax and pre-financial items whereas the U.S. GAAP CFS show adjustments to net income.

- The net financial items aggregate interest costs and interest income from various sources (including dividends and interest from associated companies and other interest income).

- Swedish GAAP CFS aggregate all changes in working capital; U.S. GAAP CFS provide detailed disclosure of the operating changes in components of working capital; non-operating changes are reported as components of investing activities.

- Swedish GAAP combines cash and cash equivalents, financial receivables (primarily receivables from associated companies) and financial liabilities (current and long-term debt) in a measure called net financial assets or liabilities. SFAS 95 shows the change in cash and cash equivalents with changes in financial receivables reported as components of CFO and CFI. Changes in current and long-term debt are reported in cash from financing activities.

b. The cash flow statement is shown on page 16.

c. Disadvantages:
(1) Aggregation of all changes in operating or working capital accounts combines cash consequences of operating and investing activities. As noted in the chapter, investing activities tend to distort cash flow from operations.
(2) The use of net financial items tends to obscures operating, investing, and financing activities. Although disclosure is available to facilitate its calculation, no separate disclosure of actual cash outflow for interest (financing) costs is provided.
(3) The inclusion of financial liabilities (borrowing and repayment) and financial receivables in liquid funds distorts cash flows from both investing and financing activities. This approach also hampers the analysis of free cash flows discussed in the chapter. It is also unclear what basis was used by the company to allocate a portion of the financial receivables to operating activities and the remainder to the net financial position category.

[Part c is continued on page 17]

b. Amounts in millions of Swedish Kronor

Swedish GAAP

Years Ending December 31	1999	1998
Operating profit	2,615	2,475
Noncash items	1,551	1,388
Change in working capital	(3)	169
Net financial items	(206)	(137)
Paid tax	(122)	253
Cash flow before capital expenditure	**3,835**	**4,148**
Capital expenditure	(1,988)	(2,557)
Effects from divested activities	3,258	0
Cash flow before dividend	**5,105**	**1,591**
Issue of warrants and convertible loan	0	46
Dividend paid: Ordinary	(889)	(800)
Extra	(3,110)	0
Currency effects	(17)	(111)
Change in net financial liability	**1,089**	**726**
Closing liquid funds	1,456	1,241
Financial receivables	3,395	0
Financial liabilities	(6,905)	(4,384)
Net financial liability	(2,054)	(3,143)
Opening liquid funds	1,241	1,636
Change in liquid funds	235	(463)
Currency effects	(20)	68
Closing liquid funds	1,456	1,241

U.S. GAAP

	1999	1998
Net income	2,287	2,591
	1,551	1,388
	(3)	169
		(137)
	0	253
Operating activities	**3,835**	**4,148**
	(1,988)	(2,557)
	(3,395)	
	3,258	0
Investing activities	**(2,125)**	**(2,557)**
	0	46
	(889)	(800)
	(3,110)	0
	2,521	0
Financing activities	**(1,478)**	**(754)**
Exchange rate effects	**(17)**	**(111)**
Change in cash and marketable securities	**215**	**726**
Cash and marketable securities:		
Beginning of period	**1,241**	**1,636**
End of period	**1,456**	**1,241**

7.   c.   (continued from page 15)

Advantages:
(1) The separate display of pre-interest and pre-tax
     cash flows permits a comparison across companies
     with different capital structures and tax regimes.
(2) Detailed disclosure of investment cash flows
     (acquisition and other) may facilitate analysis of
     free cash flows.

8. {M}a.   Differences between U.S. and IAS GAAP (see text page
           98):
           •   IAS   GAAP   is   permissive   regarding   the
               classification of interest and dividends received,
               interest paid, and dividends paid: these cash
               flows may be reported either as components of CFO
               or CFI (interest and dividends received) and CFF
               (interest and dividends paid). Roche classifies
               interest   and   dividends   received   as   CFI   and
               interest and dividends paid as CFF.
           •   Bank overdrafts may be reported as components of
               cash and cash equivalents in IAS GAAP; the change
               in bank overdrafts would not be reported as part
               of the statement of cash flows. U.S. GAAP requires
               their classification as liabilities and therefore,
               as components of financing cash flows.   Roche
               footnote 24 indicates that overdrafts are reported
               as short-term debt but is unclear as to how
               changes are reported in the cash flow statement.
           •   Companies using IAS GAAP and the direct method are
               not required to report the reconciliation from net
               income to CFO.

       b.   Cash flow statement on page 18.
            Note that conversion to SFAS 95 results in only a small
            difference in CFO as the classification differences
            largely balance. However both CFF and (especially) CFI
            are quite different (both level and trend). The major
            difference is that the large 2000 investment in
            marketable securities is shown as a CFI outflow under
            IAS 7 but an increase in cash and marketable securities
            under SFAS 95 assuming that the marketable securities
            would be considered cash equivalents under US GAAP.
            Roche footnote 19 contains general information about
            its marketable securities, but not enough detail to
            determine which investments would be considered cash
            equivalents.

b. Roche cash flow statement: IAS and US GAAP

Amounts in CHF Millions

	1999 IAS 7	1999 SFAS 95	2000 IAS 7	2000 SFAS 95
Operating profit*	6,421	6,421	7,131	7,131
Depreciation and amortization	2,453	2,453	2,848	2,848
EBITDA	8,874	N.R.	9,979	N.R.
Genentech transactions	(1,550)	(1,550)	(3,791)	(3,791)
Other non-cash transactions	619	619	(90)	(90)
Other	(3,598)	(3,598)	(2,549)	(2,549)
Interest paid		(686)		(902)
Interest and dividends received		459		743
Increase in working capital	(2,618)	(2,618)	367	367
Cash from operations	**1,727**	**1,500**	**3,916**	**3,757**
Financing transactions	541	541	(801)	(801)
Interest and dividends paid	(1,436)		(1,737)	
Dividends paid		(750)		(835)
Cash from financing activities	**(895)**	**(209)**	**(2,538)**	**(1,636)**
Capital expenditures, investments and divestitures	(906)	(906)	1,921	1,921
Interest and dividends received	459	–	743	
Change in marketable securities	(420)	–	(3,496)	–
Cash from investing activities	**(867)**	**(906)**	**(832)**	**1,921**
Net effect of currency translation on cash	**103**	**103**	**(36)**	**(36)**
Increase (decrease) in cash	**68**		**510**	
Increase (decrease) in cash and mkt. secs.		**488**		**4,006**

Note: Row headings that are right justified apply to SFAS 96 amounts.

*Actually funds from operations
N.R. Not required by US GAAP, but sometimes disclosed

c. Advantage: IAS recommends separate disclosure of cash outflows for maintenance expenditures and capital expenditures for growth; when available that can be a significant benefit.

Disadvantages:
(1) Available alternatives for the treatment of interest and dividends received, interest paid, and dividends paid (see answer to part a) may distort CFO, CFI, and CFF and hamper comparisons with companies using US GAAP or (for companies using IAS GAAP) choosing different alternatives.
(2) For companies using the direct method, when the reconciliation from net income to CFO is not reported it is impossible to determined whether changes in operating assets and liabilities (e.g. inventory) are due to operating or other factors.

9.{L}The cash flow statement shows a steady deterioration in CFO; albeit CFO remains positive. Income (before extraordinary items) on the other hand increases steadily at approximately 8%-10% per year.

To explain the discrepancy between the pattern of income and CFO, we first compute the direct method cash flow statement and then compare the cash flow components with their income statement counterparts.

The (abbreviated) cash flow statement under the direct method is presented below:

	Years Ended December 31		
	1992	1993	1994
Cash from operating activities:			
Collections from customers	$2,119,563	$2,420,961	$ 2,744,159
Payments for merchandise	(1,502,414)	(1,742,149)	(2,064,815)
Payments for SG&A	(453,449)	(523,474)	(601,575)
Interest paid	(37,883)	(33,367)	(33,948)
Taxes paid	(12,414)	(22,989)	(8,408)
Other (plug)	(13,263)	(247)	(4,619)
	$ 100,140	$ 98,735	$ 30,794
Cash for investing activities:			
Capital expenditures	(48,878)	(110,534)	(90,009)
Acquisition of leaseholds	(30,602)	(21,894)	(8,025)
	$ (85,480)	$ (132,428)	$ (98,034)
Cash for financing activities:			
Long-term borrowings	(3,276)	(23,831)	(19,432)
Revolving credit borrowings			70,243
Proceeds from sale of stock, options and warrants	1,995	54,460	1,050
	$ (1,281)	$ 30,629	$ 51,861
Net change in cash	$ 13,379	$ (3,064)	$ (15,379)

The required calculations for the operating items are presented in Exhibit 3S-2 on page 21. The last item "other" is the plug amount used to arrive at the CFO presented in the indirect cash flow statement (Exhibit 3P-4).

Exhibit 3S-2
Worksheet for Operating Items for Direct Method SoCF

	1992	1993	1994
Sales	$ 2,127,684	2,414,124	$ 2,748,634
Change in receivables	(8,121)	6,837	(4,475)
Cash Collections	**$ 2,119,563**	**2,420,961**	**$ 2,744,159**
COGS	(1,527,731)	(1,742,276)	(1,975,332)
Change in inventory	(28,401)	(60,893)	(82,863)
Change in accounts payable	53,718	61,020	(6,620)
Payments to Suppliers	**$(1,502,414)**	**$(1,742,149)**	**$(2,064,815)**
SG&A expense	(458,804)	(520,685)	(605,538)
Change in prepaid expenses	1,317	(2,137)	(3,358)
Change in accrued wages	4,038	(652)	7,321
Payments for SG&A	**$ (453,449)**	**$ (523,474)**	**$ (601,575)**
Interest expense	(39,934)	(34,904)	(34,948)
Amortization of debt issuance costs	2,051	1,537	1,000
Interest paid	**$ (37,883)**	**$ (33,367)**	**$ (33,948)**
Tax expense	(25,507)	(26,152)	(27,569)
Change in taxes payable	9,003	2,662	17,567
Deferred taxes	4,090	501	1,594
Taxes paid	**$ (12,414)**	**$ (22,989)**	**$ (8,408)**

The comparison of the cash flow and income statement components is presented below:

	1992	1993	1994	%change 1992-93	%change 1993-94	%change 1992-94
Sales	2,127,684	2,414,124	2,748,634	13.5%	13.9%	29.2%
Cash collections	2,119,563	2,420,961	2,744,159	14.2%	13.3%	29.5%
Collections/Sales	**99.61%**	**100.28%**	**99.84%**			
COGS	(1,527,731)	(1,742,276)	(1,975,332)	14.0%	13.4%	29.3%
Payments to suppliers	(1,502,414)	(1,742,149)	(2,064,815)	16.0%	18.5%	37.4%
Payments/COGS	**98.34%**	**99.99%**	**104.53%**			
SG&A expense	(458,804)	(520,685)	(605,538)	13.5%	16.3%	32.0%
Payments for SG&A	(453,449)	(523,474)	(601,575)	15.4%	14.9%	32.7%
Payments/SG&A	**98.83%**	**100.54%**	**99.35%**			

Credit and collections do not seem to be responsible for the deterioration in CFO. A comparison of cash collections with sales indicates that collections increased at a slightly faster pace than sales. The collections/sales ratio increased from 99.61% in 1992 to 99.84% in 1994.

Inventory, however, is another matter. Payments for inventory increased by 37% whereas COGS increased by only 29%. This is indicative of inventory being bought and paid for but not being sold. The proportion of payments to COGS increased accordingly from 98.3% to 104.5% in two years. This 6% increase translates (based on COGS of close to $2,000,000) to an increased annual cash requirement of $120,000.

Thus, the first cause of Radloc's problems seems to be inventories. Its income may be overstated as inventory may have to be written down if it cannot be sold. Even if inventory is eventually sold and the purchases now being made now are able to satisfy future growth, the firm may still face liquidity problems as it requires cash to purchase (and carry) the new inventory.

However, as CFO is still positive the firm may still be a good candidate for credit.

Further insights as to the impact of growth can be seen if we compare free cash flow (CFO - CFI) with income and CFO.

	1992	*1993*	*1994*
Earnings before extraordinary	$37,262	$41,378	$44,359
CFO	100,140	98,735	30,794
Free Cash Flow	14,660	(33,693)	(67,240)

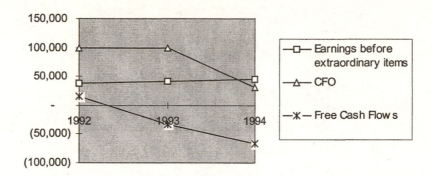

Although income rises, CFO and free cash flow fall. CFO exceeds income in 1992 and 1993 as the noncash depreciation addback increases CFO relative to income. By 1994, however, CFO, (although positive) falls below income. This indicates that the firm *may* have problems in covering the replacement of *current* productive capacity.

Free cash flow is negative in 1993 and 1994 and "barely" positive in 1992. This indicates that the firm's growth (in addition to inventory) requires cash that Radloc cannot supply internally.

Where did the cash come from?

In 1993, it met its cash requirements by issuing stock; in 1994 the firm's short term debt increased considerably as it drew down its revolving credit lines.

Thus, the loan should not be granted as the firm seems to be facing an increasing liquidity crisis..

Note: Radloc is an anagram for Caldor, a chain of discount stores. The data in Exhibit 3P-4 were taken from Caldor's published financial statements. Caldor filed for Chapter 11 bankruptcy soon after the 1994 statements were published.

10.{L}a. This part of the question requires an understanding of SFAS 95, which governs the preparation of the Statement of Cash Flows. SFAS 95 permits use of either the direct or indirect method. As an initial step under either method, the effect of the Kraft acquisition must be removed as follows:

Balance Sheet Changes ($ in millions}

	As Reported 1987	As Reported 1988	Reported Change 1987-88	Less Kraft	Adjusted Change
Receivables	$ 2,065	$ 2,222	$ 157	$ 758	$ (601)
Inventory	4,154	5,384	1,230	1,232	(2)
PPE	6,582	8,648	2,066	1,740	326
Goodwill	4,052	15,071	11,019	10,361	658
ST debt	1,440	1,259	(181)	700	(881)
A/C payable	791	1,777	986	578	408
Accrued liabilities	2,277	3,848	1,571	530	1,041
LT debt	6,293	17,122	10,829	900	9,929

The transactional analysis worksheet and statement of cash flows are shown on pages 25 and 26 respectively.

b. The simplest calculation would be operating cash flow less capital expenditures: $5,205 - $980 = $4,225 million. But many variations are possible.

The more important part of the question is the connection between free cash flow and future earnings and financial condition. Possible uses of free cash flow include:

1) Repayment of debt resulting in lower interest cost and higher earnings. This also reduces debt ratios and improves interest coverage, possibly leading to higher debt ratings.

2) Repurchase of equity may raise earnings per share and (if repurchased below stated book value or real value per share) increase these.

3) Acquisitions (such as Kraft) that may provide future growth, better diversification, lower risk, etc.

4) Expenditures to fund internal growth through capital spending, research and development, new product costs, etc.

Transactional Analysis Worksheet   ($ Millions)

Revenues	$31,742		
Decrease in receivables	601		
Cash collections		$ 32,343	
Cost of goods sold	(12,156)		
Decrease in inventory	2		
Increase in accounts payable	408		
Cash inputs		(11,746)	
Selling & admin. expense	(14,410)		
Increase in accrued liabilities	1,041		
Cash expenses		(13,369)	
Income tax expense	(1,390)		
Increase in income taxes payable	362		
Decrease in deferred income taxes	(325)		
Income taxes paid		(1,353)	
Interest expense		(670)	
Cash flow--operating activities		$ 5,205	
Depreciation expense	$ (654)		
Increase in net PPE	(326)		
Cash invested in PPE		$ (980)	
Goodwill amortization	(125)		
Increase in goodwill	(658)		
Goodwill purchased		(783)	
Decrease in investments		405	
Acquisition of Kraft		(11,383)	
Cash flow--investing activities		$(12,741)	
Dividends declared	$ (941)		
Increase in dividends payable	47		
Dividends paid		$ (894)	
Decrease in stockholders' equity (repurchase)*		(540)	
Net change in short-term debt		(881)	
Net change in long-term debt		9,929	
Cash flow--financing activities		$ 7,614	
Increase in cash and equivalents			$ 78

* The net issuance or repurchase of equity is computed by reconciling the stockholders' equity account:

                 Reconciliation of Stockholders' Equity

12/31/87 balance	$ 6,823
1988 net income	2,337
Dividends declared	(941)
Total	$ 8,219
12/31/88 balance	(7,679)
Decrease in stockholders' equity (repurchase)	$ 540

Philip Morris Companies, Inc.
Worksheet for Statement of Cash Flows
Indirect Method
Year Ended December 31, 1988   ($ Millions)

Cash flows from operating activities:

Net income	$ 2,337	
Adjustments to cash basis:		
Depreciation expense	654	
Amortization of goodwill	125	
Decrease in accounts receivable	601	
Decrease in inventory	2	
Decrease in deferred taxes	(325)	
Increase in accounts payable	408	
Increase in accrued liabilities	1,041	
Increase in income taxes payable	362	
Net cash flow from operating activities		$ 5,205

Cash flows from investing activities:

Increase in PPE (before depreciation)	$ (980)	
Increase in goodwill (before amort.)	(783)	
Decrease in investments	405	
Acquisition of Kraft	(11,383)	
Net cash used by investing activities		(12,741)

Cash flows from financing activities:

Decrease in short-term debt	$ (881)	
Increase in long-term debt	9,929	
Decrease in stockholders' equity (repurchase)	(540)	
Dividends declared	(941)	
Increase in dividends payable	47	7,614
Net cash provided by financing activities		$ 78
Net increase in cash		

Supplementary disclosure of cash flow information:

Interest paid during year	670	
Income taxes paid during year	1,353	
		$-------

Schedule of noncash investing and financing activities:

c. If the acquired inventories and receivables are sold the proceeds will be reported as cash flow from operations (CFO). As their acquisition was reported as cash used for investment, CFO will be inflated. This will occur if Kraft reduces its required level of inventories and receivables because of operating changes (such as changes in product lines or credit terms) or the use of financing techniques that remove these assets from the balance sheet.

11.{L}a. The first step is to match the items from the indirect cash flow statement with their corresponding items on the income statement as below.[1]

Indirect Method Statement		In Direct Method Statement
Net income	$ 111	offset to:
Adjustments to income		
Depreciation	280	Depreciation expense
Deferred tax	32	Tax expense
Restructuring (see Note A)	79	Restructuring expense
In COGS	1.7	Cost of products sold
Pension credit	(79)	Selling, research etc*
Asset sale gains	(18)	Other income
Currency (gains) losses	3.6	Other income
Other	3.8	Other income
Working capital changes		
Receivables	(41.1)	Sales
Inventories	24.6	Cost of products sold
Prepaid expenses etc.	(1.1)	Selling, research etc
Accounts payable	24.8	Cost of products sold
Income tax	(9.7)	Taxes paid
Cash from operations	$ 411.6	

* It is possible the pension credit may also be included in "cost of products sold."

---

[1] As a result of this matching, depreciation expense and restructuring expense offset and are eliminated from the direct method cash flow statement.

Westvaco Direct Method Cash Flow Statement

Sales	$ 2,802
Change in accounts receivable	(41)
Cash collections	**$ 2,761**
Cost of products sold	(1,970)
Change in inventories	25
Change in accounts payable and other accrued expenses	25
Inventory write down (restructuring)	2
Cash paid for inputs	**$(1,918)**
Selling, research and administrative expenses	(231)
Change in prepaid expenses	(1)
Pension credit	(79)
Adjustment for interest and taxes*	(14)
Cash expenses	**$ (325)**
Interest expense	(123)
Adjustment to interest paid (Note H)*	11
Interest paid	**$ (112)**
Tax expense	(37)
Deferred tax	32
Change in income tax payable	(10)
Adjustment to tax paid (Note H)*	3
Income taxes paid	**$ (12)**
Other**	**18**
Cash from operations	**$ 412**

* In Note H, Westvaco provides (as required by SFAS 95) the amount of interest and income tax paid. Our calculations must be adjusted to reconcile with these amounts. We have applied the adjustment to cash expenses, although it is possible that it should be applied to cash paid for inputs

** Other income of $29 from income statement less (from indirect cash flow statement) gains on asset sales $18, plus currency losses of $3.6 and "other" of $3.8. [29 − 18 + 3.6 + 3.8 = 18)

b. There are limited insights available from a single year's direct method cash flow statement. However, we can compare some cash flow relationships with their income statement analogues:

COGS to sales   70.3
Cash inputs to cash collections   69.5%

Selling, research, and admin. expense to sales   8.3%
Cash expenses to cash collections   11.8%

The second set of ratios shows the more significant difference. Westvaco's cash expenses as a % of cash collections are much higher than the income statement relationships. The explanation (see chapter 12) is that Westvaco had a large noncash pension credit, which reduced net expenses.

c. The company increased CFO (from $391 million in 1997 to $583 million in 2000) and substantially reduced its capital expenditures (see note H) from $621 million in 1997 to $229 million in 1999, generating the free cash flow needed to make acquisitions. Additional data used in Figure 3-1 tells the same story:

	1997	1998	1999	2000
CFO	$391	$407	$413	$583
FCF1	208	(9)	207	369
FCF2	202	(9)	183	(892)

FCF1 = CFO – net capital expenditures
FCF2 = CFO – CFI (where CFI = capital expenditures plus cash flows for acquisitions and from divestitures)

The company borrowed funds in 1997 but reduced that debt in 1998 and 1999; outflows for dividends are lower but not significantly so. Thus, Westvaco used higher CFO and borrowing, combined with lower capital expenditures, to finance its 2000 acquisitions.

12.{M}a. **Hertz Corp. ($ millions)**

	1989	1990	1991
Reported cash from operations	$ (117)	$ 92	$ 286
Add back: purchases of equipment	3,003	4,024	4,016
Subtract: sales of equipment	(2,354)	(3,434)	(3,784)
Adjusted cash from operations	$ 532	$ 682	$ 518

b. As reported, cash flow from operations shows steady improvement over the period 1989 - 1991, changing from a negative to a positive amount. After adjustment, the trend is eliminated; cash flow from operations is lower in 1991 than in either 1989 or 1990. The improvement in reported cash flow from operations was the result of reducing Hertz's net investment in rental equipment.

c.

	1989	1990	1991
Reported cash flow for investing	$ (133)	$ (79)	$ (72)
Subtract: purchases of equipment	(3,003)	(4,024)	(4,016)
Add back: sales of equipment	2,354	3,434	3,784
Adjusted cash flow for investing	$ (782)	$ (669)	$ (304)

d. Reported cash flow for investing shows little change over the three-year period. After reclassification of equipment purchases and sales, cash flow for investing drops by more than half in 1991. After reclassification it reflects the sharp drop in net car and truck purchases in that year.

e. Free cash flow can be defined as cash flow from operations less investment required to maintain productive capacity. If we assume that Hertz's investments are solely to maintain existing capacity, then free cash flow equals cash flow from operations less cash flow for investing:

	1989	1990	1991
Reported cash from operations	$ (117)	$ 92	$ 286
Less: reported cash for investing	(133)	(79)	(72)
Equals: free cash flow	$ (250)	$ 13	$ 214

Note that reclassification of purchases and sales of revenue equipment has no effect on free cash flow:

	1989	1990	1991
Adjusted cash from operations	$ 532	$ 682	$ 518
Less: adjusted cash for investing	(782)	(669)	(304)
Equals: free cash flow	$ (250)	$ 13	$ 214

Thus by defining free cash flow in a manner which subtracts out all expenditures required to maintain the operating capacity of the firm, whether capitalized or not and regardless of classification, the effects of accounting and reporting differences can be overcome. This solution requires, of course, the identification of the amounts of such items.

f. When equipment is purchased, the full amount is reported as an operating cash outflow. For leased equipment, only the periodic lease payments are reported as operating cash outflows. Thus, for Hertz, leasing increases reported cash flow from operations.

g. When equipment purchases are classified as investing cash flows, then leasing reduces operating cash flows relative to purchases. That is because the outflow connected with purchases (or any other capitalized expenditure) is never classified as an operating outflow. [See Chapter 11 for a detailed analysis of this issue.]

13. {M}a.

Repsol SFAS 95 Statement of Cash Flows		
€ Millions	Years ended 12/31	
	1998	*1999*
Operating activities:		
Funds from operations*	2,150	3,182
Subsidies and other revenues	92	74
Net assets from consolidation	(16)	(520)
Change in working capital	830	4,949
Cash from operating activities	**3,056**	**7,685**
Investing activities:		
Investments in property	(1,723)	(2,630)
Acquisitions	(197)	(14,277)
Other investments	(297)	(804)
Disposal of property	111	767
Disposal of investments	116	152
Minority interests	11	25
Cash from investing activities	**(1,979)**	**(16,767)**
Financing activities:		
Loans received	544	12,942
Other long-term debt	11	23
Dividends paid	(517)	(567)
Shares issued		5,665
Debt repaid or reclassified	(1,199)	(8,267)
Cash from financing activities	**(1,161)**	**9,796**
Net change	**(84)**	**714**
Net effect of currency changes	**(84)**	**714**

Assumptions:
1. Subsidies and other revenues are shown as a component of cash flows from operating activities because they include revenues and cash (subsidies) presumably received from the government. We have assumed (and it appears so from data provided) that this item was not included in income (part of funds from operations).
2. Net assets from consolidation are defined (elsewhere in Repsol's financial statements - not provided in the problem) as non-cash items resulting from accounting differences within the consolidated group. These are shown as a component of cash from operating activities to offset any items included in income.

Note that Repsol's statement of sources and applications of funds does not show the change in cash. The net change in cash in the table above reflects all changes except the effect of currency changes. If we separate out the actual change in cash and equivalents (65 in 1998, 297 in 1999) we can produce a statement that is similar to the US GAAP format:

€ Millions	1998	1999
Cash from operating activities	3,056	7,685
Plus: increase in cash and equivalents	65	297
Adjusted cash from operating activities	3,121	7,982
Cash from investing activities	(1,979)	(16,767)
Cash from financing activities	(1,161)	9,796
Net effect of currency changes	84	(714)
Change in cash and equivalents	65	297

b. A sources and uses statement does not recognize differences among operating, investing, and financing activities. SFAS 95 requires grouping of similar transactions in these three categories. Separate disclosure of the cash consequences of operating activities facilitates (1) an evaluation of the earnings and cash generating ability of the firm, (2) the quality of revenue and expense recognition principles used to prepare the financial statements, and (3) the computation of free cash flows.

Separate disclosure of investing activities permits an assessment of capital expenditures, growth, and investments in other entities. Information about financing activities shows how the company finances its capital needs and dividend payments. Although the sources and uses format provides these data (and in gross form as required by SFAS 95) for investing and financing activities, it does not provide the disclosure by category; In contrast, SFAS 95 facilitates the analysis of free cash flows and other analytical measures.

c. Separate disclosure of the components of (1) the change in working capital accounts, (2) non-cash income and expense, (3) net assets from consolidation, (4) whether any restructuring charges are included and where they were reported, and (5) debt repaid or reclassified would be useful.

d.   The total source of funds (and year-to-year changes in
     that measure) is useless as a measure of liquidity.
     Cash from operations, which aggregates cash inflows and
     outflows by type of activity, is far more useful.
     However, CFO (like any "bottom line") cannot be used
     without understanding the source of its changes. The
     following table shows the components of CFO:

Repsol Cash from Operations (€ Millions)			
Years ended 12/31	1998	1999	Difference
Operating activities:			
Funds from operations*	2,150	3,182	1,032
Subsidies and other revenues	92	74	(18)
Net assets from consolidation	(16)	(520)	(504)
Change in working capital	830	4,949	4,119
Cash from operations	3,056	7,685	4,629

At first glance, the 1999 increase in CFO suggests an
improvement in liquidity. The increase is primarily due
to the change in working capital (4,119 of the total
change of 4,629) and secondarily the increase in funds
from operations (1,032 of the total change of 4,629).
We need to know whether the change is the continuation
of a trend or a reversal. It would help to have the
components of funds from operations and the changes in
working capital to evaluate the sustainability of the
increases. For example, did the company securitize
receivables, accelerating cash collections? Has the
company delayed payments to suppliers? Has it reduced
production, decreasing outflows for production costs?

e.   (i) In its Statement of the Source and Application of
          Funds, Repsol reports the net effect of currency
          changes as a use (application) of funds. SFAS 95
          requires separate (i.e., not as a component of
          operating, investing, and financing cash flows)
          reporting of these effects.
     (ii) The net effect of currency changes reflects the
          aggregate impact of translating the assets and
          liabilities of foreign operations. Because it is
          represents exchange rate changes rather than
          actual cash consequences, the SFAS 95 treatment is
          better and in general, the amount should not
          influence valuation and investment decisions.
          However, see Chapter 15 for additional discussion
          of this issue.

14.{L}a. 2001 Direct Method Statement of Cash Flows

Sales	$ 8,000
Change in accounts receivable	(150)
Cash collections	**$ 7,850**
Cost of goods sold	(5,000)
Change in inventories	(165)
Change in accounts payable	215
Cash inputs	**$(4,950)**
SG&A	(2,000)
Change in prepaid expenses	(25)
Severance payments	(25)
Cash expenses	**$(2,050)**
Interest expense = paid	(150)
Cash flow from operations	**$ 700**

b. The adjusted income statements are presented below. After adjustment, (recurring) net income shows a declined in 2001 in contrast to the reported increase in the financial statements.

Income Statement	2000	2001
Sales	$7,100	$8,000
COGS	(4,200)	(5,000)
SG&A	(1,675)	(2,000)
Depreciation	(250)	(250)
Interest expense	(150)	(150)
Net income	**$ 825**	**$ 600**

Note: The year 2000 income statement excludes the restructuring charge of $125 ($100 has been added to COGS for the inventory write-down and $25 to SG&A for the severance payment). The 2001 gain on sale of a division has been eliminated from the computation of net income.

c. Comparison of 2000 to 2001 change in accrual-based items to the change in their cash analogs (after removal of nonrecurring items):

	2000	2001	% change
Sales	$7,100	$8,000	12.68%
Cash collections	7,000	7,850	12.14%
Cash collections/sales	0.986	0.981	
Cost of goods sold	(4,200)	(5,000)	19.05%
Cash inputs	(4,100)	(4,950)	20.73%
Cash inputs/COGS	0.976	0.990	
SG&A	(1,675)	(2,000)	19.40%
Cash expenses	(1,750)	(2,025)	15.71%
Cash expenses/SG&A	1.045	1.013	

The changes in sales exceed their cash analog, cash collections, but only marginally.
Cash inputs are higher than amounts recorded as expense – likely due to delayed recognition of expenses and/or accumulation of inventories due to declining quality of or demand for products. Again, however the difference in the changes is not significant, SG&A expense is higher on an accrual-basis; likely due to payment in 2000 of prior accruals or prepayment of 2001 expenses.

d. The decline in CFO can be a function of
1. changes in the timing of cash collections (disbursements) relative to the income (expense) components
2. lower income (after adjusting for the nonrecurring nonoperating events)

We quantify both effects below.

Effect of changes in the timing of cash collections (disbursements) relative to income (expense) components

Effect of change in cash collections/sales	
(0.981-0.986) x $8,000 =	$(40)
Effect of change in cash inputs/COGS	
(0.990-0.976) x $(5,000) =	(70)
Effect of change in cash expenses/SG&A	
(1.013-1.045) x $(2,000) =	64
Net effect	**$(46)**

As noted in part c. the differences between the income and cash flow counterparts are relatively small. Thus these differences did not contribute significantly to the drop in CFO, contributing only $46 out of the $300 decline.

The remaining decline was due to the drop in income and can be calculated as

Effect of changes in revenue and expense on CFO

Change in sales:0.986 x [$8,000 - $7,100]   = $ 887
Change in COGS: 0.976 x [(5,000) - (4,200)]   = (781)
Change in SG&A: 1.045 x [(2,000) - (1,675)]   = (340)
Net effect   **$(234)**

The decline in CFO was $300. Most of the effect ($234) was caused by a drop in income. In spite of the fact that revenues increased, expenses grew at a faster rate. (Revenue grew at a rate of 12.7% whereas expenses grew at a rate of almost 20%).[2]

e. Nonrecurring charges will not contribute to future earnings and cash generating ability, that is, they do not contribute to value and should be excluded for valuation purposes.

---

[2] The CFO decline of $300 can be reconciled as follows:
     Effect of changes in timing $(46)
     Income effect   (234)
     Nonrecurring severance payment   (25)
                                         $(305)

The difference of $5 is due to rounding errors. If the calculations were done with the cash/income ratios taken to four or five decimal places then the timing effect would be (42) and the income effect would be (233).

15.{L}a. **2001 Direct Method Cash Flow Statement**

Sales	$7,103
Change in accounts receivable	(138)
Cash collections	**$6,965**
Cost of goods sold	(4,295)
Inventories	(114)
Accounts payable	15
Restructuring charge	103
Cash inputs	**($4,291)**
SG&A**	$(1,712)
Prepaid expenses	(47)
Restructuring charge	22
Cash expenses	**$(1,737)**
Interest expense = paid	(146)
Cash flow from operations	**$791**

b. The adjusted income statements are presented below. After adjustment, (recurring) net income shows a declined in 2001 in contrast to the reported increase in the financial statements.

Income Statements	2000	2001
Sales	$7,103	$7,047
COGS	(4,192)	(4,122)
SG&A	(1,690)	(1,724)
Depreciation	(235)	(260)
Interest expense	(146)	(149)
Net income	**$ 840**	**$ 792**

c. Comparison of 2000 to 2001 change in accrual-based items to the change in their cash analogs (after removal of nonrecurring items):

	2000	2001	% change
Sales	$7,103	$7,047	-0.79%
Cash collections	6,965	7,182	3.12%
Cash collections/sales	0.981	1.019	
Cost of goods sold	$(4,192)	$(4,122)	-1.67%
Cash inputs	(4,291)	(4,097)	-4.52%
Cash inputs/COGS	1.024	0.994	
SG&A*	$(1,690)	$(1,724)	2.01%
Cash expenses	(1,737)	(1,634)	-5.93%
Cash expenses/SG&A	1.028	0.948	

The changes in sales are lower than their cash analog, cash collections, because of higher collections, i.e., a decrease in receivables – indicating more conservative revenue recognition relative to cash receipts and/or more efficient collection procedures in 2001.

Cash inputs declined more than comparable amounts recorded as expense – likely due to delayed recognition of expenses and/or prior accumulation of inventories due to declining quality of or demand for products in 2000.

Similarly cash SG&A expense fell in 2001 despite an increase in SG&A itself; possibly because of a decline in prepaid expenses or an increase in accruals.

The improvements in efficiency of cash relative to income is reflected in the cash/income ratios as each one improved (i.e. increased for cash/revenue and declined in cash/expenses – see part d.)

d. As income declined (after adjusting for the nonrecurring nonoperating events) the increase in CFO must be a function solely of changes in the timing of cash collections (disbursements) relative to the income (expense) components

Effect of changes in the timing of cash collections (disbursements) relative to income (expense) components

Effect of change in cash collections/sales
$$(1.019-0.981) \times \$7,047 = 268$$

Effect of change in cash inputs/COGS
$$(0.994-1.024) \times \$(4,122) = 124$$

Effect of change in cash expenses/SG&A
$$(0.948-1.028) \times \$(1,724) = \underline{138}$$

Net effect **530**

The overall increase in CFO was (1,280-791=) $489. The increase was solely due to more effective cash management techniques with improved collections accounting for more than half of the improvement.[3] Additionally, the company was able to control its cash payments for inventory and SG&A. Although reported income increased, income was not a contributing factor to the increased CFO. If anything income has a negative impact on CFO as after removing nonrecurring and nonoperating events income declined.

e. Nonrecurring charges will not contribute to future earnings and cash generating ability, that is, they do not contribute to value and should be excluded for valuation purposes.

---

[3] Of the $41 difference between $530 and $489, $22 is due to severance pay and $18 is due to declining income. The $18 amount can be calculated by following the procedure used in problem 3-14 part d.

16.{S}a. Direct Method Statement of Cash Flows for Year 2

Sales	$12,000
Change in accounts receivable	(240)
Cash collections	**$11,760**
Cost of goods sold	(7,100)
Change in Inventories	(200)
Change in Accounts payable	(240)
Cash inputs	**($7,540)**
SG&A	(3,700)
Depreciation	1,000
Accrued liabilities	(25)
Cash expenses	**($2,725)**
Interest expense = paid	**($300)**
Cash flow from operations	**$1,195**

b. The comparison of the income statement components with their cash flow counterparts is presented below.

	Year 1	Year 2	% change
Sales	$10,000	$12,000	20.0%
Cash collections	$9,800	$11,760	20.0%
Cash collections/sales	0.98	0.98	
Cost of goods sold	(6,000)	(7,100)	18.3%
Cash inputs	(5,800)	(7,540)	30.0%
Cash inputs/COGS	0.97	1.06	
SG&A*	(2,000)	(2,700)	35.0%
Cash expenses	(2,000)	(2,725)	36.3%
Cash expenses/SG&A	1.00	1.01	
Interest expense	(300)	(300)	0.0%
Interest paid	(275)	(300)	9.1%
Interest paid/Interest expense	0.92	1.00	

* Adjusted for depreciation expense and assuming depreciation is equivalent in both years.

From the data it is apparent that payments for inventory had the biggest impact on CFO. Although COGS only increased by 18.3%, payments for inventory increased 30%. The cash inputs/COGS ratio increased by .09 (from 0.97 to 1.06). This increase of 9% translates (based on COGS of $7,100) to an increased cash outflow of $639 accounting for the decrease in CFO[4] as the effects of the cash/income relationships of the other income statement components is small.

---

[4] The actual decrease in CFO was only $530 as the $639 outflow was offset by increases in CFO resulting from higher income.

Case 3-1 – Solution

Estimated time to complete this case is two hours.

1. Cash collections for the years 1998 – 2000:

Amounts in $thousands	1998	1999	% Δ	2000	% Δ
Revenues	$171,298	$226,290	32%	$268,836	19%
Provision for bad debts	2,295	2,079		373	
Increase in receivables	(22,733)	(27,491)		(13,549)	
Cash collections	$150,860	$200,878	33%	$255,660	27%
Cash collections/revenues	88.1%	88.8%		95.1%	

2. (i)   In 1998 and 1999, cash collections were less than 90% of revenues because OCA recognized 24% of contract revenue during the first month but patients paid in equal monthly installments. The ratio of cash collections to revenues rose to 95% in 2000 as the change in revenue recognition method reduced the lag between revenues and collections.

    (ii) As calculated in question 9 of case 2-1, 2000 revenues would have been $295.136 million if OCA had used the pre-2000 revenue recognition method. The ratio of cash collections to revenues would have been 86.6% ($255.660/$295.136), slightly below the 1999 ratio.

    (iii) Calculations assuming use of post-January 1, 2000 revenue recognition method:

$thousands	1998	1999	% Δ
Net income (NI) pro forma	$ 22,276	$ 32,326	
Pretax income (NI/.65)	34,271	49,732	
Net interest income (expense)	280	(2,204)	
Operating profit	$ 33,991	$ 51,936	
Operating expense	117,012	149,366	
Net revenue	$ 151,003	$ 201,302	33%
Cash collections/revenues	99.9%	99.8%	

    When the 2000 revenue recognition method is used, the ratio of cash collections to revenues for 1998 and 1999 is about 100%, much closer to the 95% ratio for 2000.

3. The revenue recognition method used before January 1, 2000 results in revenues that consistently exceed cash collections. While growth companies often show receivable growth, the disparity suggests that OCA's revenue recognition method was overly aggressive. It should be noted that, under either revenue recognition method, the ratio of cash collections to revenues fell in 2000. The apparent slowing of cash collections makes the significant decline in bad debt expense for 2000 something an analyst should question.

4.

In $thousands	1998	1999	Change 1998–99	2000	Change 1999–00
Revenues	$171,298	$226,290	32%	$268,836	19%
Cash collections	150,860	200,878	33%	255,660	27%
CFO	22,109	23,347	6%	39,644	70%
CFI	(43,159)	(43,075)	0%	(48,533)	13%
CFF	12,786	23,949	87%	7,884	-67%

The company's cash flow from operations (CFO) rose only 6% in 1999 but increased by 70% in 2000. The major variable was the change in accounts payable and other current liabilities, which was positive (cash outflow) in 1999 but negative (cash inflow) in 1998 and 2000. If that change were excluded, the 1999 and 2000 CFO would have risen by 84% and 13% respectively.

Reported cash for investing (CFI) was relatively stable, with almost no change in 1999 and a 13% increase in 2000. However the individual components were more variable. The large 1998 proceeds from securities sales, for example, offsets the large 1999 increase in acquisition activity.

If we assume that purchases of PPE reflect capital expenditures needed to replace productive capacity used during the year, free cash flow (FCF) can be calculated as CFO - purchases of PPE. Using this definition of free cash flow, FCF declined by 82% in 1999 and increased 2,243% the following year. Free cash flow fell in 1999 because of the low CFO increase and a 28% rise in capital expenditures, which was a result of the increase in orthodontic centers. The 2000 increase reflected the 70% increase in CFO and the 10% decline in capital expenditures, as shown in the following table:

In $ thousands	1998	1999	% Δ	2000	% Δ
Cash from operations	$22,109	$23,347	6%	$39,644	70%
Purchases of PPE	(17,638)	(22,520)	28%	(20,271)	- 10%
Free cash flow	$ 4,471	$ 827	-82%	$19,373	2243%

However, if FCF is defined as CFO less all growth expenditures, then the acquisition of intangible assets should also be deducted:

In $ thousands	1998	1999	% Δ	2000	% Δ
Cash from operations	$ 22,109	$ 23,347	6%	$39,644	70%
Purchases of PPE	(17,638)	(22,520)	28%	(20,271)	-10%
Intangible assets acquired	(42,216)	(17,178)	-59%	(28,246)	64%
Free cash flow	$(37,745)	$(16,351)	-57%	$(8,873)	-46%

Free cash flow as redefined was negative every year but it improved as the shortfall declined in both 1999 and 2000. However, as discussed in questions 5 and 6, even this definition of free cash flow is incomplete.

Cash from financing (CFF) was variable, nearly doubling in 1999 but declining by two-thirds the following year. the 1999 increase was required to finance capital expenditures and acquisitions; 1998 financing had been provided by the securities sales. Higher CFO in 2000 reduced the need for new financing.

5. (a) The total cost of acquiring all assets and liabilities (short- and long-term tangible and intangible) of other entities is the sum of the cash paid plus the notes payable and equity issued to the previous owners of those entities. The cash component of acquisition costs is reported separately in cash for investing. Because equity and notes payable issued to affect the acquisitions are reported, per SFAS 95, as non-cash investing and financing activities, they do not affect the statement of cash flows.[1] From an analytic perspective, however, this distinction is irrelevant; we should adjust cash flow for acquisitions made using all forms of payment.

The finance literature defines free cash flow as CFO less capital expenditures. Under that definition, the cost of acquired affiliates does not affect free cash flows. However, in the chapter, we noted that, when acquisitions are a part of the company's normal growth, then FCF should be measured as CFO less acquisition costs (as well as capital expenditures).

OCA's expansion entails the continued acquisition of new affiliates and hence it falls into this category. However, calculating free cash flows by deducting acquisitions as reported in the SoCF will understate (overstate) the cost of acquisitions (free cash flows) by the portion financed by debt or equity.

(b) The most significant difference is that all expenditures incurred for newly developed practices affect free cash flows.[2] Additionally, it is also likely that, to the extent certain development and startup costs are defined as operating, *cash from operations will be reduced*. Cash flows associated with acquisition of affiliates will never affect cash from operations. Free cash flows will be affected only when its definition includes the cost of acquisitions. Even then, however, the portions financed by debt and equity are excluded.

---

[1] Acquisition costs include any existing receivables, inventory, accounts payable, and other operating assets and liabilities. Changes in these accounts subsequent to acquisition are reported within OCA's cash from operations.

[2] This results when we define free cash flow as CFO minus all capital expenditures (both purchases of PP&E and acquisition costs).

6. The differing treatment of internally developed affiliates and those acquired as well as the treatment of acquisitions costs financed by debt and equity introduces confounding elements into the amounts and trends reported for the various cash flow categories. An adjusted statement of cash flows eliminating these differences is presented below.

Adjusted Statement of Cash Flows

Amounts In $thousands	1998	1999	% Δ	2000	% Δ
Cash from operations	$ 22,109	$ 23,347	6%	$ 39,644	70%
Adjusted purchases of PPE	(15,860)	(22,508)	42%	(20,271)	-10%
Acquisitions	(56,900)	(21,700)	-62%	(34,220)	58%
Adjusted free cash flow	$(50,651)	$(20,861)	-59%	$(14,847)	-29%
Net advances to orthodontic entities	(2,979)	(3,581)			
Transactions in available-for-sale securities	19,674	204		(16)	
Adjusted cash for investing	$(56,065)	$(47,585)	-15%	$(54,507)	15%
Net increase in debt, excluding acquisitions	12,191	23,835	96%	3,585	-85%
Debt issued for acquisitions	8,700	3,600	-59%	1,255	-65%
Total increase in debt	$ 20,891	$ 27,435	31%	$ 4,840	-66%
Net increase in equity excluding acquisitions	595	114	-81%	4,299	3671%
Equity issued for acquisitions	4,206	910	-78%	4,719	419%
Total increase in equity	$ 4,801	$ 1,024	-79%	$ 9,018	781%
Cash from financing	$ 25,692	$ 28,459	11%	$ 13,858	-51%
Foreign currency translation adjustment				(127)	
Net change in cash and cash equivalents	$ (8,264)	$ 4,221	-151%	$ (1,132)	-127%

Unfortunately, as we cannot separate affiliate development and start-up costs included in CFO, our focus is free cash flows. CFO is as reported by the company.

Capital expenditures for PP&E reported on the SoCF include

1. PP&E acquired directly (as part of newly developed sites) and
2. PP&E included as a portion of their acquisitions

Our adjusted statement removes the PP&E included as a portion of their acquisitions. It is calculated below:

	1998	1999	2000
Total cost of acquisitions	$(56,900)	$(21,700)	$(34,220)
Less: notes payable issued	8,700	3,600	1,255
equity issued	4,206	910	4,719
Net cash flows - acquisitions	$(43,994)	$(17,190)	$(28,246)
Allocated to intangible assets	42,216	17,178	28,246
Balance - allocated to PPE	$(1,778)	$(12)	$ 0

For acquisitions we include the total cost, irrespective of how it was financed.

Free cash flow is then calculated as CFO less capital expenditures and acquisitions. The effects of the adjustments made can best be understood if we compare it to "free cash flows" without these adjustments.

	1998	1999	% Δ	2000	% Δ
Cash from operations	**$ 22,109**	**$ 23,347**	6%	**$ 39,644**	70%
PPE purchases*	(17,638)	(22,520)	28%	(20,271)	-10%
Free cash flows (I)	**$ 4,471**	**$ 827**	-82%	**$ 19,373**	2243%
Intangible asset acquired*	(42,216)	(17,178)		(28,246)	
Free cash flows (II)	**$(37,745)**	**$(16,351)**	-57%	**$ (8,873)**	-46%
Financing of acquisitions	(12,906)	(4,510)	-65%	(5,974)	32%
Adjusted free cash flows	**$(50,651)**	**$(20,861)**	-59%	**$(14,847)**	-29%

* As reported on the Statement of Cash Flows

Free cash flow (I) calculated as CFO less capital expenditures is positive each year. It overstates free cash flows as it implies the firm has positive cash flows even after paying for its growth. That is incorrect as it ignores the firm's primary mode of growth - acquisitions. Moreover, even if the objective was to exclude acquisitions, the amount is "incorrect" as it includes PPE acquired through acquisitions.

Free cash flow (II) includes acquisitions (reported on the SoCF); it is negative but it too overstates free cash flows as it excludes the cost of acquisitions financed by debt and equity. The adjusted free cash flow calculated after subtracting all costs provides the most accurate picture. Free cash flows are negative and improving. The improvement, however, is not as great as that implied by the free cash flow (II) reported on the SoCF.

Returning to the adjusted SoCF, we turn to cash from financing. Consistent with our treatment of acquisitions, we include in cash from financing the debt and equity issued as part of the acquisition. This provides a more accurate measure of the scope and trend of the firm's financing activities.

Using 1998 - 1999 as an example, we note that in 1998, the SoCF reported debt financing of only $12,191. When we include the financing used for acquisitions, total debt financing was $20,891; 71% more than the amount reported. Similarly, the reported 1998 - 1999 trend implies a 96% increase in debt financing; the actual increase was 31%.

Chapter 4 Solutions

1.{S} a.

    (i) The identical amount is subtracted from both numerator (CA) and denominator (CL). Since the ratio (before subtraction) is greater than 1 , the effect will be to increase the ratio.

    (ii) The ratio will increase since the denominator (assets) will decrease.

    (iii) The ratio will decrease since the numerator (cash) will decrease

    (iv) The ratio will decrease since the numerator (debt) will decrease.

  b. All the answers will be the same as in A except for {i} Current ratio. Since the ratio now is less than 1, the effect will be to decrease the ratio.

2.{L} The Walt Disney Company

    (i) Accounts receivable turnover = Revenue / Receivables
= \$25,402 / \$3,599 = 7.06
This ratio measures the effectiveness of the firm's credit policies and the capital required to maintain the firm's sales level.

    (ii) Total asset turnover = Sales / Total assets
= \$25,402 / \$45,027 = 0.56
This ratio is designed to evaluate the efficiency of long-term capital investment in productive capacity by measuring sales generated by investments in total assets.

    (iii) Current ratio = current assets /current liabilities
= \$10,007 / \$8,402 = 1.19
The current ratio is the broadest measure of current and potential resources available to meet short-term obligations.

(iv) CFO to current liabilities = $6,434 / $8,402 = 0.77
Unlike the current ratio, this measure compares actual
cash flows to current obligations.

(v) Debt to equity = $6,959 / $24,100 = 0.29
A measure of risk compared to the owners' investment in
the firm. Note that this ratio should include the
current portion of financial obligations in the
numerator. An alternative computation is based on the
sum of operating and financial obligations:
($8,402 + $6,959) / $24,100 = 0.64

(vi) The times interest earned ratio =
EBIT/interest expense = ($2,526 + $558) / $558 = 5.53
is an indicator of safety for creditors as it measures
the extent to which earnings are available to meet
interest charges.

(vii) Operating income to sales = $2,848 / $25,402 = 0.11
This is a measure of the profitability of a firm's
"core" business.

(viii) Return on sales = net income / sales
= $920 /$25,402 = 3.62%
An indicator of overall profitability.

(ix) Return on assets =
(Net income + after-tax interest)/total assets =
($920 + $203[1]) /$ 45,027 = 2.49%
This ratio measures the efficiency of the use of assets
in generating operating profits and of the return
accruing to capital used in the operations. It may also
be measured on a pretax basis to exclude the impact of
differences in tax position and financial policy:
EBIT / total assets = $ 3,084 / $ 45,027 = 6.85%

---

[1] The tax-rate is estimated as (income tax expense)/(pretax income) =
$1,606/$2,526 = 63.6%. Thus after-tax interest expense = 36.4% x $558 = $203

3.{M}a. **Five component disaggregation of ROE:**

			1997	2000
1. Operating margin	EBIT/Sales	=	18.16%	12.14%
x 2. Interest burden	Pretax income/EBIT	=	0.83X	0.82X
x 3. Tax burden	Net income/Pretax income	=	0.58X	0.36X
x 4. Asset turnover	Sales/Average assets	=	0.59X	0.56X
x 5. Leverage	Average assets/Average equity	=	22.50X	1.87X
= Return on equity	Net income/Average equity	=	117.09%	3.82%

Note: Due to rounding errors, ROE computed by multiplying out the components does not equal actual ROE

     b.   The primary causes of the decline in ROE are the lower operating margin, the higher tax burden,,and the lower leverage effect as equity is substantially higher.

4.{L}a.   **Activity Ratios:**
     (i) Inventory turnover = COGS/average inventory
         = \$12,000 / \$4,100 = **2.93X**

     (ii) Accounts receivable turnover = Sales/ average receivables
         = \$19,000 / \$3,250 = **5.85X**

     (iii)Fixed asset turnover = sales/average fixed assets
         = \$19,000 / \$13,400 = **1.42X**

     (iv) Total asset turnover = sales/average assets
         = \$19,000 / \$22,850= **.83X**

     b.   **Liquidity Ratios:**
     (i) Operating cycle = 365 [1/inventory turnover + 1/receivable turnover]
         = 365 [1/2.93 + 1/5.85] = **187 days**

     (ii) Cash cycle:
         Purchases = COGS + increase in inventory
         = \$12,000 + \$200 = \$12,200'

         Number of days payable = 365 x average payables / purchases
         = 365 x \$2,520/\$12,200 = 75.4 days

         Therefore cash cycle = 187 - 75.4
         = **111.6 days**

(iii) Current ratio = current assets / current
liabilities
= $9,900 / $4,400 = **2.25X**

(iv) Quick ratio = (cash + receivables) / current
liabilities
= $5,700 / $4,400 = **1.30X**

(v) Cash ratio = cash / current liabilities
= $2,200 / $4,400 = **0.50X**

(vi) Defensive interval
= 365 x [cash + receivables] / projected
expenditures
= 365 x $5,700 / $14,200 = **146.5 days**

Where projected expenditures estimated as total
costs and expenses less depreciation
= $15,700 - $1,500 = $14,200

c. **Solvency Ratios**

(i) Debt to equity = debt (nontrade) / equity
= $15,004 / $4,296 = **3.5**

(ii) Debt to capital = debt / (debt + equity)
= $15,004/ $19,300 = **.78**

(iii) Times interest earned = earnings before interest
and tax/interest expense
= $4,500 / $1,200 = **3.75**

d. **Profitability Ratios**

(i) Gross Margin: = (sales - COGS) / sales
= ($19,000 - $12,000) / $19,000 = **36.8%**

(ii) Operating income to sales
= operating income / sales
= $ 4,500 / $19,000 = **23.7%**

(iii) Return on sales = net income / sales
= $1,860 / $19,000 = **9.8%**

(iv) Return on assets = (net income + [interest expense
      x (1-tax rate)]) / average assets
      = ($1,860 + [$1,200(1-.436)])/$22,850 = **11.1%**

      Return on assets (pretax) = earnings before
      interest and taxes/Average assets
            = $4,500 / $22,850 = **19.7%**

(v) Return on equity = net income / average equity
            = $1,860 / $3,648 = **51%**

5.{M}Three component disaggregation of ROE:

	1. Profitability	net income / sales	=	9.8%
x	2. Asset turnover	sales / average assets	=	0.83X
x	3. Leverage	average assets/average equity	=	6.26X
=	Return on equity	net income / average equity	=	51.0%

Five component model:

	1. Operating margin	EBIT / sales	=	23.7%
x	2. Interest burden	pretax income / EBIT	=	0.73X
x	3. Tax burden	net income / pretax income	=	0.56X
x	4. Asset turnover	sales / average assets	=	0.83X
x	5. Leverage	average assets / average equity	=	6.26X
=	Return on equity	net income / average equity	=	51.0%

6.{M}a.   Estimate of fixed and variable costs:
            S = Sales
            F = Fixed costs
            V = Variable costs
            v = Variable costs as a percentage of sales
            TC = total costs = F + V = F + vS

$$v = \frac{TC \ (year \ 2) \ - \ TC \ (year \ 1)}{S \ (year \ 2) \ - \ \ S \ (year \ 1)}$$

$$= \frac{\$15,700 \ - \ \$10,400}{\$19,000 \ - \ \$12,000}$$

            = 0.757

            F = TC - vS
              = $15,700 - (0.757 x $19,000)
              = $1,317

            V = TC - F
              = $15,700 - $1,317 = $14,383 for 2002
              = $10,400 - $1,317 = $ 9,083 for 2001

b.   Financial Leverage Effect (FLE)
      = operating income/pretax income

      2001: FLE = $2,900/$1,600 *2002*: FLE = $4,500/$3,300
                  = 1.81   = 1.36

      Operating Leverage Effect (OLE)
      = contribution margin/operating income

      2001: OLE = $2,917/$2,900 *2002*: OLE = $4,617/$4,500
                  = 1.01   = 1.03
      where contribution margin is pretax income plus fixed
      costs ($1,317 for both years).

      Total Leverage Effect (TLE) = OLE x FLE = Contribution
      margin/net income
      2001: TLE = $2,917/$1,600 *2002*: TLE = $4,617/$3,300
                  = 1.82   = 1.40
                  = 1.01 x 1.81   = 1.03 x 1.36

c.   The basic formula used to estimate fixed and variable
      costs assumes that the underlying relationships are
      constant. Brown's rapid growth is probably accompanied
      by increasing fixed costs, and perhaps the ratio of
      variable costs to sales.
            A partial solution would be to deduct known fixed
      costs like depreciation and interest expense from total
      costs before applying the formula. All of the problems
      discussed in Appendix 4-A, including relevant range and
      the non-linear relationship between costs and output,
      apply in this case as well.
            The calculation of OLE in part b is not meaningful
      given the inability to estimate variable and fixed cost
      components. Brown's operating leverage is surely
      greater than the OLE calculated. The total leverage
      effect (TLE) is also understated in the part b
      computation.

7.{L}

Description	Ratio	Method of Calculation
1. Inventory turnover	3.71X	Asset turnover x (COGS/sales) x (assets/inventory)
2. Receivable turnover	5.65X	Asset turnover x (assets/ receivables)
3. Days of inventory Days of receivables Operating cycle	98 days 65 163 days	365/inventory turnover 365/receivable turnover Total
4. Days of payables Cash cycle	(72)days 91 days	365/payables turnover (calculated as 5.06X using COGS instead of purchases) Operating cycle less days of payables
5. Fixed asset turnover	2.67X	Asset turnover divided by (PPE/ assets)
6. Cash ratio	0.08X	Cash/current liabilities
7. Quick ratio	0.79X	(Cash + receivables)/Current liabilities
8. Current ratio	1.67X	Current assets/Current liabilities
9. Debt-to-equity	0.60	(Debt payable + long-term debt)/ equity
10. Interest coverage	11.0X	Operating income/interest expense
11. EBIT/sales	11.0%	Given directly
12. Sales/assets	0.96	(Asset turnover) Given directly
13. EBIT/assets	10.6%	(EBIT/sales) x (sales/assets)
14. EBT/assets	9.6%	(EBT/sales) x asset turnover
15. Assets/equity	2.50X	Inverse of equity/assets (given)
16. EBT/equity	24.0%	(EBT/assets) x (assets/equity)

8.{L}a.

Company	Industry
1	Chemicals and drugs (Monsanto)
2	Aerospace (Boeing)
3	Computer software (Altos Computer)
4	Department stores (J.C. Penney)
5	Consumer foods (Quaker Oats)
6	Electric utility (SCEcorp)
7	Newspaper publishing (Knight Ridder)
8	Consumer finance (Household Finance)
9	Airline (AMR Corp.)

b.   The airline, consumer finance, and electric utility industries are service industries. They are characterized by the absence of cost of goods sold and inventories. Companies 6, 8, and 9 have the lowest ratios (COGS/sales and inventories/total assets). Newspaper publishing may also be considered a service industry; we will return to this later.

Company 8 is the consumer finance company. It has a high level of debt balanced by a high level of receivables and investments (loans and securities). Much of its debt is short-term, reflecting the short maturities of its loans. It has almost no fixed assets. The ratio of interest expense to revenues is the highest for this company.

Both the electric utility and airline firms would have high fixed assets; utilities generally have higher assets (lower asset turnover), are more profitable, and have higher debt and interest expense. Airlines, on the other hand, have high current liabilities for trade payables (payments to suppliers) and for advance ticket sales (other current liabilities). We conclude that company 6 is the electric utility and company 9 is the airline.

Companies 1, 2, and 3 have high R&D expense, consistent with the aerospace, chemicals and drugs, and computer software industries. Aerospace would have the highest inventory (low inventory turnover). Customer prepayments under long term contracts result in lower receivables and large customer advances (other current liabilities). Therefore, company 2 is the aerospace firm.

Distinguishing company 1 from company 3 is difficult. Computer software and drugs are both characterized by high R & D. The inclusion of chemicals, however, should lower the intensiveness of R&D, suggesting that company 3 is the computer software firm. Computer software, lacking manufacturing, is less capital intensive than chemicals and drugs and the latter is generally more profitable. Further, the chemical industry (being older) should have "older" plant (greater proportion depreciated). Company 1 is, therefore, the chemical and drugs firm and company 3 is in the computer software industry.

Companies 4, 5, and 7 remain. Company 4 has high inventories and COGS, the highest receivables relative to assets, and high asset turnover, all of which suggest a retailer. It has no R&D, high advertising expense, and low pretax profit margins. Company 4 is the department store firm.

Company 5 has high net property relative to assets, and the highest ratio of advertising to revenues. Company 5 must be the consumer foods company.

Company 7 is the newspaper publisher. It has very low inventory but high cost of goods sold; inventory is primarily newsprint while cost of goods sold includes the high cost of reporting and production. Company 7 has the highest intangibles (newspapers purchased) and very high pretax profit margins (most newspapers have only indirect competition).

This exercise was intended to show that industries have balance sheet and income statement characteristics that set them apart from others. These characteristics are often used to compare firms within an industry (e.g. advertising as a percentage of sales for consumer goods firms). Summarized data should be used with caution, however. Different firms (even in the same industry) classify identical items differently. Thus the analyst should examine original financial statements to achieve better comparability. Differences among firms may be due to operational or classification differences. When management is available to answer questions, these differences are often useful starting points for obtaining a better understanding of the firm.

9.{S}   Common size statements are the first step in developing insights into the economic characteristics of different industries and of different firms in the same industry. They are also used to standardize components of financial statements by expressing them as a percentage of a relevant base, e.g. total assets for the balance sheet or cash flow from operations for the cash flow statement.

10.{S}(i) Use the average of end of year and end of first quarter assets in denominator, or alternatively, use end of year assets.

   (ii) Use weighted average: .25 x opening assets + .75 closing assets; this matches the numerator that reflects a return on the additional assets for 3/4 of the year. Alternatively, use end of first quarter assets.

   (iii) Average of opening and closing assets is weighted average.

   (iv) Use weighted average: .75 x opening assets + .25 closing assets. If assets added at the end of the fourth quarter, use opening assets.

11.{S}   Operating leverage measures the effect of fixed operating costs on income whereas financial leverage measures effects of fixed financing costs. Total leverage is the product of operating and financial leverage (TL = OL x FL), measuring the effect of all fixed costs. That amount (TL) can be equal for both companies even if the individual components (OL and FL) are not. One company may have high fixed operating costs, whereas the second may have high fixed interest costs, but overall total fixed costs may be identical.

12.{S}   Can be solved by either disaggregating ROE

         ROE = NI/E = NI/S x S/E = 5.5% x 4.2 = 23.1%

         Or by use of the 3 component Dupont Model

         ROE= Profitability x Turnover x Leverage
         ROE= NI/S x S/A x A/E

         Now A/E= (S/E)/(S/A) = 4.2/2.0 = 2.1
         ROE= 5.5% x 2 x 2.1= 23.1%

13. {M}
    (i)   COGS= .55 x sales = .55 x $12 million = $6.6 million
         Therefore **Inventory =** COGS/(Inventory turnover) = $6.6/6 = **$1.1 million**

    (ii) **A/R =** Sales/Receivables turnover = $12 million/12 = **$1 million**

    (iii) Cash Cycle = # of days inventory + # of days A/R - # of days accounts payable
         45 = 60 + 30 - # of days accounts payable
         Therefore # of days accounts payable = 45 and
         A/P turnover = 8.1
         A/P = Purchases/A/P turnover = $6.6/8.1 = **$.815 million**

    (iv) Cash ratio = Cash/A/P = 1.2
         Cash = 1.2 x $.815= **$.978 million**

    (v) **Current ratio =**
         (Cash + A/R + Inventory)/Current Liabilities =
         (.978 + 1.0 + 1.1)/0.815 = **3.78**

14. {M}
    (i)   Operating Cycle =
           number of days inventory   ?
        + number of days A/R   60.83   (365/6)
                                  80.00

        Therefore the number of days inventory = 19.17 and **Inventory turnover =** 365/19.17 = **19.04**

    (ii) **Cash Cycle =**
           Operating cycle   80.0
         - number of days A/P   27.0   (365/13.5)
                             53.0

    (iii) ROE = NI/S x S/A x Assets/Equity
         56.3% = 10% x 3.5 x ?
         Therefore, **Assets/Equity = 1.61**

(iv) $$ROA = \frac{[NI + ((1 + \text{tax rate}) \times \text{interest})]}{\text{Sales}} x \frac{\text{Sales}}{\text{Assets}}$$

Now

$$\frac{[NI + ((1 + \text{tax rate}) \times \text{interest})]}{\text{Sales}} = \frac{NI}{\text{Sales}} + (1 + \text{tax rate})\frac{\text{Interest}}{\text{Sales}}$$

$$= 10\% + (.8 \times 4\%) = 13.2\%$$

Therefore **ROA** = 13.2% x 3.5= **46.2%**

(v)   EBT/sales = (NI/sales)/(1 - tax rate)
       = 10% / 0.8 = 12.5%
       EBIT/sales= EBT/sales + I/sales = 12.5% + 4%= 16.5
       EBIT/I = (EBIT/S)/(I/S)= 16.5%/4%= **4.1**

15.{M}a.

	2001	2002	2003
Current ratio	2.00X	2.00X	2.00X
Quick ratio	1.20	1.10	1.00
Cash ratio	.40	.30	.25

b.   Common size statements would show that cash as a
     percentage of (current) assets is declining; accounts
     receivable and inventory are growing. Similarly,
     current liabilities would show the proportion of
     (bank) borrowing growing relative to credit granted
     by suppliers.

c.   Although the current ratio has remained constant over
     the 2001- 2003 period, its components have not. The
     quick and cash ratios have deteriorated. The firm's
     liquidity position has weakened over the period as
     its current assets are less liquid (more inventory
     and receivables, less cash). At the same time its
     debt financing relative to trade credit has grown.

d.   The CFO to current liabilities and turnover ratios
     would be used to measure the length of the operating
     and cash cycle. We would expect slower turnover and
     therefore longer operating and cash cycles.
     Similarly, CFO and the CFO to current liabilities
     ratio would be expected to decline.

16. {M} a. Purchases = COGS + change in inventory

1999 = $1,349 + ($221 - $30) = $1,540
2000 = $2,106 + ($171 - $221) = $2,056

b.

		1999	2000
Inventory turnover	COGS / Average inventory	10.75	10.74
A/P turnover	Purchases / Average A/P	5.35	4.34
# of days inventory = operating cycle*	365 / Inventory turnover	33.96	33.97
# of days A/P	365 / A/P turnover	(68.26)	(84.15)
Cash cycle		(34.30)	(50.18)

*Because Amazon has no receivables, its cash cycle is equal to the number it takes to convert inventory into sales.
Note: The # of days are calculated from the unrounded turnover ratios rather than the rounded ratios shown.

c. Like other companies doing business on the Internet, Amazon is able to finance operations through its operating and cash cycles. Amazon's turnover ratio is high, perhaps because most of its sales are in a relatively small number of items. Amazon collects cash from its customers immediately (through credit cards) but takes two to three months to pay its suppliers.

17.{M} a.

	Company 1	Company 2	Common size statements Company 1	Company 2
Sales	$ 1,084	$ 977	100%	100%
COGS	(536)	(644)	(49)%	(66)%
Gross margin	$ 548	$ 333	51%	34%
Oper. expense	(414)	(241)	(38)%	(25)%
Oper. income	$ 134	$ 92	12%	9%

b. ROA equals asset turnover times profitability:

	Company 1		Company 2	
Asset turnover	Sales / Assets $1,084 / $765	= 1.42	Sales / Assets $977 / $413	= 2.37
Profitability	Oper. income / Sales $134 / $1,084	= 12%	Oper. income / Sales $92 / $977	= 9%
ROA		17.5%		22.3%

c. and d.

Company 1 has higher gross margin, higher operating expense relative to sales, higher operating profit margin, and lower turnover than Company 2. This indicates that Company 1 is Ann Taylor and Company 2 is the Limited.

The Limited appeals to a larger target audience and therefore sells lower priced items (that carry lower profit margins). Its operating expenses are low as it provides limited service to its customers. Ann Taylor aims for the higher end of the market and charges higher prices, resulting in higher gross margins. Operating expense is high, reflecting services expected by customers for high price clothing. However, this strategy involves a lower volume of sales as evidenced by the sales turnover. Overall, based on ROA, the Limited's (Company 2) strategy was more profitable for the year (ending January 2000) shown.

18.{M}a.

	1997	1998	1999
Income/equity = ROE	$2,664/$12,766 = 20.87%	$603/$11,833 = 5.10%	$1,177/$12,042 = 9.77%

b.

		1997	1998	1999
Operating margin	EBIT/sales	8.51%	3.64%	5.96%
X Interest burden	EBT/EBIT	0.86	0.62	0.85
X Tax burden	Net income/EBT	0.80	0.86	0.66
X Asset turnover	Sales/assets	1.53	1.08	1.21
X Leverage	Assets/equity	2.32	2.41	2.41
= ROE		20.78%	5.05%	9.75%

Note that, due to rounding errors, the ROEs calculated above are slightly lower than ROE calculated directly as net income/ending equity.

Operating margin, and asset turnover are the prime factors responsible for the changes in ROE. The interest burden contributed somewhat to the drop in ROE in 1998. Leverage (assets/equity) and the tax burden are relatively constant over the three years.

c.   Operating leverage effect (OLE) =
     % change in EBIT / % change in sales.
     For 1998 = [($1,124 - $3,847)/$3,847]/[($30,910 - $45,187)/$45,187] = **2.24**

     For 1999 (relative to 1997) = [($2,083 - $3,847)/$3,847]/[($34,975 - $45,187)/$45,187] = **2.03**

     OLE is similar for both years.

d.   OLE reflects the impact of fixed costs on profits as a result of changes in volume. Thus, for companies such as Texaco with high OLE, sales volume decreases impact profit margin percentages. Thus, the activity component and the operating margin component (for companies with high fixed costs) are not distinct.

19.{L}a.

	1998	1999
Activity ratios		
A/R turnover	7.9	8.2
Inventory turnover	3.1	2.3
Asset turnover	1.1	0.9
Liquidity ratios		
Operating & cash cycle		
# of days receivables	46.4	44.4
# of days inventory	116.6	155.9
Operating cycle	163.1	200.3
# of days payables	(99.5)	(120.2)
Cash cycle	63.5	80.1
Current ratio	1.04	1.36
Quick ratio	0.44	0.45
Solvency ratios		
Debt to equity	0.76	2.37
Interest coverage	1.35	2.84
Profitability ratios		
Operating margin	4.4%	10.9%
Profit margin	0.7%	4.6%
EBIT/Average assets	5.0%	10.1%
ROE	1.1%	8.6%

The financial statements and ratios send mixed signals. While there are warning signs, the ratios do not unformly indicate that the company is facing bankruptcy. Sales grew at a rate of 8% whereas profits increased by more than 600%! Accordingly, all the profitability ratios improved considerably.

The ratios and financial data do however point out some concerns:

(1) *Activity*: Inventory turnover declined sharply, despite the sales increase. Asset turnover also fell. The 1999 increase in Warnaco's inventories and assets greatly exceeded the sales increase.

(2)   *Liquidity*: The operating and cash cycles are high and increasing. The primary factor is the number of days of inventory (see activity analysis above), partly offset by the increase in the number of days of payables. However, the latter may not be a positive development. That increase as well as the increase in short-term debt and the longer operating cycle may all be symptoms of a firm having trouble meeting its obligations. The increase in number of days payables results in a misleading view of the cash cycle; if the company is in financial distrees, suppliers will reduce the flexibility given to the company. We should expect the number of days payables to decline and the cash cycle to lengthen. The higher current ratio, which reflects higher inventories, may also be a sign of difficulty rather than of financial strength.

(3)   *Solvency*: Although, interest coverage improved (as a result of higher profits) the debt-to-equity ratio increased three-fold as the company added debt in 1999 and short-term debt increased almost 400%.

(4)   *Rapid Growth:* Finally, it should be noted that during 1999, the company's fixed assets, inventory and debt all increased substantially. All of the above are indicative of rapid expansion that may lead to cash flow shortages.

Ratio analysis is incomplete without cash flow data. Such data may shed some light on the issues raised above.

b.   (1)   COGS is the same for 1998 and 1999 even though sales increased substantially.

(2)   The allowance for doubtful accounts declined although gross receivables increased 47%. This raises the question of whether the company's provision for doubtful accounts is sufficent.

(3)   Interest expense rose 28% although total debt tripled, indicating that most of increase took place late in 1999. Interest coverage for 2000 should decline even if operating income is unchanged.

c. The increase in the provision for bad debts may indicate that the company may have used "aggressive" estimates, indicating low quality of earnings. Note that, even after restatement, the 1999 provision is still much lower relative to gross receivables than the 1998 and 1997 levels. The other revisions are also troublesome, although insufficient information is presented in the problem to evaluate them. Given the high debt level, the reduction in equity increases the reported financial leverage even further.

20.{L}a. **Identification of common-size statements**: Company C is highly automated with higher gross plant assets ($175,000 versus $65,000). Therefore it would tend to have higher fixed operating costs. As sales drop, COGS as a percentage of sales should increase more than for a firm with lower fixed costs. As Company C is more capital intensive it would be expected to have higher debt and (as a percentage of sales) interest costs. *Thus, the second set of common size statements is for Company C. The first set belongs to Company L.*

Identification of ratios: As Company C operates in a JIT inventory environment and has prompt payments and collections, it should have the higher turnover ratios:

Turnover	Company L	Company C
Inventory	6.667	16.667
Receivables	7.409	11.111
Payables	4.444	25.000

Similarly Company C would be expected to have more long-term debt as it is more capital intensive. Therefore the debt to capital ratio of .429 (.195) applies to Company C (Company L).

b. **Creation of income statement, Company C, 2002:**
Since CFO/current liabilities = 5.275 and CFO = $52,750, then current liabilities = $10,000

Since the current ratio (current assets/current liabilities) = 9.475 and current liabilities = $10,000, then current assets = $94,750

Similarly the quick ratio [(cash + receivables)/current liabilities] = 8.875 yields cash + receivables = $88,750 and therefore:

Inventory (2002) = (current assets less quick assets)
                 = ($94,750 - $88,750) = $6,000

As there was no inventory change in 2002, inventory(2001) = $6,000

As average inventory = $6,000, and 2002 inventory turnover was 16.667, then

COGS(2002) = 16.667 x $6,000 = $100,000

Using COGS and the common size statement for Company C, we can now reconstruct the income statement for 2002:

Sales	100.00%	$ 150,000
COGS	66.67%	$ 100,000
SG&A	20.00%	30,000
Interest	4.67%	7,000
Taxes	2.17%	3,250
Total Expense	93.50%	$ 140,250
Net Income	6.50%	$ 9,750

Creation of income statement, Company C, 2001:

Since sales dropped by 1/6 from 2001 to 2002, and sales in 2002 were $150,000; sales in 2001 were $180,000. This amount and the common size income statement for 2001 can be used to prepare the income statement for 200

Sales	100.00%	$ 180,000
COGS	58.33%	$ 105,000
SG&A	17.78%	32,000
Interest	3.89%	7,000
Taxes	5.00%	9,000
Total Expense	85.00%	$ 153,000
Net Income	15.00%	$ 27,000

Creation of income statement, Company L, 2002:

This follows the methodology used for Company C.

Since CFO/current liabilities = .807 and CFO = $28,250, then current liabilities = $30,000

Since current ratio = 3.592, and current liabilities = $30,000, then current assets = $107,750

Similarly the quick ratio of 3.192 yields quick assets of $95,750 (3.192 x $30,000) and therefore inventory(2002) of $12,000 ($107,750 - $95,750).

As the 2002 change in inventory was (6,000), inventory(2001) was $18,000.

As average inventory = $15,000 and inventory turnover = 6.667, then COGS (2002) = 6.667 x $15,000 = $100,000

We can now reconstruct the income statement for 2002:

Sales	100.00%	$ 150,000
COGS	66.67%	$ 100,000
SG&A	20.00%	30,000
Interest	2.00%	3,000
Taxes	2.83%	4,250
Total Expense	91.50%	$ 137,250
Net Income	8.50%	$ 12,750

Creation of income statement, Company L, 2001:

Since sales dropped by 1/6, sales in 2001 were $180,000. The income statement for 2001 is:

Sales	100.00%	$ 180,000
COGS	63.89%	$ 115,000
SG&A	19.44%	35,000
Interest	1.67%	3,000
Taxes	3.75%	6,750
Total Expense	88.75%	$ 159,750
Net Income	11.25%	$ 20,250

c. Interest costs (Company C = $7,000; Company L = $3,000) are fixed for both companies. The breakdowns for COGS and SG&A follow:

Company C: 2002 sales decreased by $30,000, COGS decreased by $5,000, and SG&A decreased by $2,000. Therefore, variable costs as a percentage of sales are:

COGS = $5,000/$30,000   =   16.67%
SG&A = $2,000/$30,000   =   6.67
    Total   23.34%

Therefore, (using 2001 income statement), fixed costs equal

COGS = $105,000 - (.1667 x $180,000)   = $75,000
SG&A = $ 32,000 - (.0667 x $180,000)   =   20,000
    Total $95,000

Company L: 2002 sales decreased by $30,000, COGS decreased by $15,000, and SG&A decreased by $5,000. Therefore, variable costs as a percentage of sales are:

COGS = $15,000/$30,000   =   50.00%
SG&A = $ 5,000/$30,000   =   16.67
    Total   66.67%

Therefore, (using 2001 income statement), fixed costs equal

COGS = $115,000 - (.5000 x $180,000)   = $25,000
SG&A = $ 35,000 - (.1667 x $180,000)   =   5,000
    Total $30,000

Taxes are a constant 25% of pretax income.

d. The 2003 sales forecast is .8 x 2002 sales = .8 x
    $150,000 = $120,000 for both companies. Projected
    income statements for 2003 follow:

	Company C	Company L
Sales	$ 120,000	$ 120,000
COGS[1]	95,000	85,000
SG&A[2]	28,000	25,000
Interest	7,000	3,000
Total expenses	$ 130,000	$ 113,000
Pretax income	(10,000)	7,000
Taxes (25%)	2,500	(1,750)
Net income	$ (7,500)	$ 5,250

[1] Company C: $75,000 + (.1667 x $120,000) = $95,000
    Company L: $25,000 + (.5000 x $120,000) = $85,000
[2] Company C: $20,000 + (.0667 x $120,000) = $28,000
    Company L: $ 5,000 + (.1667 x $120,000) = $25,000

e. With higher fixed operating costs and interest costs,
    Company C has higher operating as well as financial
    leverage. The effects can be demonstrated by reference
    to the following schedule that uses 2002 as its
    reference point:

	2001	2002	2003
Sales (both)	$180,000	$150,000	$120,000
% change from 2002	20%	---	(20%)
Net income: Company C	$ 27,000	$ 9,750	$ (7,500)
% change from 2002	177%	---	(177%)
Net income: Company L	$ 20,250	$ 12,750	$ 5,250
% change from 2002	59%	---	(59%)

With higher sales in 2001, the leverage effect works in
Company C's favor and its income is higher. However,
when sales decline in 2002 and 2003, Company L's income
is higher as it does not bear the burden of high fixed
costs.

Using 2002 as the base period, (since percentage changes in sales are symmetric to that year) we find that Company C's total leverage effect is 8.85 as a 20% change (higher or lower) in sales results in a 177% change in net income.

% Change in income = TLE x % change in sales
177% = 8.85 x 20%

Company C's TLE is three times as large as Company L's whose TLE (with a 2002 base) is only 2.95:

% Change in income = TLE x % change in sales
59% = 2.95 x 20%

Note: The components of the TLE, the Operating Leverage Effect (OLE) and Financial Leverage Effect (FLE), can be calculated by converting the 2002 income statements into the following format (on a pretax basis):

	Company C	Company L
Sales	$150,000	$150,000
Variable COGS & SG&A	(23.33%) (35,000)	(66.67%) (100,000)
Contribution	$115,000	$ 50,000
Fixed costs	(95,000)	(30,000)
Operating income	$ 20,000	$ 20,000
Interest	(3,000)	(3,000)
Pretax income	$ 13,000	$ 17,000

As the following breakdown indicates, the OLE is the major contributor to the TLE for both companies and is the primary difference between the two companies as well. The difference in OLE is then further magnified by the difference in FLE:

	Co. C	Co. L
OLE = Contribution/operating income	5.75	2.50
FLE = Operating income/pretax income	1.54	1.18
TLE = OLE x FLE = Contribution/pretax income	8.85	2.95

The calculations can also be done on a posttax basis but that would require "tax effecting" the contribution margin and operating income as well as net income. For example, for Company C, the contribution margin is $86,250 (.75 x $115,000), operating income is $15,000 (.75 x $20,000) and net income is $9,750 (.75 x $13,000).

21.{L}a. **Balance Sheet - Company C:**

	2001	2002
Cash	$ 25,000	$ 76,750
Receivables	15,000	12,000
Inventory	6,000	6,000
Property	175,000	175,000
(Depreciation)	(80,000)	(120,000)
Totals	$141,000	$149,750
Payables	$ 4,000	$ 4,000
Short-term debt	7,000	6,000
Long-term debt	60,000	60,000
Equity	70,000	79,750
Totals	$ 141,000	$ 149,750

These amounts can be calculated from the data provided as follows:

Property, Plant and Equipment:
Given at $175,000 for 2002. Since cash for investing is zero, the same level applies to 2001.

Accounts Receivable:
For 2002, A/R turnover of 11.1111 and sales of $150,000 imply average receivables of $13,500. Since receivables decreased by $3,000 in 2002, they must have been $15,000 in 2001 and $12,000 in 2002.

Inventory:
From the answer to problem 11-B, Inventory (2002) = Inventory (2001) = $6,000

Cash:
Since current assets = $94,750, and cash = current assets less receivables and inventory, then cash (2002) = $94,750 - $12,000 - $6,000 = $76,750.
   Since the 2002 change in cash = CFO + cash from financing + cash from investment = $52,750 - $1,000 + $0 = $51,750, then cash (2001) = $76,750 - $51,750 = $25,000.

Accounts Payable:

With no change in inventory and COGS = $100,000, 2002 purchases must be $100,000.

2002 accounts payable turnover of 25 and purchases of $100,000 imply an average accounts payable of $4,000. Since there was no 2002 change in payables, then A/P (2001) = A/P (2002) = $4,000.

Short-term debt (S.T.Debt):

Short term debt = Current liabilities - accounts payable

For 2002, current liabilities of $10,000 imply short term debt of $10,000 - $4,000 = $6,000. Given a decrease of $1000 in 2002, S.T.Debt (2001) = $7,000.

Equity:

ROE = 0.13 and net income of $9750 imply average equity = $75,000

Since only change in equity is net income of $9,750, equity (2001) = $70,000, and equity (2002) = $79,750.

Long-term Debt (L.T.Debt):

With L.T.Debt/capital of 0.429 and equity of $79,750, L.T.Debt = $60,000.

Accumulated Depreciation:

Total liabilities + equity = $141,000 and $149,750 for 2001 and 2002 respectively.

Total assets must be same, yielding accumulated depreciation of $80,000 and $120,000 for those years. The 2002 increase must be depreciation expense for that year (as no property was sold or retired) of $40,000.

Alternate Method of Calculation:

CFO = income + noncash items + changes in operating assets

$52,750 = $9,750 + noncash items + $3,000

Therefore, noncash items (depreciation expense in this case) = $40,000

Balance Sheet - Company L:

	2001	2002
Cash	$ 54,500	$ 77,750
Receivables	22,500	18,000
Inventory	18,000	12,000
Property	65,000	65,000
(Depreciation)	(30,000)	(40,000)
Totals	$ 130,000	$ 132,750
Payables	$ 23,650	$ 18,650
Short-term debt	16,350	11,350
Long-term debt	20,000	20,000
Equity	70,000	82,750
Totals	$ 130,000	$ 132,750

The methodology is the same as for Company C:

Property, Plant and Equipment:
Given at $65,000 for 2002. Since cash for investing is zero, the same level applies to 2001.

Accounts Receivable:
For 2002, A/R turnover of 7.409 and sales of $150,000 imply average A/R = $20,250.
    Since A/R decreased by $4,500, A/R (2001) = $22,500 and A/R (2002) = $18,000

Inventory:
From 11-B, inventory (2002) = $12,000 and inventory (2001) = $18,000

Cash:
Since current assets = $107,750, cash (2002) = $107,750 - $12,000 - $18,000 = $77,750

2002 change in cash
= CFO + cash from financing + cash from investment
= $28,250 - $3,000 + $0
= $23,250

and cash (2001) = $77,750 - $23,250 = $54,500

Accounts Payable:
With inventory change of $(6,000) and COGS of $100,000; purchases = $94,000

For 2002, accounts payable turnover of 4.444 and purchases of $94,000 imply an average A/P of $21,150. Since the change in A/P was (5,000), A/P (2001) = $23,650 and A/P (2002) = $18,650

Short-term Debt:
Short-term debt = Current liabilities - accounts payable = $30,000 - $18,650 = $11,350

Since S.T.Debt decreased by $5,000 in 2002, S.T.Debt (2001) = $16,350

Equity:
ROE = 0.167 and net income = $12,750, therefore average equity = $76,350.

Since only change in equity is net income of $12,750, equity (2001) = $70,000, and equity (2002) = $82,750.

Long-term Debt (L.T.Debt):
L.T.Debt/capital = 0.195 and equity = $82,750; L.T.Debt = $20,000.

Accumulated Depreciation:
Total liabilities + equity = $130,000 and $132,750 for 2001 and 2002 respectively.

Total assets must be same, yielding accumulated depreciation of $30,000 and $40,000. Change is depreciation expense of $10,000:

Alternate Method of Calculation:
CFO =   income + noncash items + changes in operating assets
28,250 = $12,750 + noncash items + $5,500
Therefore noncash depreciation expense = $10,000

b. **2003 Forecast Balance Sheet - Company C:**

Cash	$111,650	Accounts payable	$ 4,000
Acct. receivable	9,600	Short-term debt	6,000
Inventory	6,000	Long-term debt	60,000
Property, plant	175,000		
(Depreciation)	(160,000)	Equity	72,250
Total assets	$142,250	Total equities	$142,250

Explanation: Given the JIT environment, and the patterns for 2001 and 2002, we assume that inventory and payables stay at the same level even with the decline in sales. These levels are presumably "minimum" working levels. To maintain the receivable turnover ratio of 11.111, accounts receivable (2003) = $9,600. Assuming no new investments or debt repayment implies a change in cash solely due to cash flow from operations. In 11-D, 2003 net income was projected at $(7,500).

2003 CFO = Net income + depreciation + Δ in operating accounts = $(7,500) + $40,000 + $2,400 = $34,900
Therefore, cash (2003) = $76,750 + $34,900 = $111,650.

2003 Forecast Balance Sheet – Company L:

Cash	$ 96,700	Accounts payable	$ 20,250
Accounts receivable	14,400	Short-term debt	11,350
Inventory	13,500	Long-term debt	20,000
Property, plant	65,000		
(Depreciation)	50,000	Equity	88,000
Total assets	$139,600	Total equities	$139,600

Explanation: For Company L, we assume that all turnover ratios are maintained.

A/R turnover of 7.409 with sales of $120,000 implies average inventory of $16,200. From part A, we have A/R (2002) = $18,000. Thus A/R (2003) equals $14,400.

Inventory turnover of 6.667 with COGS of $85,000 (see 11-D) implies average inventory of $12,750. Given inventory (2002) of $12,000, inventory (2003) = $13,500.

Purchases = COGS + increase in inventory = $85,000 + $1,500 = $86,500.

With accounts payable turnover of 4.444, average payables = $19,450. Since 2002 payables are $18,650, A/P for 2003= $20,250.

Assuming no new investment or debt repayment implies a change in cash solely due to cash from operations. In 11-D, 2003 net income was projected at $5,250.

CFO = Net income + depreciation + change in operating accounts = $5,250 + $10,000 + [$3,600 + $(1,500) + $1,600] = $18,950

Cash (2003) = $77,750 + $18,950 = $96,700

c.   Although both companies have positive CFO and "seem" to
     be cash rich, the picture is not as rosy as it appears.
     CFO does not make allowance for the replacement of
     productive capacity. The fixed assets of both companies
     are almost fully depreciated and may have to be
     replaced soon. Also any improvement in sales will
     require additional working capital, especially for
     Company L. Thus, cash is not really "excess" as it may
     be needed for working capital and future capital
     expenditures to maintain present productive capacity.

22.{M}a. As there is no debt, ROA and ROE are identical at 10%.

b.   ROE = ROA + D/E [ROA - cost of debt] where cost of debt
     is measured on an after-tax basis. This formula is used
     to prepare the following table showing the expected ROE
     at each level of debt:

	{A} Debt/ Equity	{B} Pretax Interest	{C} = .80 x {B} Aftertax Interest	{D} = 10% + [{A}(10%-{C})] ROE
(1)	0.25X	6.0%	4.8%	11.3%
(2)	0.50	8.0	6.4	11.8
(3)	1.00	10.0	8.0	12.0
(4)	1.50	12.0	9.6	10.6
(5)	2.00	15.0	12.0	6.0

c.   Detailed calculations for cases (1) and (5):

Case Number	(1)	(5)
Debt	$200,000	$666,667
Equity	800,000	333,333
Income before interest and taxes	$125,000	$125,000
Interest expense	(12,000)	(100,000)
Income before tax	$113,000	$ 25,000
Tax expense	(22,600)	(5,000)
Net income	$ 90,400	$ 20,000
ROE	$ 90,400 = 11.3% $800,000	$ 20,000 = 6.0% $333,333

d.   Leverage works up to a point. As a firm takes on more debt the interest rate tends to rise (riskiness of debt increases). When the interest rate exceeds the firm's ROA then the benefits of leverage are lost. This trend is accelerated when ROA declines with increasing amounts of investment as more attractive (higher ROA) investments are made first.

In theory, the firm should borrow as long as the expected ROA exceeds the cost of debt. In practice, firms place their "hurdle rate" for new investments above the cost of capital to allow for risk. Many investments fail to achieve their expected ROA. When the realized ROA falls short of the cost of debt, the investment reduces ROE.

23.{L}   In this problem the debt/equity ratios and cost of debt have to be adjusted to include all the debt (even that which is non-interest bearing).

a.   The D/E ratio without any *bank* borrowing is
$200,000/$800,000 = .25
Therefore ROE = 10% + .25[10% - 0] = 12.5%

b.   Calculations for the table that follows can be illustrated using case (1) with a D/E ratio of 25% and interest rate of 6%.

Total assets are $1,000,000 and trade payables equal $200,000. That leaves $800,000 to be divided between bank debt and equity. A D/E ratio of 25% implies bank debt of $160,000 and equity of $640,000.
    The actual D/E ratio (including trade payables) is therefore: $360,000/$640,000 = 0.56.
    Interest (on bank debt only) at 6% = $9,600. The interest rate on total debt of $360,000 (bank debt + trade payables) can be computed as:
        $9,600/$360,000 = 2.67%

Therefore, ROE = ROA + D/E [ROA - (1-tax rate)cost of debt] = 10% + .56 [10% - .8 x 2.67%] = 14.4%

Data for all five cases follows:

	Stated D/E Ratio	Stated Interest Rate	Bank Loan Amount	Actual D/E Ratio	Actual Interest Rate	ROE
(1)	0.25	6.0%	$160,000	0.56	2.67%	14.4%
(2)	0.50	8.0	266,667	0.88	4.57	15.6
(3)	1.00	10.0	400,000	1.50	6.67	17.0
(4)	1.50	12.0	480,000	2.13	8.47	16.9
(5)	2.00	15.0	533,333	2.75	10.91	13.5

c.

Case Number	(1)	(5)
Debt	$160,000	$533,333
Equity	640,000	266,667
Income before interest and taxes	$125,000	$125,000
Interest expense	(9,600)	(80,000)
Income before tax	$115,400	$ 45,000
Tax expense	(23,080)	(9,000)
Net income	$ 92,320	$ 36,000
ROE	$ 92,320 = 14.4% $640,000	$ 36,000 = 13.5% $266,667

d.   Trade debt appears to be interest free credit (in fact
the cost of credit is often included in the price of
the goods sold). The result of such debt is a higher
return on equity as the same return is earned on a
smaller investment. While the numbers change from
problem 13, the conclusion is the same. Leverage
enhances returns only when the cost of credit is less
than the return on assets. As in problem 13, the
highest ROE is earned at a debt/equity ratio of 1.

24.{M}a.and b   The following liquidity, solvency, and profitability ratios can be used to support the conclusions reached in Problem 6 of Chapter 3:

	1996	1997	1998	1999	2000
M COMPANY					
Turnover Ratios:					
Inventory	3.60	3.43	3.27	3.17	2.96
Receivables	3.34	3.22	3.09	3.24	3.25
Payables	7.87	7.47	7.76	10.85	12.79
Number of days:					
Inventory	101.29	106.51	111.54	115.02	123.33
Receivables	109.20	113.25	118.00	112.70	112.00
Payables	(46.40)	(48.90)	(47.00)	(33.60)	(28.50)
Cash cycle	164.09	170.86	182.54	194.12	206.83
Current ratio	1.71	1.57	1.75	1.55	1.60
Quick ratio	1.09	0.99	1.11	0.91	0.93
Debt-to-equity	0.78	0.97	1.17	1.60	2.14
Interest coverage	6.33	4.84	4.94	4.00	1.35
Return on equity	0.14	0.13	0.11	0.11	0.03
G COMPANY					
Turnover ratios:					
Inventory	3.43	3.84	3.87	3.84	4.73
Receivables	5.38	6.07	6.11	6.07	6.10
Payables	10.19	10.61	10.52	10.34	12.47
Number of days:					
Inventory	106	95	94	95	77
Receivables	68	60	60	60	60
Payables	(36)	(34)	(35)	(35)	(29)
Cash cycle	138	121	119	120	108
Current ratio	2.23	2.13	1.95	2.29	2.30
Quick ratio	1.07	1.01	0.92	1.08	1.05
Debt-to-equity	0.38	0.49	0.63	0.71	0.74
Interest coverage	4.27	5.77	4.70	4.62	4.27
Return on equity	0.05	0.09	0.11	0.12	0.12

c. The deterioration in M company's liquidity and financial position can be seen from the cash cycle, which increased to 207 days in 2000 from 164 days in 1996. Also see the decline in the current and the quick ratios. M company's debt-to-equity ratio has more than doubled from 0.78 to 2.14, accompanied by a decline in interest coverage from 6.33x to 1.35x. That decline resulted from both the increasing leverage and the decreasing ROE (from .14 in 1996 to .03 in 2000).

G company's cash cycle has declined (improved) and its liquidity ratios remained steady. The problem here is the higher leverage and low interest coverage (albeit, a steady 4.27 with modest change during the five years shown). Profitability (ROE) increased from .05 to .12. The substantial growth has been managed well so far but it remains to be seen whether the firm can manage future growth as well.

25{L} a. Five-component duPont model:

ROE Component	Description	1986	1987	1988	1989	1990
x EBIT/sales	Operations	5.7%	8.2%	9.3%	9.0%	8.6%
x EBT/EBIT	Financing	0.44	0.55	0.65	0.75	0.85
x Net income/EBT	Tax burden	0.59	0.57	0.59	0.62	0.61
= Net income/sales	Profitability	1.5%	2.6%	3.6%	4.1%	4.4%
x Sales/assets	Activity	1.34	1.94	1.94	2.03	2.20
x Assets/equity	Solvency	14.34	7.95	4.24	2.81	2.21
= ROE		27.9%	39.7%	29.4%	23.5%	21.6%

The ratios used in the above are based on income before extraordinary items and discontinued operations. We start from 1986 as average balances can only be calculated from that point forward

b. The interesting overall result shown by the disaggregation is that ROE declined sharply at the same time that profit margins (net income/sales) and activity ratios were rising. The steady decline in equity turnover explains this apparent contradiction. Equity grew from a nominal amount in 1985 (4% of assets) to nearly half of total assets by the end of 1990. Not only did Harley pay nominal if any dividends to stockholders but the firm sold equity as well. (Net income was about $120 million over the 1986-1990 period while equity increased by $194 million.)

Harley is a classic case of deleveraging. Total debt (current + long-term) declined by $138 million, from about $210 million at the end of 1986 to barely $72 million four years later. Thus more than 70% ($138/$194) of the equity increase over the 1986-1990 period was used for debt reduction rather than for investment purposes. The firm's 21.6% return on equity in 1990, while very respectable, is far below what it would have been if Harley had remained highly leveraged.

When we analyze the components that lead to the increase in the overall profit margin, we find that the greatest contributor is the financing component (EBT/EBIT). This, of course, is a direct result of the deleveraging as interest expense was reduced dramatically as debt was paid off.

Thus, the question remains – did the drive to "world-class management techniques" improve Harley's operations or is the improvement solely do to financing effects. The answer can be found by focusing on the operating component of profitability and on sales turnover – the components that make up ROA on a pre tax basis.

ROA (pretax)	Description	1986	1987	1988	1989	1990
EBIT/Sales	Operations	5.7%	8.2%	9.3%	9.0%	8.6%
x Sales/Assets	Activity	1.34	1.94	1.94	2.03	2.2
= ROA (pretax)		7.6%	15.9%	18.0%	18.3%	18.9%

ROA (as noted in the text) is designed to focus on a firm's operations. Harley's ROA did increase almost threefold over the 1986-1990 period. The improvement came first from operating profitability which increased substantially from 1986 to 1988 but subsequently tapered off. Improvements in the period 1988-1990 came from asset turnover.

26.{S}a. Basic EPS =

$$\frac{\text{Earnings available to common shareholders}}{\text{Weighted average number of common shares outstanding}}$$

$$= \frac{\text{Net income less preferred dividends}}{\text{Weighted average number of common shares outstanding}}$$

$$= \frac{\$10.5 \text{ million} - (\$.40 \times 5 \text{ million})}{20 \text{ million} + (.75 \times 6 \text{ million})}$$

$$= \$8.5 \text{ million}/24.5 \text{ million} = \mathbf{\$0.35 \text{ per share}}$$

b. DEPS = $\frac{\text{Adjusted income available for common shares}}{\text{Weighted average common and potential common shares}}$

$$= \frac{\$10.5 \text{ million}}{24.5 \text{ million} + 7.5 \text{ million}}$$

$$= \mathbf{.33 \text{ per share}}$$

Adjusted income is net income before preferred dividends as the preferred shares are assumed to be converted.

The number of shares is increased by the number of common shares into which the preferred shares are assumed converted.

c. Book value per share =

$$\frac{\text{Common shareholders' equity}}{\text{Common shares outstanding}}$$

$$= (\$100 \text{ million} - \$25 \text{ million})/26 \text{ million}$$

$$= \mathbf{\$2.88 \text{ per share}}$$

d. The preferred shares are assumed to be converted; the numerator reverts to $100 million and the denominator is now (26 million + 7.5 million) = 33.5 million. Book value per share is now ($100/33.5)= **$2.98 per share**.

e. Given the profitability of the company, it is likely that the preferred shares will be converted at some point (the market price of the common and the stated conversion terms would be useful indicators of the likelihood of conversion). Thus the company should be valued assuming conversion.

27.{S}
a.   Basic EPS   =   Earnings available for common
                        Average common shares

        = $50 million - $5 million
            50 million + (½ x 20 million)

        = $.75

Earnings available for common must be reduced by preferred dividends. The shares issued on June 30 are outstanding for one-half year.

b.   Diluted EPS =
                Adjusted income available for common
        Weighted average common and potential common shares

        = $50 million + ($100 million x 6.5% x 60%)
                    (60 + 8 + 10 + 5) million

        = $.65

As the diluted calculation assumes that both the preferred shares and the convertible bonds are converted into common, the numerator excludes the preferred dividends and is increased by the (after-tax) bond interest. The denominator must be increased to reflect the shares issued on conversion of the preferred shares (4 million x 2), the convertible bonds ($100 million/$10) and exercise of the options. The treasury stock method calculates the additional option shares as:

        ($12 - $9.60) x 25 million = 5 million
                $12

Note: Under SFAS 128, the treasury stock method uses the average market price for the period. The standard permits the use of the closing market price if the price is stable and the method is applied consistently. As only the closing price was provided in the problem, it is used to compute the answer here.

c.   Stated book value per share

  = $\dfrac{\$500 \text{ million} - \$100 \text{ million}}{70 \text{ million}}$

  = $5.71

Total equity must be reduced by the redemption value of the preferred shares. The denominator is the year-end number of shares outstanding.

d.   Diluted book value per share

  = $\dfrac{\$500 \text{ million} + \$100 \text{ million}}{(70 + 8 + 10 + 5) \text{ million}}$

  = $6.45

Book value must be increased by the face amount of convertible bonds that are now assumed to be converted into common shares. The denominator is increased by the shares resulting from conversion of the preferred shares and convertible bonds and exercise of the options (see part b for calculations).

e.   The diluted calculations reflect the conversion of the preferred shares and convertible bonds and the exercise of options. As all of these are likely to take place, given the stock price, valuation should be based on the diluted earnings and book value amounts. Note that the diluted book value per share is above the stated amount. This increase is due to assumed conversion of the convertible bonds.

Case 4-1 Solution

Estimated solution time: three hours

1. and 2. Solutions for Takeda's 1999 activity, liquidity, solvency, and profitability ratios are provided in Exhibit 4CS-1(a)-(d). The exhibits also provide the corresponding ratios for Pfizer 1999 (as calculated in Chapter 4). A comparison of the Takeda and Pfizer ratios accompanies each exhibit followed by an overall summary at the end. Takeda amounts in Yen millions.

Exhibit 4CS-1(a)

Activity Ratios	Numerator	Denominator	Takeda	Pfizer
Inventory turnover	Cost of sales 435,787	Average inventory 107,408	4.06	1.45
No. of days	365 365	Inventory turnover 4.06	90	251
Receivable* turnover	Sales 844,463	Average receivables 203,206	4.16	4.78
No. of days	365 365	Receivable turnover 4.16	88	76
Fixed asset turnover	Sales 844,463	Average fixed assets 228,161	3.70	3.32
Total asset turnover	Sales 844,463	Average assets 895,536	0.94	0.83

* Receivables include trade notes and trade receivables only.

Comparison of Takeda and Pfizer: Takeda's operations seem to be more efficient than Pfizer's. Other than receivables turnover, Takeda's activity ratios are superior to those of Pfizer. The most pronounced difference is the inventory ratio.[1] JIT inventory systems prevalent in Japan as well as other (superior) management techniques used in Japan may be responsible for the differences. It is also possible that the inventory turnover differs because of Takeda's chemical business, whose operating characteristics may differ from the drug business. The fixed asset and total asset turnover ratios may be affected by differing accounting methods.[2]

---

[1] As noted in the chapter, Pfizer inventory turnover seems abnormally low. However, see question 5 below where Roche's inventory turnover is similar to that of Pfizer.

[2] Examples include faster depreciation methods (chapter 8), accounting for acquisitions (chapter 14), and the greater use of unconsolidated subsidiaries (chapter 13), permitting it to record lower assets (showing only net assets of unconsolidated subsidiaries).

Exhibit 4CS-1(b)

Liquidity Ratios	Numerator	Denominator	Takeda	Pfizer
Days inventory			90	251
Days A/R			88	76
Operating cycle			178	328
- # of days payables	365 365	Payables turnover[*] 4.79	(76)	(149)
Cash cycle			102	179
Current ratio	Current assets 913,263	Current liabilities 280,058	3.26	1.22
Quick ratio	Cash + MS + A/R 736,849	Current liabilities 280,058	2.63	0.90
Cash ratio	Cash + MS 540,830	Current liabilities 280,058	1.93	0.48
Cash from operations ratio	CFO 104,979	Current liabilities 280,058	0.37	0.33
Defensive interval no. of days	365 365	Projected expenditures[**] Cash + MS + AR 0.91	402	273

[*] A/P turnover = Purchases/(Average A/P)

Purchases = Cost of sales + Δ inventory = 435,787 + (107,767 - 107,049)

Average A/P = Average (Trade notes & accounts)= ½ (11,277+80,154+78,287+12,373)

[**] Projected expenditures assumes same level as 1999. Calculated as cost of sales + selling, general & administrative - depreciation & amortization = 435,787 + 266,636 - 32,651 = 669,772

Comparison of Takeda and Pfizer: Takeda's superior inventory turnover ratio results in a more favorable operating and cash cycle. As noted in the chapter, (with respect to Exhibit 4-1 - common-size balance sheets of Takeda and Pfizer), Takeda had a much stronger cash position than Pfizer. Over 41% of its assets are cash and marketable securities as compared to 23% for Pfizer. The strong cash (and MS) position is the primary factor responsible for Takeda's superior liquidity ratios. However, note that the cash from operations ratio does not exhibit the same superiority (0.37 compared to 0.33) The difference in defensive intervals may reflect significant differences in R&D expenditures as a % of sales (9% for Takeda versus 19% for Pfizer in 1999 - both companies report R&D in SG&A).

Exhibit 4CS-1(c)

Solvency Ratios	Numerator	Denominator	Takeda	Pfizer
Debt to equity	ST + LT debt 21,338	Equity 907,373	0.02	0.46
Debt to capital	ST + LT debt 21,338	Capital 928,711	0.02	0.31
Debt (including trade payables)				
To equity	Debt (incl. trade payables) 151,467	Equity 907,373	0.17	0.83
To capital	Debt (incl. trade payables) 151,467	Capital 1,058,840	0.14	0.45
Times interest earned	EBIT 183,201	Interest expense 1,059	173	20
Capital expenditure ratio	CFO 104,979	Capital expenditures 27,847	3.77	2.06
CFO to debt ratio	CFO 104,979	ST + LT debt 21,338	4.92	0.56

Debt = Bank loans + long-term debt (including current portion)
= 9,361 + 2,119 + 9,858 = 21,338

Debt (including trade)
= Debt + trade notes + trade accounts + income tax payable
= 21,338 + 11,277 + 80,154 + 38,698 = 151,647

Capital = equity + debt (as defined above)

Comparison of Takeda and Pfizer: Consistent with Takeda's strong cash position, Takeda has very low debt. Thus, its capitalization ratios, (*debt to equity* and *debt to capital*) are far superior to those of Pfizer. Similarly, its times interest earned is 173, almost 9x that of Pfizer's. The low debt also contributes to Takeda's strong *CFO to debt* ratio (at 4.92, almost 9x that of Pfizer.) Takeda's superiority, however, is not solely due to its strong cash/low debt position. Its *capital expenditures ratio*, which is independent of the above factors, is also stronger than Pfizer's.[3]

---

[3] Takeda's reported superiority may also reflect benefits from its extensive use of unconsolidated subsidiaries, keeping debt off the parent's balance sheet. To the extent that some debt is held by those subsidiaries, interest expense is understated as well.

Exhibit 4CS-1(d)

Profitability Ratios	Numerator	Denominator	Takeda	Pfizer
Gross margin %	Gross margin 408,676	Sales 844,463	48.4%	84.4%
Operating margin %	Operating income 142,220	Sales 844,463	16.8%	28.9%
Pretax margin %	Pretax income 182,142	Sales 844,463	21.6%	27.4%
Profit margin %	Net income 91,755	Sales 844,463	10.9%	19.7%
Return on assets (pre-interest)				
After-tax %	Net income + interest (1-t) 92,606	Average assets 895,536	10.3%	17.3%
Pretax %	EBIT 183,201	Average assets 895,536	20.5%	24.1%
Return on equity				
After tax %	Net income 91,755	Average equity 868,377	10.6%	36.2%
Pretax %	Pretax income 182,142	Average equity 868,377	21.0%	50.2%
Return on total capital				
After tax %	Net income 91,755	Average capital 901,287	10.2%	25.5%
Pretax %	Pretax income 182,142	Average capital 901,287	20.2%	35.3%

Tax rate (t) = 89,019/182,142 = 48.9%

Comparison of Takeda and Pfizer: The first three categories examined (activity, liquidity and solvency) indicate that Takeda is stronger than Pfizer. However, in the profitability category, Pfizer's performance is far superior to that of Takeda in every area. The superiority stems from the firms' respective gross margins, much higher for Pfizer than for Takeda. As noted in the chapter (see p. 117), this is partially due to the Japanese environment wherein firms are subject to "price controls" limiting their ability to mark-up pharmaceutical products. Additionally, 29% of Takeda's revenues are non-pharmaceutical (with lower gross margins) compared to 8% for Pfizer.

Takada's lower returns also reflect its high cash position as returns on cash equivalents are far lower than returns on operating activities. Return on equity for Pfizer is also enhanced by its debt leverage, which Takeda lacks.

Comparison of Takeda and Pfizer - Overall summary: Financial statement analysis is carried out by and for creditors as well as equity investors. In comparing Pfizer and Takeda we come across an interesting dichotomy. Because of its strong liquidity and solvency position, Takeda would be the stronger candidate for a credit granting decision. It is less risky than Pfizer.[4] On the other hand, the lower risk implies a potentially lower return as seen in Takeda's lower profitability relative to that reported by Pfizer. Thus for the equity investor, (assuming the risk differential is not onerous) Pfizer maybe be a preferred investment.

The comparative analysis of Takeda and Pfizer is limited insofar as it ignores the following factors:

- Takeda's large chemicals business limits its comparability to a pure drug company like Pfizer.
- Ratios are based on financial data that reflect differing accounting methods and assumptions.
- Economic, political and cultural environments in which the two firms operate (i.e. United States versus Japan) affect the firms' risk and return profiles.

For these reasons, ratio analysis is just the beginning. The analyst should examine these factors to determine the extent to which ratio differences reflect underlying operating differences rather than accounting methods or other factors.

---

[4] This does not imply that Pfizer is a risky credit decision - only that it is riskier compared to Takeda.

3. and 4. *The integrated ratio analysis for 1999 Takeda is provided in Exhibit 4CS-2(a) and (b). The exhibits also provide the corresponding ratios for Pfizer 1999 (as calculated in Chapter 4).*

Exhibit 4CS-2(a)

Disaggregation Of ROA and ROE On a Pretax Basis	Takeda	Pfizer
Pre-interest and tax margin	21.7%	28.9%
X asset turnover	0.94	0.83
= Pre-interest and tax ROA	20.5%	24.1%
Less: interest on assets	0.1%	1.2%
Post-interest ROA	20.3%	22.9%
X leverage	1.03	2.20
Pretax ROE	21.0%	50.2%

- Pre-interest and tax margin = EBIT/sales = (182,142 + 1,059)/84,463
- Asset turnover: see Exhibit 4CS-1(a)
- Interest on assets = interest/average assets = 1,059/895,536
- Leverage = Average assets/average equity = 895,536/868,377

Exhibit 4CS-2(b)

ROE Disaggregation: 3- and 5-Component Dupont Models					
Total components					
3	5			Takeda	Pfizer
	1	Tax burden(Net income/EBT)		0.50	0.72
	2	X Financing (EBT/EBIT)		0.99	0.95
	3	X Operations (EBIT/Sales)		21.7%	28.9%
1		= Net income/sales		10.9%	19.7%
2	4	X Asset turnover		0.94	0.83
3	5	X Leverage		1.03	2.20
		= Return on equity		10.6%	36.2%

- Net income/EBT = 91,755/182,142
- EBT/EBIT = 182,142/(182,142 + 1,059)
- Other variables defined in Exhibit 4CS-2(a)

Consistent with the analysis used to answer questions 1 and 2, Pfizer reports stronger profitability ratios whereas Takeda's reports better solvency and activity ratios.

Both *stronger* and *better* are relative terms. Leverage is 1.03 for Takeda and 2.20 for Pfizer. The lower ratio for Takeda reflects less debt and hence higher solvency. However, from the point of view of profitability, the lower leverage translates into lower ROE and in that sense, Pfizer's leverage is preferred. The effects of leverage can be seen when we compare Takeda and Pfizer's ROA and ROE. Takeda's (pretax) ROA at 20.5% is virtually identical to its (pretax) ROE of 21.0%. Pfizer, on the other hand, has an ROE of 50.2%, considerably above its ROA of 24.1%.

There is one other striking difference; Pfizer's tax burden is far lower than Takeda's.[5]

5. The 5-component disaggregation[6] of Roche's 1999 - 2000 ROE as well as Pfizer's 1999 ROE is presented below. All amounts are in CHF millions.

Exhibit 4CS-3

	5-Component Disaggregation Of ROE		
		Roche	Pfizer
		2000	1999	1999
1. Tax burden (Net income/EBT)	0.76	0.75	0.72
2. X Financing (EBT/EBIT)	0.86	0.86	0.95
3. X Operations (EBIT/Sales)	38.2%	31.9%	28.9%
= Net income/sales	25.1%	20.5%	19.7%
4. X Asset turnover	0.41	0.39	0.83
5. X Leverage	2.52	2.61	2.20
= Return on equity	26.1%	21.0%	36.2%

---

[5] Pfizer's effective tax rate is discussed on pages 310 - 311 of the text.

[6] The following data used in the calculations was taken directly from Roche's financial statements. Year-end values were used for assets and equity. For net income, profit after taxes was used to avoid the effects of the accounting change in 2000.

	2000	1999	Source
Net income	7,196	5,653	Given (profit after taxes)
EBT	9,468	7,555	Given (profit before taxes)
Interest	1,487	1,237	Footnote 10
EBIT	10,955	8,792	EBT + interest
Sales	28,672	27,567	Given
Assets	69,535	70,431	Given
Equity	27,608	26,954	Given

(i) Roche's ROE increased by 5.1% (a 25% increase) in 2000. A review of the five components that make up ROE indicates that the improvement was due primarily to operations as operating profitability increased 6.3% (from 31.9% to 38.2%). The other four components were virtually unchanged.[7]

Following the top-down approach, we now focus on operating profitability and analyze the components that contributed to the improvement in Roche's ROE by preparing common-size income statements for 1999-2000.

Common size statements -- Roche

	2000		1999	
Sales	28,672	**100.0%**	27,567	**100.0%**
Cost of sales	(9,163)	**-32.0%**	(8,874)	**-32.2%**
Gross profit	19,509	**68.0%**	18,693	**67.8%**
Marketing and distribution	(8,746)	**-30.5%**	(7,813)	**-28.3%**
Research & development	(3,950)	**-13.8%**	(3,782)	**-13.7%**
Administration	(1,242)	**-4.3%**	(1,174)	**-4.3%**
Amortization of intangible assets	(1,474)	**-5.1%**	(1,207)	**-4.4%**
Operating profit before special items and financial income	4,097	**14.3%**	4,717	**17.1%**
Special items	3,034	**10.6%**	1,704	**6.2%**
Operating profit before financial income	7,131	**24.9%**	6,421	**23.3%**
Financial income	3,824	**13.3%**	2,371	**8.6%**
EBIT	10,955	**38.2%**	8,792	**31.9%**

Analysis of the common-size statements serves to reveal some surprising results. On an (ongoing) operational level, Roche's profitability did not improve - it actually declined 2.8% in 2000 from 17.1% to 14.3%. The decline was primarily due to increased marketing and distribution costs that increased 2.2% (from 28.3% to 30.5%). Thus, the improvement in EBIT/Sales is illusory as it is solely due to one-shot "special items" and increases in financial income. On the contrary, on an ongoing basis it is possible that Roche's profitability is declining!

---

[7] Leverage did change somewhat but in the opposite direction; i.e. the decrease in leverage serves to reduce ROE rather than improve it.

(ii) Referring to Exhibit 4CS-3, we find that Pfizer's 1999 ROE is 36.2% whereas Roche's is 21.0%. Examining the five components that make up ROE, we find that the major factor contributing to Pfizer's higher ROE is asset turnover.[8] At 0.83, Pfizer's turnover is more than twice that of Takeda's turnover ratio of 0.39.

Following the top-down approach, we now focus on activity ratios and analyze the components that contribute to the differences between Roche and Pfizer.

Activity	Numerator	Denominator	Roche	Pfizer
Inventory turnover	*Cost of sales* 8,874	*1999 Inventory* 6,546	**1.36**	**1.45**
No. of days	*365* 365	*Inventory turnover* 1.36	**269**	**251**
Receivable* turnover	*Sales* 27,567	*1999 Receivables* 6,178	**4.46**	**4.78**
No. of days	*365* 365	*Receivable turnover* 4.46	**82**	**76**
Fixed asset turnover	*Sales* 27,567	*1999 fixed assets* 14,240	**1.94**	**3.32**
Total asset turnover	*Sales* 27,567	*1999 assets* 70,431	**0.39**	**0.83**

* Receivables include trade notes and trade receivables only.

As the above data indicate, Pfizer's activity ratios are more efficient in every respect. Differences in inventory and receivables ratios are not that large. The major efficiency seems to be with respect to fixed asset turnover. However, as noted earlier these differences may result from differences in accounting methods (e.g. differing patterns of depreciation.)

---

[8] Taxes and financing are identical, whereas differences in profitability and leverage would result in higher ROE for Roche.

Chapter 5 - Solutions

Overview:

Problem Length	*Problem #'s*
{S}	*1,4,5,6,12-15*
{M}	*2,3,7,8,10,11*
{L}	*9*

NOTE: The problems in this chapter are designed primarily as a basis for discussion of the issues covered in this chapter. There are no absolutely right/wrong answers. The solutions that follow should be viewed in that spirit.

1.{S} The FASB view of neutrality is consistent with the classical approach, that takes the position that an "ideal" accounting paradigm can and should be designed disregarding potentially adverse impacts.

Market-based researchers, however, argue that the costs and benefits of accounting policy setting should be subject to economic analysis. Neutrality as defined in the quotation is therefore *not a desirable objective*. The fact that certain firms would be adversely affected by accounting standards renders the standard non (pareto[1]) optimal. Thus, although the efficacy of an accounting system is measurable by its market impact (information content), that same impact means that it is not possible to use information content to determine accounting policy.

The "positive" approach argues that *de facto* neutrality is *not a feasible objective*. The accounting standard setting process is influenced by the impact, favorable or unfavorable, that standards have on firms. Firms lobby (in many cases successfully) for or against certain standards precisely for that reason. This is not necessarily bad. Rather it is a "fact of life" and in this view, accounting standards and the standard setting process cannot be determined exogenously of firms' production-investment decisions.

---

[1] Pareto optimality is defined as the condition where a change to a new equilibrium leaves nobody worse off and at least one participant is better off.

2.{M}a. This question is difficult to answer without knowing the total information set provided by each system in its first report. However, assuming that in other respects they are identical, information system Alpha is a superior system insofar as it provides a better prediction of the second report.

b. Since, under the Alpha system, the second report could be forecasted better, at the time of its issuance it would contain fewer "surprises" and show less information content. The Gamma system, however, would contain a greater degree of "surprise" and, therefore, show greater information content.

c. The answers to parts a and b point out the problems of focusing only on the market reaction to one report at a specific point in time. Although market reaction may tell us something about the information content of that given report, it does not tell the whole story. Accounting reports may contain information that will only be known at a later point in time (outside the "window" examined). Similarly, nonreaction may be due to knowledge generated by previous information provided by the system (alone or in conjunction with external information sources); the better a system predicts, the less "information" content in subsequent reports.

d. Ingberman and Sorter viewed accounting systems as part of an overall data base whose purpose is to aid in forecasting the impact on the firm of changes in the firm and the environment. Thus, their view suggests the following "scenario":

1. Financial statements provide information as to how previous changes in the environment impacted the firm.

2. A change occurs in the environment. Market participants use their previous knowledge (see #1) to assess the potential impact of that change on the firm. Market reaction occurs at this time.

3. Subsequent reports update and confirm the extent to which the environmental change affected the firm. A small (or nonexistent) market reaction at the time of issuance of these reports means that most (or all) of the reaction occurred earlier.

4.   The measures of the effects on the firm provided by the subsequent reports are then used to update the database and make projections.

Similar to the situation described by the Alpha and Gamma information systems, Ingberman and Sorter argued that focusing on the specific point in time when a given accounting report is issued may be the wrong way to assess the value of the information provided by accounting reports.

3.{M}a.   (i)   The efficient market hypothesis (EMH) states that a market is efficient if security prices immediately and fully reflect all available relevant information. If the market fully reflects information, the knowledge of that information would not allow anyone to profit from it because stock prices already incorporate the information.

The weak form asserts that stock prices already reflect all information that can be derived by examining market trading data such as the history of past prices and trading volume.

Technical analysis in the form of charting involves the search for recurrent and predictable patterns in stock prices to enhance returns. The EMH implies that this type of analysis is without value. If past prices contain no useful information for predicting future returns, there is no point in following any technical trading rule for timing the purchases and sales of securities. According to weak-form efficiency, no investor can earn excess returns by developing trading rules based on historical price and return information. A simple policy of buying and holding will be at least as good as any technical procedure. Tests generally show that technical trading rules do not produce superior returns after making adjustments for transactions costs and taxes.

(ii)   The semistrong form says that a firm's stock price already reflects all publicly available information about a firm's prospects. Examples of publicly available information are annual reports of companies and investment advisory data. Empirical evidence mostly supports the semistrong form, but occasional studies are inconsistent with this form of market efficiency.

Fundamental analysis uses earnings and dividend prospects of the firm, expectations of future interest rates, and risk evaluation of the firm to determine proper stock prices. The EMH predicts that most fundamental analysis is doomed to failure. According to semistrong-form efficiency, no investor can earn excess returns from trading rules based on any publicly available information. Fundamental analysis is no better than technical analysis in enabling investors to capture above-average returns. Only analysts with unique insight earn superior returns.

The strong form of the EMH holds that market prices incorporate both publicly available and privately held (insider) information. [However, empirical evidence suggests insiders may earn abnormal returns using inside information.] Both technical and fundamental analysis would not be able to earn abnormal returns under the strong form.

In summary, the EMH holds that the market appears to adjust so quickly to information about individual stocks and the economy as a whole that no technique of selecting a portfolio -- using either technical or fundamental analysis-- can consistently outperform a strategy of simply buying and holding a diversified group of securities, such as those making up the popular market averages,

b. Even in perfectly efficient markets, portfolio managers have several roles. Two of these deal with the crux of any investment decision risk and return.

   1. *Identify the risk/return objectives for the portfolio given the investor's constraints and develop a well-diversified portfolio with the selected risk level.*

       In an efficient market, portfolio managers are responsible for tailoring the portfolio to meet the investor's needs rather than to beat the market, which requires identifying the client's requirements and risk tolerance. Although an efficient market prices securities fairly, each security still has firm-specific risk that portfolio managers can eliminate through diversification. Therefore, rational security selection requires selecting a well-diversified portfolio that provides the level of systematic risk that matches the investor's risk tolerance.

2. *Develop capital market expectations for appropriate asset-allocation decisions.*

As part of the asset-allocation decision portfolio managers need to consider their expectations for the relative returns of the various capital markets to choose an appropriate asset allocation.

c. The empirical evidence generally supports the weak form and to a great degree the semistrong firm. However, the existing anomalies suggest that *superior* analysis of available information may result in excess or abnormal returns. Furthermore, as market efficiency is often explained as being the product of the plethora of analysts analyzing information, neglected areas such as smaller firms, firms that have fallen "out of favor" or sources of information not readily available to (or used by) all analysts are areas that analysts can most readily exploit. A word of caution - however - if many analysts simultaneously try to exploit these sources, then once again efficiency will prevail.

4.{S}a. Standard research procedures abstract from (i.e. eliminate) general market conditions to test for (market) reaction specific to a firm or sample of firms. If an accounting standard affects all firms equally, then a test looking for firm-specific reaction will not find anything, as the informational impact is (inadvertently) included in "general" market conditions. Even if the standard does not affect all firms, but only a sizable proportion of them, then standard research designs would be unlikely to find (significant) market reaction.

b. Somewhat paradoxically, the more pervasive the impact of an accounting change the less likely that market reaction will be found. Only if studies are designed to measure the differential effect of such changes on particular firms can a market reaction be found.

c. Examples of pervasive accounting standards are:
1. Changing prices (SFAS 33*)
2. Pension plans (SFAS 87)
3. Income taxes (SFAS 109)
4. Postretirement benefits (SFAS 106)

* This argument may explain the insignificant results found by studies that examined the impact of SFAS 33 (see Appendix 8-A).

5.{S} This statement is most consistent with the positive approach to accounting theory. Proponents of the classical and market-based approaches might agree with the descriptive validity of the statement. Classicists, however, view the political process as an undesirable 'fact of life' to be overcome and as irrelevant by the market-based proponents. The positive approach, on the other hand, holds that the ramifications and implications of this political process are an essential element in understanding how accounting standards are developed and the motivation of firms in opting for alternative choices.

6.{S} Pharmaceutical companies are often the subject of attack by politicians and consumer groups that drug prices are too high. The political cost hypothesis argues that firms may choose to "artificially" depress earnings if they fear legislative or regulatory actions would be taken against them if it was perceived that their earnings were excessive.

1993, at the beginning of President Clinton's term was the year that his wife Hillary Rodham Clinton headed a committee whose objective was to create a nation-wide health care system. As part of that process, drug prices (and profits) were under extreme scrutiny. This environment may explain why the Pfizer company "managed down earnings."

7.{M} *Note: Most, if not all, of the items listed have analytical implications that are independent of financial statements, i.e., they would have to be considered whether or not the firm issued financial statements. We focus here only on the implications of these items in the context of financial statements.*

(i)   To the extent that a firm's labor costs are related to profitability, (e.g. profit sharing plans), management may have an incentive to select accounting policies that dampen reported profits. Lower reported profits may also keep down demands for higher wages and benefits. Thus, the analyst should be prepared to "adjust" the firm's reported performance upwards as the firm may have been too conservative.

Similarly, if a labor contract is coming up for renewal, and the firm's financial statements show strong performance, then one can expect higher demands from labor, increased probability of a strike, and increased labor costs in the future. (Also see iii below)

(ii) Market efficiency is increased by analysts competing to "beat the market." This motivation and the resultant behavior (somewhat paradoxically) leads to information being immediately impounded in prices. If this is true then the degree of efficiency should be (positively) related to the number of analysts covering the firm. Thus, an analyst who wants to uncover and exploit information not recognized by the market should look for firms that are covered by few other analysts. (Also see iv below)

(iii) The bonus plan hypothesis is that managers will act to enhance their well being even if it may not be in the firm's best interest. For example, managers may opt for financial reporting methods that increase income if their compensation is directly (or indirectly) tied to the firm's income. Analysts need to be aware of this phenomenon to better understand the effect of this behavior on the firm's reported performance. (Also see v below)

More sophisticated manifestations of this behavior include:

(1) taking a "big bath" in a year when performance is below some threshold anyway, thereby increasing the probability that the threshold level will be achieved in the future.

(2) alternatively, if a threshold has been achieved and no further benefit (to managers) accrues from exceeding that threshold, they may engage in income smoothing to "store" income for future years when adverse business conditions make the threshold harder to achieve.

(iv) (1) One of the documented anomalies of the efficient market hypothesis is the small firm effect. Small firms tend to earn abnormal positive returns (even after compensating for risk). This phenomenon may be related to item ii, the number of analysts covering the firm, as larger firms tend to have more of an analyst following. This argues for more emphasis on the analysis of smaller firms.

However, there is a cost-benefit tradeoff. An investor with $100 million to invest may have to choose between investing in ten larger firms or 100 smaller firms. The additional return earned on the latter may not compensate for the higher research costs (especially time) and lower liquidity. For a given research effort that results in an additional 1% return, the benefits will differ considerably depending on the size of the firm. The 1% additional return for a firm whose capitalization is $100 million is considerably greater than a 1% return on a firm whose capitalization is only one million dollars. The $10,000 return earned on the latter may not compensate for the research time and money expended.

(2) On the other hand, the political cost hypothesis argues that larger firms are more sensitive to certain accounting changes and patterns of income. Analysts should be on the lookout to see if large firms have chosen accounting methods that shield them from political costs.

(v)　As noted earlier (item iii) managers may have incentives to take actions that enhance their position at the expense of the firm. The incentives for this behavior are reduced when managers are also owners of the firm. Thus, the more a firm is controlled by its owners, the lower the potential effects of agency costs.

(vi)　Companies in the same industry tend to choose similar accounting methods. When a company deviates from these policies, in addition to adjusting for the alternative methods the analyst should ask what motivates these divergences and what can be learned about the company's "corporate profile." Do the changes signal a shift in emphasis from one segment (industry) to another?

Additionally, for firms in certain industries (oil and gas, banking) the political cost hypothesis discussed earlier is a relevant consideration.

8.{M}a.b.　Assuming external validity and generalizability of the survey, there are three possible explanations for the results:

(1)　Firms were not aware of the magnitude of their postretirement health benefits until they were forced to calculate them by the new accounting rule.

(2)　The mandated balance sheet recognition and disclosure of health care liabilities was directly responsible for their curtailment by firms.

(3)　There is no direct cause and effect between balance sheet recognition and the curtailment of benefits. The events are only correlated with another.

The first explanation assumes that managers (as well as investors) are "fixated" on annual reports and that managers have no appreciation of actual costs unless and until they are contained in the financial reporting system. Previous research on leases and foreign currency translation suggest that managers do pay more attention to events that they must account for. Similarly, field tests carried out when the health cost disclosure was first introduced indicated that (some) managers had difficulty in complying with the requirements because of a lack of data availability.

Because of this lack of data and the complexity of calculating the present value of these benefits (see Chapter 12) it is possible that some firms had only the haziest idea of the cost of these benefits. Postemployment benefits were often granted to unionized employees as trade offs for current wages that had to be recognized as expense immediately. Managers had a clear incentive to trade future costs for present costs. [A senior manager of one Fortune 100 company told one of the authors that he thought the benefits would not have been granted if management had known their cost.]

The second explanation is consistent with the "economic consequences" branch of the positive accounting approach. By adversely affecting the company's reported performance, the new accounting standard may impact one or more of the following:

(1) management compensation,
(2) bond covenants on existing debt,
(3) the terms of any new debt,
(4) future labor negotiations, and
(5) internal resource allocation decisions.

All of these factors can have real costs associated with them and may be incentives for management to reduce health care costs.

Somewhat less likely in our opinion, is the possibility that managers reduced their health care costs because they feared the market reaction to the accounting recognition and disclosure. This is not necessarily inconsistent with the efficient market hypothesis as it is possible that even though the market is efficient, managers may not perceive it to be so. However, in this case, prior disclosure requirements (SFAS 81) and the long gestation period of the exposure draft, comment period and standard may have taken some of the surprise out of the actual accounting.

The third explanation is the most likely. Under this view, the benefit curtailments were not caused by new accounting standards. Rather, both events were influenced by the same underlying factor--the explosion of health care costs in recent years. The growth in these costs was a major factor that triggered the FASB project that resulted in new accounting standards. Similarly, the higher costs induced firms to reduce the health care benefits offered to employees. Thus the coincidence of these events is an example of *association and correlation not causation*.

c.   One would not expect to see any market reaction to the survey as companies had already been disclosing the effect of the new standard. As far as reaction to the accounting rule itself and subsequent disclosures, any market reaction observed and its direction (positive or negative) would result from one of three factors:
(1) the disclosure requirement itself,
(2) the curtailment of benefits, or
(3) the level and trend of health care costs.

Under the efficient market hypothesis, *ceteris paribus*, one would not expect to see any market reaction to the rule itself or the subsequent balance sheet disclosures unless the market (analysts) had previously done a poor job of estimating the level of a firm's health care liabilities. Then the actual disclosure may contain surprises ("good" and "bad") triggering market reaction.

Under the "economic consequences" hypothesis one would expect to see market reaction, primarily at the time of the adoption of the new rule. The direction would presumably be negative, unless it is assumed that the market anticipates that the disclosure rule will force firms to curtail future benefits. The curtailment may be perceived as being positive as it lowers future costs.

Under any approach, the results must be understood in the context of rising health care costs. Any results indicating that firms that have a higher burden of health care costs perform poorly relative to firms whose health care costs are not as high may be measuring reaction to rising health care costs rather than to the new accounting and disclosure requirement. This point would be especially relevant if the research did not focus on the period (days) immediately surrounding the new disclosure requirement.

9.{L}a. To determine abnormal returns, one must abstract from general market conditions as well as industry factors. Overall market indices rose by 1% to 2%, much less than the increases in Amgen (6.3%) and Deere (5.2%) and, in the opposite direction, the 16.9% decline in Dell. Thus, ignoring industry factors all three firms could be said to exhibit abnormal returns.

When we consider industry factors, the answers become more complicated. As the index for computer stocks increased slightly, it would be safe to argue that the decline in Dell is firm-specific and would qualify as an "abnormal" return. To a lesser extent, a similar argument can be made for Deere as the overall industry index for heavy machinery increased by only 2.9%; Deere's increase was substantially higher. However, this conclusion would depend on Deere's "beta" relative to the industry index. If it was very high then Deere's high return would be considered industry rather than firm related.

For Amgen, it would seem that its increase of 6.3% was industry-specific (rather than firm-specific) as the biotechnology index increased by a similar 5.4%. However, the industry index may itself be affected by firm-specific events (see Part E to this problem). Amgen is a component of the biotechnology index. Thus the change in that index may reflect the firm-specific change in Amgen rather than industry wide factors. To remedy this problem, an industry index without Amgen would have to be constructed and used. Additionally, to the extent that news about one firm provides information about other firms in the industry, it is difficult to argue that the market reaction was not related to Amgen simply because it affected the shares of other firms in the same industry. Similar arguments can, of course, be made for the other industry indices.

b. The efficient market hypothesis does not hold that the market is omniscient; only that it correctly and rapidly processes available information. If the information about Amgen's earnings was not known earlier, then the negative reaction at the time of the announcement would be totally consistent with the efficient market hypothesis. Only if there existed prior public information,[2] in the form of lower orders for example, that could have permitted the market to anticipate the earnings disappointment, would the lack of anticipation be an example of market inefficiency.

For Dell, the question of market inefficiency seems to be more relevant. Only a month earlier, Dell had hit an all-time high of approximately $50. This raises the first question: how did this happen? What news (seemingly completely contrary to present news about the firm) did the market react to then? Since then, the stock had declined by about 30% prior to February 24. Obviously, the market had wind of the negative news prior to the February 24th announcement. The question now becomes: why wasn't the full reaction immediate? Why did the decline take over a month? To answer these questions, more information would be required as to the pattern of news relating to Dell appearing in the last month.

c.   The existence of abnormal returns would be an indicator of reaction to firm-specific news. Thus, as argued in part a, it appears that Dell's market reaction was related to the news item.

However, the strongest argument can be made for Amgen. The reaction was over a very short time horizon (one half-hour) *after* the normal market close, it immediately followed the release of the news item, and it was in the opposite direction to the stock's movement prior to the news release.

d.   It is difficult to determine the "cause" of the market reaction because there are confounding news items:

(i)   the reduction of the long-term profit goal; and
(ii) the withdrawal of the stock issue.

Which of these items is "responsible" for the market reaction is difficult if not impossible to determine.

---

[2] We are ignoring the strong form of the efficient market hypothesis, which holds that even nonpublic information is reflected in prices as insiders trade on it. In Amgen's case, one would have to know when the insiders became aware of the disappointing earnings expectation and whether they had the time or opportunity to trade on it.

e. (i) In this part, we assume that the Amgen effect is not large enough to significantly affect the Biotechnology index.

   The actual change in Amgen occurred after the market closed on February 24. On that day the biotechnology index was positive, and as we argued in part C, Amgen's reaction is surely a result of the news item. However, by using February 25 as the announcement date, when the index was negative, a researcher may erroneously conclude that the reaction was industry related.

  (ii) The evidence about the components of the index clearly indicates that the index was significantly affected by Amgen. The assumption made in (i) does not hold. However, since Amgen affects the index, by using the index to abstract industry wide effects, the researcher would erroneously conclude that the Amgen effect was industry related when the correct conclusion was the reverse. Amgen caused the industry effect! (Also see discussion earlier for questions 4 and 9a.)

f. One would expect to see little or no market reaction after the financial statements are released as all the information was anticipated by then. The market reaction will depend on how the actual earnings report compares with that expected (not just with prior year earnings).

   This does not mean that financial statements in general are irrelevant. As discussed in previous questions (see #2), relevance should not be based on one statement but rather on the whole system of accounting reports. After all, the market reacted to a forecast of a number produced by that system. It is difficult to argue then that financial statements are irrelevant. Moreover, the detailed income statement will contain the components of earnings and may explain why earnings were disappointing (were gross margins too low, was selling expense too high, did research expense increase, did the tax rate rise, etc.). Taken together with the balance sheet (e.g. inventory levels) and cash flow statement (cash from operations) the statements may contain data that help the market forecast future earnings and cash flows. [At times, the market may first react to an earnings release in one direction, then reverse direction when details of the earnings report become available, casting new light on the results.]

g. Changes in production (and demand) ultimately affect profitability. Financial statements are useful in determining how such changes affect profitability. They provide information about a firm's operating and financial leverage, and provide a historical record of how previous changes in volume affected profitability.

10.{M}a. Negative reaction would be expected at the time of the 8-K filings, with the second filing have a greater effect due to KPMG's negative views of the company's accounting and internal controls. As changing auditors is generally negatively viewed by the market, even the first filing would be expected to have a negative effect.

b. No reaction would be expected at the time Bloomberg reported the 8-K filings as, two weeks later, the information should be widely known and stock prices would have adjusted to it.

c. There was, as expected, (muted) negative reaction at the time of the original 4/20 announcement and the negative reaction continued to 4/24. However following 4/24, the stock price recovered for a day or two. Afterwards, however, there was a steep drop as the stock price lost over 20% of its value. Thus, while the market did react negatively, there seemed to be a "delayed" reaction. The most surprising result is the reaction following the Bloomberg report. As noted in part b., one would not expect any reaction, as by 5/09 the filings were "old" news. If, however, for some reason the news were not widely known, the reaction would be expected to be negative. The actual market reaction, however, was sharply positive, recovering approximately 50% of the previous losses.

d. The delayed negative reaction may be a function of the market "digesting" and analyzing the news. The initial announcement only spoke in generalities about the accounting problems and auditor conflict. The nature or magnitudes were not disclosed then and it may have taken a while for these details to become known.

The surprising price recovery in mid-May may be due to overreaction to the initial news. The initial drop may have reflected increased risk as the market anticipated more bad news. When the Bloomberg report came in without any more bad news, the market may have been relieved and buying offset some of the initial overreaction.

11. {M} This question is based on the notion that, as there are market incentives to disclose financial data, market forces will result in rational managers providing such information.

Beaver's approach to this question is based on the concept of information as an economic good and explores three potential reasons why market forces alone will not provide the "sufficient" or "right amount" of information. The reasons offered attempt to explain why market forces by themselves do not result in the "appropriate" amount of information being produced. These reasons, however, do not necessarily mean that levels of disclosure mandated by regulation result in an optimal amount of information production and disclosure. Beaver's three reasons follow:

(1) An economic commodity will be produced so long as the benefits from the commodity outweigh its production cost (marginal cost equal marginal benefits). This holds so long as those who benefit from a good also bear its cost. Information, however, is a *public good*. Access to it cannot [and perhaps should not (see (2) below)] be limited. Thus, there will be some who benefit from disclosure without having to pay for it. Two examples are given:

   (i) Competing firms who obtain information from annual reports without bearing the cost of information production; and

   (ii) Investors who, based on the information provided, decide *not* to invest in the company. They obtain the benefit without paying any of the cost.

This so-called *free rider problem* reduces the incentive to disclose, as those bearing the cost are not fully compensated.

(2) The second reason is usually couched in terms of equity or fairness. Without regulation, there may be selective disclosure and uneven distribution of information. Some

investors will be better informed than others.[3] Regulation is needed to "protect" the uninformed from the informed.

(3) There exists *information asymmetry* as managers are better informed about the firm than investors. Moreover, managers have incentives to suppress (unfavorable) information. As investors know that some firms suppress information but do not know which firms are doing so, they will treat all firms in some "average" fashion. Hence, poorer performing (below average) firms will be priced "too high" and better (above average) firms will be priced "too low". Poorer (better) performing firms will want to offer more (fewer) shares to investors as a result. To combat this, managers of better performing firms may offer warranties on their information (audited statements) and other guarantees to investors to distinguish themselves. The result may be that managers of "better" firms absorb too much risk leading to an *inefficient* sharing of risk in the economy. Regulation is designed to mitigate this information asymmetry.

12.{S}a. The actual reserve additions should not result in any market reaction, assuming that the market knew about the potential losses. However, the rule change itself could cause market reaction, not so much from the actual requirement to recognize losses, but from the associated *requirement that increased the level of required reserves*. This tightening up would increase the risk of a firm becoming "technically insolvent".

b. This article would probably not result in any market reaction. Any reaction (as described in part a) would occur at the time of the announcement of the rule change itself.

---

[3] One can debate, as does Beaver, whether this is inherently unfair. Presumably, those who are better informed have paid for more information. The only thing stopping others from becoming as well informed is their unwillingness to pay (or lack of funds). This may be unfortunate but, as with any other good, it is a fact of life. Should all goods be distributed equally? Certainly some have put forth this argument. Its ramifications are clearly beyond the scope of this text.

c. Positive accounting theory views a firm and its environment as consisting of a "nexus of contracts". The terms of these contracts, in many cases, are determined by accounting based numbers. RAP rules are a perfect example of this concept. Regulators set the rules for the contract between the firm and its environment. RAP rules determine not only the amount of profits that regulators (the environment) allow the firm to report but also the terms (net worth requirements) permitting the firm to operate at all.

13.{S}*The arguments below are summarized from Christopher Farrell "The 'Efficient Market' was a Good Idea - and Then Came the Crash," Business Week (February 22, 1988), page 140.*

There is considerable divergence of opinion regarding the implications of that crash for the Efficient Market Theory (EMT). Detractors of the EMT cite the crash as evidence that the theory is not a good description of financial markets. They argue that there was no significant news prior to the crash, certainly not sufficient news to justify a 25% decline in New York Stock Exchange prices. The market reacted, they contend, to sharp declines experienced the previous two days. Thus panic set in, there was no rationality and a herd instinct took over.

Defenders of the EMT, on the other hand, say that the crash does not invalidate the EMT. Market volatility had increased in the weeks prior to the crash. Then when a sell-of began, the exchanges broke down. The computers could not keep up with the flow of orders and specialists panicked. Thus, institutional factors helped turn a normal decline into a panic.

14.{S}From a positive accounting perspective, it is consistent for managers to engage in behavior leading to an increase in their compensation. If they perceived that using aggressive accounting techniques would increase share prices (and hence the value of their options), they would certainly do so.

From an efficient markets perspective, however, it should not have been possible for managers to engage in practices that would "fool the market" over an extended period. This view holds that market prices reflect all information, even non-public information, and therefore should not be "misled" by aggressive accounting techniques.

15. {S}a. Managers have superior information as to the nature of a firm's operations including the recurring (and nonrecurring) nature of its earnings/cash flows. A proponent of the EMH could view pro forma earnings as a means whereby managers provide additional information to investors. The motivation may be to dampen the volatility (risk) of market returns by "guiding" investors to appropriate valuation decisions.

From a positive accounting perspective, pro forma earnings may be viewed as an example of managers managing expectations as the manager is saying "here is how I really performed" and "ignore the nonrecurring factors." Note that managing expectations, *per se*, does not necessarily mean that managers are being dishonest;[4] similar to the EMH approach, managers may have superior knowledge that they are conveying to investors. The difference lies in their motivation. Under the EMH, their motivation is not tied to their pecuniary or other rewards.

b. As stated above, it can serve as a mechanism to convey superior information to the market, thereby reducing risk.

c. Managers would probably argue that pro forma data provide superior inputs to the forecasting model envisioned by Ingberman and Sorter. Whether this is the case would be shown as future financial statements are issued and models are updated and revised accordingly.

---

[4] At the same time, it does not preclude it.

Chapter 6 - Solutions

1.{S}a.   Start with the basic inventory relationship

$$BI + P = COGS + EI$$

Opening inventory	400 units @ $20	$ 8,000
Purchases	1,000	25,000
Total	1,400 units	$33,000

    (i)   Under FIFO, ending inventory consists of 600 units:

100 purchased in second quarter at $24	$2,400
300 purchased in third quarter at $26	7,800
200 purchased in fourth quarter at $28	5,600
600 units total	$15,800

    (ii) Under LIFO, ending inventory consists of 600 units:

400 inventory at January 1 at $20	$8,000
200 purchased in first quarter at $22	4,400
600 units total	$12,400

    (iii) Under average cost, ending inventory consists of 600 units with an average cost of $33,000/1,400 = $23.5714 per unit or $14,142.84 total.

    b.   COGS for the year equals the $33,000 total of opening inventory plus purchases, less closing inventory under the method chosen:

    (i)   FIFO: $33,000 less $15,800 = $17,200
    (ii) LIFO: $33,000 less $12,400 = $20,600
    (iii) Average cost: $33,000 less $14,142.84 = $18,857.16

    c.   (i)   Reported income is highest under FIFO (lowest COGS) and lowest under LIFO (highest COGS). Average cost is in between FIFO and LIFO.

        (ii) Stockholders' equity is highest under FIFO (highest inventory and retained earnings) and lowest under LIFO (lowest inventory and retained earnings), with average cost in between.

2.{S}Using FIFO instead of LIFO when prices are rising and inventory quantities are stable has the following effects:

(i) Gross profit margins are higher under FIFO than under LIFO because revenues at higher current prices are matched with cost-of-goods-sold measured using older (lower) prices.

(ii) Net income is lower under LIFO than under FIFO because cost-of-goods-sold is higher.

(iii) Cash from operations is higher under LIFO than under FIFO because income tax paid is lower.

(iv) Inventory balances are lower under LIFO than under FIFO because cost-of-goods-sold is higher and lower prices remain in inventory.

(v) Inventory turnover is lower under FIFO than under LIFO because cost-of-goods-sold is lower and inventory balances higher. Both factors decrease the inventory turnover ratio.

(vi) Working capital is lower under LIFO than under FIFO because inventory balances are lower, despite partial offset from higher cash balances (because of lower tax payments).

(vii) Total assets are higher under FIFO because FIFO inventory balances are higher.

(viii) The debt-to-equity ratio is lower under FIFO than under LIFO because equity is higher, reflecting higher retained earnings.

3.{M}a.   Start with the basic inventory relationship

$$BI + P = COGS + EI$$

Since opening inventory is zero, both BI and P (purchases) are identical under FIFO and LIFO; the difference in COGS equals the difference in ending inventory. That difference can be computed as follows:

Total purchases in units = (3 x 100,000) + (3 x 125,000)
    + (3 x 150,000) + (3 x 200,000) = 1,725,000

Total sales in units = (6 x 100,000) + (6 x 150,000)
            = 1,500,000.

Therefore units in ending inventory =
        1,725,000 - 1,500,000 = 225,000

(i)   Purchases are identical; there is no difference between
        methods.

(ii)   Closing inventory under FIFO uses the latest costs of
        $15; under LIFO uses the earliest costs of $25; the
        difference is $10/unit x 225,000 = $2,250,000 (LIFO
        higher).

(iii)   COGS is $2,250,000 lower under LIFO, as the total of
        COGS and ending inventory is identical.

(iv)   As a result of lower COGS, LIFO pretax income is
        $2,250,000 higher.

(v)   Income tax expense is higher under LIFO by

        .40 x $2,250,000 = $900,000

(vi)   Net income is higher under LIFO by

        .60 x $2,250,000 = $1,350,000

(vii)   Since income tax is higher under LIFO, cash flow from
        operations is lower by $900,000 (assuming taxes paid in
        same year).

(viii) From (ii) ending inventory is higher by $2,250,000, but
        from (vii) cash is lower by $900,000. Therefore, LIFO
        working capital is higher by $2,250,000 - $900,000 =
        $1,350,000

        The problem illustrates that, when prices are
        declining, LIFO results in higher inventory and higher
        net income than FIFO. This solution would, however, be
        modified in practice as all inventory must be reported
        at the lower of cost or market. Thus inventory would
        have to be written down to market value for financial
        reporting purposes (but not for tax).

b.   If all inventory units were liquidated, FIFO and LIFO
      would be identical in all respects.

4. {M} We start by computing total inventory available for sale, using the second part of the identity BI + P = COGS + EI. Using the average cost amounts provided, the total must be $10,500 + $3,500 = $14,000. We also know that Metro purchased:

On February 1, 1,000 units @ $2	$ 2,000
On April 1, 2,800 units @ $3	8,400
Total	$10,400

We can now infer that the August 1 purchase must be for $3,600 ($14,000 less $10,400).

a. The unit price for the August 1 purchase must be $3,600/1,000 = **$3.60**.

b. First, we need to determine the number of units in ending inventory. From the average cost data, 25% of costs ($3,500/$14,000) remain, implying 25% of the 4,800 units purchased. Thus 1,200 units remain in ending inventory.

[Alternate solution: as the average cost is $2.9167, 3,600 units ($10,500/$2.9167 were sold.]

Under LIFO, these 1,200 units must be those *first* purchased:

1,000	units purchased February 1 @ $2	$2,000
200	units purchased April 1 @ $3	600
1,200	total	$2,600

Therefore COGS must be $14,000 less $2,600 = **$11,400**

Under FIFO, these 1,200 units must be those *last* purchased:

1,000	units purchased August 1 @ $3.60	$3,600
200	units purchased April 1 @ $3	600
1,200	total	$4,200

Therefore COGS must be $14,000 less $4,200 = **$9,800**

5.{L}a. This problem tests the interrelationships among accounting methods and differentiates between the flow of units and the flow of costs. Keep in mind that some factors are affected by the choice of accounting method but others are not.

Opening inventory (in this problem), purchases, and actual inventory turnover are not a function of accounting method. *Physical* turnover is based on units while *reported* turnover is based on dollars and is affected by the choice of accounting method. Thus the accounting method can only approximate the physical turnover.

Opening inventory is $500 for all methods. Since the firm replenishes inventory every month, its *actual* inventory turnover is 12. Thus, in units, its cost of goods sold is 12 times its inventory level. That is, 12 months of inventory were sold; one month remains.

The solution begins with the weighted average method:

Cost-of-goods sold = units sold x average cost = $12,000

As closing inventory = units in inventory x average cost, and, units sold are 12 times units in inventory; then closing inventory equals $1,000.

We can now solve for purchases:
Opening Inventory + Purchases = COGS + Closing Inventory
        $500   +   ?   = $12,000 + $1,000

Therefore, purchases equal $12,500.

Reported turnover = COGS/Average Inventory = $12,000/$750 = 16.

Under the LIFO method:

Since inventory in units does not change:

Closing Inventory = Opening Inventory = $500

Therefore, Cost of Goods Sold = Purchases = $12,500

Reported turnover = COGS/Average Inventory = $12,500/$500 = 25.

Under the FIFO method:

First, note that under the weighted average method, closing inventory is greater than opening inventory. As cost changes were only in one direction, they must have gone up during the year. Therefore, use of FIFO must result in higher net income (lower COGS) and higher income taxes. Since the cash flow difference is $400 (all attributable to taxes), the income/COGS difference must be $1000. Therefore, $COGS_{FIFO}$ is $11,500 and Closing Inventory is $1,500.

Reported turnover = COGS/Average Inventory = $11,500/$1,000 = 11.5.

The completed table is:

	FIFO	Weighted Average	LIFO
Opening inventory	$ 500	$ 500	$ 500
Purchases	12,500	12,500	12,500
Cost of goods sold	11,500	12,000	12,500
Closing inventory	1,500	1,000	500
Inventory turnover (reported)	11.5X	16.0X	25.0X
Inventory turnover (actual)	12.0X	12.0X	12.0X

b. Reported turnover under the FIFO method most closely approximates the actual physical turnover whereas LIFO is farthest away. The preferred (current cost) turnover ratio (LIFO COGS/Average FIFO inventory) $12,500/1,000 = 12.5 also approximates the physical turnover.

c. The choice of method affects reported income, income taxes paid, and (therefore) the change in cash. The LIFO method reports the lowest net income but highest cash flow from operations (because of lower tax payments). Neither cash for investment nor cash for financing are affected. Thus LIFO reports the highest net cash flow. The FIFO method reports the lower cash from operations and, therefore, the lowest net cash flow. The average cost method is halfway between the other two methods.

6.{L}a.   The first step is to obtain FIFO cost-of-goods-sold:

Pretax income = sales - COGS - other expenses

$5,000 = $25,000 - COGS - $12,000

Solving: COGS = $8,000

Purchases are equal to COGS + Closing Inventory
= $8,000 + $10,000 = $18,000.

The key to this problem is to distinguish between the flow of units and the flow of costs. Purchases are independent of the accounting method used.

Since half the units were sold, half remain in inventory. Under LIFO, therefore, the cost allocations to inventory and COGS are the reverse of those allocated under FIFO. That is, under LIFO, COGS = $10,000 and Closing Inventory = $8,000.

Under the weighted average method, as total purchases equal $18,000, the allocation between COGS and closing inventory will be equal: COGS = Closing Inventory = $9,000.

Recalling that pretax CFO depends on purchases, not COGS, we can now fill in the rest of the table.

	FIFO	Weighted Average	LIFO
Sales	$25,000	$25,000	$25,000
Cost of goods sold	8,000	9,000	10,000
Other expenses	12,000	12,000	12,000
Pretax income	5,000	4,000	3,000
Tax expense	2,000	1,600	1,200
Net income	3,000	2,400	1,800
Retained earnings	3,000	2,400	1,800
Cash from operations[1]	(7,000)	(6,600)	(6,200)
Cash balance[2]	3,000	3,400	3,800
Closing inventory	10,000	9,000	8,000
Purchases	18,000	18,000	18,000

[1] Cash from operations = Sales - Other expenses - Purchases - Tax expense.
[2] Cash balance = $10,000 + Cash from operations

b. **M & J Company**
   Balance Sheet, December 31, 20X0

	FIFO	Weighted Average	LIFO
Cash	$ 3,000	$ 3,400	$ 3,800
Inventory	10,000	9,000	8,000
Total assets	$ 13,000	$ 12,400	$ 11,800
Common stock	$ 10,000	$ 10,000	$ 10,000
Retained earnings	3,000	2,400	1,800
Total equities	$ 13,000	$ 12,400	$ 11,800

c. The advantages of LIFO are that it results in the highest cash flow (by reducing income taxes) and it best measures net income by matching the cost of sales with most recent costs to replace inventory sold. The disadvantage of LIFO is that inventory on the balance sheet is understated.

The advantage of FIFO is that inventory is measured at most recent costs. Its disadvantages are the reduced cash flow and overstatement of reported income.

Average cost has the disadvantage of misreporting both the balance sheet inventory and net income. Income taxes are higher than under the LIFO method (but lower than under FIFO). The "advantage" of average cost is that it is "less wrong" than LIFO on the balance sheet and "less wrong" than FIFO on the income statement.

7.{S}a. The number of units in inventory at December 31, 20X2 = 475 (100 + 500 - 125). Beginning inventory plus fourth quarter purchases equal $25,000 ($4,400 + $8,600 + $12,000). How that amount is allocated between ending inventory (EI) and cost-of-goods-sold (COGS) depends on the inventory method.

(i) FIFO EI equals:

	175 units @ $43	$ 7,525
	300 units @ $40	12,000
Total EI	475 units	$19,525

(ii) LIFO EI equals:

	100 units @ $44	$ 4,400
	200 units @ $43	8,600
	175 units @ $40	7,000
Total EI	475 units	$20,000

b. Cost of goods sold equals beginning inventory plus purchases less ending inventory:

   FIFO: $25,000 - $19,525 = $5,475

   LIFO: $25,000 - $20,000 = $5,000

Therefore, FIFO pretax income is $475 lower and income taxes are lower by $190 (40% of $475).

c. As the market price is now $40, the lower of cost or market (LOCOM) rule applies, and inventory with a cost exceeding $19,000 ($40 x 475) must be written down to that amount.

(i) FIFO: Inventory must be written down by $525, increasing COGS, decreasing pretax income and income taxes.

(ii) LIFO: Inventory must be written down by $1,000, increasing COGS. But as LOCOM writedowns are not permitted for tax purposes when LIFO is used, income taxes are not affected by the writedown.

8.{L}a. Adjusting Zenab to FIFO:

Since the LIFO reserve increased by $1,500, the LIFO effect is $1,500. Under FIFO, COGS is $1,500 lower at $59,800 ($61,300 - $1,500). Pretax income is $1,500 higher at $6,500.

A comparison of both companies on a FIFO basis is presented below:

	Zenab	Faybech
Sales	$ 92,700	$ 77,000
Cost of goods sold	59,800	52,000
Gross profit	$ 32,900	$ 25,000
Selling and general expense	26,400	21,500
Pretax income	$ 6,500	$ 3,500

b. Adjusting Faybech to LIFO/Current Cost is more complicated. The first step is to calculate an implied inflation rate using Zenab's statements. On a FIFO basis, Zenab's inventories are $24,900 + $3,600 = $28,500 at the beginning of the year. Of that inventory, 70%or $19,950 (.70 x $28,850) are carried on LIFO. The increase in the LIFO reserve implies a specific inflation rate of $1,500/$19,950 = 7.52%. Therefore, Faybech's COGS (pretax income) on an LIFO/current cost basis increases (decreases) by .0752 x $22,300 = $1,675. This decrease in pretax income is close to 50%.

A comparison of both companies on a LIFO basis is presented below:

	Zenab	Faybech
Sales	$ 92,700	$ 77,000
Cost of goods sold	61,300	53,675
Gross profit	$ 31,400	$ 23,325
Selling and general expense	26,400	21,500
Pretax income	$ 5,000	$ 1,825

Note that this solution is incomplete as Faybech is 100% on LIFO while Zenab is only 70% on LIFO. To complete the solution, convert the remaining 30% of Zenab's inventories to LIFO using the same inflation rate:

Thirty percent (30%) of Zenab inventory is FIFO (.30 x $28,500) or $8,550. Applying the same inflation rate of 7.52% increases COGS (reduces pretax income) by $643. The comparison now becomes:

	Zenab	Faybech
Sales	$ 92,700	$ 77,000
Cost of goods sold	61,943	53,675
Gross profit	$ 30,757	$ 23,325
Selling and general expense	26,400	21,500
Pretax income	$ 4,357	$ 1,825

c. It depends on the purpose of the comparison. There are three possibilities:

(1) Comparison of firms' operations.
(2) Comparison of firms' operations and tax policy.
(3) Analysis of firm's "economic" status.

If the purpose is a comparison of a firm's operations with another firm's, then the adjustment should be "as if" and a tax adjustment should be made. If the purpose is to compare operations and tax policy, then no tax adjustment should be made. Finally, for evaluation of the economic status no tax adjustment should be made unless liquidation is considered to be imminent.

9.{L}a.

Year	Zenab (LIFO) 20X1	20X2	Faybech (FIFO) 20X1	20X2
Current ratio	2.89	2.65	3.24	3.68
Inventory turnover		2.45		1.98
Gross profit margin		.339		.32
Pretax income/sales		.054		.045

b. Faybech's liquidity (as measured by the current ratio) appears to be better. Its inventory turnover is lower, however, implying lower efficiency. Faybech appears to be slightly less profitable as well.

c. (i) Using the FIFO income statements from problem 8, we compute the following ratios:

Year	Zenab (FIFO) 20X1	20X2	Faybech (FIFO) 20X1	20X2
Current ratio[1]	3.20	3.04	3.24	3.68
Inventory turnover[2]		2.03		1.98
Gross profit margin		.355		.32
Pretax income/sales		.070		.045

[1] 20X1 = ($33,500 + $3,600)/$11,600
     20X2 = ($33,600 + $5,100)/$12,700

[2] $$\frac{\$59,800}{(\$25,200 + \$5,100 + \$24,900 + \$3,600)/2}$$

(ii) Using the LIFO income statements from problem 8 (using the Zenab statement after conversion to 100% LIFO), we compute the following profitability ratios:

Year	Zenab (100% LIFO) 20X2	Faybech (LIFO) 20X2
Gross profit margin	.332	.303
Pretax income/sales	.047	.024

Balance sheet adjustments are not possible for Faybech and the 30% of Zenab inventories on FIFO. Thus adjusted current and inventory turnover ratios cannot be computed.

(iii) The current cost method of computing the inventory turnover ratio uses the FIFO measure of inventory and the LIFO measure of COGS. The ratios are:

	Zenab	Faybech
LIFO cost of goods sold	$61,943	$53,675
FIFO average inventory	29,400	26,300
Inventory turnover ratio	2.11X	2.04X

d. Balance sheet values are most meaningful when FIFO is used. For the income statement, however, LIFO should be used. Therefore for the current ratio, we use the FIFO amounts. For the gross profit margin, and pretax/sales we use the 100% LIFO amounts. For the inventory turnover ratio, the current cost approach is preferred. However that ratio and the FIFO based ratio are similar in this case:

	Zenab		Faybech	
Year	20X1	20X2	20X1	20X2
FIFO current ratio	3.20	3.04	3.24	3.68
FIFO inventory turnover		2.03		1.98
Current cost turnover		2.11		2.04
LIFO gross profit margin		.332		.303
LIFO pretax income/sales		.047		.024

Notice that, based on these ratios, Zenab is clearly more profitable than Faybech. The inventory turnover ratios are, however, virtually identical. While Faybech still has a higher current ratio, the difference is smaller than it appears based on the reported balance sheet data.

10.{M}a. The LIFO Reserve increased by $4,000. If the company used FIFO, its pretax income would be $4,000 higher. After-tax income would be higher by .65 x $4,000 = $2,600.

b. Inventory turnover is COGS/average inventory:

LIFO $3,800,000/[.5($748,000 + $696,800)] = 5.26X
FIFO $3,796,000/[.5($794,000 + $746,800)] = 4.93X

c. Since the firm's ROE is 4.6% and net income is $340,000, then average equity = $340,000/.046 = $7,391,304

If the company used FIFO, equity would be higher by the LIFO reserve amount adjusted for taxes. The average LIFO reserve is $48,000. Therefore, average equity should be higher by $31,200 (.65 x $48,000) after tax.

FIFO average equity = $7,391,304 + $31,200 = $7,422,504
ROE_{FIFO} = $342,600/$7,422,504 = 4.62%

The adjustment of ROE is insignificant in this case because the increase in the numerator (income) and denominator (equity) are proportionate.

d. There are two reasons to make adjustments for accounting methods:

1. To more accurately measure the firm's operations
2. To facilitate comparisons of different firms on the same basis

For inventory turnover, the adjustment results in a more accurate measure of performance. However, the main purpose of the LIFO to FIFO adjustment is to enable the analyst to compare Zeta to other firms that use FIFO.

e. The current cost method (inventory and equity at FIFO, COGS and net income at LIFO) should be used for both inventory turnover and ROE. For inventory turnover, this method better approximates the actual (physical) turnover. The argument for ROE is that FIFO equity better reflects the Company's current value, while LIFO income reflects the current operating profit earned on that equity. For Zeta, these adjustments offset. In some cases, however, the current cost method ratios are quite different.

11.{M}a.

LIFO	1998	1999	2000
Sales	$ 8,413	$ 9,889	$ 14,062
Cost of sales	5,646	7,365	10,819
Gross profit	$ 2,767	$ 2,524	$ 3,243
Gross profit %	32.9%	25.5%	23.1%

b. As calculated below, price levels were very volatile over the 1997 - 2000 period. Oil prices fell by 33% in 1998, followed by a sharp increase of almost 125% in 1999. The increase continued into 2000, but at a more moderate level of 10%

	1997	1998	1999	2000
	(See Exhibit 6-3)			
LIFO inventory	$ 364	$ 403	$ 321	$ 381
LIFO reserve	492	205	763	873
FIFO inventory	$ 856	$ 608	$1,084	$1,254
Change in LIFO reserve		(287)	558	110
Price level change*		**-33.5%**	**123.5%**	**10.1%**

* For 1998 and 2000 estimated as:
    change in LIFO reserve/opening FIFO inventory

For 1999, the above calculation was adjusted for the decline in inventory (see text P. 205-206)

c. FIFO cost of sales is calculated by subtracting the change in the LIFO reserve (part b) from LIFO cost of sales

FIFO	1998	1999	2000
Sales	$ 8,413	$ 9,889	$ 14,062
Cost of sales	5,933	6,807	10,709
Gross profit	$ 2,480	$ 3,082	$ 3,353
Gross profit %	29.5%	31.2%	23.8%

The gross profit margin percentages calculated in part a more accurately reflects Sunoco's real profitability as by using LIFO (i.e. current cost) for cost of sales, inventory-holding gains (losses) are removed from gross profit.

d. Sunoco's gross profit decreased in 1999-2000 as prices increased. This indicates that Sunoco is not able to "pass on" price increases immediately or in full to customers. Gross profit was highest (1998) when price levels fell, consistent with prices not being decreased as quickly as costs fell.

e.

		LIFO	*FIFO*	*CURRENT COST*
2000	Cost of sales / average inventory = **turnover**	$10,819 / $351 = **30.8**	$10,709 / $1,169 = **9.2**	$10,819 / $1,169 = **9.3**
1999	See text P. 209	**20.3**	**8.0**	**8.7**
1998	See text P. 209	**14.7**	**8.1**	**7.7**

Turnover on a LIFO basis is clearly overstated and continues to climb as price levels increase. The FIFO and current cost based turnover calculations are better measures and paint a similar picture – turnover increased in 2000 from 1998-1999 levels – number of days inventory is now (just under) 40 days

12.{M}a.

LIFO Basis	*1997*	*1998*	*1999*
COGS		$ 27,444	$ 27,212
Inventory	$ 5,044	4,816	5,069
Average inventory		4,930	4,943
Inventory turnover		**5.57 X**	**5.51 X**
Number of days		**65.6**	**66.3**

b. In adjusting inventories to a FIFO basis one can calculate turnover on a
   • FIFO basis by adjusting COGS to FIFO as well, or
   • Current cost basis by leaving COGS on a LIFO basis.

The differences are often minimal (see below)

	1997	1998	1999
LIFO reserve	$ 713	$ 679	$ 595
FIFO Basis			
COGS (FIFO)[1]		$ 27,478	$ 27,296
Inventory (FIFO)[2]	$ 5,757	5,495	5,664
Average inventory		5,626	5,580
Inventory turnover		**4.88 X**	**4.89 X**
Number of days		**74.7**	**74.6**
Current Cost Basis			
COGS (LIFO)		$ 27,444	$ 27,212
Inventory (FIFO)[2]	$ 5,757	5,495	5,664
Average inventory		5,626	5,580
Inventory turnover		**4.88 X**	**4.88 X**
Number of days		**74.8**	**74.8**

[1] COGS (LIFO) less change in LIFO reserve.
[2] Inventory (LIFO) plus LIFO reserve

c. The FIFO-based measure(s) of turnover are better as they more closely measure the actual physical turnover. The LIFO-based measure overstates turnover, as there is a mismatch of costs with current costs in the numerator and historical costs in the denominator. Thus, the LIFO-based turnover measure is upwardly biased due to price increases.

d. The LIFO adjustment is the change in the LIFO reserve which, when added to FIFO COGS, yields LIFO COGS. (Like most companies, Sears keeps track of its inventories on a day-to-day basis using FIFO. At year-end they adjust the FIFO amounts to arrive at the LIFO amounts reported in their financial statements).

     Based on the balance sheet data, the adjustments are
■ 1998: = ($679 - $713) = ($ 34) and
■ 1999: = ($595 - $679) = ($ 84)

The $34 credit reported by Sears in 1998 is identical to that calculated above. For 1999, there is a discrepancy of $11 million as Sears reported a $73 million credit and our calculations yield an $84 million credit. The discrepancy could be due to a divestiture - Sears may have sold a subsidiary or division, thus removing its inventory and LIFO reserve from its books.

13.{M}a. **Inventory turnover** = Cost of sales/Average inventory =

$$\frac{\$2,512}{.5 \times (249 + 333)} = \textbf{8.63}$$

Gross profit margin = ($3,663-$2,512)/$3,663 = **31.4%**

ROE = Net income / Average equity =

$$\frac{\$255}{.5 \times (2,171 + 2,333)} = \textbf{11.3\%}$$

b.   FIFO Cost of sales
 = $2,512 - change in LIFO reserve
 = $2,512 - [($469 - $333)- ($368 - $249)])
 = **$2,495**

Inventory turnover = Cost of sales/Average inventory =

$$\frac{\$2,495}{.5 \times (368 + 469)} = \textbf{5.96}$$

Gross profit margin = ($3,663 - $2,495)/$3,663 = **31.8%**

The effect on net income for the year would be
$17 x (1 - tax rate) = $17 (0.65) = $11, therefore
FIFO net income would be $255 + $11 = $266

The adjusted equity equals the reported equity plus the
   LIFO reserve x (1 - tax rate)

1999 adjustment: $119 x 65% = $77, therefore
Equity = $2,171 + $77 = $2,248

2000 adjustment: $136 x 65% = $88
          Equity = $2,333 + $88 = $2,421

ROE = Net income / Average equity =

$$\frac{\$266}{.5 \times (\$2,248 + \$2,421)} = \textbf{11.4\%}$$

c.   LIFO artificially inflates the inventory turnover ratio
as the denominator is depressed. The gross margin is
slightly lower using LIFO as COGS is higher. ROE is
little changed as both the numerator and denominator are
lower using LIFO.

d.   The FIFO measure (part b) is a more useful measure of the
turnover ratio as it removes the inflation effect. On the

other hand LIFO COGS (part a) is a more useful measure than FIFO COGS as it reflects current costs. For ROE, the ideal would be to have LIFO income in the numerator and FIFO equity in the denominator, as both would measure current costs; the analyst should use neither the "pure" FIFO nor the LIFO ROE measure.

14.{S}a.   First, calculate the change in the LIFO reserve:

Total inventories	1999	2000	Change
Current cost	$ 368	$ 469	
Carrying value	(249)	(333)	
LIFO reserve	$ 119	$ 136	$ 17

The rate of price change equals the year 2000 change in the LIFO reserve compared with current cost LIFO inventories at the end of 1999:

LIFO inventories	1999
Carrying value	$ 157
LIFO reserve	119
Current cost	$ 276

The year 2000 rate of price change equals $17/$276 = 6.2%

b.   Opening FIFO Inventory = Total inventories − LIFO inventories = $249 − $157 = $92 million

Adjustment to COGS = $92 x 6.2% = $6 million
Adjusted COGS = $2,512 + $6 = $2,518

Adjusted gross profit = $3,663 − $2,518 = **$1,145**
Adjusted net income   = $255 − $6(.65) = **251**

c.   It provides a current cost measure of income for all of the company's sales

d.   The assumption is reasonable if the FIFO inventories are similar to those carried on LIFO but are located in jurisdictions where LIFO is not permitted or there are other reasons for not using LIFO. On the other hand, the reason the company carries these inventories on a FIFO basis may be that they face a lower inflation rate.

15.{S}a. Pulp, Paper increased by (185.1/177.0 - 1)= 4.6%
          Chemical & Allied increased by (151.9/147.0 - 1) = 3.3%

          For Westvaco, therefore, the rate should be
              (.9 x 4.6%) + (.1 x 3.3%) = 4.5%

     b. Westvaco's inventory disclosures (see Problem 14a.)
         suggest a slightly higher estimate of 6.2%.

     c. The mostly likely explanation for the different estimates
         is that Westvaco's product mix differs from that used to
         compute the Pulp, Paper and Allied Products Index. That
         index may, for example, include products that Westvaco
         does not produce, whose prices rose less rapidly than the
         prices of those produced by Westvaco.

         The lesson here is that, when commodity prices are used
         to estimate the effect of price changes on company
         inventories, care must be taken to ensure that product
         mixes between the chosen index and inventories are
         similar.

16.{M}a. Inventory turnover
         = Cost-of-goods (and services) sold/average inventory

	(i) FIFO		(ii) LIFO	
	1999	2000	1999	2000
Cost of goods*	$ 34,638	$ 39,394	$ 34,554	$ 39,312
Average inventory	6,521	7,358	5,552	6,472
Turnover	**5.31**	**5.35**	**6.22**	**6.07**
Cost of goods and services sold	$ 46,042	$ 51,905	$ 45,958	$ 51,823
Average inventory	6,521	7,358	5,552	6,472
Turnover	**7.06**	**7.05**	**8.28**	**8.01**

*Note that COGS has been adjusted for the FIFO calculation to
reflect the change in the LIFO reserve as calculated below.

	1998	1999	2000
Inventory FIFO	$6,316	$6,725	$7,991
Inventory LIFO	5,305	5,798	7,146
LIFO reserve	$1,011	$ 927	$ 845
Change in LIFO reserve		(84)	(82)

b. When sales is used instead of cost-of-goods-sold:

	(i) FIFO		(ii) LIFO	
	1999	*2000*	*1999*	*2000*
Sales of goods	$ 47,785	$ 54,828	$ 47,785	$ 54,828
Average inventory	6,521	7,358	5,552	6,472
Turnover	**7.33**	**7.45**	**8.61**	**8.47**
Sales of goods and services sold	$ 64,068	$ 72,954	$ 64,068	$ 72,954
Average inventory	6,521	7,358	5,552	6,472
Turnover	**9.83**	**9.91**	**11.54**	**11.27**

c. None of these computations match those reported by management. Our understanding (from prior year conversations with GE's management) is that GE uses sales and FIFO inventories to calculate turnover. Those ratios [b(i) above] have the right trend but are almost exactly 1 turn higher than our computed ratios.

d. The preferred measure of inventory turnover uses the current cost method:

COGS (LIFO)/Average inventory (FIFO)

As the turnover ratio is intended to measure the relationship between goods sold during the period and the stock of goods held for sale, COGS (without cost of services) should be the numerator. Using sales in the numerator inflates the turnover ratio as sales always exceed COGS. In addition, when sales is the numerator, the ratio is affected when COGS fluctuates relative to sales.

COGS should be at LIFO to measure it at current cost.

FIFO inventory should be the denominator as LIFO inventory understates the inventory on hand. As discussed in the chapter, using LIFO inventory to compute turnover results in a ratio that is too high and that systematically increases over time.

The preferréd calculations are:

	1999	2000
Cost of goods sold at LIFO	$ 34,554	$ 39,312
Average inventories at FIFO	6,521	7,358
Turnover ratio	5.30	5.34

Under any measure, GE's turnover ratio remained relatively stable over the 1999-2000 period. Management's chosen method shows a higher turnover ratio than the preferred method. Comparisons with other firms are misleading when turnover ratios are computed differently.

The point of this problem is that ratios reported by management cannot be used blindly (especially for comparisons with other firms). The analyst must determine how management calculates its ratios and ensure that those calculations accord with calculations made by other firms and, most important, by the analyst.

17.{S}a. January 1, 20X3 inventory = $2,700,000 ($2,000,000 + $700,000).

b. To maintain its inventory balance at $2,700,000, Jofen would have had to increase its purchases by $1,000,000 ($700,000 + $300,000); $300,000 is the difference between the LIFO and FIFO inventory cost. The choice of inventory method does not affect purchases, which reflect actual prices paid.

c. Ignoring taxes and any change in accounts payable, reported cash flow from operations increased by $1,000,000 due to lower purchases.

d. COGS should be increased by $300,000 to exclude the effect of the LIFO liquidation.

e. The LIFO liquidation is likely not a recurring event. Excluding that income makes net income more useful for evaluating operating performance (net income and cash from operations) and forecasting future performance.

18.{M}a. The LIFO adjustment refers to the change in the LIFO reserve (or as Noland calls it 'Reduction to LIFO')

	1997	1998	1999
LIFO Reserve	$32,495	$32,876	$34,267
Change in LIFO reserve		381	1,391

b. $COGS_{FIFO} = COGS_{LIFO}$ - change in LIFO reserve

For 1998: $372,033 - $ 381 = $371,652
For 1999: 385,892 - 1,391 = 384,501

c. Income would decline if prices in previous years were higher than current prices and the higher priced layer was liquidated.

d. (i) 1998:   COGS = $372,033 - $150 = $371,883
       1999:   COGS = 385,892 +   47 = 385,939

   (ii) For FIFO, COGS is the same as in part b –
        "liquidations" do not affect FIFO COGS

e. The most appropriate measure is the calculation computed in part d(i): LIFO COGS after eliminating effects of liquidation. That measure of COGS is closest to replacement cost.

f. By adding the LIFO reserve to equity; i.e. add $32,876,000 to 1998 equity and $34,267,000 to 1999 equity. Depending on the purpose of analysis, it may be appropriate to tax-adjust these values i.e. add [$32,876,000 x (1-tax rate)] to 1998 equity and [$34,267,000 x (1-tax rate)] to 1999 equity.

19.{S}a. The company wrote down the carrying values of the inventories to market value. The write-downs of $36 and $18 million in 1997 and 1998 respectively were charged to income.

b. There may have been market value adjustments (write-downs) prior to 1997 that were reversed in 1999 in addition to those of 1997-1998.

c. Income would decline if prices in previous years were higher than current prices and the higher priced layer was liquidated.

d. The market value and liquidation adjustments do not relate to current year COGS and therefore should be excluded:

	1998	1999	Growth rate
Market value	$ (18)	$ 71	
Liquidation	(4)	41	
Total effect	$ (22)	$ 112	
Reported net income	$ 193	$ 390	102%
Less: total effect	22	(112)	
Adjusted net income	$ 215	$ 278	29%

Before adjustment the growth rate of net income is overstated at 102%. After adjustment, the actual growth rate is 29%, respectable but considerably below the reported growth rate.

20.{S}a. The cost of inventory may have declined due to deflation.

b. (1) They might believe that the price decrease is temporary and in the future prices will increase again.

(2) Since the LIFO reserve is large, a switch to FIFO would require a large tax expense (equal to tax rate times the LIFO reserve) immediately. Thus, even if they felt that prices would continue to decrease in the future, they are still better off paying the higher taxes slowly over time (as the LIFO reserve declines) rather than paying the full amount immediately.

21.{S}

		1997	*1998*	*1999*
a.	Sales	$ 515,728	$ 539,413	$ 572,696
	Gross margin	187,556	190,826	210,588
	Gross margin %	**36.4%**	**35.4%**	**36.8%**
b.	LIFO liquidation	$ 3,379	$ 1,733	none
	Pretax liquidation*	**5,198**	**2,666**	
	Adjusted			
	Gross margin	$ 182,358	$ 188,160	$ 210,588
	Gross margin %	**35.4%**	**34.9%**	**36.8%**

* Equals LIFO liquidation (net of tax)/.65

c.   The adjusted gross margin percentage is more indicative of the longer-term trend of the company. By removing the effects of the LIFO liquidation(s), COGS and subsequently gross margin are more reflective of current cost income. Removing the effect of the liquidation shows that gross margins improved significantly from 1997-1998 to 1999.

22.{S} The last sentence in the statement is patently absurd. The accounting method for inventory should have nothing to do with a company's pricing strategy. Pricing should be based on current market conditions. Companies that ignore the cost of replacing inventory when setting prices will suffer from poor cash flows and, in some cases, will fail.

23.{S}a.   For service companies, inventory is an insignificant component of assets and COGS an insignificant cost. The main inputs of service companies are capacity and people. Thus inventory turnover is not a useful measure for such companies.

b.   Capacity utilization is an important measure of operating efficiency for firms with fixed capacity. The fixed cost of such capacity means that utilization is an important determinant of profitability. An airline seat, rental car, or hospital bed that goes unused generates no revenue; the variable cost saved may be very low. This phenomenon explains why airlines sell discount tickets; such sales are profitable as long as the marginal revenue exceeds the variable cost.

It is also important to measure costs in relation to either capacity or utilization. As revenues are subject to competitive and regulatory constraints, lower costs are important to profitability. Thus an airline's costs relative to available seat-miles (or to passenger revenue miles) measures the efficiency of its operations. For a car rental company, cost per available car would be a similar measure. For a hospital the analogous metric would be cost per available bed.

24. {M} Contracts can provide strong incentives that affect the choice of inventory method. However different contracts may provide incentives for different choices. The following discussion assumes rising prices.

The management compensation plan provides a mixed incentive. Use of LIFO reduces income but increases cash from operations. Assuming a tax rate t, and a LIFO effect L, net income decreases by $(1-t)L$ while cash from operations increases by tL. The net effect $(2t-1)L$ is positive only at tax rates above 50%. Thus management contracts argue against use of LIFO.

Bond covenants also argue against LIFO. Working capital is reduced by the LIFO reserve less taxes saved. The annual amount is $(t-1)L$ which is always negative. Retained earnings are also lower under LIFO.

Union employee profit sharing payments are lower under LIFO, assuming that profits would exceed the minimum level. This would seem to argue for LIFO, to reduce compensation paid.

However, there are also second and third order effects that must be considered. Lower profit sharing payments, for example, increase net income (and cash from operations), increasing management compensation and easing the effect of bond covenants. These effects require complex calculations and are highly firm-specific.

Some effects are non-quantitative. Lower profit sharing payments may result in higher wage demands from workers. For management, use of FIFO may raise questions about why they failed to obtain tax savings by using LIFO.

Thus, while we can identify many of the factors that motivate the choice of inventory method, the controller's choice will depend on how these factors affect Sechne; there is no simple answer.

Case 6-1 - Solution

Estimated solution time: three hours
Note: The calculations required for this case are shown in Exhibit
6CS-1, and appear in question order. The calculations are explained
in the solution. All data are in $thousands.

1. Gross margin equals sales less cost-of-products-sold (COPS).
    The adjusted COPS is derived by reducing the reported amount
    by the change in the LIFO reserve during the year. As the LIFO
    reserve declined in 1996 and 1998 (due to declining prices),
    FIFO COPS exceeds LIFO COPS for those years.

2. Over the 1995 - 1999 period, LIFO gross margins declined,
    except for an increase in 1997. GM as a percent of sales
    followed a similar pattern.

    Adjusted (FIFO) gross margins show a similar trend, except
    that the 1997 increase was greater and there was another
    increase in 1999. FIFO GM are more volatile (range 11.2% -
    16.6%) relative to sales than the reported amounts (range
    13.2% - 16.2%), as price changes magnify operating changes.
    The contrast between reported and adjusted amounts is
    particularly striking in 1998 vs. 1997 (the FIFO decline is
    much higher) with its sharp decline in prices and 1999 vs.
    1998 (higher margins using FIFO but lower margins under LIFO).
    The exclusion of price change effects under LIFO affects
    profitability trends.

3. The adjustment to gross margins must be carried down to net
    income on an after tax basis. This step entails multiplying
    the pretax adjustment by $(1-t)$, where the marginal tax rate t,
    is provided in Exhibit 6C-1.

    The net income (and earnings per share) trends are similar to
    those of gross margins. The reported (LIFO) amounts are lower
    in all years except 1996 and 1998, and are more stable as they
    exclude the price change effects.

4. The adjustment to Nucor's book value per share (BVPS) is
    simply the LIFO reserve. As elsewhere in the text and
    problems, we make this adjustment pretax as there is little
    indication that the LIFO reserve will be liquidated. The
    adjusted BVPS is computed using the same number of shares
    Nucor uses to report (unadjusted) BVPS.

Exhibit 6CS-1. INVENTORY ANALYSIS OF NUCOR, ADJUSTMENT FROM LIFO TO FIFO
Years Ended December 31 (data in $thousands)

	1994	1995	1996	1997	1998	1999
Sales		$3,462,046	$3,647,030	$4,184,498	$4,151,232	$4,009,346
COPS		2,900,168	3,139,158	3,578,941	3,591,783	3,480,479
1 Reported gross margin		$ 561,878	$ 507,872	$ 605,557	$ 559,449	$ 528,867
1 % of sales		16.2%	13.9%	14.5%	13.5%	13.2%
LIFO reserve	$ 81,662	$ 93,932	$ 73,901	$ 100,576	$ 5,121	$ 28,590
Change in LIFO reserve		12,270	(20,031)	26,675	(95,455)	23,469
Adjusted COPS		$2,887,898	$3,159,189	$3,552,266	$3,687,238	$3,457,010
1 Adjusted GM		574,148	487,841	632,232	463,994	552,336
1 % of sales		16.6%	13.4%	15.1%	11.2%	13.8%
Net income		$ 274,535	$ 248,169	$ 294,482	$ 263,709	$ 244,589
Earnings per share		$ 3.14	$ 2.83	$ 3.35	$ 3.00	$ 2.80
Change in LIFO reserve		12,270	(20,031)	26,675	(95,455)	23,469
Tax rate		35%	35%	35%	35%	35%
3 Adjusted net income		$ 282,511	$ 235,149	$ 311,821	$ 201,663	$ 259,844
Adjusted EPS		$ 3.23	$ 2.68	$ 3.55	$ 2.29	$ 2.97

		(1)	(2)	(3)	(4)	(5)	(6)
	Stockholders' equity	$2,262,248	$2,072,522	$1,876,426	$1,609,290	$1,382,112	$1,122,610
	LIFO reserve	28,590	5,121	100,576	73,901	93,932	81,662
	Adjusted equity	2,290,838	2,077,643	1,977,002	1,683,191	1,476,044	1,204,272
	Book value per share	$ 25.96	$ 23.73	$ 21.32	$ 18.33	$ 15.78	$ 12.85
4	**Adjusted BVPS**	**$ 26.29**	**$ 23.79**	**$ 22.46**	**$ 19.17**	**$ 16.85**	**$ 13.78**
	Cash from operations	$ 604,834	$ 641,989	$ 577,326	$ 450,611	$ 447,160	
	Tax effect of LIFO	8,214	(33,409)	9,336	(7,011)	4,295	
5	**FIFO CFO**	**$ 596,620**	**$ 675,398**	**$ 567,990**	**$ 457,622**	**$ 442,866**	
	LIFO inventory	$ 464,984	$ 435,885	$ 397,048	$ 385,799	$ 306,773	$ 243,027
	LIFO reserve	28,590	5,121	100,576	73,901	93,932	81,662
	FIFO inventory	$ 493,574	$ 441,006	$ 497,624	$ 459,700	$ 400,705	$ 324,689
	Current assets	$1,538,509	$1,129,467	$1,125,508	$ 828,381	$ 830,741	
	Current liabilities	531,031	486,987	524,454	465,653	447,136	
	Working capital	$1,007,478	$ 642,480	$ 601,054	$ 362,728	$ 383,605	
6	**Current ratio**	**2.90**	**2.32**	**2.15**	**1.78**	**1.86**	
	Adjusted current assets	1,567,099	1,134,588	1,226,084	902,282	924,673	
	Adjusted working capital	1,036,068	647,601	701,630	436,629	477,537	
6	**Adjusted current ratio**	**2.95**	**2.33**	**2.34**	**1.94**	**2.07**	
6	**Return on equity**	11.3%	13.4%	16.9%	16.6%	21.9%	
6	**Adjusted ROE**	11.9%	9.9%	17.0%	14.9%	21.1%	
7	LIFO turnover	7.73	8.62	9.14	9.07	10.55	
7	FIFO turnover	7.40	7.86	7.42	7.34	7.96	
7	Current Cost turnover	7.45	7.65	7.48	7.30	8.00	

The adjustment increases BVPS each year, although the percentage adjustment is lowest in 1998 and 1999, when the LIFO reserve declined considerably (relative to the previous years). The adjustment slightly reduces the growth rate of BVPS (using 1994 as the base year). Given the variability of the LIFO reserve, the effect on BVPS varies with the choice of base and ending years.

5. The effect of LIFO on cash from operations (CFO) is the tax effect, equal to the LIFO effect (change in LIFO reserve) multiplied by the tax rate t. When the cash effect is removed, FIFO CFO is lower in all years except 1996 and 1998 (when prices declined).

    Over the entire five-year period, the LIFO reserve decreased $53 million, resulting in a tax increase of approximately $18 million. The year-to-year changes in CFO are significantly affected, especially 1998 versus 1997.

6. LIFO reduces the carrying value of inventory, lowering working capital and the current ratio. The adjusted amounts are, therefore, higher as the LIFO reserve is added (pretax) to current assets. The adjusted current ratio is always higher.

    The adjusted amounts are, however, more volatile, as they include the effect of price changes on Nucor's inventory. Note however that the differences between FIFO and LIFO disappear in 1998 and are much smaller in 1999 as a result of the sharp decline in the LIFO reserve.

    LIFO also affects return on equity. Adjustments to FIFO always increase the denominator (equity); the effect on return (net income) varies. The most striking differences are in 1996 and 1998. In those years, when prices declined, the adjusted ROE is significantly lower

7. The inventory turnover ratios calculated in exhibit 6CS-1 vary, as expected, with the inventory method. The LIFO ratios are always higher as the ratio denominator (average inventory) is understated by the LIFO reserve. The FIFO and current cost ratios are similar, as discussed in the text.

    The current cost method, using LIFO COPS in the numerator and FIFO inventory in the denominator, is the best measure of economic turnover. By this measure, Nucor's inventory turnover declined over the period, from 8.00 to 7.45. Growth in inventory was greater than growth in sales.

8. The major advantages to Nucor of using the LIFO method are:
   - Reduced volatility of reported gross margin and income (answers 2 and 3 above)
   - Higher cash flow due to tax savings (answer 5)
   - Higher reported inventory turnover ratio (answer 7)

   The major disadvantages of the LIFO method are:
   - Reduced reported income in most years (answer 3)
   - Lower reported stockholders' equity (answer 4) Ratios that use equity (such as the debt-to-equity ratio) are understated.
   - Lower current ratio (answer 6). Ratios that use total assets are also understated.

9. (a) Prices have declined dramatically, especially in 1998

   (b) The major implication is the reduced cash flows in the years the LIFO reserve declined (1996 and 1998) as Nucor had to pay higher taxes. Declining prices in some years offset the benefits of LIFO when prices rise. On the other hand, the price declines increase LIFO income as well as balance sheet ratios, as the difference between FIFO and LIFO inventory declines.

10. When a company switches from LIFO to FIFO, it must pay taxes on the accumulated LIFO reserve. Thus, the best time to switch would have been at the end of 1998 when the LIFO reserve was smallest - mitigating the tax consequences.

11. A switch to FIFO would have signaled that Nucor expects the price of steel scrap to continue to decline. In that environment, the switch to FIFO would be motivated by the desire to lower taxes, and the elimination of the record keeping requirements of the LIFO method.

12. (a)

	1997	1998	1999
Sales		$514,786	$618,821
COGS		428,978	487,629
Gross margin		**$ 85,808**	**$131,192**
% of sales		**16.7%**	**21.2%**
Net income		$ 31,684	$ 39,430
Ending equity	$337,595	351,065	391,370
Average equity		344,330	371,218
Return on equity		**9.2%**	**10.6%**
Ending inventory	60,163	$126,706	$106,742
Average inventory		93,435	116,724
Turnover ratio		**4.59**	**4.18**

(b) We should convert STLD results to LIFO. We start by using Nucor data to estimate the 1998 and 1999 (de)inflation rates:

For 1998:

$$\frac{\text{Change in LIFO Reserve}}{\text{FIFO Opening Inventory}} = \frac{\$(95,455)}{\$497,624} = (19.2)\%$$

For 1999:

$$\frac{\text{Change in LIFO Reserve}}{\text{FIFO Opening Inventory}} = \frac{\$ 23,469}{\$441,006} = 5.3\%$$

STLD's LIFO effect is estimated by applying these percentages to the opening inventory for each year:

1998: (19.2%) x $60,163 = $(11,551)

Thus LIFO COGS is estimated at $428,978 - $11,551 = $417,427

1999: 5.3% x $126,706 = $6,715

Thus LIFO COGS is estimated at $487,629 + $6,715 = $494,344

Recomputing STLD's ratios:

	1997	1998	1999
Sales		$514,786	$618,821
Adjusted COGS		417,427	494,344
Adjusted gross margin		**$ 97,359**	**$124,477**
% of sales		18.9%	20.1%
Net income reported		$ 31,684	$ 39,430
After tax LIFO effect			
(using 35% tax rate)		7,508	(4,365)
Adjusted net income		$ 39,192	$ 35,065
Ending equity	$337,595	351,065	391,370
Average equity		344,330	371,218
Adjusted return on equity		**11.4%**	**9.4%**
Ending inventory	$ 60,163	$126,706	$106,742
Average inventory		93,435	116,724
Adjusted turnover ratio		**4.47**	**4.24**

We use LIFO adjusted COGS to estimate the gross margin ratio as it better measures current costs. Relative to reported numbers, the ratio improves for 1998 and declines in 1999. In keeping with the policy of using LIFO for income statement values and FIFO for balance sheet numbers, the ROE and inventory turnover are calculated with net income and COGS on a LIFO basis and equity and inventory using FIFO. As a result, all the ratios are on a current cost basis.

(c) Since prices declined in 1998, COGS on a LIFO basis was lower than COGS on a FIFO basis; when prices increased in 1999 the reverse was true.

(d) The adjusted (current cost) ratios provide a more useful comparison as they remove the effects of the volatile price changes. Using the gross margin percentage as an example, the reported numbers indicate a sharp increase of 4.5% from 1998 to 1999 (16.7% -> 21.2%). After removing the effects of inflation (holding gains and losses) we find a more stable year-to-year relationship; an increase of only 1.2% as the gross margin percentage rose from 18.9% to 20.1%.

(e) The effects of adjustment can be illustrated by comparing the two companies' ROE over the two years on a reported as well as adjusted basis.

| ROE | AS REPORTED | | BOTH COMPANIES | | | |
| | | | ON LIFO | | ON FIFO | |
	1998	1999	1998	1999	1998	1999
Nucor	13.4%	11.3%	13.4%	11.3%	9.9%	11.9%
STLD	9.2%	10.6%	11.4%	9.4%	9.2%	10.6%
Difference	4.2%	0.7%	2.0%	1.9%	0.7%	1.3%

On a reported basis, relative to STLD, Nucor's 1998 ROE is superior by almost 50%. In 1999, however, the ROE differences almost disappear, as Nucor's ROE declined and STLD's ROE increased. These effects primarily reflect the difference in inventory accounting methods, rather than real changes in relative profitability.

When we use the same accounting methods for both companies, we find that:

- Nucor's 1998 ROE is still superior to STLD's but by a much smaller amount (18% on a LIFO basis and 8% on a FIFO basis rather than 50% as reported).
- The differences between Nucor and STLD's ROE remained stable in 1999 as the change of ROE was similar for both companies.[1]

This example illustrates the difficulty of comparing firms using different inventory methods. Reported data cannot be compared without adjustment. Some adjustments can be made simply; others are difficult or impossible given lack of data. Some ingenuity may be required to obtain meaningful comparisons. Once reported data have been made comparable, the analyst can focus on real operating differences.

---

[1] The direction of change depended on whether LIFO or FIFO was used; i.e. whether price changes (inventory holding gains or losses) were included or excluded. On a LIFO basis, excluding price changes, ROE fell for both companies. On a FIFO basis, with inventory profits included (as prices rose in 1999), ROE increased.

Chapter 7 Solutions

Overview:
Problem Length   *Problem #s*
   {S}   2, 3, 5, 8, and 10
   {M}   1, 4, 6, 7, 9, 11, 12, and 13
                                       Appendices
   {M}   7A-1 and 7B-1
   {L}   7A-2 and 7B-2

1.{M}   Exhibit 7S-1 contains the calculations required.

Exhibit 7S-1. Chevron
Adjustments for Capitalization of Interest
Amounts in $ millions

	Year 1995	1996	1997	1998	1999	**part c** **1999/95**
As reported						
Interest expense	$ 401	$ 364	$ 312	$ 405	$ 472	**1.18**
Pretax income	1,789	4,740	5,502	1,834	3,648	**2.04**
Net income	930	2,607	3,256	1,339	2,070	**2.23**
Capitalized interest	141	108	82	39	59	
Amortization of capitalized interest	47	24	28	35	9	
a. Calculations						
EBIT	$2,190	$5,104	$5,814	$2,239	$4,120	
Times interest earned	**5.46**	**14.02**	**18.63**	**5.53**	**8.73**	**1.60**
b. Adjusted						
Net capitalized interest	$ 94	$ 84	$ 54	$ 4	$ 50	
After 35% income tax	61	55	35	3	33	
Interest expense	542	472	394	444	531	**0.98**
EBIT	2,237	5,128	5,842	2,274	4,129	
(i) Times interest earned	**4.13**	**10.86**	**14.83**	**5.12**	**7.78**	**1.88**
(ii) % reduction from reported ratio	**-24.4%**	**-22.5%**	**-20.4%**	**-7.4%**	**-10.9%**	
Pretax income	$1,695	$4,656	$5,448	$1,830	$3,598	**2.12**
(iii) Net income	**869**	**2,552**	**3,221**	**1,336**	**2,038**	**2.34**
% reduction from reported	-6.6%	-2.1%	-1.1%	-0.2%	-1.6%	

b.   (iv) Expensing all interest reduces net income for each
            year. However the effect diminishes over time.

c.   (i)   Because the amount of interest capitalized
             declined over time, restatement reduces the rate
             of increase in interest expense.
       (ii) While the interest coverage ratio is lower after
             restatement, its trend improves due to the lower
             growth rate of interest expense.
       (iii) Both pretax and net income are lower after
             restatement but their growth rate improves due to
             the lower growth rate of interest expense.

d.   The restated data are more useful for financial
       analysis because they are based on actual interest
       expense. They provide better comparability with firms
       that do not capitalize interest.

2.{S}a. (i)   Interest cost can be capitalized on borrowings
               directly associated with the project or when the
               company has debt equal to or exceeding the cost of
               construction.
         (ii) Start-up costs must be expensed under U.S. GAAP.
         (iii) Shipping costs are considered part of the cost of
               acquisition.
         (iv) Increases in the market value of land and
               buildings may not be recognized under U.S. GAAP.

b.   (i)   While the benchmark treatment under IAS 23 is to
             expense all interest, capitalization of borrowing
             costs directly attributable to a project is an
             allowed alternative.
       (ii) Same as U.S. GAAP except that the benchmark The
             capitalization of interest is an allowed
             alternative under IAS 23 (paragraph 11)
       (iii) Same as U.S. GAAP.
       (iv) While revaluation is an allowed alternative under
             IAS 16, it must be applied to all assets in a
             particular class and could be selectively applied
             to a particular project.

3.{S}a. Under SFAS 86 (text page 242), computer software
         development costs can be capitalized only when economic
         feasibility has been established.

b.   Under IAS 38 (paragraph 45), intangible assets such as
       computer software can be recognized when the enterprise
       can demonstrate technical and economic feasibility.

4.{M}   Exhibit 7S-2 contains the calculations required by parts a through c.

```
┌──────────────────────────────────────────────────────────────────┐
│ Exhibit 7S-2                                                       │
│ Ericsson                                                           │
│ Amounts in SEK millions                                           │
│                                        1997      1998      1999    │
│ a. Under Swedish GAAP:                                            │
│                                                                    │
│ Net sales                           167,740   184,438   215,403   │
│ Pretax income                        17,218    18,210    16,386   │
│ Total assets                        147,440   167,456   202,628   │
│ Stockholders' equity                 52,624    63,112    69,176   │
│ Average total assets                          157,448   185,042   │
│ Average stockholders' equity                   57,868    66,144   │
│ Asset turnover                                    1.17      1.16   │
│ Pretax ROE                                        0.31      0.25   │
│                                                                    │
│ b. Adjustments:                                                   │
│ Development costs for software to be sold:                        │
│ Capitalization                        5,232     7,170     7,898   │
│ Amortization                         (3,934)   (3,824)   (4,460)  │
│ Write down                                                 (989)   │
│ Net effect                            1,298     3,346     2,449   │
│                                                                    │
│ Development costs for software for internal use:                  │
│ Capitalization                                             1,463   │
│ Amortization                                                (152)  │
│ Net effect                               –         –       1,311   │
│                                                                    │
│ Total pretax effect                   1,298     3,346     3,760   │
│ Adjusted pretax income               18,516    21,556    20,146   │
│ (i) % change                            8%       18%        23%    │
└──────────────────────────────────────────────────────────────────┘
```

```
Exhibit 7S-2 (continued)
Year-end balances:
Software to be sold          7,398     10,744   13,193
Internal use software                            1,311
Total                        7,398     10,744   14,504
Less: deferred tax @ 35%    (2,589)    (3,760)  (5,076)
Increase in equity           4,809      6,984    9,428

Adjusted total assets      154,838    178,200  217,132
(ii) % change                  5.0%       6.4%     7.2%
Adjusted equity             57,433     70,096   78,604
(iii) % change                 9.1%      11.1%    13.6%

c:
Adjusted average assets                166,519  197,666
Adjusted average equity                 63,764   74,350
(i) Adjusted asset turnover               1.11     1.09
(ii) Adjusted pretax ROE                  0.34     0.27
```

d. The adjustments for Ericsson show that capitalization
    of software development costs can have a significant
    effect on reported income and equity, and on financial
    ratios. Therefore comparability requires that all firms
    be restated to the same basis.

e. The amounts capitalized highlight expenditures and
    enable the analyst to inquire about the new products
    under development. The amortization period used may be
    useful as a forecast of the useful life of the product.
    In both cases (capitalization and amortization)
    significant changes from prior periods may provide
    useful signals of impending change.

5.{S}a. The capitalization of the investment in displays delays their impact on income as compared with expensing. In addition, cash from operations is permanently increased as the expenditures are classified as cash flows for investment. Finally, if these expenditures are volatile, capitalization and amortization smoothes the impact on reported income.

b. (i) In 2000, the capitalized amount increased by $1,648,000. Had promotional displays been expensed, net income would be $1,071,200 (after 35% tax) lower. Expensing would have reduced net income by 7.4% ($1,071.2/$14,467).

(ii) Shareholders' equity would be reduced by 65% of $10,099,000 equal to $6,564,350 or 7.1%.

(iii) Reported return on (average) assets equals
$14,467/[($166,656 + $140,609)/2] = 9.42%
Adjusted return on (average) assets equals
($14,467 - $1,071)/[($166,656 - $10,099) + ($140,609 - $8,451)/2] = 9.28% as assets must be reduced by the investment in promotional displays.

6.{M}a. Brand names are clearly an asset. However, it is not clear that these assets should be shown on corporate balance sheets.

One advantage of recognizing brand names is completeness; a balance sheet that ignores major firm assets is of limited use for analysis. Another advantage is that the cost of acquiring or developing a brand name should be recorded as an investment (asset) in order to properly match revenues and expenses.

The major disadvantage of brand name recognition is the difficulty of proper measurement. As each brand name is unique, market transactions are not available to value the brand. Thus, the value recognized is subjective; differences across firms may reflect either real differences in the value of the brands or different measurement decisions.

One approach involves capitalization of the acquisition cost (for purchased brands) or the advertising and other development costs (for internally developed brands). In the latter case, it is unlikely that the value of the brand will be equal to the cost of development. A successful brand will be worth much more than the cost of its development; an unsuccessful brand may have no value at all. (These characteristics may also describe acquired brands.)

Further, the value of brands changes over time. Despite the quotation from Laing, brands can also become "dilapidated" if they are neglected, if the advertising is poor, or if the products are defective. The value of brands will also be affected by changes in market conditions, e.g., pricing decisions and the inroads made by generic products.

From the point of view of financial analysis, therefore, it is not clear that reporting management's estimate of brand value would be helpful. The "proof of the pudding is in the eating" and a valuable brand should be highly profitable. The evaluation of that profitability might be better left to the marketplace.

b. The advantage of amortization is that the income statement should reflect all expenses that help produce income. If profitability is due to the brand name, the amortization of its acquisition cost should be an element of expense.

On the other hand, given the subjectivity of brand name valuation, the amortization amount (also affected by the choice of method and life) may be a poor measure of the expired value. In addition, brand names may not decline in value over time; any decline is likely to be irregular.

For purposes of analysis, therefore, the amortization of brand name intangible assets should be excluded from income. The evaluation of profitability, however, should consider the role of brand names.

Exhibit 7S-3
Norsk Hydro
Amounts in NOK millions

Pretax income:

Norwegian GAAP	6,292
Capitalized exploration costs	(107)
Depreciation	(729)
Capitalized interest	614
Other differences (net)	(239)
US GAAP	5,831

Parts a and b:

(i) Pretax ROE:

Norwegian GAAP	**14.5%**
US GAAP	**12.1%**

Part c:

Capitalized exploration costs	(107)
Depreciation	(729)
Capitalized interest	614
Net effect	(222)

Norwegian GAAP adjusted:

Pretax income	6,070
(i) ROE	**12.5%**

Shareholders' equity:

Norwegian GAAP	43,532
Property, plant, equipment	7,999
Other differences (net)	(3,290)
US GAAP	48,241
Total debt	30,842

(ii) Debt-to-equity ratio:

Norwegian GAAP	**0.71**
US GAAP	**0.64**

Property, plant, equipment	7,999
Deferred tax @ 35%	(2,800)
Net effect on equity	5,199
Shareholders' equity:	48,731
(ii) Debt-to-equity ratio:	**0.63**

7.{M}   Exhibit 7S-3 (previous page) contains the calculations required by parts a through c.

d.   Capitalization policy can significantly affect both pretax income and shareholders' equity. Capitalization rather than expensing always increases equity and, therefore, reduces the debt-to-equity ratio. The effect on ROE varies as capitalization increases both return and equity.

In the case of Norsk Hydro, Norwegian GAAP adjusted to exclude non-capitalization produces the lowest debt-to-equity ratio as the expensing of exploration, environmental, and interest costs increases reported equity. ROE is highest under Norwegian GAAP (unadjusted) as income is highest and equity lowest. US GAAP produces the lowest ROE as income is lowest and equity highest.

e.   The negative adjustment means that exploration costs were higher under US GAAP than under Norwegian GAAP. This suggests that exploration costs that Norwegian GAAP expenses (but US GAAP capitalizes) were below normal. As a result the amortization of past expenditures capitalized under US GAAP exceeded the current year's capitalized expenditures.

8.{S}a.   (i)   Given rapidly rising expenditures, Nokia will report higher net income as current year capitalization will exceed amortization of prior year capitalized amounts.
(ii)   Regardless of trend, Nokia will report higher cash from operations as expenditures are reported as cash for investment and never affects cash from operations (see Figure 7-4 on page 232).
(iii) Capitalization of development costs results in higher equity for Nokia, regardless of the trend of expenditures.

b.   (i)   Capitalization of development cost increases operating income (EBIT) and, therefore, the interest coverage ratio.
(ii)   Higher equity under capitalization reduces the debt-to-equity ratio.

c.	These steps are described in Box 7-2 of the chapter.
One can adjust Nokia's reported amounts to those for an
"expensing" firm by:
- 	Eliminating the capitalized costs from assets
- 	Eliminating the capitalized costs (net of taxes)
from equity
- 	Deducting the (tax-adjusted) difference between
expenditures and amortized cost from income
- 	Transferring expenditures from CFI to CFO

Alternatively, one can adjust Ericsson's reported
results by assuming that it capitalizes development
costs and:
- 	Choosing an appropriate amortization period
- 	Increasing assets by the unamortized portion of
previous years' expenditures
- 	Increasing equity by the (tax adjusted) assets
calculated above
- 	Adding the (tax-adjusted) difference between
expenditures and amortized cost to income
- 	Transferring expenditures from CFO to CFI

9. {M}	Exhibit 7S-4 (page 10) contains the calculations
required by parts a and b.

a.	R&D is clearly very important to Pfizer's business. Its
R&D expenditures are very high relative to sales and
the percentage has been growing even though sales
growth is rapid. These expenditures, at least in the
short run, reduce Pfizer's reported earnings given the
long time lag between discovery and profitable sales of
prescription drugs.

c.	Capitalization and amortization of R & D increases net
income each year, the expected result given rising
expenditures. There is little impact on ROE as higher
equity offsets higher net income. (This latter result
is not surprising given the findings of Sarath et. al,
discussed in footnote 3 on page 233.)

d.	(i)	Asset turnover will decline under capitalization
due to the higher level of assets; sales are
unchanged.
	(ii)	Cash from operations will rise under
capitalization as R&D expenditures will be
classified as investing cash flows and will never
be reported as a component of cash flows from
operations.

Exhibit 7S-4
Pfizer

		Years ended December 31			
Amounts in $millions	*1995*	*1996*	*1997*	*1998*	*1999*
Net sales	$ 8,684	$ 9,864	$ 10,739	$ 12,677	$ 14,133
R & D expense	1,340	1,567	1,805	2,279	2,776
a. % sales	**15.4%**	**15.9%**	**16.8%**	**18.0%**	**19.6%**

b. Adjustments

3 year amortization:

1/3 current year			$ 602	$ 760	$ 925
1/3 prior year			522	602	760
1/3 2nd prior year			447	522	602
Total amortization			$ 1,571	$ 1,884	$ 2,287
Expense less amortization			(234)	(395)	(489)
Adjusted pretax income			$ 3,101	$ 2,989	$ 4,937
Adjusted tax expense			(857)	(780)	(1,415)
(i) Adjusted net income			**$ 2,244**	**$ 2,209**	**$ 3,522**
Reported net income			2,092	1,952	3,204
R & D asset (net)	$ 1,239	$ 1,491	$ 1,726	$ 2,121	$ 2,610
R & D asset after-tax	805	969	1,122	1,379	1,697
Shareholders' equity	5,506	6,954	7,933	8,810	8,887
Adjusted equity	$ 6,311	$ 7,923	$ 9,055	$10,189	$10,584
Adjusted average equity	5,637	7,117	8,489	9,622	10,386
(ii) Adjusted ROE			**26.4%**	**23.0%**	**33.9%**
Reported ROE			28.1%	23.3%	36.2%

10.{S}a. Because SB expenses the cost of developing new drugs, their carrying amount on SB's balance sheet is extremely low. As a result, the proceeds of sale are virtually all profit.

b. The drugs were developed over a number of years and the income from their sale was really earned during that time period rather than completely in the year of sale.

c. For valuation purposes, it would be more logical to spread the sale income over the time period during which the drug was developed. Valuation based on 2000 income that includes the entire gain will overvalue the company.

11.{M}a. Debt to total assets = $15,431/$65,585 = 23.5%
Debt to equity = $15,431/$32,660 = 47.2%

b. Debt to total assets = $15,431/$61,056 = 25.3%
Debt to equity = $15,431/$28,131 = 54.8%

c. (i) Because the revaluation increment increases equity, and has no effect on income, ROE is reduced.
(ii) Because the revaluation increment increases assets, and has no effect on sales, asset turnover is reduced.
(iii) There is no effect on EPS as income is unchanged.
(iv) Revaluation has no effect on cash flow or any of its components.

d. (i) The initial effect of amortization would be to reduce income and, therefore, ROE. Longer term the lower equity base would tend to increase ROE so that the net effect is difficult to predict.
(ii) Initially and over time, asset turnover would increase as amortization reduced the carrying amount of assets.
(iii) Amortization would reduce the level of earnings per share initially and over time.
(iv) Cash from operations would be unchanged as amortization is a noncash expense.

e. Increased competition would be likely to reduce the current stock price almost immediately as stock prices discount future events as soon as information is known. The financial statement effects would be slower to occur. Initially there would be reduced profitability. At some point the intangible asset would be revalued downward.

f. Revaluation facilitates disclosure of management's view of the value of the firm's assets. This disclosure allows the financial analyst to measure operating results against the real investment in these assets rather than an obsolete cost. This permits the analyst to evaluate the "opportunity cost" of using the assets in operations rather than selling them.

    However, revaluations are subjective by their nature. Management can manipulate revaluations and provide a misleading indication of the value of the firm. The lack of amortization means that changes in economic value are reflected only when management chooses to write down the assets, which may be well after the market price of the company's shares has recognized the change.

12.{M} Exhibit 7S-5 (page 13) contains the calculations required by parts a through e.

a. ROE: SUA = 14.2%   May = 15.6%   Difference = 1.4%

b. MAY's reported data is adjusted by increasing R&D expense by the 2002 increase in R&D assets and reducing assets by the amount of capitalized R&D.

c. After adjustment, MAY's ROA is higher at 16.2 %, widening the gap between the two companies.
    ROE: SUA = 14.2%   May = 16.2%   Difference = 2.0%

d. Capitalizing R&D requires that R&D expense for 2002 be replaced by one-third of total R&D expenditures over the 2000 to 2002 period. R&D assets at the end of 2002 equals one-third of the 2001 expenditures plus two-thirds of the 2002 expenditures.

e. Capitalizing R&D for SUA reduces ROA to 13.8%, widening the gap between the two companies relative to the reported numbers.
    ROE: SUA = 13.8%   May = 15.8%   Difference = 1.8%

The effect of the differing accounting methods is to make ROA for the two companies seem closer than it really is. Adjustment of either company to the method used by the other makes the disparity clearer.

Exhibit 7S-5

Reported Data:

SUA	2000	2001	2002
R&D expense	$ 15,200	$ 16,500	$ 18,100
Net income	27,000	29,000	32,000
R&D assets	–	–	–
Total assets	200,000	210,000	225,000
a. Return on assets[1]			14.2%

MAY	2000	2001	2002
R&D expense	$ 29,500	$ 32,400	$ 35,600
Net income	48,600	52,200	57,600
R&D assets	28,800	31,500	34,600
Total assets	330,000	346,000	370,000
a. Return on assets			15.6%

b. **MAY: Adjustment to expense R&D**

Change in R&D expense	$ 3,100
Adjusted net income	**54,500**
Change in R&D assets	(34,600)
Adjusted total assets	**335,400**
c. **Adjusted ROA**	**16.2%**

d. **SUA: Adjustment to capitalize R&D**

Change in R&D expense	$ (1,500)
Adjusted net income	**33,500**
Change in R&D assets	17,567
Adjusted total assets	**242,567**
e. **Adjusted ROA**	**13.8%**

---

[1] As can be seen when part b is done, calculation of Sua's 2001 assets would require R&D expenditures for 1999 – 2001.

13.{M}a.   (i)   1999 income is reduced as prior year startup expenses are amortized but there were no startup costs incurred.
   (ii) Cash from operations for 1999 is unaffected as amortization is a noncash expense.
   (iii) Return on equity is reduced because of lower income and because equity was increased by the capitalization of startup expenses in prior years.
   (iv) Asset turnover is reduced as assets were increased by capitalization of startup costs in prior years.

   b.   (i)   Initial year income was increased as startup costs were capitalized rather than expensed.
   (ii) Cash from operations was also increased as startup expenses were reported as investments rather than operating expenses.
   (iii) Return on equity was increased because of higher income from the initial application of the method.
   (iv) Asset turnover was reduced as ending assets were increased by capitalization of startup costs.

   c.   When a company capitalizes startup costs, the initial financial statement effects are mostly favorable. However if startup expenses are not incurred each year, then later year effects are negative. The exception is cash from operations, where the initial favorable effect is never reversed.

a.

Ratios	1998	1999	2000
United States GAAP			
Net income/sales	37.2%	-63.8%	-47.8%
Return on ending equity	83.3%	-41.1%	-62.2%
Asset turnover	0.56	0.37	0.28
Book value per share	$ 0.50	$ 2.15	$ 1.81
Canadian GAAP			
Net income/sales	31.8%	30.9%	26.1%
Return on ending equity	164.6%	13.0%	9.7%
Asset turnover	0.49	0.26	0.21
Book value per share	$ 0.19	$ 3.15	$ 6.38

b.   Biovail appears to be much more profitable using the Canadian GAAP data. Further, the declines in 1999 and 2000 are much milder under Canadian GAAP.

Asset turnover is higher under U.S. GAAP, with a similar declining trend.

Book value per share is higher under Canadian GAAP in 1999 and 2000, with much larger increases from the 1998 level.

c.   The rise in the market price of Biovail shares appears to be more closely related to the Canadian GAAP data that show a rising book value per share and rising earnings per share (see Exhibit 7A-1). The rise may have been due to announcements related to drugs that received regulatory approvals or marketing arrangements.

d.   The answer to part c suggests that capitalization and amortization of IPRD comes closer to reflecting the economic impact (measured by share price) of the acquisition of drug rights.

e.   The answer to part d assumes that the acquired rights eventually prove to result in profitable drugs. If the rights proved to be worthless, then immediate write off would more accurately forecast the eventual decline in the share price.

f.   The answers to the preceding parts suggest that
      internal drug research expenditures should also be
      capitalized, assuming that (in the aggregate) they
      result in profitable drugs.

7A-2{L}   Exhibit 7AS-1 (page 17) contains the calculations
          required by parts a through d.

          The adjustments shown remove (from ALZA's income
          statement) the payments from Crescendo, payments to
          Crescendo, and IPRD write off. These adjustments are
          carried forward to operating and pretax income.

e.   (i)   The Crescendo transactions reduced the revenue
            growth rate as payments from Crescendo declined in
            1999 and 2000. The effect on the growth rate of
            profitability was negative for the same reason.

      (ii) The Crescendo transactions increased the reported
            profitability of ALZA for all three years by all
            measures (operating profit and margin, pretax
            profit and margin). This was because ALZA
            effectively converted much of the cost of drug
            development from an expense to revenue.

      (iii) The volatility of ALZA's profitability was reduced
            by the transactions as their net effect was
            relatively stable. ALZA's pretax profit margin,
            for example, would have fallen more than 50% in
            1999 and then quadrupled in 2000. The reported
            margin was less volatile.

      (iv) The return portion of ROE increased as a result of
            the Crescendo transactions. However equity also
            increased due to higher retained earnings. Unless
            ALZA's equity was very low, it is likely that the
            earnings effect dominates and ROE increased.

f.   The benefit to AlZA is clearly higher and more stable
      profitability, as discussed in part e, subparts ii and
      iii. Higher ROE (subpart iv) may be an additional
      benefit. While not shown numerically, the Crescendo
      transactions may have shifted some of the risk of drug
      development to Crescendo shareholdings.

      One drawback is a reduced revenue growth rate. More
      important, the cost of capital was very high, as
      discussed in the appendix.

Exhibit 7AS-1
ALZA Corp.
All data in $millions, except per share

Adjustments for Crescendo	Years ended December 31			% change	
	1998	1999	2000	98/99	99/00
Reported revenues	$ 646.9	$ 795.9	$ 988.5	23.0%	24.2%
Payments from Crescendo	(105.9)	(97.4)	(71.2)		
Adjusted revenues	$ 541.0	$ 698.5	$ 917.3	29.1%	31.3%
% reduction	-16.4%	-12.2%	-7.2%		
Reported expenses	(450.4)	(646.7)	(732.8)	43.6%	13.3%
In-process R & D			9.4		
Payments to Crescendo	–	2.4	4.5		
Adjusted expenses	$(450.4)	$(644.3)	$(718.9)	43.1%	11.6%
% reduction	0%	0.4%	1.9%		
Operating income	$ 196.5	$ 149.2	$ 255.7	-24.1%	71.4%
Adjusted operating income	90.6	54.2	198.4	-40.2%	266.1%
% reduction	-53.9%	-63.7%	-22.4%		
Interest and other income	26.4	41.6	59.0		
Interest expense	(56.7)	(58.1)	(58.0)		
Net other expense	$ (30.3)	$ (16.5)	$ 1.0		
Pretax income	$ 166.2	$ 132.7	$ 256.7	-20.2%	93.4%
Adjusted pretax income	60.3	37.7	199.4	-37.5%	428.9%
% reduction	-63.7%	-71.6%	-22.3%		
Reported Ratios					
Operating margin	30.4%	18.7%	25.9%		
Pretax margin	25.7%	16.7%	26.0%		
Times interest earned	3.47	2.57	4.41		
Adjusted Ratios					
Operating margin	16.7%	7.8%	21.6%		
Pretax margin	11.1%	5.4%	21.7%		
Times interest earned	1.60	0.93	3.42		

g.	ALZA effectively controlled Crescendo. While it may have shifted some development risk to Crescendo shareholders, it is unclear that ALZA could have "walked away" if no marketable drugs had resulted as Crescendo had licensed ALZA technology. This technology may well have alternative uses that would make ALZA unwilling to see it fall into the hands of competitors. Therefore the risk transfer may have been limited.

Given these factors, ALZA's reported financial data may not portray the company's underlying economics. Adjusted data that exclude the Crescendo transactions may be more useful for evaluating ALZA's performance and valuing its shares.

7B-1{M}a.(i)	Because all exploration costs are capitalized and amortized under the full cost method, earnings are no longer immediately affected by dry hole costs.

(ii)	Dry hole costs are unpredictable and volatile; amortization is predictable and varies only with the level of production.

(iii)	Because capitalized cost includes all exploration costs, the carrying amount is higher.

(iv)	Higher earnings resulting from capitalizing rather than expensing dry hole costs results in higher stockholders' equity.

b.	

January 1, 1996 retained earnings effect	$ 199,196
1996 earnings effect	18,006
1997 earnings effect	130,584
1998 earnings effect	(258,351)
Total effect of accounting change	$ 89,435

c.	(i)	Debt-to-equity ratio declines as equity increases.

(ii)	Asset turnover declines as assets increase.

(iii)	Book value increases as equity increases.

d.	In theory, capitalizing dry hole costs would increase cash from operations. However Sonat, like most firms in its industry, considers all exploration costs to be investing cash flows.

e.	Sonat's accounting change was clearly intended to improve the level and stability of reported earnings.

f. When energy prices decline, use of the full cost method increases the risk that impairment charges will be required. The SEC requires that the "ceiling test" be based on *discounted* present values (rather than *undiscounted* present values used by successful efforts firms). The 1998 ceiling test charges were presumably greater under the full cost method as restated 1998 net income was significantly lower than net income reported under the successful efforts method.

g. The 1991 accounting change suggests that the company views accounting methods as a free choice and that it can change methods whenever it believes that the new method will make its results look better.

7B-2{L} Exhibit 7BS-1 (page 20) contains the calculations required by part a.

b. U.S. reserve lives increased as production fell and reserves fell less (oil) or increased (gas). Worldwide reserves grew for both oil and gas, increasing reserve lives, especially for gas.

c. Exhibit 7BS-2 (page 21) contains the calculations required by part c.

d. Capitalized cost per BOE in the United States was stable at $3.22. However worldwide capitalized cost per BOE rose slightly each year. Lower capitalized costs and upward reserve estimates reduce those amounts while lower reserve balances increase them.

e. Over the four years ending December 31, 2000, the standardized value rose from less than $18 billion to more than $26 billion. Price changes accounted for $7.6 billion, or virtually all of the net increase as 1999 and 2000 price increases more than offset 1997 and 1998 declines. Revisions were upward each year, adding $3.3 billion to the standardized measure. Income taxes of $4.8 billion over the four-year period offset a portion of the net gain.

```
Exhibit 7BS-1
Texaco Reserve Lives in Years


                              United States
                    1997      1998      1999      2000
Oil reserves       1,767     1,824     1,782     1,560
Production           157       144       144       130
Ratio              11.25     12.67     12.38     12.00


Gas reserves       4,022     4,105     4,205     4,430
Production           643       633       550       494
Ratio               6.26      6.48      7.65      8.97


                              Worldwide
                    1997      1998      1999      2000
Oil reserves       3,267     3,573     3,480     3,518
Production           317       351       336       307
Ratio              10.31     10.18     10.36     11.46


Gas reserves       6,242     6,517     8,108     8,292
Production           839       879       786       730
Ratio               7.44      7.41     10.32     11.36


Data for 2000 from Table I; oil in millions of barrels,
   gas in billions of cubic feet

Data for 1997-1999 from Appendix 7-B
```

f. If we use the standardized measure as a guide, Texaco increased the economic value of its reserves significantly over the four-year period. However price increases account for more of the gain than any other factor. Sales and transfers greatly exceeded new discoveries. While Table I in Exhibit 7BP-1 shows that the company replaced more than 100% of its production over the past five years, that performance is due more to upward reserve estimates than to exploration success.

```
Exhibit 7BS-2
Texaco Capitalized Cost per BOE


December 31              U.S.        Worldwide
      1998
Oil reserves            1,824         3,573
Gas reserves            4,105         6,517
BOE                     2,508         4,659
Capitalized costs      $8,086       $12,190
Costs per BOE            3.22          2.62


      1999
Oil reserves            1,782         3,480
Gas reserves            4,205         8,108
BOE                     2,483         4,831
Capitalized costs      $7,933       $13,038
Costs per BOE            3.20          2.70


      2000
Oil reserves            1,560         3,518
Gas reserves            4,430         8,292
BOE                     2,298         4,900
Capitalized costs      $7,412       $13,544
Costs per BOE            3.22          2.76


Data for 2000 from Tables I and IV of Exhibit 7BP-1
Data for 1998-1999 from Appendix 7-B
Oil reserves and BOE in millions of barrels, gas reserves
 in billion cubic feet, capitalized costs in $millions
```

g.   Exhibit 7BS-3 (page 22) contains the calculations
     required by part g.
     (iii) The adjustment increased the debt-to-equity ratio
           in 1998 but reduced it in 1999 and 2000. Overall
           the adjusted ratio shows a sharp declining trend
           while the unadjusted ratio declined modestly.
     (iv) The adjustment would decrease the asset turnover
           ratio for 1999 and 2000 as the excess of the
           standardized measure over the carrying amount
           would increase total assets.

```
Exhibit 7BS-3
Texaco
Adjustment of Stockholders' Equity
```

Amounts in $ millions Standardized measure	Years Ended December 31		
	1998	1999	2000
United States[1]	$ 4,879	$ 15,604	$ 27,159
Europe[1]	1,382	4,990	4,656
Other areas[2]	1,116	3,909	4,984
Total	$ 9,375	$ 26,502	$ 38,799
Carrying amount	12,190	13,038	13,544
(i) Excess	**$ (2,815)**	**$ 13,464**	**$ 25,255**
Reported equity	11,833	12,042	13,444
Adjusted equity	$ 9,018	$ 25,506	$ 38,699
% change	-24%	112%	188%
Total debt	$ 7,291	$ 7,647	$ 7,191
(ii) Debt-to-equity ratio			
Reported	**0.62**	**0.64**	**0.53**
Adjusted	**0.81**	**0.30**	**0.19**

```
1 Pretax basis
2 Posttax basis
```

h. (i) The change in the standardized measure could be
         added to income for each year, and the sum,
         divided by adjusted equity, would be a measure of
         current cost ROE.

    (ii) Current cost ROE would compare a more complete
         measure of income with a better measure of the
         company's equity.

    (iii)One drawback to this current cost ROE would be its
         volatility. As both the numerator and denominator
         could change significantly from year to year, it
         would be difficult to use this measure to evaluate
         management. In addition, when energy prices
         change, changes in current cost ROE would be
         largely determined by a factor outside of
         management's control, limited the usefulness of
         ROE further.

Case 7-1 - Solution

Estimated time to complete this case is two hours.

Exhibit 7CS-1 shows the required computations.

1. For each year, net income is adjusted by the difference between new software investment and amortization, reduced by the tax effect.

2. Cash from operations reduced by the new investment in software as amortization is excluded from cash from operations. The adjustment reduces CFO substantially in 1992 through 1994 but less so in later years as capitalized expenditures decline. Thus, while adjusted CFO is lower each year, the growth rate increases due to the greater reduction in early years.

   Cash for investment is reduced by the same amount, increasing the level (reducing the outflow). Again the early year effects are greatest. Over the 1992 to 2001 period, the reported amounts show a small change (< 4%) while the adjusted amounts show modest growth (33%).

3. Total spending declined from 1992 through 1996 and then rose to the 1993 level by 2001. The percentage capitalized declined to as low as 10% for 1998, rising thereafter as IBM implemented new standards as discussed in the chapter.

4. External software revenues showed virtually no change after 1995, although annual fluctuations remain.

5. As shown in Exhibit 7CS-1, gross profit rose approximately 50% from 1992 to 2001, mainly due to lower costs in the later years. Gross profit margins rose from a low of 59% in 1994 to over 80% for the years 1998 to 2001.

6. Total software revenues showed some growth over the 1996 to 2001 period. Profit margins peaked in 1999 but then declined.

7. Segment assets rose in 2001 after declining steadily through 2000. Pretax ROA averaged close to 100% over the entire time period. ROA is greatly affected by capitalization policy. If IBM expensed all software costs, the asset base would remain low and large changes in software expenditures would directly affect ROA. If IBM capitalized all expenditures, the asset base would be higher and volatility lower as variations in spending affect pretax income only indirectly through amortization.

8. (i) In years with large capitalized amounts, ROA is higher. Income is high as expenditures are capitalized rather than expensed. This effect is partially offset by the larger asset base resulting from capitalization.

(ii) When capitalization is relatively low, then ROA is reduced as amortization of prior year capitalized amounts exceeds the amount that would have been expensed. Again, the effect of capitalization on the asset base mitigates the income effect.

9. Total expenditures (including purchased IPRD) declined from the high levels of the early 1990's to approximately 6.5% of revenues; the 2001 increase probably reflects disappointing revenue growth rather than a change in budgeted amounts. Questions that may be worth asking include:
   a. What are IBM's future plans for R&D spending?
   b. Will the percentage of IBM's future spending that qualifies for capitalization change?
   c. Has there been a shift in spending between software intended for sale and for internal use?
   d. How does IBM's spending level and growth rate compare with those of its competitors?
   e. How is the result of R&D spending expected to change IBM's revenue mix and profitability?

10. See exhibit 7CS-1.

11. The amount of software expenditures than can be capitalized reflects changes in accounting standards.

The nature of expenditures also affects the amount that can be capitalized. Pure research must be expensed while the cost of developing new products can often be capitalized.

Corporate policy also affects these decisions. A conservative policy would require, for example, more confidence that a software product is commercially feasible before starting to capitalize development costs.

Specifically for IBM, while accounting standards allowed more capitalization over the period, the percentage of software spending that was capitalized declined thru 1998. IBM's profitability increased substantially, despite lower capitalization. While the nature of expenditures (and reduced R&D due to more licensing, for example) may account for some of the reduced capitalization, it is likely that IBM shifted to a more conservative policy.

The desire of large firms to keep reported earnings from appearing too large, especially as IBM had a history of government scrutiny, may have accounted for the apparent policy change. The increase in the capitalization rate starting in 1999 may reflect the desire to accelerate EPS growth to meet the stock market's demand for rapid growth.

Exhibit 7CS-1 IBM: Software Capitalization   (Amounts in $millions)

Years Ended December 31	1992	1993	1994	1995	1996	1997	1998	1999	2000	2001
1. Adjusted net income										
Investment in software	$ 1,752	$ 1,507	$ 1,361	$ 823	$ 295	$ 314	$ 250	$ 464	$ 565	$ 655
Amortization of software	1,466	1,951	2,098	1,647	1,336	983	517	426	482	625
Net pretax effect	$ 286	$ (444)	$ (737)	$ (824)	$(1,041)	$ (669)	$ (267)	$ 38	$ 83	$ 30
Less: 35% income tax	(100)	155	258	288	364	234	93	(13)	(29)	(11)
Net income effect	$ 186	$ (289)	$ (479)	$ (536)	$ (677)	$ (435)	$ (174)	$ 25	$ 54	$ 20
Net income	(6,865)	(7,987)	3,021	4,178	5,429	6,093	6,328	7,712	8,093	7,723
Adjusted net income	(7,051)	(7,698)	3,500	4,714	6,106	6,528	6,502	7,687	8,039	7,704
% change	-2.7%	3.6%	15.9%	12.8%	12.5%	7.1%	2.7%	-0.3%	-0.7%	-0.3%
2. Adjusted cash flows										
Cash from operations	$ 6,274	$ 8,327	$11,793	$10,708	$10,275	8,865	$ 9,273	$10,111	$ 9,274	$14,265
(i) Adjusted cash from operations	4,522	6,820	10,432	9,885	9,980	8,551	9,023	9,647	8,709	13,610
% change	-27.9%	-18.1%	-11.5%	-7.7%	-2.9%	-3.5%	-2.7%	-4.6%	-6.1%	-4.6%
Cash for investment	$(5,878)	(4,202)	(3,426)	(5,052)	(5,723)	(6,155)	(6,131)	(1,669)	(4,248)	(6,106)
(ii) Adjusted cash for investment	(4,126)	(2,695)	(2,065)	(4,229)	(5,428)	(5,841)	(5,881)	(1,205)	(3,683)	(5,451)
% change	29.8%	35.9%	39.7%	16.3%	5.2%	5.1%	4.1%	27.8%	13.3%	10.7%
3. Computer software investment										
Investment in software	$ 1,752	$ 1,507	$ 1,361	$ 823	$ 295	$ 314	$ 250	$ 464	$ 565	$ 655
Software-related R & D.	1,161	1,097	793	1,157	1,726	2,016	2,086	2,036	1,948	1,926
Total software investment	$ 2,913	$ 2,604	$ 2,154	$ 1,980	$ 2,021	$ 2,330	$ 2,336	$ 2,500	$ 2,513	$ 2,581
% capitalized	60.1%	57.9%	63.2%	41.6%	14.6%	13.5%	10.7%	18.6%	22.5%	25.4%

Exhibit 7CS-1 (continued) IBM: Software Capitalization   (Amounts in $millions)

Years Ended December 31	1992	1993	1994	1995	1996	1997	1998	1999	2000	2001
Software Segment										
External revenue	$11,103	$10,953	$11,346	$12,657	$11,426	$11,164	$11,863	$12,662	$12,598	$12,939
4. % change		-1.4%	3.6%	11.6%	-9.7%	-2.3%	6.3%	6.7%	-0.5%	2.7%
Cost of external revenue	3,924	4,310	4,680	4,428	2,946	2,785	2,260	2,240	2,283	2,265
5. Gross profit	$ 7,179	$ 6,643	$ 6,666	$ 8,229	$ 8,480	$ 8,379	$ 9,603	$10,422	$10,315	$10,674
Gross profit margin	64.7%	60.7%	58.8%	65.0%	74.2%	75.1%	80.9%	82.3%	81.9%	82.5%
Internal software revenue					$ 593	$ 671	$ 749	$ 767	$ 828	$ 981
Total software revenue					12,019	11,835	12,612	13,429	13,426	13,920
Pretax income					2,466	2,034	2,742	3,099	2,793	2,794
6. Pretax profit margin					20.5%	17.2%	21.7%	23.1%	20.8%	20.1%
Segment assets					$ 2,813	$ 2,642	$ 2,577	$ 2,527	$ 2,488	$ 3,356
7. Pretax ROA					87.7%	77.0%	106.4%	122.6%	112.3%	83.3%
Investment in software	$ 1,752	$ 1,507	$ 1,361	$ 823	$ 295	$ 314	$ 250	$ 464	$ 565	$ 655
Total R & D expense	6,522	5,558	4,363	4,170	4,654	4,877	5,046	5,273	5,151	5,290
9. Total R&D expenditures	$ 8,274	$ 7,065	$ 5,724	$ 4,993	$ 4,949	$ 5,191	$ 5,296	$ 5,737	$ 5,716	$ 5,945
% total corporate revenue	12.8%	11.3%	8.9%	6.9%	6.5%	6.6%	6.5%	6.6%	6.5%	6.9%
IBM Totals										
Revenue	$64,523	$62,716	$64,052	$71,940	$75,947	$78,508	$81,667	$87,548	$88,396	$85,866
Net income*	(6,865)	(7,987)	3,021	4,178	5,429	6,093	6,328	7,712	8,093	7,723
10. Net profit margin	-10.6%	-12.7%	4.7%	5.8%	7.1%	7.8%	7.7%	8.8%	9.2%	9.0%
Stockholders' equity	$27,624	$19,738	$23,413	$22,423	$21,628	$19,816	$19,433	$20,511	$20,624	$23,614
Return on average equity	-21.4%	-33.7%	14.0%	18.2%	24.6%	29.4%	32.2%	38.6%	39.3%	34.9%

Chapter 8 Solutions

Overview:

Problem Length	*Problem #s*
{S}	2, 4, 5, 6, 7, 8, 9 and 15.
{M}	1, 3, 10, 12, 13, 14 and 16.
{L}	11 and 8A-1.

1.{M}(i)   Straight-line depreciation
     (ii) Sum-of-years' digits

Depreciable base	$10,000,000	$10,000,000
Sum-of-years'-digits		15
Year	Straight line Method	Sum-of-years' Digits
1	$ 2,000,000	$ 3,333,333
2	2,000,000	2,666,667
3	2,000,000	2,000,000
4	2,000,000	1,333,333
5	2,000,000	666,667
Total	$10,000,000	$10,000,000

(iii) Double declining balance

Depreciable base	$12,000,000	Rate = 40%
	Double-declining balance	
Year	Depreciation	Balance
1	$ 4,800,000	$ 7,200,000
2	2,880,000	4,320,000
3	1,728,000	2,592,000
4	592,000	2,000,000
5		2,000,000
Total	$10,000,000	

2.{S}
(i)   Straight-line methods report constant depreciation
        expense throughout the life of the asset. Accelerated
        methods result in higher depreciation expense
        initially, but a declining trend thereafter. The effect
        on total depreciation expense depends on the growth
        rate of capital spending (whether the effect of higher
        depreciation expense on new assets offsets the impact
        of declining depreciation expense on old ones). Using
        the same economic life, accelerated methods will report
        higher depreciation expense than the straight-line
        method during the early years and lower expense
        thereafter.

(ii)   The effect on net income is the reverse of the above.
        Net income is lower initially. Its reversal will depend
        on the level and growth of capital expenditures in the
        future.

(iii)   Accelerated depreciation methods report lower net
        income (higher depreciation expense), lower assets, and
        lower equity (higher accumulated depreciation) than the
        straight-line method. The numerator effect may
        dominate, producing lower return ratios. For a growing
        firm with increasing capital expenditures, the early
        years' depreciation expense difference will persist,
        resulting in lower return ratios.

(iv)   Accelerated depreciation methods report lower income in
        the first year but higher income in later years as
        depreciation expense declines. Reported assets are
        lower throughout. Companies with rapidly growing
        capital expenditures are likely to report lower ROA as
        the income effect dominates. As they mature, however,
        slowing capital expenditures and the growing effect of
        the reduced denominator (assets) is likely to result in
        higher ROA than under the straight-line method.

(v)   For financial reporting purposes, the choice of method
        has no effect on reported cash flows, as depreciation
        is a noncash expense. However, for tax purposes, the
        use of accelerated methods rather than the straight-
        line method reduces taxes paid, increasing cash from
        operations.

(vi)   As depreciation expense has no effect on revenues,
        accelerated depreciation methods increase reported
        asset turnover, as the denominator is lower.

3.{M}a. and b. As discussed on page 276 of the text, Baxter must use a two-step process. First, it must determine whether the asset is impaired, by comparing the machinery's carrying amount with the *undiscounted* future cash flows expected from its use and disposal. If the carrying value exceeds the undiscounted cash flows, it must measure the impairment loss by comparing the asset's carrying amount with its fair value. When the fair value of the asset is not available, Baxter must use the fair value of a similar asset. When neither is available, the carrying amount of the asset must be compared to the *discounted* present value of the expected future cash flows from its use and disposal.

c. (i) Reported net income declines in the year of impairment recognition but rises in following years due to lower depreciation expense.

(ii) Same as part (i) as impairment charges are reported as part of income from continuing operations, although they may be reported on a separate line of the income statement.

(iii) There is no effect on cash from operations as impairment charges that reduce the carrying amount of fixed assets have no impact on reported cash flows either in the year of recognition or in following years.

(iv) Shareholders' equity is reduced when impairment charges are recognized as income is reduced. The difference declines in following years as income is increased but equity remains below what it would have been without impairment recognition until the asset is fully depreciated.

(v) Return on equity is reduced in the recognition year as income is lower. In following years, however, ROE is increased as income is higher and equity lower.

(vi) Asset turnover is lower each year as the impairment write down reduces the machinery's carrying amount, reducing total assets. The effect disappears only when the machinery is fully depreciated.

d. Same as part c, except that the asset must be written down to fair value (PV of expected cash flows) less cost to sell. Because the fair value of the impaired asset must be measured at each subsequent reporting date, declines in value below the amount recognized initially and subsequent increases (no higher than original carrying amount at impairment date) must be recognized, increasing the volatility of reported net income and income from continuing operations.

4.{S} a.
   (i) **Depreciation expense: 2000**   **2001**

   Sum-of-years' digits: depreciable cost = $8,000 ($9,000
   - $1,000), SYD = 15
                5/15ths = **$2,666.67**   4/15ths = **$2,133.33**

   (ii) Double declining balance: 2000 depreciable cost =
        $9,000, rate = 40% (2x20%)

                .40 x $9,000 = **$3,600**   .40 x $5,400* = **$2,160**

   * Balance at the end of 2001 is ($9,000 - $3,600)

   (iii) Straight line: depreciable cost = $8,000 ($9,000 -
         $1,000), rate is 20%

                .20 x $8,000 = **$1,600**   (same) **$1,600**

   b. (i) Depreciation expense declines over the machine's
           life under the DDB method but remains constant
           over the straight line method.

       (ii) Other things being equal, net income will be the
            same each year when the straight line method is
            used but will increase each year when the DDB
            method is used (as depreciation declines).

       (iii) Cash from operations is unaffected by the choice
             of depreciation method.

       (iv) The debt-to-equity ratio is lower when the DDB
            method is used as lower income reduces equity.

       (v) Fixed asset turnover is higher when the DDB method
            is used as higher depreciation reduces net assets.

5.{S}a. Computation of depreciation expense:

	Cost	Salvage	Base	Years	*Expense*
(i)	$ 10,000	$ 1,000	$ 9,000	10	**$ 900**
(ii)	10,000	1,000	9,000	15	**600**
(iii)	10,000	2,500	7,500	10	**750**
(iv)	10,000	2,500	7,500	15	**500**

   b. If Juliet chooses the assumptions in (iv) rather than
       (i), its depreciation expense will be lower, increasing
       reported income. The longer depreciable life and the
       higher salvage value lower Juliet's quality of
       earnings.

6.{S}a. The present value of the cash flows, discounted at 10%, is $60 for each asset.

b. Asset A:

Year	Net Asset	Cash Flow	Depreciation Expense	Income	ROA
1	$ 60	$ 36	$ 30	$ 6	10%
2	30	23	20	3	10%
3	10	11	10	1	10%

Asset B:

Year	Net Asset	Cash Flow	Depreciation Expense	Income	ROA
1	$ 60	$ 26	$ 20	$ 6	10%
2	40	24	20	4	10%
3	20	22	20	2	10%

c. The pattern for Asset A is the sum-of-the-years' digits method. The pattern for Asset B is the straight-line method.

7.{S}a. Boeing uses accelerated depreciation methods: 150% declining balance for buildings and land improvements and sum-of-the-years' digits for machinery and equipment. As a result early year depreciation resulting from capital expenditures is high keeping net plant and equipment low. The second reason is that, from 1995 to 1999, total depreciation expense was $6,286 while net additions to plant and equipment were $6,010 or $176 lower.

b. Accelerated depreciation methods result in low balance sheet carrying values for fixed assets, increasing the likelihood that asset sales will result in gains.

c. (i) If Boeing adopted the straight-line method in 1999, depreciation expense for both 1998 and 1999 will most likely be reduced. Depreciation on assets acquired in recent years will be reduced although depreciation on older assets will be higher under the straight-line method. As 1998 capital spending was relatively high, the more recent year effects are likely to be greater than the older year effects of the accounting change. As 1999 capital spending was reduced, the effect on that year's depreciation will be less than on 1998.

(ii) Stockholders' equity at December 31, 1999 will be higher due to lower prior year depreciation that increases net income and, therefore, retained earnings.

(iii) Cash from operations is unaffected by the choice of depreciation method.

(iv) Fixed asset turnover for 1999 will be decreased by the accounting change as lower prior year depreciation expense increases net fixed assets.

d. (i) If Boeing adopted the straight-line depreciation method prospectively at January 1, 2000, net income for 2000 would increase as depreciation of current year capital additions is lower under the new method.

(ii) Depreciation expense would be likely to decline due to the combined effect of lower depreciation expense on current year capital additions and the declining trend of depreciation expense on older assets for which accelerated methods remain in use.

e. As the accounting change would increase reported income without any effect on cash flows, an analyst might conclude that the company expects
(i) future earnings trends to be negative
(ii) capital spending to rise sharply
Either of these expectations might lead the company to change its accounting method to improve near-term reported earnings.

8.{S}a.

Reported net income	$ 342,000
Cumulative effect of change	(700,000)
Net income before cumulative effect	**$(358,000)**

b.

1998 effect of change	$ 800,000
Less: 35% income tax	(280,000)
1998 effect net	$ 520,000
Net income before cumulative effect	$(358,000)
1998 effect net	(520,000)
Net income before accounting change	**$(878,000)**

c. Pope and Talbot had an operating loss of $(878,000) in 1998. The accounting change enabled POP to report net income of $342,000.

9.{S}a. Because both companies use ranges to describe their depreciation policy, it is difficult to compare DAL with AMR. AMR used a depreciable life of 20 years for the (unspecified) aircraft types disclosed in Exhibit 8-7, the midpoint of the DAL range of 15 - 25 years. However AMR's residual value of 5% was clearly more conservative than the DAL range of 5 - 25%. Thus we conclude that AMR's depreciation was most likely higher than DAL's. This conclusion leads to the following answers:

(i) Higher depreciation expense for AMR

(ii) Lower stockholders' equity for AMR due to lower income.

(iii) Same cash from operations as depreciation is a noncash expense.

(iv) Higher quality of earnings for AMR as its depreciation assumptions are more conservative.

b. In 1999 AMR changed its depreciable life to 25 years, equaling the high end of the DAL range, suggesting that DAL now uses the higher depreciation rate. However AMR's residual value assumption of 10% is still near the bottom of the DAL range of 5 - 25%. Given the long aircraft lives, the effect of residual value assumptions is small. We conclude that, after the 1999 change, that AMR's depreciation is most likely lower than DAL's. This conclusion leads to the following answers:

(i) Lower depreciation expense for AMR

(ii) Stockholders' equity for AMR tends to rise relative to that of DAL due to higher income.

(iii) Same cash from operations as depreciation is a noncash expense.

(iv) Higher quality of earnings for DAL as its depreciation assumptions are now more conservative.

10.{M}a.

1999 income from vessel operations	$34,189
Change in accounting estimate	(22,500)
1999 income before accounting change	$11,689

b.

Percent change from 1998 as reported	-67%
Percent change from 1998 before change	-89%

c.   (i) Shareholders' equity is increased because of the positive effect of the change on 1999 income.

(ii) Cash from operations is unaffected as depreciation expense is a noncash expense.

(iii) Asset turnover is reduced as lower depreciation expense increases net fixed assets at year-end.

(iv) The depreciation change lowers Teekay's quality of earnings by increasing reported income.

d.   In 2000, Teekay will continue to use longer estimated useful lives for its vessels, reducing depreciation expense and increasing income from vessel operations.

11.{L}a.   Ratios based on reported data

	1997	1998	1999
Interest coverage ratio	3.66	3.04	2.96
Operating margin	11.2%	11.3%	12.5%

b.c.   Assuming that depreciation expense = 3.4% of gross plant and equipment for all years, 1998 and 1999 must be adjusted as follows:

$thousands	1998	1999
Adjusted depreciation	$ 26,950	$ 28,421
Reported depreciation	(25,310)	(21,490)
Excess	$ 1,640	$ 6,931

Using the excess depreciation to adjust EBIT and operating income produces the following ratios:

$thousands	1998	1999
Adjusted EBIT	$ 62,963	$ 54,085
Interest coverage ratio	2.96	2.63
Adjusted operating income	$ 61,824	$ 54,558
Adjusted operating margin	11.0%	11.1%

d.   Reported interest coverage in 1998 and 1999 declined from the 1997 ratio. The adjusted ratios show even greater declines. The reported improvement in the operating ratio (especially for 1999) completely disappears after adjusted for the change in depreciation. This change masked a significant decline in the interest coverage ratio and produced a misleading improvement in the operating ratio.

e.   As regulators are concerned with public reaction to rate increases, accounting changes are viewed as beneficial alternatives. Accounting changes enable the regulated utility to earn its permitted rate of return without increasing rates.

      However mandating accounting changes rather than rate increases may be short sighted. Accounting changes have no cash effect. Ultimately, bond rating agencies will downgrade the utility's bond ratings, increasing its borrowing costs and requiring offsetting rate increases.

f.   Accounting changes do not change the utility's cash flows. When accounting changes are made instead of needed rate increases, the quality of earnings is reduced. From the stockholder/bondholder perspective, the utility's securities are less attractive investments.

g.   Reduced depreciation expense increases the net carrying value of Laclede's utility plant. Deregulation, which removes the guaranteed profitability of utility operations, is likely to result in write-downs of utility plant and increased depreciation rates.

12. {M} a.- c.

As shown in the table below, the accounting change improved the 2000 gross margin ratio by 0.5% and the operating ratio by 0.9%.

| | As Reported | | Accounting | Adjusted |
	1999	2000	Change	2000
Net revenues	$1,452	$1,545		$1,545
Cost of sales	(835)	(845)	$ 8	(853)
Gross profit	$ 617	$ 700	$ 8	$ 692
S, D, & A expense	(575)	(625)	6	(631)
Operating income	$ 42	$ 75	$ 14	$ 61
% of Sales				
Net revenues	100.0%	100.0%		100.0%
Cost of sales	-57.5%	-54.7%	0.5%	-55.2%
Gross margin	**42.5%**	**45.3%**	**0.5%**	**44.8%**
S, D, & A expense	-39.6%	-40.5%	0.4%	-40.8%
Operating margin	**2.9%**	**4.9%**	**0.9%**	**3.9%**

d. (i) Fixed asset turnover is reduced as lower depreciation expense increases the net carrying amount of fixed assets.

   (ii) The accounting change improves the reported income trend as 2000 and following years benefit from the reduced depreciation expense.

   (iii) PBG's quality of earnings is reduced as the accounting change increases reported earnings.

   (iv) Cash from operations is unchanged as depreciation is a noncash expense.

e. If the company believes that its performance is best measured using cash flow data, the accounting change has no benefit whatsoever. However reported income is increased, reducing the reported price-earnings ratio.

13. {M}a. and b.   As shown in the table below, the accounting change improved the operating margin by 1.1 percentage points. Only 0.7 percentage points of the 1999 - 2000 operating margin increase of 1.8% was due to operating changes.

| | As reported | | Accounting | Adjusted |
	1999	2000	Change	2000
Net revenues	$14,406	$14,750		$14,750
Cost of sales	(9,015)	(9,083)	92	(9,175)
Gross profit	$ 5,391	$ 5,667	$ 92	$ 5,575
S, D, & A expense	(4,552)	(4,541)	69	(4,610)
Operating income	$ 839	$ 1,126	$ 161	$ 965
% of Sales				
Net revenues	100.0%	100.0%		100.0%
Cost of sales	-62.6%	-61.6%	0.6%	-62.2%
Gross margin	**37.4%**	**38.4%**	**0.6%**	**37.8%**
S, D,& A expense	-31.6%	-30.8%	0.5%	-31.3%
Operating margin	**5.8%**	**7.6%**	**1.1%**	**6.5%**

Note: depreciation expense allocated between cost of sales and S, D, & A expense using the same ratio as for PBG in problem 12:
8/14 x $161 million = $ 92 million to cost of sales
6/14 x $161 million =   69 million to S, D, A expense
     Total effect   = $161 million

c. (i) The PBG disclosures in Exhibit 8P-2 are more informative as they provide precise information on the depreciable lives by asset class. The CCE disclosures are vague and have little analytical value.

(ii) It appears that PBG's quality of earnings is higher but we cannot be certain without better data. CCE reports that asset lives for machinery and equipment are as long as 20 years, while the PBG data show maximum lives of 15 years, suggesting more conservative accounting. But without having lives (and salvage values) by asset class, all we can do is guess.

d. The change suggests that both companies are concerned about their level of profitability, perhaps expecting lower operating margins. As the companies are competitors, it is also possible that one company changed first and the other followed in order not to be "disadvantaged" by more conservative depreciation assumptions.

14. (M) a. Calculations below use the following definitions:

   (i)   Average depreciable life (years) = Gross
         investment/depreciation expense
   (ii) Average age (years) = Accumulated
         depreciation/depreciation expense
   (iii) Average age (%) = Accumulated depreciation/gross
         investment

	1997	1998	1999
Buildings and land improvements			
(i) Average depreciable life (years)	32.5	40.8	40.8
(ii) Average age (years)	11.1	13.8	14.0
(iii) Average age (%)	34.1%	33.9%	34.3%
Machinery and equipment			
(i) Average depreciable life (years)	15.2	12.0	12.7
(ii) Average age (years)	8.3	6.4	6.8
(iii) Average age (%)	54.7%	53.6%	53.2%

   b. The average depreciable life for buildings and land
       improvements is just over 40 years for 1998 and 1999,
       very close to the 40 year stated life. The 1997 ratio
       is much lower. The high depreciation for that year
       suggests that there was some special factor accounting
       for the discrepancy.

       The average for machinery and equipment varies over the
       three-year period but is consistent with the 15-year
       maximum stated life. The ratio suggests that most
       assets in this category are depreciated over 15 years
       despite the stated policy of 5 - 15 years.

   c. The average age (years) of buildings and land
       improvements has been increasing but is still low (and
       stable) compared with the average depreciable life
       (average age (%)). For machinery and equipment the
       average age fell in 1998 and was stable in 1999. These
       ratios suggest that Roche's physical facilities are
       modern, although it would be useful to compare the
       ratios with those of Roche competitors.

d.   Questions worth asking include:
- Why was 1997 depreciation on buildings and land improvements abnormally high?
- Was 1997 depreciation on machinery and equipment abnormally low and, if so, why?
- What types of machinery and equipment are depreciated over 15 years versus shorter time periods?
- What is the breakdown of future capital expenditures between land and land improvements and machinery and equipment?
- Will future capital expenditures change the average depreciable life due to changes in the asset mix?

15 {S}a.   (i)   Income before the effect of accounting changes was increased because intangible amortization was reduced.

(ii) Net income was reduced by the impairment charge, partly offset by reduced amortization.

(iii) Stockholders' equity was reduced by lower net income.

(iv) Cash from operations was unchanged as both the impairment charge and amortization are noncash expenses.

b.   (i)   2001 net income will be increased as amortization of the reduced intangible assets is lower as a result of the accounting change.

(ii) Return on equity is increased by the accounting change as net income is increased and equity is reduced (see answer to a(iii)).

(iii) Cash from operations is unchanged as amortization is a noncash expense.

16.{M}a. Given the 1998 and 1999 losses on declining revenue, the impairment charge should not have been a surprise (the company had reported losses for the first three quarters of fiscal 1999). Operating losses are a frequent indicator of impending impairment charges. The depreciation change is less obvious as declining use of fixed assets does not necessarily change their useful life.

b. (i) Cash from operations is unchanged as impairment charges and depreciation are noncash expenses.

(ii) Fixed asset turnover increases as the carrying amount of fixed assets has been reduced.

(iii) IEC's debt-to-equity ratio increases as equity is reduced by the charges.

c. (i) Year 2000 income will be decreased by higher depreciation expense. The company will continue to compute depreciation expense using the new, shorter lives. There is some offset from lower depreciation of the impaired assets.

(ii) Cash from operations is unchanged (see b(i)).

(iii) Fixed asset turnover remains higher as the accounting change reduces the carrying amount of fixed assets.

(iv) The debt-to-equity ratio remains higher due to the impairment charges and increased depreciation expense.

8A-1{L}a. As forest and agricultural property is not depreciated, we must make adjustments only for other fixed assets. If we use the assessed tax values as a measure of the current cost of these assets, we can make the following calculations (all in SKr millions) using data from Exhibit 8A-2.

	12/31/99
Net carrying value	1,805
Accumulated depreciation	1,640
Gross carrying amount	3,445
Estimated current cost	5,155

The assessed tax value of $2,701 is 896 in excess of the *net* carrying amount. If we apply that ratio to the *gross* carrying amount, the estimated current cost is equal to (2,701/1,805) x 3,445 = 5,155.

This calculation understates current cost as it the assessed values are for Swedish assets only and Holmen has some fixed assets in other countries.

Holmen's 1999 income statement reports depreciation expense of 1,387. Note 10 reports depreciation for the category of buildings, other land, etc. equal to 159. Using the average of the opening and closing balance for the year of acquisition values (cost) plus revaluations less the Modo divestment [(5,065 − 1,659) + 3,341 + (108 − 4) + 104/2] = 3,478 produces a depreciation rate of 4.6% [159/3,478].

Applying the same depreciation rate to the current cost computed above produces depreciation expense of 237 [4.6% x 5,155], an increase of SKr78 million. However most depreciation (footnote 10) relates to machinery and equipment for which no current value data are provided. If we assume that current cost is only 25% above carrying amount (the buildings increment is at least 50%), then depreciation for machinery and equipment would increase from 1,223 (Note 10) to 1,529, an increase of 306 or 25%.

Adding the two adjustments together, depreciation expense for 1999 rises by 384 {78 + 306} to 1,771 [1,387 + 384].

b. The increased depreciation expense of SKr384 million reduces net income by 288 (using the 25% reported tax rate) to SKr1,526 million, a reduction of 15.9%.

c.   As depreciation is a noncash expense, there is no effect on cash from operations.

d.   The adjustments to net income, assets, and equity are summarized in the following table

SKr millions	1998	1999	Average
Net turnover		20,508	
Net income reported		1,814	
Net income adjusted		1,526	
Total fixed assets	20,707	14,825	17,766
Total excess values	2,912	3,018	
Adjusted fixed assets	23,619	17,843	20,731
Total assets	30,434	29,172	29,803
Total excess values	2,912	3,018	
Adjusted total assets	33,346	32,190	32,768
Stockholders' equity	18,377	15,883	17,130
Total excess values	2,912	3,018	
Adjusted equity	21,289	18,901	20,095

These data produce the following ratios, based on reported and adjusted data:

1999 Ratios	Reported	Adjusted
(i) Fixed asset turnover	1.15	0.99
(ii) Total asset turnover	0.69	0.63
(iii) Return on equity	10.6%	7.6

Chapter 9 - Solutions

Overview:
Problem Length   *Problem #s*
     {S}   1 - 4, 6, 11, 15
     {M}   5, 7 - 9, 13, 14, 16
     {L}   10, 12

1.{S}Deferred taxes can be found in all of the categories listed. Examples are:
   (i)   Current liabilities may include deferred tax liabilities arising from an installment sale with cash payments expected within one year.
   (ii) Deferred income tax credits resulting from the use of accelerated depreciation for tax purposes and straight line for financial reporting are reported in long-term liabilities.
   (iii) The stockholders' equity account may include the deferred tax offset to the valuation allowance for available-for-sale securities or the cumulative translation adjustment account.
   (iv) The deferred tax asset (debit) due to accrued compensation with cash payment expected within one year is a component of current assets.
   (v)   Long-term assets would include deferred tax assets (debits) recognized, (for example for, postretirement benefits or restructuring charges), but not expected to be funded within one year.

2.{S}(i)   Correct: Under SFAS 109, changes in tax laws must be reflected in the deferred tax liability in the period of enactment.
   (ii) Correct: Answer to (i) also applies to deferred tax assets.
   (iii) Correct: The tax consequences of events that have not been reflected in the financial statements (such as future earnings or losses) are not recognized.
   (iv) Incorrect: See answers to (i) and (ii) above. This statement is true for the deferral method (see footnote 2 on text page 292).
   (v)   Incorrect: Changes in deferred tax assets and liabilities are included in income tax expense except for those charged directly to stockholders' equity.

3.{S}a. Permanent differences are items of income or expense that affect *either tax return income or financial income, but not both.* Examples include:

- Tax-exempt interest income (not reported on the tax return,

- Interest expense on amounts borrowed to purchase tax-exempt securities (not deductible on the tax return),

- Tax or other nondeductible government penalties (not reported on the tax return),

- Statutory mineral depletion in excess of cost basis depletion (not reported in the financial statements),

- Premiums on key-person life insurance policies (not deductible on the tax return),

- Proceeds from key-person life insurance policies (not reported on the tax return).

b. Permanent differences, depending on their nature, either increase or decrease the firm's effective tax rate relative to the statutory rate. For example, tax-exempt interest income (the first example listed) reduces the effective tax rate as there is no tax expense associated with this income.

4.{S}a. (i) If the deferred tax liability is not expected to reverse, there is no expectation of a cash outflow and the liability should be considered as equity.

(ii) If the deferred tax liability is the result of a temporary difference that is expected to reverse, with consequent tax payment, it should be treated as a liability.

b. Because both the amounts and timing of tax payments resulting from the reversals of temporary differences are uncertain, deferred taxes should be excluded from both liabilities and equity.

c. The portion of the deferred tax liability that represents (the present value of) expected payments should be treated as debt. Accounting-based timing differences that are not expected to reverse should be treated as equity.

5.{M} We begin by determining the cost of each asset using the information about asset L. Year 2 depreciation under the sum-of-the-years' digits method with a five-year life is 4/15ths. Therefore, the depreciable base (cost - salvage value) must be $12,000/(4/15) = $45,000 and the cost must be $48,000 because salvage value is $3,000. We can now prepare a depreciation schedule for each method:

Depreciation Expense			
	Asset K	Asset L	Asset M
Year	Straight-line[1]	SYD[2]	DDB[3]
1	$ 9,000	$15,000	$19,200
2	9,000	12,000	11,520
3	9,000	9,000	6,912
4	9,000	6,000	4,147
5	9,000	3,000	3,221
Total	$45,000	$45,000	$45,000

[1] Base = $45,000 {cost -salvage value}; expense = $45,000/5 = $9,000.

[2] Base = $45,000; expense = 5/15ths, 4/15ths, 3/15ths, etc.

[3] Base = $48,000 (salvage value ignored); rate = 40%

Year 1 expense = .40 x $48,000 = $19,200, leaving $28,800

Year 2 expense = .40 x $28,800 = $11,520, leaving $17,280

Year 3 expense = .40 x $17,280 = $ 6,912, leaving $ 10,368

Year 4 expense = .40 x $ 10,368= $ 4,147, leaving $ 6,221

Year 5 expense = $ 3,221 leaving $ 3,000

a. The double declining balance method is used on the tax return for all three assets; year 2 depreciation expense under that method is **$11,520**.

b. Financial statement depreciation expense in year two (from table on previous page) is:

Asset K (straight line)   **$ 9,000**

Asset M (double declining balance)   **11,520**

c. (i) At the end of year two, accumulated depreciation equals (from table on previous page):

Asset K (straight line) $18,000

Asset L (SYD)   27,000

Asset M (DDB)   30,720

Tax return (DDB)   30,720

Therefore, the deferred tax liability is:

Asset K: .34 ($30,720 - $18,000) =   **$ 4,324.80**

Asset L: .34 ($30,720 - $27,000) =   **1,264.80**

Asset M: No deferred tax as the same method is used for financial and tax reporting.

(ii) At the end of year five, accumulated depreciation is the same under all methods and there is no deferred tax asset or liability.

6.{S}a.b. Assuming that Mother Prewitt continues to buy machines in the future, the depreciation timing difference will never reverse and there is no expected cash consequence. In this case, the deferred tax can be treated as equity.

If the installment sale is not expected to recur, the tax on that sale will be paid in 2001 and will require cash. For that reason, the $27,200 of deferred taxes should be considered a liability when calculating liquidity, solvency, and leverage ratios.

If, on the other hand, installment sales are expected to recur, such sales are no different from the depreciation case. The cash consequences of deferred tax items depend on the probability of their reversal, not on their nature.

c. Under SFAS 109 (liability method), enacted changes in tax rates are recognized, and the deferred tax liabilities must be restated to amounts based on the 40% tax rate. The incremental liability is recorded as a component of income tax expense regardless of when (or if) paid.

7.{S}

	Years ended June 30			
Amounts in $millions	1997	1998	1999	2000
Deferred tax assets due to depreciation	$ 57.7	$ 40.3	$ 49.2	$ 37.7
Effect on fixed assets of:				
Impairment of long-lived assets		47.0		
Write-downs of operating assets		47.0	4.2	26.6
Write-downs of capitalized software		–	16.0	–
Total effect on fixed assets		$ 94.0	$ 20.2	$ 26.6
Tax rate		34%	35%	35%
a. Expected effect on deferred tax asset		$ 32.0	$ 7.1	$ 9.3
Reported change in deferred tax asset		(17.3)	8.9	(11.6)
Difference between expected effect and reported change in deferred tax asset		$ 49.3	$ (1.8)	$ 20.9

Write-downs reduce the carrying amount of the assets on the financial statements but have no effect on the tax basis. Even if the company uses the straight-line depreciation method for both tax and financial reporting, tax depreciation would be higher than book depreciation after a write-off, generating deferred tax liabilities (credits) or lowering deferred tax assets (debits). In each year, therefore, write-downs increase the deferred tax asset but depreciation expense tends to reduce it.

In the table above, we compute the effect of the asset changes on the deferred tax asset for each year by multiplying the impairment plus the write-off amount by the tax rate for that year. We then compare that effect with the reported change in the deferred tax asset related to depreciation.

For 1998, the non-cash impairment of long-lived assets and the write-down of operating assets would generate a $32 million *increase* in deferred tax assets. However, the company reported a *decrease* of $17.3 million in deferred tax assets due to depreciation. The difference is much too high to result from current year depreciation expense. The most likely explanation is that the company sold fixed assets during the year, eliminating the book-tax difference relating to those assets. If those assets had a higher tax basis than book basis, sale would reduce the deferred tax asset by that difference multiplied by the tax rate.

In 1999, the difference is smaller and in the right direction, since we have an expected $7.1 million increase due to write-downs and a reported increase of $8.9 million. Regardless of whether internal-use software was capitalized on the tax return, its write-off should generate a deferred tax debit. This difference is probably due to a combination of current year depreciation (reducing the deferred tax asset) and asset sales (increasing the deferred tax asset).

In 2000, instead of an increase of $9.3 million, the company reports a decrease of $11.6 million in deferred tax assets. As for 1998, asset sales provide the most likely explanation.

8.{M}a. (i) Income tax expense is lower than it would be if SGI provided taxes on the undistributed earnings of its foreign subsidiaries.

(ii) Income tax paid was not affected because those earnings are undistributed, that is, SGI did not pay U.S. income tax on them.

(iii) The effective tax rate is lower than it would have been because income tax expense is lower (see answer a(i)).

(iv) Earnings per share are higher because income tax expense is lower.

(v) Book value per share is higher because retained earnings (and therefore, equity) are higher.

b. In the year that the foreign subsidiaries remitted previously undistributed earnings:

(i) Pretax income would not change because SGI had previously recognized those earnings.

(ii) Income tax expense would increase by the amount of the income tax payable on the remitted earnings.

(iii) Income tax paid would increase by the U.S. tax paid on the remitted earnings.

(iv) The effective tax rate would increase to reflect higher income tax expense and no change in pretax income.

(v) Earnings per share would decline due to higher income tax expense, resulting in lower net income.

(vi) Book value per share would be reduced; because income tax expense would increase, net income and retained earnings would decline.

c. Reported financial data should not be adjusted if the undistributed earnings are not expected to be remitted. However, if repatriation is likely, (the company needs funds for debt repayment, an acquisition, or operations), the reported data should be adjusted to establish a deferred tax liability, reducing equity.

d. It is likely that SGI recognized tax expense for deferred taxes on previously undistributed earnings because it changed its policy and now expected to repatriate earnings of foreign subsidiaries, perhaps to meet the liquidity needs of its operations.[As shown in the data provided for problem 9, the company reported large operating losses in fiscal 1998 - 2000.]

9.{M}a. As of June 30, 1999 Silicon Graphics [SGI] needed to generate nearly $900 million in taxable income to realize reported net deferred tax assets of $489 million. However, for fiscal 1998 and 1999 combined, the company reported net losses of $406 million. It is, therefore, difficult to support the company's assertion that because of forecasted income from operations it *is more likely than not* that the deferred tax asset will be realized.

The company's sale of a 35% interest in MIPS generated a $272 million gain; if not for that gain, SGI would have reported a significant pretax loss for 1999, casting further doubt on its assumption of future taxable income. SGI's plan to divest its remaining 65% interest in MIPS technologies may enable it to generate a portion of the required income, but that is unlikely to be sufficient.[2] Thus, the valuation allowance at June 30, 1999 was unlikely to be adequate.

---

[2] Profit on 35% was $272 million; at that rate profit on the remaining 65% would be ($272 x 65%/35%) $505 million, far below the required $900 million.

b. (Amounts in $thousands)

Years ended June 30	1998	1999	2000
Reported:			
Gross deferred tax assets	$ 643,307	$ 593,965	$ 743,916
Valuation allowance	(90,705)	(105,364)	(632,324)
Net deferred tax assets	$ 552,602	$ 488,601	$ 111,592
Adjusted:			
Gross deferred tax assets	$ 643,307	$ 593,965	$ 743,916
Reported valuation allowance	(90,705)	(105,364)	(632,324)
Adjustment to valuation allowance	$ 552,602	$ 488,601	$ 111,592
(i) **Adjusted income tax expense**	$ (415,310)	$(560,493)	$(559,252)
(ii) **Adjustment to income tax paid**	**none**	**none**	**none**
Reported pretax income	$ (596,919)	$ 125,721	$(381,884)
Adjusted income tax expense	(415,310)	(560,493)	(559,252)
(iv) **Adjusted net income**	$(1,012,229)	$(434,772)	$(941,136)
(iii) **Effective tax rate**	**(70)%**	**446%**	**(146)%**

(i)   The increase in valuation allowance required to offset all of its deferred tax assets is added (the increase is a negative adjustment) to the reported tax expense to compute the adjusted income tax expense.

(ii) Because it is only a financial reporting effect and does not affect taxable income, the change in the valuation allowance has no impact on tax paid.

(iii) The effective tax rate is calculated as income tax expense/pretax income.

(iv) Net income is calculated by deducting adjusted income tax expense from pretax income.

c. The tax-free distribution of the remaining shares of MIPS to shareholders no longer allows Silicon Graphics to include a gain from that sale in evaluating the sufficiency of the valuation allowance. Therefore, a significant portion of the increase in the valuation allowance ($527 million) must be due to the tax-free distribution. [The company disclosed that it added $369 million to the valuation allowance as a result of the MIPS transaction. The remaining increase in the valuation allowance probably reflects the 2000 operating loss, which increased operating loss carryforwards and makes it more difficult to justify an assumption of future profitability.]

10. {L}a. (i) Using the format of Exhibit 9-3 on text page 311, we convert the tax rate effect of lower foreign tax rates to the dollar effect. For example, the 1998 dollar effect equals the rate effect times total pretax income = -3.0% x $2,263 = $(68) million.

Amounts in $millions	1998	1999	2000
Statutory rate	35.0 %	35.0 %	35.0 %
Effect of lower foreign tax rate	(3.0)%	(2.7)%	(3.0)%
Pretax income			
United States	$1,629	$2,771	$2,126
Foreign	634	885	1,084
Total	$2,263	$3,656	$3,210
Tax @ statutory rate	$ 792	$1,280	$1,124
(i) Effect of lower foreign tax rate	**(68)**	**(99)**	**(96)**

(ii) - (v): Exhibit 9S-1 (next page) is based on the following computations:

- To compute foreign income tax expense, we multiply foreign pretax income by the statutory rate and subtract the answer to (i). We assume that all other effects apply to U.S. income. For example, the 1998 calculation is [(.35 x $634) - $ 68] = $154 million. The effective rate on foreign income is calculated as foreign tax expense divided by foreign pretax income (1998: $154/$634 = 24.3%).

- Foreign net income is obtained by subtracting foreign tax expense from foreign pretax income.

- U.S. tax expense and U.S. effective rate are calculated by subtracting foreign tax expense from the total tax expense.

- U.S. net income is obtained by subtracting U.S. tax expense from U.S. pretax income.

```
Exhibit 9S-1
         Amounts in $millions    1998      1999      2000
         Foreign income - pretax  $  634   $  885   $1,084
         Foreign tax expense        (154)    (211)    (283)
(iii)    Foreign net income       $  480   $  674   $  801

(ii)     Foreign tax rate          24.3%    23.8%    26.1%

         U.S. income - pretax     $1,629   $2,771   $2,126
         U.S. tax expense           (115)  (1,394)    (744)
(iv)     U.S. net income          $1,514   $1,377   $1,382

(v)      U.S. tax rate             7.1%    50.3%    35.0%
```

b. Percent change from prior year	% Change	
	1999	2000
(i) Foreign income - pretax	39.6%	22.5%
Foreign tax expense	37.0%	34.1%
(ii) Foreign net income	40.4%	18.8%
(i) U.S. income - pretax	70.1%	-23.3%
U.S. tax expense	1109.1%	-46.6%
(ii) U.S. net income	-9.0%	0.3%

c. Percent changes in foreign net income are only slightly different from the pretax percent changes. The effect is greater for 2000 due to the increased tax rate, which reduced the growth rate of net income relative to pretax income.

The differences are far greater for U.S. income due to more significant tax rate changes. The increased (versus 1998) 1999 tax rate (due to the absence of the two settlements and a higher rate on bottling transactions) in tax rates converted pretax income growth of 70% to a 9% decline in net income. As the tax rate fell in 2000 (no bottling transactions), the decline in pretax U.S. income was converted to a minor increase in net income.

d. The "other effects" increased the effective tax rate in both 1998 and (to a lesser extent in) 1999. The analyst should ask management about the nature of these effects, their sources, and the likelihood of future impacts.

An analyst should ask about the effect of the bottling transactions. The high effective tax rate suggests that PepsiCo was assuming that reinvested income would be received as dividends (see Box 13-2 on text page 471) but realized them via sale instead. The analyst should evaluate the possibility that there will be other such transactions in the future.

Foreign effective tax rates depend on the "mix" of earnings from various jurisdictions with different tax rates. The analyst should ask which foreign jurisdictions apply tax rates that are higher (lower) than the average, whether any tax "holidays" are due to expire (or may be extended), and how mix changes have affected the effective foreign tax rate over the 1998 to 2000 period. The answers to these questions also help earnings forecasts. Specifically, they enable the analyst to forecast the aftertax impact of assumed changes in pretax income from major foreign subsidiaries.

e. The most likely explanation is that a portion of these charges had no tax effect, thus reducing pretax income but not taxable income. One example would be the writedown of nondeductible acquisition goodwill. Another example would be an asset writedown in a tax jurisdiction where the loss must be carried forward, and a valuation allowance offsets the resulting deferred tax asset.

f. In the absence of any nonrecurring transactions (for example, settlements, bottling transactions, and asset impairments), PepsiCo should face an effective tax rate of the statutory rate of 35%, less the average effect of lower foreign tax rate of 2.9%, or 32.1%.

This is nearly identical to its 2000 effective tax rate.

g. In 1998, management must have considered the effects of the two settlements, the asset impairment and restructuring charge, and the "other effects" as nonrecurring. These adjustments result in an effective tax rate of 32% (11.9 + 5.7 + 21.8 – 3.4 – 4.0); it is likely that management used one or more components of the "other effects – net" to estimate a 31% effective rate on comparable operations.

For 1999, we need only to eliminate the effect of bottling transactions and "other – net" to arrive at management's 32.2% rate. Finally, the actual and assumed comparable 2000 rates are identical; they both adjust the statutory rate only for the effect of lower foreign tax rates.

h. The tax effects of the Puerto Rico settlement (tax case) and the bottling transactions should be excluded in earnings used to value PepsiCo because neither effect can be expected to recur.

11.{S}a. In the U.S., zero-coupon debt should not result in deferred tax effects because there is no difference between tax and financial statement computation and reporting of interest expense. Internal Revenue Service rules require the use of the effective tax rate for the tax return and GAAP mandates the use of the effective tax rate for financial statements.

A deferred tax credit (liability) implies that financial reporting deductions are lower than the amounts reported on the tax return. The zero coupon debt must have been issued in a (foreign) tax jurisdiction that permits the use of straight-line amortization of the difference between the face amount of the debt and its issue price. Straight-line amortization results in higher expense in the early years (see text pages 329 – 332 for discussion of zero-coupon debt).

Another reason may be the differential treatment of issuance costs. If issuance costs are immediately expensed for taxes but amortized (using the interest method) for financial reporting, a deferred tax liability would be created. However, we do not expect this tax-book difference to generate deferred tax credits of the magnitude reported by PepsiCo because issuance costs rarely exceed 3 to 5% of the proceeds.

b.   The deferred tax credit (liability) can be expected to decrease each year by the amount of imputed interest expense difference (between book and tax amounts) multiplied by the marginal tax rate for that tax jurisdiction. The amounts reported by PepsiCo for 1998 to 2000 reflect that trend. When the debt matures and the full amount of the accrued interest is paid (and deducted on the tax return), the deferred tax credit (liability) attributed to that debt issue will decline to zero.

c.   The primary reason for the decline is most likely the increasing interest expense reported on the financial statements (due to the application of the effective interest rate to an increasing carrying amount of debt) whereas the straight-line method interest expense on the tax return remains constant.

A second reason for the decline may be repurchase of a portion of the zero coupon debt in some years, eliminating a corresponding amount of the accumulated interest differential and therefore the deferred tax credit.

12.{L}a. The first step converts the effective tax rate analysis from Exhibit 9P-1 into a pretax income-based reconciliation, following the format of Exhibit 9-3 on text page 311. Exhibit 9S-2 shows the results for each year and three-year totals.

Exhibit 9S-2. Honda Motor
Reconciliation of Effective and Statutory Rates

| In ¥ millions except percentages | Years ended March 31 | | | 3 Year |
	1999	2000	2001	Total
Pretax income – Japanese	199,848	127,562	133,166	460,576
Pretax income – Foreign	320,663	288,501	251,810	860,974
Pretax income – Total	520,511	416,063	384,976	1,321,550
Statutory tax rate	48.0%	41.0%	41.0%	43.3%
Valuation allowance	1.2	2.8	5.2	
Difference in normal foreign tax rates	(3.0)	(1.3)	(1.0)	
Changes in tax laws and rates	(4.2)	0.0	0.0	
Reversal of valuation allowance	(0.1)	(0.1)	(0.1)	
Other	2.2	(1.4)	1.3	
Effective tax rate	44.1%	41.0%	46.4%	43.8%
Income tax expense at statutory rate	249,845	170,586	157,840	578,271
Effects of:				
Valuation allowance	6,246	11,650	20,019	37,915
Difference in tax rates of foreign subsidiaries	(15,615)	(5,409)	(3,850)	(24,874)
Changes in tax laws and rates	(21,861)	0	0	(21,861)
Reversal of valuation allowance due to operating loss carryforwards	(521)	(416)	(385)	(1,322)
Other	11,451	(5,825)	5,005	10,631
Income tax expense*	229,545	170,586	178,629	578,760
Calculation below required for part c.				
Pretax income – Foreign	320,663	288,501	251,810	860,974
Foreign tax expense**	(138,303)	(112,877)	(99,392)	(348,215)
Foreign net income	182,360	175,624	152,418	512,759
Foreign tax rate	43.1%	39.1%	39.5%	40.4%

* Numbers differ from Exhibit 9P-1 due to rounding

** Calculated as (statutory rate x foreign pretax income) – differences in tax rates of foreign subsidiaries. Using 1999 as an example: (48% x $320,663) – $15,615 = $138,303

b. The reconciliation in Exhibit 9S-2 shows the following:

   (i) Net changes in the valuation allowance increased tax expense by ¥36,593 (37,915 – 1,322) million over the three year period increasing from ¥5,725 (¥6,246 – ¥521) million in 1999 to ¥19,634 (¥20,019 – ¥385) in 2001.

   (ii) Changes in tax law decreased 1999 income tax expense by ¥21,861 million. There were no changes in tax laws and rates for other years.

   (iii) Honda's disclosures are unclear. It appears that the decision not to recognize deferred taxes on reinvested subsidiary earnings decreased 2001 tax expense by ¥856 million [5,987 – 5,131] or 0.2% of pretax income. However the reported amounts are extremely low relative to the reported reinvested earnings (¥663,540 million at 3/31/01). A better understanding of this issue is required before meaningful adjustments can be made.

c. (i) Although lower non-Japanese tax rates reduced Honda's tax expense in each year, 1999-2001, that reduction declined from 1999 to 2001.

   (ii) As Japanese tax rates declined from 48% in 1999 to 41% in 2000 and 2001, they are now closer to non-Japanese rates reducing the difference.

d. Factors an analyst must consider when forecasting Honda's effective tax rate for 2002 include the following:

   • The mix of Japanese and foreign pretax income,

   • Any possible changes in Japanese and foreign tax rates,

   • The impact of the valuation allowance, and

   • The composition of and trends in "other" tax differences.

13.{M}a.

	1991 tax rate	1992 tax rate
Q1	$1,224/$4,797 = 25.5%	$232/$1,123 = 20.7%
Q2	$ 624 /$2,600 = 24.0	$934/$3,723 = 25.1
Q3	$ 848 /$3,244 = 26.1	$583/$98 = (594.9)

b. Using a tax rate of 17% for 1992 Q3 alone, tax expense would have been $16,660. The actual tax credit for Q3 was $ 583,000, for a difference of $600,000.

c. On a pretax basis, 1992 Q3 declined by 97% from 1991 Q3 ($98 versus $3,224). Net income, however, declined by only 72% ($681 versus $2,396) because 1992 Q3 included the tax benefit of revising the tax rate on earnings already reported for the first two quarters of 1992.

d. One possibility is to make comparisons only on a pretax basis to avoid distortions due to changes in the estimated tax rates. Another approach would use post-tax data to analyze the trends by applying the change to each quarter of 1992.

e. (i)

	1992		
	Q1	Q2	Q3
Pretax income	$1,123	$3,723	$ 98
Income tax expense @17%	(191)	(633)	(17)
Net income	$ 932	$3,090	$ 81

(ii) The assumption has a marginal effect on Q1; it continues to reflect a significant decline relative to 1991 Q1. For Q2, we see the improvement in performance augmented by a lower tax rate (17% compared to 25%, but presumably a better indicator of future tax rates). The analyst should attempt to determine the causes of the decline in income in Q1 and Q3, the recovery in Q2 and better understand the implications for future performance.

14.{M}a. The following questions should enable the analyst to better understand trends in earnings and permit a more informed forecast of earnings and firm value.

- Lower foreign rates were not as beneficial in 2000 as they have been in the three previous years (7% compared to an average of more than 14% (see Exhibit 9S-3 below). To what extent does this change reflect the 1999 expiration of the tax holiday? What tax rate on foreign income does management expect in 2001 and future years.

- Explain why state tax expense has been so variable, and seems to be unrelated to US pretax earnings. Although US pretax income rose significantly in 2000, state tax expense declined by 50%.

- What is the reason for the substantial decline in the effects of the valuation allowance from 1997 to 2000? For which tax jurisdictions is the valuation allowance provided? Under what conditions would the deferred tax assets for which the valuation allowance has been provided be realized?

- Which tax jurisdictions have deferred tax assets for which a valuation has not been provided? What are the amounts, is there a deadline for realization, and what management assumptions result in the decision not to provide a valuation allowance?

- What are the components of nondeductible and "other" items?

- Are changes in tax rates under consideration in any jurisdiction in which the company operates?

b. Exhibit 9S-3 provides all the required calculations.

Exhibit 9S-3. Coca Cola Enterprises in $millions	1997	1998	1999	2000
Income tax expense reconciliation				
U.S. federal statutory expense	$ 62	$ 59	$ 31	$ 117
State expense, net of federal benefit	2	0	4	2
European and Canadian operations, net	(21)	(21)	(17)	(22)
Rate change benefit	(58)	(29)	0	(8)
Valuation allowance provisions	15	8	3	7
Nondeductible items	5	6	7	7
Other (net)	2	4	1	(6)
Total provision for income taxes	$ 7	$ 27	$ 29	$ 97
Pretax earnings				
Total	$ 178	$ 169	$ 88	$ 333
Foreign	(162)	(151)	(49)	(141)
U.S.	$ 16	$ 18	$ 39	$ 192
Statutory rate	35%	35%	35%	35%
State expense, net of federal benefit	1	0	5	1
European and Canadian operations, net	(12)	(12)	(19)	(7)
Rate change benefit	(33)	(17)	0	(2)
Valuation allowance provisions	8	5	3	2
Nondeductible items	3	4	8	2
Other (net)	1	2	1	(2)
Total provision for income taxes	4%	16%	33%	29%
Foreign operations: pretax income	$ 162	$ 151	$ 49	$ 141
Income tax expense*	(35)	(32)	(0)	(28)
Net income	$ 127	$ 119	$ 49	$ 113
Effective foreign tax rate	**21.9%**	**21.0%**	**0.5%**	**19.5%**
U.S. Operations: pretax income	$ 16	$ 18	$ 39	$ 192
Income tax expense**	28	5	(29)	(69)
Net income	$ 44	$ 23	$ 10	$ 123
Effective U.S. tax rate	**-177.7%**	**-26.2%**	**73.7%**	**36.2%**

* Calculated as (Statutory rate x Foreign pretax income) – European and Canadian operations, net. Using 1997 as an example: (35% x 162) – 21 = 35

** Calculated as Total provision less foreign income tax expense. Using 1997 as an example: $7 – $35 = $(28)

c. The tax effect of rate changes is clearly nonrecurring (certainly nonoperating) even though there have been such effects in three of the four years presented. This effect appears to apply only to foreign income so that the U.S. tax rate is unaffected.

If we remove this effect from the foreign income tax expense computed in part b, we obtain the following:

in $millions	1997	1998	1999	2000
Adjusted foreign tax expense	$(93)	$(61)	$(0)	$(36)
Adjusted foreign tax rate	57.7%	40.2%	0.5%	25.2%

The adjusted tax rate is much closer to CCE's statutory rate, especially in 1997 and 1998.

		1997	1998	1999	2000
d.(i)	Total pretax income	$ 178	$ 169	$ 88	$ 333
	Actual tax expense	(7)	(27)	(29)	(97)
	Net income	$ 171	$ 142	$ 59	$ 236
(ii)	Total pretax income	$ 178	$ 169	$ 88	$ 333
	Adjusted tax expense (part c)	(65)	(56)	(29)	(105)
	Adjusted net income	$ 113	$ 113	$ 59	$ 228

Adjusted net income is significantly lower for 1997 and 1998, reflecting the exclusion of the rate change benefits. There is no effect for 1999 and a small one for 2000.

e. The 2001 effective tax rate for CCE should contain the following components:

Statutory rate	= 35%
State rate effect	2
Lower foreign operations rate	(7)
Valuation allowance	5
Nondeductible items	4
Effective rate	= 39%

This calculation has the following components:

- Statutory rate assumed unchanged

- State rate: average four year rate[3]

- Foreign effect: use 2000 rate as end of tax holiday makes prior year effect less relevant

- Valuation allowance: average four year rate

- Nondeductible items: average four year rate

Assuming that the federal statutory rate and the state rates remain constant, the foreign rate is 7% (consider the 1999 expiration of the tax holiday), the continued impact of the valuation allowance (assumed to continue until unless we get information that suggests an improvement in the ability to generate taxable income) and nondeductible items (assumed to relate to franchise rights that the company considers indefinitely long-lived) gives us a 39% effective rate.

f.   The effective tax rates developed in (e) is six percentage points higher than that stated in the Management Review. The most likely reason for that difference is that management may assume no further increases in the valuation allowance; omitting the valuation allowance would reduce our estimated rate to 34%. However, the actual long-run effective rate will depend on the earning mix (U.S. versus foreign, see part g.), the trend of the valuation allowance, and the long-run effect of nondeductible items. Although impossible to estimate, the contribution of "other - net" is another variable.

---

[3] Average rate calculations are:

	1997	1998	1999	2000	Average
Statutory rate	35%	35%	35%	35%	35%
State expense, net	1%	0%	5%	1%	2%
Foreign operations, net	-12%	-12%	-19%	-7%	-13%
Valuation allowance provisions	8%	5%	3%	2%	5%
Nondeductible items	3%	4%	8%	2%	4%

g. In 1997 and 1998, foreign operations contributed most of the pretax income reported by CCE (approximately 90% in both years). In those years, tax law and rate changes in foreign jurisdictions also helped lower the effective tax rates. In 1999, foreign income fell significantly while domestic income rose relative to the prior years. However, an absence of rate changes resulted in a substantial increase in the effective tax rate. In 2000, U.S. pretax rose sharply, reducing foreign pretax income to 42% of the total. Because of this decline, another beneficial foreign rate change did not provide a benefit similar to that of previous years.

Thus, both the proportion of foreign income to domestic income and foreign rate changes have been the principal factors in the changing effective rates faced by the firm.

15. {S} The benefit of a tax deduction for the 1997 loss is a one-time occurrence and as such, would increase the value of the firm and its common shares by the amount of the benefit. However, the post-announcement impact on the value of the firm and its common shares will depend on whether (and the extent to which) the market had assumed a successful resolution of the case.

16.{M}   The answers to parts a and b are shown in the
          following table:

	Repsol		
	Effective tax rates, profit margin, and ROE under		
a.	Spanish GAAP		
	(in €millions)	1998	1999
	Stockholders' equity	€ 6,043	€12,526
	Net sales	18,573	25,633
	Pretax income	1,411	1,743
	Income tax expense	(397)	(557)
	Net income	€ 1,014	€ 1,186
(i)	**Effective tax rate**	**28.1%**	**32.0%**
(ii)	**Net profit margin**	**5.5%**	**4.6%**
(iii)	**Return on ending equity**	**16.8%**	**9.5%**
	Effective tax rates, profit margin, and ROE under		
b.	U.S. GAAP		
	(in €millions)	1998	1999
	Stockholders' equity	€ 5,653	€12,140
	Net sales	18,573	25,633
	Pretax income	1,277	1,622
	Income tax expense	(402)	(488)
	Net income	€ 875	€ 1,134
(i)	**Effective tax rate**	**31.5%**	**30.1%**
(ii)	**Net profit margin**	**4.7%**	**4.4%**
(iii)	**Return on ending equity**	**15.5%**	**9.3%**

- The effective tax rate was calculated as income tax
  expense/pretax income.

- Return on ending equity is derived as follows: net
  income/ending equity.

c. The effective tax rate under US GAAP is significantly higher in 1998 but lower in 1999. The tax rate also appears to be more variable under Spanish GAAP. The net profit margin is lower under US GAAP for both years, as is the return on equity. These differences would tend to reduce valuation of Repsol shares as net profit is lower as is estimated growth.[4]

d. The calculations are:

(in millions)	1998	1999	% change
Spanish GAAP			
Pretax income	€ 1,411	€ 1,743	23.5%
Net income	1,014	1,186	17.0%
US GAAP			
Pretax income	$ 1,277	$ 1,622	27.0%
Net income	875	1,134	29.6%

The growth rate is higher for both pretax and after-tax income. A major factor in the higher growth rate for net income is that the effective tax rate rose under Spanish GAAP but was relatively unchanged under US GAAP.

---

[4] Growth rate estimates are usually based on sustainable growth rates derived from return on equity.

Chapter 10 - Solutions

Overview:
Problem Length   *Problem #s*
  {S}   *1 - 2, 6 - 22, and 25*
  {M}   *3 - 5, and 23 - 24*

1.{S}a.   When full-coupon debt is issued, interest paid reduces cash from operations (CFO). When zero-coupon debt is issued, however, no cash interest is paid. CFO is unaffected, and is therefore higher than when full-coupon debt is issued. In addition, when imputed interest on zero-coupon debt is tax deductible, CFO is further increased by the tax benefit.

   b.   When full-coupon debt is issued, the proceeds are included in cash from financing (CFF). When that debt matures, the amount paid reduces CFF. Assuming the debt is issued and redeemed at par, the net effect on CFF is zero over the life of the debt.

        Zero-coupon debt is issued at a discount; CFF is below the full-coupon case. However at maturity the full face amount is paid (same as full-coupon case). The net amount of CFF (outflow) is therefore greater than when full-coupon debt is issued.

   c.   No effect.

   d.   Interest on the zero-coupon bond rises each year as the carrying amount rises, increasing the base on which each year's interest expense is computed. All other things being equal, net income declines each year.

2.{S}(i)   Net income declines as interest expense increases, reflecting the higher level of interest rates.

   (ii) The market value of the firm's debt should remain unchanged. As the interest rate adjusts to changes in market rates, investors will pay the face amount for the debt, assuming no change in credit risk.

3.{M}a. Reported data

	AMR Corp		US Airways	
	1998	1999	1998	1999
Cash and short-term investments	$ 2,073	$ 1,791	$ 1,210	$ 870
Net receivables	1,543	1,134	355	387
Inventories	596	708	228	226
Other current assets	663	791	571	613
Current assets	$ 4,875	$ 4,424	$ 2,364	$ 2,096
Accounts payable	1,152	1,115	430	474
Accrued liabilities	2,122	1,956	1,016	1,276
Air traffic liability	2,163	2,255	752	635
Notes payable and current portion LT debt	202	538	71	116
Current liabilities	$ 5,639	$ 5,864	$ 2,269	$ 2,501
Net working capital	(764)	(1,440)	95	(405)
Current ratio	0.86	0.75	1.04	0.84
Quick ratio	0.64	0.50	0.69	0.50
Cash ratio	0.37	0.31	0.53	0.35

b. Unlike other payables, the air traffic liability will
    not require cash outlays (other than low marginal
    costs); instead this obligation is satisfied as
    customers use their tickets on flights. The air traffic
    liability should therefore be excluded from
    computations of short-term liabilities.

c.   Adjusted data

	AMR Corp		US Airways	
	1998	1999	1998	1999
Current liabilities (reported)	$5,639	$5,864	$2,269	$2,501
Air traffic liability	(2,163)	(2,255)	(752)	(635)
Current liabilities (adjusted)	$3,476	$3,609	$1,517	$1,866
Net working capital (adjusted)	1,399	815	847	230
Current ratio	1.40	1.23	1.56	1.12
Quick ratio	1.04	0.81	1.03	0.67
Cash ratio	0.60	0.50	0.80	0.47

As expected, all of American Airlines' liquidity measures improve when the air traffic liability is removed from current liabilities.

However the adjustments in the table above overstate the firms' liquidity, especially for AMR. A portion of the air traffic liability relates to frequent flyer programs (37% of AMR's 1999 liability and 13% of US Airways' 1999 liability). AMR's frequent flyer obligation is based on the incremental costs of fuel, food, and reservations/ticketing costs (US Airways' approach is similar but includes insurance and other compensation). Thus some portion of the air traffic liability does represent near-term cash outlays.

d.   US Airways' short-term liquidity position appears to be stronger than American's at December 31, 1999 as its current ratio and cash ratio are both higher and the quick ratio is that same. However, the higher current and quick ratios evaporate when the air traffic liability is eliminated. This liability is lower for US Airways (relative to total current liabilities). The adjusted data show that all three liquidity ratios are higher for AMR than for US Airways.

While not part of the question, it is worth noting that two of the three 1998 ratios are higher for US Airways than for AMR. While the ratios of both companies declined in 1999, the decline in US Airways' ratios was greater.

10-3

e. The 1999 decline in US Airways' air traffic liability indicates that fewer customers were willing to purchase tickets in advance, presumably due to the deterioration in the company's financial position. In contrast, American's air traffic liability increased, although the growth should be compared to past fluctuations and to growth for the rest of the industry.

US Airways filed for bankruptcy in August 2002.

4.(M}a. Proceeds equal $100,000/(1.12)^5$ = **$56,742**

b.	2000	2001	2002	2003	2004
EBIT	$50,000	$50,000	$50,000	$50,000	$50,000
CFO before interest & taxes	60,000	60,000	60,000	60,000	60,000
Interest expense	6,809	7,626	8,541	9,566	10,714
CFO	60,000	60,000	60,000	60,000	60,000
Times interest earned	7.34	6.56	5.85	5.23	4.67
Times interest earned (cash basis)	[Infinite, since no interest is paid. In 2004, when the bond is retired, the payment will be reported as a financing cash outflow.]				

c. For a full-coupon bond, annual interest expense paid in cash would be $56,742 x .12 = $6,809

	2000	2001	2002	2003	2004
EBIT	$50,000	$50,000	$50,000	$50,000	$50,000
CFO before interest & taxes	60,000	60,000	60,000	60,000	60,000
Interest expense	6,809	6,809	6,809	6,809	6,809
CFO	53,191	53,191	53,191	53,191	53,191
Times interest earned	7.34	7.34	7.34	7.34	7.34
Times interest earned (cash basis)	8.81	8.81	8.81	8.81	8.81

d. Cash flow from operations is higher when zero-coupon bonds are issued because interest is never reported as an operating cash outflow. [Note the infinite cash-basis coverage ratio.] Interest coverage, however, is lower after the first year, and declines as interest expense increases over time, reflecting the steadily increasing principal amount. Full-coupon bonds (if sold at par) result in a constant cash outflow from operations and constant interest expense. Given the Null Company's "steady state," the interest coverage ratio is constant on both accrual and cash flow bases.

e. Given the tax deductibility of accrued but unpaid interest on zero-coupon bonds, cash flow from operations will be higher for both cases. The reported cash flow differences will remain unchanged. For the zero-coupon case, cash flow from operations is even more misleading as the firm must generate sufficient cash from operations to repay the debt at maturity. The obligation must be repaid, regardless of its cash flow classification.

5.{M}a. The $US carrying amount = 1,282/1.37 = **$936 million**.

b. Because the notes have no coupon, they were issued at a discount. The difference between the face amount and the amount computed in part a must be unamortized discount.

c. Interest expense (CHF millions) would be 7% X 1,282 = **CHF 90**

d. Adding the 1999 interest computed in part c to the carrying amount at December 31, 1998: 90 + 1,282 = **CHF 1,372 million**

e. The most obvious explanation is the change in the exchange rate from 1.37 to 1.60.

In $US, 1999 interest expense = 7% X $$936 = $65 million, making the carrying amount at December 31, 1999 equal to $1,001 million [$936 + $65]. This is much closer to the carrying amount computed at 1,618/1.60 = $1,011 million.

A second factor is that interest expense in CHF is computed quarterly, based on average rates for each period. The CHF carrying value at December 31, 1999 equals the 1998 carrying value + 1999 interest expense + translation loss [Swiss franc decline increases the CHF debt amount].

f. (i) Cash from operations is higher each year when zero coupon notes are issued because there is no cash interest.

(ii) Interest expense rises each year (excluding the effect of exchange rates) because it is based on a (rising) $US carrying amount.

g. The rise in the value of the dollar (decline in Swiss franc) increases interest expense in CHF.

6.{S}(i) Interest expense = Interest paid + change in bond discount

$8,562 = $7,200 + $1,362

(ii) = Market rate x [face value - discount]
= .12 x [face value - $8,652]

Therefore, face value = ($8,562/.12) + $8,652 = **$80,000**

(iii) Coupon rate = interest paid/face value
= $7,200/$80,000 = **9%**

7.{S}a. An interest rate rise would decrease the market value of the fixed rate bonds but have no effect on the variable rate bonds. The effect on the fixed rate bonds would depend on their duration.

b. An interest rate rise would increase FIF's interest expense because more than half of its bonds have variable rates as well as a small portion of its bank loans.

c. A finance company seeks to match the interest rate sensitivity of its debt to that of its earning assets. It is likely that FIF's fixed rate receivables increased over the 1996 - 2000 period and the company increased its fixed rate debt to lock in the spread between fixed rate interest income and expense.

d. For a finance company, an analyst is interested in knowing how well the company has matched the interest rate sensitivity of its financial assets and liabilities. When fair value estimates of financial assets are not provided the fair value of debt has very limited usefulness.

8.{S}a. FIF has swapped variable rate interest payments for fixed rate (5.2%) payments on a notional amount of $25 million.

b.

($ thousands)	1999	2000
Interest received	$ 1,375	$ 1,750
Interest paid	(1,300)	(1,300)
Net receipt	$ 75	$ 450

Interest received = $25 million X receive rate
Interest paid = $25 million X 5.2% (both years)

c. The swap reduced the sensitivity to changes in interest rates by converting part of the variable rate obligation to one with fixed rates.

9.{S}a. and b. *In ¥ millions*

Years	1998	1999	% *increase*
Issue			
2.14%, 2005	6,248	6,356	1.72%
1.73%, 2003	6,134	6,356	3.61%

The yen amounts were obtained by multiplying the dollar amounts by the exchange rate. For example, for the 2.14% bond at December 31, 1998, $55 X 113.60 = 6,248. [*Note:* the yen amounts are rounded.]

c. It appears that both bonds were issued at a discount, creating amortization that increases the carrying amount each year. If we add the 1999 increase to the coupon rate, it appears that the effective interest rates are 3.86% and 5.34% respectively.

d. One possible motivation is to finance Japanese operations that are conducted in yen. A second is that, as a well-known company, BMY may be able to borrow more cheaply by borrowing in yen and swapping the yen proceeds into US dollars.

10.{S}a. The advantage is that, when Takeda's share price rose, the debt was converted into equity, strengthening the balance sheet. As convertible notes are issued with a conversion price that exceeds the then market price, the company effectively sold common shares at a premium. In addition, because of the conversion feature, the interest rate would have been below the rate required by nonconvertible notes.

The disadvantage is that the debt was converted into common shares at a time when Takeda could have sold new shares at a much higher price, obtaining the same capital at a lower cost.

b. Reported data (Yen millions)

	1998	1999
Total debt	44,482	21,338
Equity	829,381	907,373
Total capital	873,863	928,711
Debt/total capital	5.1%	2.3%

The more than 50% debt decrease was the largest factor reducing the debt/total capital ratio.

c. As the market price of Takeda shares was well above the conversion price in 1998, the convertible debt should be classified as equity. After that adjustment (subtracting 22,000 from debt and adding the same amount to equity) Takeda's debt was virtually unchanged from 1998 to 1999 and the decline in the debt/total capital ratio was small:

Adjusted data (Yen millions)

	1998
Total debt	22,482
Equity	851,381
Total capital	873,863
Debt/total capital	2.6%

This analysis underscores the discussion in the chapter; the analyst must classify convertible debt based on market considerations. Proper classification results in a more appropriate leverage measure.

11. {S}a. There were two benefits: a lower interest rate than on nonconvertible debt of the same maturity and the possibility of future conversion. If conversion takes place Roche will have sold shares for 25% more than their then market price.

b. First, you must compute the effective rate on the bonds considering their coupon rate and the discount from face value at which they were sold. Interest expense for 2000 would equal the effective rate multiplied by the issue amount of 101.22 billion Yen (105 x 96.4%) prorated for the portion of the year for which the bonds were outstanding.

The carrying amount at December 31, 2000 would equal the issue amount (101.22) plus the excess of interest expense over interest at the coupon rate.

c. If the Yen appreciates (declines) against the Swiss franc, then both interest expense and the carrying amount of the debt will rise (fall).

d. At the issue date the bonds should be considered debt because their conversion price is well above the market price. They should be considered equity only when the market price is sufficiently above the market price that conversion can be considered highly likely.

12. {S}a. The advantages to Network Associates compared with full-coupon nonconvertible bonds were:
(i)   Lower interest rate
(ii) No cash interest expense
(iii) Higher cash flow from operations
(iv) The likelihood that the debt would be converted to common shares before its maturity in 20 years

b. The first year interest expense on the bonds is $16.44 million [4.75% X $346 million (39.106% X $885)]. As the bonds were issued in February 1998 interest expense for 1998 would have been below that amount. Assuming 1998 interest expense of $15 million results in a carrying amount of $361 million ($346 + $15).

Thus 1999 interest expense can be estimated as $17.15 million (4.75% X $361 million), close to the amount in the cash flow statement. This represents, therefore, the noncash interest expense for 1999.

c. At a common stock price of $66.25, the conversion value of the bonds was:
    $1,280 million [$885 X ($66.25/$45.80)]
    At this price conversion is highly likely and the convertible bonds should be treated as equity.

d. At a common stock price of $4, the conversion value of the bonds was $77.3 million [$885 X ($4/$45.80)]. At this price conversion is highly unlikely and the convertible bonds should be treated as debt.

e. Issuing bonds with an embedded put option has the advantage of lowering the interest rate, as investors will accept a lower rate in return for the put option. The disadvantage is that NET may be required to redeem some or all of the bonds if bondholders exercise the put option. As option exercise is likely only if the company's financial condition has weakened and the shares are selling at a low price, option exercise may strain the company's financial condition further.

13.{S}(i) If Munich Re had sold its shares of Allianz in June 2000 it would have incurred a large capital gains tax. In addition, it would have had to sell the large block of shares at a discount to the market price of Allianz.

By selling the exchangeable notes, Munich has postponed the effective sale date, in the expectation that capital gains taxes would be reduced (they were). In addition, assuming the bonds are exchanged for Allianz shares, it sold those shares at a premium of 28% to the market price.

The major disadvantage is that Munich Re retains the risk of ownership of Allianz shares. If Allianz shares do not rise by the maturity date of the notes, Munich will still hold the shares and will be required to repay the debt. In addition, Munich will have to pay interest expense on the notes until they mature or are exchanged, although it will also receive any dividends declared by Allianz. [*Note*: in December 2002 the market price of Allianz shares was €100, far below the €509 price at which the bonds are exchangeable.]

(ii) If Munich Re had sold notes without the exchange feature it would have had to offer a higher interest rate, incurring higher interest expense. In addition, if the notes are exchanged, Munich Re will not have to repay the debt and interest expense will decline as bonds are exchanged for Allianz shares.

The disadvantage is that Munich Re has given up the possibility of a large increase in the value of Allianz shares. Munich has also lost the flexibility of being able to choose the period in which is recognizes the gain on the sale of Allianz shares.

14. {S}a. Future redemption depends on conditions in the credit markets at each "reset" date. Investors would choose redemption if more attractive Swiss franc (SFR) investments were available. That would be the case, for example, if PepsiCo's credit rating had declined.

PepsiCo would redeem bonds if alternative financing sources are available or if SFR debt is no longer desirable. The latter depends on PepsiCo's exposure to SFR assets at that time or, if the debt was swapped for debt in another currency, conditions in the swap market at that time.

b. The obligations should be classified as debt. One might argue that, because there is no stated maturity date, these bonds are "permanent" capital and should be considered equity. However the periodic reset provisions suggest that, at some point, either PepsiCo or investors will choose the redemption option. As investors can force redemption, the bonds should be classified as debt.

15. {S}a. An investor who is willing to accept the risk of loss of principal might find the high returns on these bonds attractive.

b. In a period without insurance losses, Scor will be required to pay the high stated interest rates on these bonds, increasing interest expense, reducing reported income, and reducing the interest coverage ratio.

c. In a period with insurance losses, Scor will be required to pay little or no interest on these bonds, increasing net income and the interest coverage ratio.

d. These bonds hedge Scor's insurance risk. Interest expense on these bonds will be high in periods without losses and low in periods with losses. As a result they reduce the variability of Scor's reported net income.

16.{S}a. The preferred shares should be categorized as debt. The dividend is set by periodic auctions and the company may redeem them at any time. In effect, they are a form of short-term debt that the company can extend as long as it is willing to pay the rate demanded by the market. Should the company find a cheaper source of financing, it is likely to call the preferred issue. [They were called in June 2001.]

b. The ratio calculation before and after adjustment is:

Amounts in $ millions	Reported	Adjusted
Total debt	$ 7,647	$ 7,947
Minority interest	710	710
Stockholders' equity	12,042	11,742
Total capital	$ 20,399	$ 20,399
Total debt/total capital	37.5%	39.0%

17.{S}a. The fair value of Wal-Mart's debt declined relative to book value from 1-31-99 to 1-31-00. Interest rates must have risen during that time period, as higher rates reduce the present value of future payments.

b. The fair value at 1-31-99 was above book value, implying that (on that date) interest rates were below the average rate of 7.2% on Wal-Mart debt. Thus the company could have borrowed at those lower rates, before rates increased, reducing its average rate.

18. {S}a. Wal-Mart may have believed that variable rates were likely to fall and/or remain below fixed rates over the swap period. Swapping fixed for variable rates would, under that assumption, reduce interest expense.

   b. One risk that variable rates would rise so that the swaps would increase interest expense. The second risk is counterparty risk - the risk that the other party to the swap would be unwilling to pay. The second risk would apply only when interest rate changes require payments to Wal-Mart.

   c. When interest rates rise, the value of the right to receive the fixed rate of 5.75% declines, reducing the fair value of the swap. We know from problem 17a that interest rates rose from 1-31-99 to 1-31-00.

19. {S}a. The market value of AMR's fixed rate debt issues fell relative to book value at December 31, 1999, implying that interest rates must have risen. Higher rates reduce the present value of payments associated with fixed rate debt.

   b. The interest rate must have been below 10.2% as the present value exceeds book value.

   c. Because the interest rate on variable rate debt floats, fair value should not change except as a result of changes in credit quality.

20. {S}a. Because the average floating rate was below the average fixed rate, the swaps reduced AMR's interest expense.

   b. AMR's swaps convert fixed rate to variable rate debt; AMR exchanged the right to received fixed rates for an obligation to pay variable rates. When interest rates rise, the value of the right to receive fixed rates declines, reducing the fair value of the swap. From the answer to problem 19a, we know that interest rates fell in 1999. The rise in interest rates therefore decreases the fair value of the swaps.

   c. AMR's debt nearly doubled in 1999, increasing its exposure to changes in interest rates as much of its debt is fixed rate. Both the notional and fair value of AMR's swaps declined in 1999, reducing their offsetting effect on market risk. Both of these factors increased AMR's exposure.

21. {S}a. An argument for inclusion is that, for Fannie Mae, the issuance and retirement of debt are recurring operating activities whose consequences should be included in operating earnings.

An argument for exclusion is that gains or losses from debt repurchase reflect economic changes during the entire period the debt was outstanding and should not be included in operating earnings for the period in which management chose to realize the gain.

b. An argument for including the hedging loss is that hedging activities are part of Fannie Mae's normal operating activities.

An argument for exclusion is that the hedging loss was unusually large and inclusion distorts the trend of operating earnings.

c. We believe that gains and losses from debt retirement should be excluded from operating earnings for most firms. These gains and losses result from management decisions and because (as discussed in the chapter) refinancing may not yield any economic gain or loss despite the accounting gain or loss. Hedging results should be included in operating earnings as hedging gains and losses should offset other economic effects that are also included.

However, Fannie Mae may be an exception. As stated in part a, the company routinely issues and retires debt, suggesting that gains and losses should be included in operating earnings. Before doing so, the analyst should try to determine whether the gains or losses for the particular quarter are unusual or reflect interest rate changes over multiple periods, suggesting that the gains or losses should (analytically) be spread over several quarters.

22.{S}a. The $300 million gain should be excluded from Arco's operating earnings for 1997 because the gain results from the appreciation of Lyondell shares in prior years (possibly including years prior to the bond issuance).

b. Arco may have chosen to issue the exchangeable notes to
   (i)   maintain its controlling interest in Lyondell for strategic reasons
   (ii) postpone the income tax consequences of sale
   (iii) obtain a higher price for the shares than the market price at that time
   (iv) avoid an unfavorable impact on sale proceeds due to the effect on Lyondell's share price of selling a large block of shares
   (v)   retain the flexibility to report the gain in a period of management's choice

c. On Arco's balance sheet, the investment in Lyondell shares is reduced by the cost basis of the shares exchanged; debt is reduced by the carrying value of the notes retired; equity is increased by the (after-tax) gain.

The income statement reports the gain on the sale and the related income tax expense.

The transaction is noncash. However Arco's cash flow statement will report (as an adjustment to net income in the cash from operations section) the amount of the gain and any deferred income tax effect.

23.{M}a. Adding principal and interest payments:

PV of $20 million, payable in 10 years[1] = $ 9,127,800
+ PV of 20 payments of $1 million each[2] =   13,590,330
Financing cash inflow = proceeds = $22,718,130

[1]PV factor (n=20, r=.04) = .45639 x $20,000,000 = $ 9,127,800
[2]PV factor (n=20; r=.04) = 13.59033 x $1,000,000 = $13,590,330

On January 1, 2000, cash and debt liability are each
increased by $22,718,130

Years Ended December 31	2000	2001
Long-term debt	$ 22,626,855	$ 22,433,206
Accrued interest	905,074	897,328
Total liability	$ 23,531,929	$ 23,330,534
Interest expense	1,813,799	1,798,605
Cash from operations	(1,000,000)	(2,000,000)

Calculations:

<u>*Interest expense* (income tax ignored)</u>

<u>Year ended December 31, 2000:</u>
July 1: $22,718,130 x .04 = $908,725
Interest payment of $1,000,000 (no impact on expense)
Reduction of bond premium = $1,000,000 - $908,725 =
$91,275
Debt balance on July 1 = $22,718,130 - $91,275 =
$22,626,855

December 31: $22,626,855 x .04 = $905,074 interest
expense, shown as accrued interest on December 31, 1994
balance sheet

January 1, 2001:
Interest payment of $1,000,000 (no impact on expense)
Reduction of bond premium = $1,000,000 - $905,074 =
$94,926
Debt balance on Jan. 1 = $22,626,855 - $94,926 =
$22,531,929

Year ended December 31, 2001:
July 1: $22,531,929 x .04 = $901,277 interest expense
Interest payment of $1,000,000 (no impact on expense)
Reduction of bond premium = $1,000,000 - $901,277 = $98,723
Debt balance on July 1 = $22,531,929 - $98,723 = $22,433,206

December 31: $22,433,206 x .04 = $897,328 interest expense, shown as accrued interest on December 31, 1995 balance sheet.

January 1, 2002:
Interest payment of $1,000,000 (no impact on expense)
Reduction of bond premium = $1,000,000 - $897,328 = $102,672
Debt balance on January 1 = $22,433,206 - $102,672 = $22,330,534

Operating cash outflow
2000: One interest payment on July 1, 1994, $1,000,000
2001: Two interest payments of $1,000,000 each, on January 1 and July 1, $2,000,000

Balance sheet impacts
2000: effect of bond issuance
      reduction of bond premium at July 1
      interest payable at December 31
      interest expense reduces equity

2001: reduction of interest payable and bond premium at January 1
      reduction of bond premium at July 1
      interest payable at December 31
      interest expense reduces equity

b. The purchase price must be equal to the face amount
    since the market interest rate is equal to the coupon
    rate.[3]

    The carrying amount of the bonds on July 1, 2003 will
    be $21,997,050.[4] The gain from repurchase is the
    difference between the purchase price and carrying
    amount: $20,000,000 - $21,997,050 = $1,997,050. It is a
    gain because a liability has been extinguished for a
    lesser asset amount. Because of the change in interest
    rates since the bonds were issued, Derek has captured
    the remaining bond premium. The journal entry would be:

    Bonds payable   20,000,000
    Premium on bonds payable   1,997,050
        Cash   20,000,000
        Gain on extinguishment   1,997,050

    [3] This can be shown, as well, by using present values: purchase
    price = present value of $20,000,000, to be repaid in 6.5 years:
    PV factor (n=13, r=.05) = .53032 x $20 million = $10,606,400
    plus PV of 13 payments of $1,000,000 each: PV factor (n=13,
    r=.05) = 9.39357 x $1,000,000 = $9,393,570; total is
    $20,000,000.

    [4] Present value of $20,000,000, to be repaid in 6.5 years: PV
    factor (n=13, r=.04) = .60057 x $20 million = $12,011,400 plus
    PV of 13 payments of $1,000,000 each: PV factor (n=13, r=.04) =
    9.98565 x $1,000,000 = $9,985,650; total = $21,997,050. The
    carrying amount could also be determined by extending the
    analysis in part A (reducing the bond premium at the time of
    each interest payment) to July 1, 2003.

c. The gain is not a component of continuing, operating
    income but should be considered nonrecurring. It is a
    consequence of the change in interest rates rather than
    the firm's operating activities, and cannot be expected
    to recur.

d. 1. The gain provides a one-time increase in reported
        net income.

    2. The decrease in leverage (as a lower amount of
        higher coupon debt is issued to replace the lower
        coupon debt) may help the firm avert or delay
        technical default on bond covenants. The
        repurchase may also allow the firm to eliminate
        limiting covenants on this specific debt issue.
        Thus even if new debt must be issued to raise the
        funds needed for repurchase, the firm may wish to
        retire the bond issue.

24.{M}a. The data needed to calculate the ratios for each of the three options follows ($ thousands):

Financing Method Number		1 Preferred Shares	2 Full Coupon Bond	3 Zero Coupon Bond
CFO before interest		$ 390	$ 390	$ 390
Interest paid[1]	Given	$ 200	$ 200	$ 200
	New	0	100	0
Total		$ 200	$ 300	$ 200
Preferred dividends	Given	$ 0	$ 0	$ 0
	New	100	0	0
Total		$ 100	$ 0	$ 0
Long-term debt[2]	Given	$2,000	$2,000	$2,000
	New	0	1,000	1,100
Total		$2,000	$3,000	$3,100
Tangible fixed assets	Given	$5,000	$5,000	$5,000
	New	1,000	1,000	1,000
Total		$6,000	$6,000	$6,000

[1] No cash interest is paid on the zero coupon bond (see note 2).
[2] Unpaid interest on the zero coupon bond increases the liability.

Times interest earned (cash basis):			
CFO Before interest / Interest paid	1.95	**1.30**	1.95

Fixed charge coverage (cash basis):			
CFO Before interest / Interest paid + preferred dividends	**1.30**	**1.30**	1.95

Debt to gross tangible assets:			
Long-term debt / Gross tangible fixed assets	0.33	0.50	**0.52**

The resultant ratios for each of the three options are shown above, with ratios that violate the applicable covenant in boldface. Note that each of the options violates at least one of the covenants and the conventional bond violates two.

The zero-coupon bond seems to be the "best" as it results in high coverage ratios (no cash interest payment) and the debt to assets limit is barely violated. It violates this covenant because debt increases to reflect the unpaid interest.

b.   The best approach is to combine the zero-coupon bond, which violates only the debt/assets covenant, with another financing method that brings down that ratio without lowering either of the other ratios excessively. Preferred stock dominates conventional bonds as it has a lower debt/assets ratio and its coverage ratios are at least as high. Thus the optimal choice is a combination of preferred stock and zero coupon bonds. Because the times interest coverage ratio is identical at 1.95 for both we need only consider the last two ratios:

CFO/(interest + preferred dividends) must exceed 1.80

Long-term debt/gross assets must be less than 0.50

If P dollars are raised via preferred shares and Z dollars via zero coupon bonds, then P + Z = $1,000,000. For the zero coupon bonds, the amount of debt at year-end is 1.1Z because of the accrual of unpaid interest. These constraints reduce to the following equations (amounts in $thousands):

I: $390/($200 + $100p) > 1.80 where p = P/$1,000,000

II: $$\frac{\$2,000 + \$1,100\ (1-p)}{\$6,000} < 0.50$$

These reduce to the following constraints:

I: .167 > p   II: p > .091

Thus, .167 > p > .091

> **One possibility would be to issue 85% zero coupon bonds and 15% preferred (p = .15):**
>
> CFO = $390 (neither issue reduces CFO)
> Interest paid = $200 (neither issue creates interest payments)
> Preferred dividends = $15 ($150 x 10%)
>
> Long-term debt = $2,935 [$2,000 + ($1,100 x .85)]
> Tangible fixed assets = $6,000 (same for both choices)
>
> Times interest earned ($390/$200) = 1.95
> Fixed charge coverage ($390/$215) = 1.81
> Debt to tangible fixed assets ($2,935/$6,000) = .489

> **Another possibility would be 90% zero coupon bonds and 10% preferred (p = .10):**
>
> CFO = $390
> Interest paid = $200
> Preferred dividends = $10 ($100 x 10%)
>
> Long-term debt = $2,990 [$2,000 + ($1,100 x .90)]
> Tangible fixed assets = $6,000 (same for both choices)
>
> Times interest earned ($390/$200) = 1.95
> Fixed charge coverage ($390/$210) = 1.86
> Debt to tangible fixed assets ($2,990/$6,000) = .498

Thus there is a tradeoff between the two ratios. As p increases, Sleepman reduces its debt ratio but also its coverage ratio. At the extremes (p = .167 and p = .091), the firm will be right on the edge of violating one covenant. The decision would be based on management's view of which ratio has the lower risk of being violated (or which ratio the lender considers more significant). Note, however, the zero coupon bond increases in amount as interest accrues and (all other things being equal) puts increasing pressure on the debt-to-fixed-assets ratio over time.

25.{S}a. The calculated dividend capacity equals:

Minimum shareholders' equity, 12/31/93	$650.0 million
50% of 1994 net income of $48 million	24.0
Minimum shareholders' equity, 12/31/94	$674.0 million
Actual shareholders' equity, 12/31/94	717.3
Unrestricted amount	**$ 43.3 million**

b. Without any increase in income, the current dividend can be maintained for only two years:

	1995	1996	1997
Estimated Stockholders' Equity ($millions)			
Opening	$717.3	$723.3	$729.3
Income	48.0	48.0	48.0
Dividend	(42.0)	(42.0)	(42.0)
Closing	$723.3	$729.3	$735.3*
*Below minimum stockholders' equity required.			
Minimum Stockholders' Equity ($millions)			
Opening	$674.0	$698.0	$722.0
Addition (50% of income)	24.0	24.0	24.0
Closing	$698.0	$722.0	$746.0

As the table above shows, in 1997 the minimum equity requirement will be violated.

c. To maintain dividend payments at the 1994 level through 1998, income would have to increase. The required income for 1997 and 1998 is $69.4 million and $84.0 million respectively.[1] These amounts result in the following table for those years:

	1997	1998
Estimated Stockholders' Equity ($millions)		
Opening	$729.3	$756.7
Income	69.4	84.0
Dividend	(42.0)	(42.0)
Closing	$756.7	$798.7
Minimum Stockholders' Equity ($millions)		
Opening	$722.0	$756.7
50% of income	34.7	42.0
Closing	$756.7	$798.7

[1] These amounts can be calculated as follows:
1997: Increase = 2 X shortfall in equity = 2 X ($746.0 − 735.3)
           = 2 X $10.7 = $21.4 million
1998: Income must equal $84 million, twice the dividend, to maintain equity at the required level.

d. The answer would depend on the shareholder's view of
    the market price of NorAm's shares. Issuance of new
    shares to maintain the current dividend makes no sense
    given finance theory, which states that the two are
    equivalent. In an imperfect world, however, NorAm's
    shares may have been fully valued but the shareholder
    may not have wished to sell and incur capital gains
    taxes. If NorAm had attractive investment opportunities
    not reflected in its stock price, then issuing new
    shares to increase the firm's borrowing capacity would
    have been desirable.

Case 10-1 - Solution

Estimated time to complete this case is one hour.

1. The calculations are:

Amounts in $millions	1997	1998	1999	2000
Total debt	$ 357.6	$367.5	$ 503.1	$ 30.9
Net debt	59.5	259.1	276.7	(23.7)
Total debt at market	357.6	205.3	304.4	23.8
Net debt at market	59.5	96.9	78.0	(30.8)
Equity plus minority interest	618.8	275.9	126.1	290.5
Equity (MV) plus MI	1,363.5	380.8	219.1	1,316.4
Ratios				
(i) Total debt to equity	**58%**	**133%**	**399%**	**11%**
(ii) Net debt to equity	**10%**	**94%**	**219%**	**(8)%**
(iii) Total debt to equity (MV)	**26%**	**54%**	**139%**	**2%**
(iv) Net debt to equity (MV)	**4%**	**25%**	**36%**	**(2)%**

Calculations for 2000:
    (i) $ 30.9/ $ 290.5
    (ii) $(23.7)/$ 290.5
    (iii) $ 23.8/ $1,316.4
    (iv) $(30.8)/$1,316.4

2. All of the ratios show rising financial leverage through 1999 with a significant decline in 2000. However the levels are quite different. When the market value of equity is used in the denominator, the 1997 leverage ratio seems quite reasonable, especially when net debt is used in the numerator. However the gross debt-to-equity ratio for 1998 is high and rises to an alarming level in 1999, even using the market value of equity. This comparison highlights one problem with using market values in the debt-equity ratio: changes in market price may result in significant changes in the ratio over time.

3. There is no simple answer to that question. Normally, the last ratio (net debt at market and equity at market) is most informative. However, using that ratio makes several implicit assumptions.

First, it assumes that all cash equivalents and short-term investments can be used to repay debt. If the cash equivalents are not available for that purpose (for example, because they are in a subsidiary and cannot be used without regulatory permission or tax payments) then gross debt should be used. In the case of Read-Rite it appears that large cash equivalents (in excess of operating requirements) were maintained for liquidity purposes (to reassure customers and suppliers) rather than because of any restrictions.

The second implicit assumption is that declines in the market value of debt can be realized. When a company is financially troubled, creditors may be willing to forgive a portion of the debt or restructure the debt (reducing the interest rate, for example). Subordinated creditors (such as bondholders) are more likely to do so because of their weaker security position. Banks and other senior lenders rarely make such concessions unless the firm is close to bankruptcy.

The answer, therefore, requires an analysis of the company and the purpose of the calculation (i.e. for which creditor). Our point is that, while ratio (iv) appears to be the best measure of Read-Rite's debt burden, it should not be used without additional analysis, leading to an understanding of operating and other liquidity needs.

4. The required calculations are:

Amounts in $millions	1997	1998	1999
Gross margin	$ 238.8	$(132.8)	$ (23.2)
Gross margin %	21%	-16%	-3%
Operating income	$ 119.7	$(352.9)	$(182.2)
Interest coverage ratio	7.6X	(11.9)X	(5.7)X
Free cash flow	$ (82.7)	$(195.0)	$ (24.8)

Gross margin % = gross margin/sales [1997 = $238.8/$$1162.0]
Operating income = sales − (cost of sales + operating expenses) [1997 = $1162.0 − ($923.2 + $119.1)]
Interest coverage ratio = operating income/interest expense [1997 = $119.7/$15.7]
Free cash flow = cash from operations − capital expenditures [1997 = $190.1 − $272.8]

All three statistics reflect Read-Rite's poor operating results. Gross margin for 1998 and 1999 was negative; revenues did not even cover the costs of production. The interest coverage ratio was negative for 1998 and 1999, reflecting negative operating income. Free cash flow (cash from operations less capital expenditures) was negative for all three years. Cash from operations was negative for 1998 (see exhibit 10C-1).

The company's sales were declining and its debt burden (by any measure) rising. Thus it is not surprising that the auditor gave a going concern qualification at September 30, 1999.

5. There were at least six benefits (to Read-Rite) from the exchange offer:
   a. The face amount of the convertible debt was reduced by 50% from $1,000 per old bond to $500 per old bond.
   b. The interest burden of the convertible debt was reduced from $65 per old bond (6.5% coupon rate) to $50 per old bond (10% coupon on $500 face amount).
   c. Read-Rite was permitted to pay interest on the new bonds in common shares, increasing cash flow. [In fact the company did pay interest in common shares until the new bonds were converted.]
   d. As part of the exchange offer, Read-Rite was able to raise $61 million from the sale of additional new notes.
   e. Read-Rite was relieved from complying with any of the debt covenants of the old bonds.
   f. The lower conversion price of the new bonds increased the likelihood that they would be converted into common shares, eliminating that portion of the company's debt burden and improving its financial condition.

   The last "benefit" for Read-Rite is also the cost borne by the stockholders. As can be seen from the 2000 data in Exhibit 10C-1, the conversion of the bonds into common shares (and the additional shares issued as interest payment on the new bonds) more than doubled the number of common shares outstanding, diluting the interest of the existing Read-Rite common shareholders. Any future earnings would be spread over more shares, reducing earnings per share.

   The conversion effect of the new bonds exchanged and sold can be calculated as ($162.6 + $61.2)/$4.51 = 49.6 million shares ($4.51 is the conversion price).

6. The gain can be estimated as follows:

Face amount of old bonds exchanged	$ 325.2 million
Face amount of new bonds	(162.6)
Gross gain on exchange	$162.6 million
Write-off of unamortized issue cost	(5.0)
Net gain on exchange	$157.6 million

There is an unexplained $1 million difference between this amount and the $158.6 million recognized.

7. The $158.6 million gain really originated in prior years (mostly 1998 as shown in exhibit 10C-1), when the market value of the convertible bonds declined. Its recognition in the year of realization (2000), while required by GAAP because it was realized in that year by the exchange offer) is arbitrary.

There is also some question as to whether there was any economic gain, as well as the amount of the gain at the time of the exchange. At that time, Read-Rite exchanged new bonds with a market value no lower than that of the old bonds (otherwise bondholders would not have been willing to make the exchange). In addition, while the face amount of the new bonds was one-half the face amount of the old bonds, the conversion option was much more valuable.

As discussed in the chapter (page 337, including footnote 26) a convertible bond should be viewed as a full coupon bond issued at a discount plus a warrant. The market value of the warrant portion of the old bonds was virtually zero while the warrant portion of the new bonds had substantial value due to the conversion price that was only 15% above market. If the bonds were accounted for using this component approach, the gain would be much lower than the gain computed simply by comparing the face amounts.

8. The advantages of the new notes were
   a. Read-Rite was able to survive
   b. The lower conversion price increased the possible gain on the bonds.

   The disadvantages were:
   a. The lower face amount of the new bonds reduced the (face) amount that would be received at maturity.
   b. The bondholder would receive lower coupon interest (see answer 5b).
   c. The bondholder might receive Read-Rite shares instead of cash interest.

   Presumably bondholders believed that the two advantages outweighed the disadvantages and that the exchange offer was more likely to result in recovery of their in investment.

   That decision was vindicated by subsequent events. At the fiscal 2000 year-end stock price of $11.25, the new bonds had a conversion value of $2,494.50 per bond ($11.25 x $1,000/$4.51) or $1,247.20 ($2,494.50/2) per old bond. Despite the lower face value, the subsequent rise of the common share price enabled them to more than recover the (old) face value.

Chapter 11 Solutions

Overview:

Problem Length   *Problem #s*
{S}   *1 - 4, 9, 11, 12, 15, 16, 21, 22*
{M}   *5, 7, 8, 10, 13, 14, 17, 18, 20, 23, 24*
{L}   *6, 19, 25*

1.{S}(i)   Interest expense = 12% x $10,000 (beginning balance of lease obligation) = $1,200.

(ii) The lease obligation will be reduced by $100 ($1,300 - $1,200) leaving an obligation of $9,900.

(iii) Cash from Operations will be reduced by the interest payment of $1,200. Cash from investing activities will not be affected. (However, the firm will report the capital lease as a "noncash investment and financing activity." Cash from financing will be reduced by the amount of the principal payment of $100.

(iv) Under an operating lease there is no lease obligation on the balance sheet. The only effect on income is Rent Expense of $1,300. Similarly, CFO is reduced by $1,300. (CFI and CFF are not affected).

2.{S}(i)   In a take-or-pay arrangement, a company contracts to buy or pay for a certain amount of a supplier's commodity at a predetermined price over a stated time period. The company, by entering the contract, incurs an economic liability. However, since it is only a contract, no accounting liability is recorded on the balance sheet - it is off balance sheet.

(ii) In a sale of receivable, a company "sells" its receivables to a third-party, usually a financial institution. Typically, the sale is made at a discounted price from the face value and the seller may retain some or all of the default risk. The sale, in substance, is a financing arrangement with the receivables being used as collateral. However, under GAAP, the transaction is treated as a sale and the debt does not appear on the balance sheet.

(iii) A joint venture represents an investment of 50% or less by one company (the "investor") in another company. Under GAAP, since ownership is not over 50%, the assets and liabilities of the joint venture need not be consolidated with the parent's assets and liabilities. Hence, any debt taken on by the joint venture remains off balance sheet even when the investor is liable for the debt.

11-1

3.{S} Effect of choice of interest rate on lessee:

		9% versus 10%	
		First Year	Lease Term
(i)	Interest expense: Lower interest rate reduces interest expense.	Lower	Lower
(ii)	Amortization expense: Lower interest rate increases present value of minimum lease payments, creating higher asset amount to be amortized over lease term.	Higher	Higher
(iii)	Total lease expense: The net effect for the first year depends on the lease amounts; over the lease term, however, total expense equals total lease payments regardless of the choice of interest rate.	Indeterminate	Equal
(iv)	Cash from operations: Lower interest rate shifts expense from interest to amortization (see i and ii); as cash from operations is decreased only by interest expense, a decrease in interest expense increases CFO, both in the first year and over the leas term.	Higher	Higher
(v)	Average assets: Lower interest rate increases present value (see ii) resulting in higher average assets, both in first year and over lease term.	Higher	Higher
(vi)	Average liabilities: Lower interest rate increases present value recognized as liability, both in first year and over lease term.	Higher	Higher

4.{S}a.   Pallavi must capitalize the lease because the lease agreement contains a bargain purchase option. Note that the lease also meets one other capitalization criterion: The present value of minimum lease payments exceeds 90% of the fair market value of the equipment (see part b for computations).

   b.   The fair market value of the asset is $125,000. The present value of the MLPs is $127,785 (at 8%, the lower of the lessee and lessor rates); the asset must be capitalized at the (lower) fair market value. (Note that the lease obligation is the sum of the present values of the MLPs and the bargain purchase option - the latter is not provided.)

c.   Leases must be capitalized at the lesser of the present value of lease payments or the fair value of the lease; in this case, the lease must be capitalized at the fair value of $125,000.

d.   The existence of the bargain purchase option requires depreciation over the estimated economic life of the asset rather than the (shorter) lease term.

e.   The option creates the presumption that the asset will be held past the expiration date of the lease. Otherwise it must be assumed that use of the asset will revert to the lessor at expiration, requiring the lessee to depreciate the leased asset over the (shorter) lease term.

5.{M}a.   The following states the effects of Tolrem using the capital lease method as compared with the operating lease method.

(i)   Cash from operations is higher as only the interest portion of lease expense is deducted from operating cash flows; total lease expense is deducted for operating leases.

(ii)   Financing cash flow is lower for capital lease, as part of lease rental is treated as amortization of liability and classified as financing cash outflow.

(iii) Investing cash flow is not affected by the lease treatment. However, the firm will report capital leases in the statement of cash flows (or a footnote) as noncash investment activities.

(iv)   Net cash flow reflects the actual rental payment and is unaffected by the financial reporting treatment of the lease.

(v)   Debt/equity ratio is higher for capital lease, as it records the present value of minimum lease payments as debt *and* reduces net income (and therefore equity) in first year.

(vi)   Interest coverage ratio is usually (not always) lower for capital lease method, which reports interest expense but also higher EBIT, see (vii). For coverage ratios well above 1.0, the ratio will decline. If the increase in interest expense exceeds the increase in EBIT, the ratio will decline even for firms with very low coverage ratios.

(vii) Operating income is lower for operating lease because the total lease payment is an operating expense; for capital lease, interest portion of lease expense is nonoperating.

(viii) Net income is higher for operating lease; total lease expense (interest plus depreciation) is higher for capital lease.

(ix) Deferred tax assets are higher for capital lease; as lease treatment for tax purposes is unaffected by accounting choice, capital lease will generate a deferred tax asset as taxable income (operating lease) exceeds pretax income (capital lease).

(x) Taxes paid are unaffected by choice of method.

(xi) Pretax return on assets is higher for operating leases as pretax income is higher and no assets are reported as the result of the lease; a capital lease reduces income and reports lease assets. Post-tax return on assets is higher for the same reasons.

(xii) Pretax return on equity: both pretax income and equity are higher for operating than for capital leases. The higher pretax income should increase the ratio in all but exceptional cases. Post-tax return on equity should be higher for same reason. However as increase in post-tax income equals (for first year) increase in equity, there may be more exceptional cases.

b. Net income (viii) will be lower for the operating lease after the "crossover" point. As total net income over the life of the lease is unaffected by the accounting choice, higher net income (operating lease) in the early years must be offset by lower net income in later years.

c. Consistent use of the operating lease method in place of capitalization will not change the direction of the effects shown in part A, but will increase their magnitude. In aggregate, new leases will keep Tolrem from reaching the crossover point for net income, keeping net income and return ratios higher than if the leases were capitalized.

6.{L}a. and b.

	Caramino	Aglianico	Difference
Operating income	$ 20,000	$ 20,000	$ None
Depreciation expense[1]	(8,624)		(8,624)
Lease rental expense		(10,000)	10,000
EBIT	11,376	$ 10,000	$ 1,376
Interest expense[2]	(2,650)		(2,650)
Earnings before tax	$ 8,726	10,000	$ (1,274)
Income tax expense	(3,490)	(4,000)	510
Net income	$. 5,236	$ 6,000	$ (764)

[1] The present value of the minimum lease payments is $43,121 ($10,000 + 4 payment annuity of $10,000 per year at 8%). Assuming zero residual value, depreciation = $43,121/5 = $8,624.

[2] Interest expense = 8% x ($43,121 - $10,000) = $2,650

Caramino's EBIT is $1,376 higher; Aglianico reports rental expense but no depreciation expense since it does not record an asset. Because total lease expense (depreciation plus interest) is higher than the lease rental, Caramino's EBT is lower by $1,274. After a deferred income tax offset of $510, Caramino's net income is $764 lower.

Caramino's deferred tax debit (asset) results from the difference between financial reporting (capital lease) and tax reporting (operating lease). The $1,274 timing difference results in a deferred tax debit of $1,274 x .40 = $510

c. and d. Comparison of Cash Flow Statements

	Caramino	Aglianico	Difference
Net income	$ 5,236	$ 6,000	$ (764)
Addback:			
Depreciation expense	8,624		8,624
	$ 13,860	$ 6,000	$ 7,860
Other adjustments:			
Deferred taxes	(510)		(510)
Interest payable	2,650		2,650
Cash from operations	**$ 16,000**	**$ 6,000**	**$ 10,000**
Investment cash flow	-0-	-0-	-0-
Financing cash flow	**(10,000)**	**-0-**	**(10,000)**
Net cash flow	$ 6,000	$ 6,000	$ -0-

Note: We assume that all revenues generated by the firm have been collected by the end of the year.

Caramino reports higher cash from operations by $10,000. Since the tax rate is 40%, Aglianico (operating lease firm) reports aftertax operating cash *outflow* of $6,000. Caramino (capital lease firm) pays no interest but, since it uses the operating lease method for taxes, receives a tax deduction of $4,000 for the annual payment of $10,000. Caramino's aftertax operating cash *inflow* is $4,000.

The difference ($6,000 + $4,000 = $10,000) is recorded by Caramino as a *financing* cash outflow; this is the amount of the lease payment considered a reduction of the capitalized lease liability for 2002. [Note that the lease payment made on January 1, 2002 has no interest component; there is no accrued interest as the lease has just begun. Interest accrued during the year will be paid January 1, 2003.]

e. There is no impact on investing cash flow for either firm. Caramino would report the present value of the capital lease as a noncash investment activity.

f. The net cash outflow for each firm is the lease payment of $10,000 less the tax deduction of $4,000 (40% tax rate). Only the classification of cash flow components is affected by the lease method used.

g. By using the capital lease method, Caramino reports higher debt and lower income. However the firm also reports higher cash from operations. The choice of method may reflect different debt covenants or simply a preference among financial characteristics.

7. (M) a. Since it is the first year:

Capital lease obligations	$2,596,031
Repayment of capital lease obligations	3,969
Capital lease at inception	$2,600,000

b. Amortization expense =
$2,600,000 - $2,479,570 = $120,430

Assuming the asset is being amortized on a straight line basis over the lease term, the lease term =
$2,600,000/$120,430 = 21.6 or 22 years

Total expense = interest + amortization =
$120,430 + $223,733 = $344,163

c. CFO was reduced by the interest expense of $223,733 and CFF was reduced by the "repayment of capital lease obligations" of $ 3,969

d. Free cash flows should be reduced by $2,600,000 - the "cost" of the leased asset.

e. (i) Lease expense would be lease payment =
$223,733 + $3,969 = $227,702

(ii) CFO would be reduced by lease payment of $227,702

f. Using 1999 payment only: $223,733/$2,600,000 = 8.6%

Using all the payments, we have exact MLP's for the six years 1999 - 2004. The "thereafter" MLP's totaling $4,596 thousand are spread over 16 years; i.e. $287.25 thousand/year. Equating this stream to the present value of $2,600,000 yields a rate (IRR) of 9.3%.

The two methods yield rates within "range" of each other especially when we consider that the rate derived from the first method is typically downward biased.

8.{M}a.   The adjustment involves the addition of the interest component of minimum lease payments to stated interest expense. The adjustment reflects a partial, *de facto* capitalization of operating leases.

(i) Unadjusted Ratio of Earnings to Fixed Charges:

Pretax earnings	$ 2,363,646
Interest on indebtedness	68,528
Earnings before interest and taxes (EBIT)	$ 2,432,174
Fixed Charges:	
Interest on indebtedness	$ 68,528
Unadjusted Ratio of Earnings to Fixed Charges	35.5X

(ii) The unadjusted ratio is almost four times the adjusted ratio. *Note*: the SEC rule that governs this calculation assumes that the interest component is one-third of the MLP. The true interest component may be higher or lower, changing the coverage ratio.

b.   Reported debt-to-equity = $550,000/$2,233,303 = **0.25**

c.   Calculation of amounts adjusted for lease capitalization:

The Limited, Inc.
1999 Working Capital Position and Capitalization Table

	Reported	Adjusted
(i) Working capital	$1,070,249	$ 633,579[1]
Capitalization:		
Long-term debt	550,000	550,000
Add: Capitalized lease payments		3,452,628[2]
(ii)Adjusted long-term debt		**$4,002,628**
Shareholders' equity	2,233,303	2,233,303
Total capitalization	$2,783,303	$6,235,931
(iii) Debt-to-equity	**0.25**	**1.80**

[1] Working capital is reduced by the principal component of the 2000 MLPs calculated as
$436,670 = [($643,828 - (.06 x $3,452,628)],
where $3,452,628 is the present value calculated in note 2 below.

[2] Present value of MLPs using an interest rate of 6%. The "thereafter" MLPs are spread using the constant rate assumption; ($502,880 in 2005 and 2006 and $422,102 in 2007).

9.{S} Note: all amounts in $millions
    a.   Debt to equity = ($2,416 + $235)/$4,448 = **0.60**

    b. (i)   Interest portion of 2001 payment = $63-$39 = $24
               Therefore interest rate = $24/$235 = **10.2%**

        (ii) Using the constant rate assumption yields the
            following stream:

YEAR	2001	2002	2003	2004	2005	2006	2007
MLP	$63	$57	$57	$48	$32	$32	$ 8

            The IRR that equates the above to $235 is **7.9%**

    c.   Under the constant rate assumption, the payment stream
        to be discounted at 10.2% is

YEAR	2001	2002	2003	2004	2005 - 2014	2015
MLP	$1,020	$1,030	$1,040	$1,020	$980	$620

    The present value is **$7,435**

    d.   Adjusted debt-to-equity is
            ($2,416 + $235 + $7,435)/$4,448 = **2.27**
    The adjustment increases the ratio almost four-fold.
    The real effect is greater as equity would be lower if
    Delta had capitalized its operating leases at their
    inception.

    e.   After adjustment, both AMR's and Delta's ratios are at
        similar levels of 2.3x.

Debt-to-equity ratio	AMR	Delta
Reported data	0.9	0.6
Adjusted for operating leases	2.3	2.3

    Had the lower rate been used, the present value of
    Delta's operating lease would be significantly higher
    as would its debt-to-equity ratio.

    f.   The adjustments are appropriate for two reasons
        (1) To obtain the appropriate levels of the ratio for
           each firm. For both companies, the reported ratios
           understate their financial leverage.

        (2) For comparison purposes. Before adjustment,
           Delta's ratio at 0.6x is 50% lower than AMR's
           0.9x. After adjustment, that superiority is
           removed as both firms have similar ratios.

10.{M}a. The following MLP stream is assumed (€ million):

YEAR	1	2-4	5-7	8
MLP	€166.5	€68.8	€68.8	€ 5.8

At a rate of 7%, the present value is **€505.3 million**

b. (i) €1,294/€14,145 = **0.09**

(ii) (€1,294 + €505)/€14,145 = **0.13**

c. Another assumption would be to find a decline rate
from the initial payment of €166.5 such that the sum
of the years 2 to 5 payments using that decline rate
equals €275.2; i.e. solve for d in the following
equation
$$(d + d^2 + d^3 + d^4) \times €166.5 = €275.2$$

The above can be solved by trial and error and the
solution is d = 67.66% with a MLP stream of €112.6,
€76.2, €51.5 and €34.9.

Using this MLP stream would increase the present value
of the operating lease obligation.

11.{S}a. We use the constant rate assumption, yielding the
following payment stream (€ millions)

YEAR	2000	2001	2002	2003	2004-2012	2013
Payments	1,718	1,740	1,433	1,292	1,370	1,168

At a discount rate of 7%, the present value is
€12,543.

b. (i) Reported debt-to-equity = €1,294/€14,145 = 0.09
Adjusted for part a:
(€1,294 + €12,543)/€14,145 = **0.98**

(ii) Adjusting for operating leases as well
(€1,294 + €12,543 + €505)/€14,145 = **1.01**

12.{S}a. The cash outflow of $25.6 million represents the decrease in the balance of sold but uncollected receivables ($192.8 - $167.2). It represents net collections (by Arkla as the firm continues to service the receivables) of receivables sold; amounts collected from previously sold receivables were paid to the purchasers of those receivables.

b. Receivables sold but uncollected as of 12/31/93 can be deduced to be:

Outstanding 3/31/94 $118.7 million
Decrease during quarter   107.7
Outstanding 12/31/93 $226.4 million

c. The required adjustments to Arkla's CFO for quarters ended:

	March 31, 1994	March 31, 1995
Cash outflow	$107.7	$25.6

These amounts are the decrease in receivables sold during the respective quarters. The adjustment is required because the cash flow was recognized when the receivables were sold rather than when customers paid. This adjustment produces a measure of CFO based on when the receivables were collected.

13.{S}   All amounts in $millions
    a.   (i)   Current ratio was increased by 15% from 1.61 to 1.86 as a result of receivable sale.

Reported = $686/$369 = 1.86

Adjusted = ($686 + $153.1)/($369 + $153.1) = 1.61
(ii) & (iii)
Average receivables as reported =
           .5($546 + $312) = $429
Adjusting for sale of receivables would increase average receivables by
         .5($153.1 + $115) = $134 to $563

Reported turnover = $2,951/$429 = **6.88**
       # of days = 365/6.88 = **53 days**

Adjusted turnover = $2,951/$563 = **5.24**
       # of days = 365/5.24 = **70 days**

As a result of the receivable sale the cash cycle looked better than it really was by (70 - 53) = **17 days** and the receivables turnover "improved" from 5.24 to 6.88

b. Reported debt/equity = $1,096/$950 = **1.15**
    Debt should be adjusted upwards by the receivables
    sold to ($1,096 + $153.1 =) $1,249.1 with a resultant
    debt to equity ratio of $1,249.1/$950 = **1.31**.

c. Reported cash flow from operations increased by $154
    million from ($96) million to $58 million. These
    amounts were inflated by the increase in receivables
    sold and should be adjusted by that increase:

    Adjusted CFO 1998 = ($96) − ($115 − $103.3) = ($107.7)
    Adjusted CFO 1999 = $58 − ($153.1 − $115) = $19.9

    After removing the effects of the receivable sales,
    CFO increased by $127.6 million from ($107.7) million
    to $19.9 million. The actual level and trend in CFO is
    considerably lower than the amounts reported.

14.{M}a. All amounts in $ millions

	1997	1998	1999
Receivables reported	$ 664.0	$ 720.0	$ 739.0
Receivables sold	–	38.4	50.0
Adjusted receivables	$ 664.0	$ 758.4	$ 789.0
Average receivables			
as reported		692.0	729.5
adjusted		711.2	773.7
Sales		$4,537.0	$3,867.0
Receivable turnover			
Reported		6.56	5.30
Adjusted		6.38	5.00
# of days receivable			
Reported		56 days	69 days
Adjusted		57 days	73 days
Cash cycle effect		**1 day**	**4 days**

The sale of receivables allowed the company to show an improved receivable turnover and cash cycle; the improvement was more significant for 1999 as the amount of receivables sold increased and sales declined.

b. The effect on the current ratio is minimal as the same amount is added to both numerator and denominator of the ratio and that ratio is close to 1. The debt-to-equity ratio adjustment is more significant in 1999 due to the increase in receivables sold and the lower equity amount.

	1998	1999
Current assets	$ 1,673.0	$ 1,615.0
Current liabilities	1,492.0	1,472.0
Current ratio	**1.121**	**1.097**
Adjusted (add receivables sold)		
Current assets	$ 1,711.4	$ 1,665.0
Current liabilities	1,530.4	1,522.0
Current ratio adjusted	**1.118**	**1.094**
Debt reported	$ 963.0	$ 961.0
Debt adjusted	1,001.4	1,011.0
Equity	572.0	376.0
Debt-to-equity reported	**1.68**	**2.56**
Debt-to-equity adjusted	**1.75**	**2.69**

c. As the calculation below indicates, both the level and trend in CFO are overstated as a result of the sale of receivables.

	1997	1998	1999
CFO as reported	$(113.0)	$ (59.0)	$ (6.0)
Change in receivables sold	---	38.4	11.6
CFO adjusted	$(113.0)	$ (97.4)	$ (17.6)

15.{S}a. The cash from investment amounts are equivalent to the change in the "Receivables sold by Funding to purchaser". (Recall that 1997 was the first year of receivable sales.)

b.

RECEIVABLES	1997	1998	1999
Reported	$ 174.0	$ 169.7	$ 154.1
Add: Receivables sold by Funding to purchaser	37.0	36.8	41.8
Adjusted	$ 211.0	$ 206.5	$ 195.9
Percentage decline	-17.5%	-17.8%	-21.3%

The sale of receivables allowed the company to show receivable balances 17% to 21% less than their actual levels.

c. The sale of receivables should be reported as cash from financing as they are, in effect, borrowings (using receivables as collateral).

16.{S} Aluminum producers that have take-or-pay contracts for energy and/or bauxite have converted significant variable costs into fixed costs. Therefore, their marginal costs are much lower than if these contracts had not been entered into. Under these conditions, aluminum producers will continue production as long as revenue exceeds *marginal costs*, even though they lose money based on *total costs*.

17.{M}a. By transferring receivables to a (unconsolidated) subsidiary, Lucent removed the receivables from its receivable balance and reported them as "Investments," a somewhat different asset category. Analytical adjustment is required to eliminate the artificial reported "improvements" in receivables turnover, the current ratio and the cash cycle.

b. The adjustment requires adding $700 million (in addition to the balance of uncollected receivables) to the 1999 accounts receivable and current assets. The effect is to increase the growth in receivables, reduce the receivable turnover and increase the number of days receivables outstanding. This adjustment reinforces the conclusion (see text page 381) that Lucent's receivables growth outpaced the growth in sales. On the other hand, the adjustment improves the 1999 current ratio.

		REPORTED			ADJUSTED	
	1998	1999	2000		1999	2000
Balance of uncollected receivables	$ 0	$ 625	$ 1,329			
Receivables transferred to QSPE		**700**				
					Adjustment: Add	
					$1,325	*$1,329*
Accounts receivable	7,821	9,097	10,059		**10,422**	11,388
Current assets		19,240	21,490		**20,565**	22,819
Current liabilities		9,150	10,877		9,775	12,206
Sales	24,367	30,617	33,813			
Selected Trends and Ratios						
% Change in sales from 1998		26%	39%		26%	39%
% Change in A/R from 1998		16%	26%		**33%** (24%)	46%
# of days A/R outstanding	117	101	103		**109** (105)	**117** (114)
Current ratio	1.45	2.10	1.98		**2.10** (2.03)	1.87

Note: The bold values indicate which amounts were altered from Exhibit 11-4. The Exhibit 11-4 amounts for those items affected by the adjustment are shown in parentheses.

18.{M}a. Debt should be increased by:

$ 20 million   (present value of operating lease)
    5   (guarantee)
    7   (present value of take-or-pay agreement)
$ 32 million

There is no effect on equity as each obligation is offset by a corresponding asset:
    Leased assets for operating lease
    Receivable for Crockett's obligation to repay debt
    Supply agreement

The recomputed debt-to-equity ratio is:
($12 + $32)/$20 = **2.2X** as compared to .6X before adjustment

b. Additional interest expense is:

Lease (effective interest rate is about 18%)
                                    .18 x $20 = $3.6 million
Bond guarantee   .10 x   5 =   0.5
  Total $ 4.1 million

Before adjustment, the interest expense is $1.0 million and the times interest earned ratio is 5.0, implying EBIT of $5.0 million.

After adjustment, the ratio is:
($5.0 + $4.1)/($1.0 + $4.1) = **1.78X**

No adjustment has been made for the take-or-pay contract, as it does not affect 1993 interest expense. Adjustments in future years will be based on the implicit interest rate of 21%.

c. Reasons for entering into off-balance-sheet obligations:

1. Avoidance of or mitigation of the risk of violating debt covenant restrictions.
2. Leased assets revert to lessor after eight years, limiting risk of obsolescence.
3. Guarantee of Crockett's debt may lower interest costs, increasing profitability of investment.
4. Contract with PEPE secures source of supply and possibly advantageous pricing.

d. Additional information needed for full evaluation:

1. (Lease) Useful life of leased assets; conditions under which lease can be canceled; nature of leased assets.
2. (Guarantee) Financial condition of Crockett; bond covenants.
3. (Take-or-pay) Alternate sources of supply; quantity to be purchased relative to total needs; price provisions of contract.

19.{L}a. As the table below indicates, the declining payment assumption using a 92% declining rate (the average rate over the first five years (2000 - 2004)) is a good approximation for JC Penney. The present value is $3,320; a deviation of one-half of one percent from the stated present value of $3,302. If the constant payment assumption is made, the error is about four percent.

| | PAYMENT ASSUMPTION | |
YEAR	CONSTANT PAYMENT	DECLINING PAYMENT (92%)
2000	$620	$620
2001	568	568
2002	521	521
2003	492	492
2004	454	454
2005	454	418
2006	454	384
2007	454	354
2008	454	325
2009	454	299
2010	454	275
2011	375	253
2012	–	233
2013	–	214
2014	–	197
2015	–	146
Total	$5,754	$5,754
Present Value @ 9.7%	**$3,436**	**$3,320**
% deviation from present value of $3,302	**4.1%**	**0.5%**

11-17

b. **Using only the first year payment**: Payment = $66 and current portion = $16; therefore interest portion = $50 and interest rate = $50/$417 =12%.

Using all payments:
Constant payment assumption implies MLP's of $54 from 2004 through 2017 and $12 in 2018. Equating this payment stream to $417 yields an IRR of 11.8%

For the declining payment assumption, we would use a declining rate of 95%, the average of (2000 - 2004). Using this rate yields an IRR of 10.44%

The rate seems to be between 10.4%-12%. Given that two of the methods yield estimates closer to the high end of the range, using a rate of approximately 11.5% would be an appropriate estimate.

c. The rate used by Sears is somewhat higher than that of J.C. Penney. That may be a function of (1)higher credit rating for Penney, (2)differing risk characteristics of the leased properties, or (3) Sears leases were entered into in periods of higher interest rates.

d. Given the rapid decline over the first four years, we choose to use the declining payment assumption. Using a decline rate of .86 (the average over the first five years) and a discount rate of 11.5% (from part b), the present value of the operating leases is $1,375 million.

20.{M}   Adjusting for the operating lease results in a deterioration of the ratios in each case.

		REPORTED	ADJUSTMENT FOR OPERATING LEASE	ADJUSTED
(i)	Current assets	$28,667		$28,667
	Current liabilities	13,701	$194[*]	13,895
	Current ratio	**2.09**		**2.06**
(ii)	Debt	$18,038	$1,375[**]	$19,413
	Equity	6,839		6,839
	Debt-to-equity ratio	**2.64**		**2.84**
(iii)	Pretax income	$ 2,419		$ 2,419
	Assets (year-end)	36,954	$1,375[**]	38,329
	Pretax ROA	**6.5%**		**6.3%**
(iv)	EBIT	$3,687	$158[†]	$3,845
	Interest	1,268	158[†]	1,426
	Interest coverage	**2.91**		**2.70**

* Year 2000 MLP = $352. Interest portion is equal to 11.5% x $1,325 = $158; Therefore, current portion of debt = $352 − $158 = $194

** Present Value of operating leases as calculated in Problem 19 part d.

† Assumes interest this year (1999) is approximately equal to next year's (2000) interest levels.

Note: No adjustment is made for pretax income, which may be higher or lower depending on the age" of the lease. The earlier (later) in the lease term, expense is higher (lower) for the capital lease. On average the expense is identical. As we do not know the relative age of the leases we assume no change.

21.{S} Sears' MDA reports securitized (credit card) balances sold of $6,579 and $6,626 million in 1999 and 1998 respectively. Adjusting for these balances (in 1999) requires adding $6,579 to accounts receivable and current liabilities (assuming the debt is short-term) and increasing CFO by ($6,626 − $6,579) $47 million. As the table below indicates, the impact on these three ratios is considerable.

		REPORTED	ADJUSTMENT FOR SECURITIZATION	ADJUSTED
(i)	Current assets	$28,667	$6,579	$35,246
	Current liabilities	13,701	6,579	20,280
	Current ratio	**2.09**		**1.74**
(ii)	CFO	$ 3,697	$ 47	$ 3,744
	Current liabilities	13,701	6,579	20,280
	CFO to CL ratio	**0.27**		**0.18**
(iii)	Debt	$18,038	$6,579	$24,617
	Equity	6,839		6,839
	Debt-to-equity ratio	**2.64**		**3.60**

22.{S} The adjusted ratios are poorer than those based on Sears' reported data. The adjustment for securitization of receivables accounts for far more of the impact than the operating leases.

		REPORTED	ADJUSTMENTS	ADJUSTED
(i)	Current assets	$28,667	$6,579	$35,246
	Current liabilities	13,701	$6,579 + $194	20,474
	Current ratio	**2.09**		**1.72**
(ii)	Debt	$18,038	$6,579+$1,375	$25,992
	Equity	6,839		6,839
	Debt-to-equity ratio	**2.64**		**3.80**

Note: See problems 11-19, 11-20, and 11-21 for explanation of these adjustments

23. {M}a. Using the constant rate assumption (MLP's of $59 million from 2004 - 2017 and $8 million in 2018), the implicit interest rate is **4.19%**.

Note that Texaco has not guaranteed all of this lease. The total present value of the guaranteed portion of the lease is approximately ($336/44%) $764 million.

   b. The rate is somewhat lower than the 5% - 5.5% rate calculated for Texaco in the chapter (page 385).

   c. Equilon may have less debt (in relation to their assets) than Texaco, or the nature of its business (or of the leased assets) may be operationally less risky. The leases may have been entered into when interest rates were especially low.

24. {M}

		1st Year	**9th Year**
(i)	Assets	Higher	Higher
(ii)	Revenues	Higher	Lower
(iii)	Expenses	Higher	Lower
(iv)	Asset turnover ratio	Higher	Lower
(v)	Interest income	Higher	Higher
(vi)	Cost of goods sold	Higher	No effect
(vii)	Net income	Higher	Lower
(viii)	Retained earnings	Higher	Higher
(ix)	Taxes paid	No effect	No effect
(x)	Post-tax ROA	Higher	Lower
(xi)	Cash from operations	Higher	Lower
(xii)	Investment cash flow	Lower	Higher

Assets are higher because inventory is replaced with (higher) receivables because of the recognition of manufacturing profit. Assets remain higher throughout the lease term.

Revenues are higher in Year 1 as the sales-type lease recognizes a sale whereas the operating lease method does not. In later years, interest revenue from the sales-type lease should be lower than lease revenue for the operating lease. This effect is more pronounced over time; in year 9, interest income is low given the small remaining receivable. The revenue effect increases the asset turnover ratio in the first year. But the revenue effect reduces turnover in the ninth year.

Expenses are higher in year 1 due to the recognition of cost of goods sold. In later years, there is no expense for the sales-type lease; the operating lease method reports depreciation expense in every year, however.

Initial period income and income-related ratios are higher for the sales-type lease because the sale (and income) is recognized at the inception of the lease. In later years, however, income is higher for the operating lease.

Income taxes paid are the same since the lease cannot be considered a completed sale for tax purposes.

Cash from operations is higher for the first year due to recognition of the sale (the investment in the lease is classified as an investing cash outflow). In later years the operating lease method shows higher cash from operations as rental income exceeds the interest income recorded for the sales-type lease (income taxes paid are the same).

[See Exhibit 11-8 and the accompanying text for further explanation of these effects.]

25.{L}a. The present value of the minimum lease payments receivable of $170,271 (at 10%, the lower of lessee and lessor rates) is more than 90% of the fair market value of $185,250. Therefore, the lessee, Baldes, should capitalize the lease. It would be useful to know whether the lessee has guaranteed the residual value of the leased asset.

b. Leased assets $ 170,271

Long-term lease obligation   167,298
Current portion of lease obligation   2,973
   Total lease obligation $ 170,271

Note that there are no income or cash flow statement effects at the inception of the lease.

c. (i) Balance sheet effects of capital lease:

	01/01/01	12/31/01	12/31/02
Leased assets	$170,271	$170,271	$170,271
Accumulated depreciation	0	(8,514)	(17,028)
Leased assets (net)	$170,271	$161,757	$153,243
Current portion of lease obligation	$ 2,973	$ 3,270	$ 3,597
Long-term portion of lease obligation	167,298	164,028	160,431
Total lease obligation	$170,271	$167,298	$164,028

No impact on balance sheet if operating lease method applied. [Deferred tax assets reflecting the difference between total expense under the two methods would also be reported.]

(ii) Income statement effects of capital lease:

Years ended December 31	2001	2002
Interest expense[1]	$ 17,027	$ 16,730
Depreciation expense[2]	8,514	8,514
Total expense	$ 25,541	$ 25,244

[1] Interest expense for: 2001 = .10 x $170,271
                          2002 = .10 x $167,298
[2] Deprecation expense = $170,271/20 for each year
  The income statement would show lease expense of $20,000 each year under the operating lease method.

(iii) Statement of cash flow effects of capital lease:

Years ended December 31	2001	2002
Cash from operations	$(17,027)	$(16,730)
Financing cash flow	(2,973)	(3,270)

The operating lease method reports $20,000 cash outflow from operations for each year.

d.	As in part A, the PV of the MLPs is more than 90% of the fair market value, permitting capitalization. However, for the lessor to capitalize the lease, revenue recognition criteria must be satisfied as well. These conditions are:

(i) Collectibility of MLPs is reasonably assured, and

(ii) There are no significant uncertainties regarding the amount of costs yet to be incurred by the lessor or other obligations under the provisions of the lease agreement.

To evaluate these issues, information would be needed regarding the financial condition of Baldes and any remaining obligations of Malbec.

e.	The operating lease method has no effect on Malbec's balance sheet at the inception of the lease since the lessor has merely entered into a rental arrangement - an executory contract.

f.	Sales-type lease reporting by lessor:

Malbec's gross investment in the lease:
MLPs ($20,000 x 20)	$ 400,000
Unguaranteed residual value	5,500
Gross investment	$ 405,500

Net investment:
Present value of 20 payments at 10%	$ 170,271
PV of $5,500, 20 periods hence at 10%	818
Net investment	$ 171,089

Unearned income: $405,500 - $171,089 = $ 234,411

Journal entry at inception (1/1/01):
Gross investment	$ 405,500	
Cost of goods sold	149,182	
Sales revenue		$170,271
Inventory		150,000
Unearned income		234,411

Balance Sheet Effects, January 1, 2001:
Inventory (reduction due to sale)	$(150,000)

Gross investment in sales-type lease	$ 405,500
Less: unearned interest income	(234,411)
Net investment	$ 171,089

Income Statement Effects, Year Ended December 31, 2001:

Sales revenue	$ 170,271
Cost of goods sold	(149,182)
Income effect	$ 21,089

g.

Balance Sheet Effects:	12/31/01	12/31/02
Sales-type lease:		
Net investment in lease, current	$ 3,180	$ 3,498
Net investment in lease, long-term	159,518	156,020
Operating lease:		
Assets under lease	$150,000	$150,000
Accumulated depreciation	(7,225)	(14,450)
Net assets	$142,775	$135,550

Income Statement Effects:	12/31/01	12/31/02
Sales-type lease:		
Sales revenue	$ 170,271	$ ---
Cost of goods sold	(149,182)	---
Sales profit	$ 21,089	---
Interest income	17,109	$ 16,820
Pretax income	$ 38,198	$ 16,820
Operating lease:		
Rental income	$ 20,000	$ 20,000
Depreciation expense	(7,225)	(7,225)
Pretax income	$ 12,775	$ 12,775

Cash Flow Statement Effects:	12/31/01	12/31/02
Sales-type lease:		
Cash from operations:		
Sales profit	$ 21,089	$ ---
Inventory reduction	150,000	---
Interest income	17,109	16,820
Cash from operations	$ 188,198	$ 16,820
Investment cash flow:		
Net investment in lease	$(171,089)	$ ---
Reduction in net investment	2,891	3,180
Investment cash flow	$(168,198)	$ 3,180
Net cash flow	$ 20,000	$ 20,000
Operating lease:		
Rental income	$ 20,000	$ 20,000
Cash from operations	$ 20,000	$ 20,000

Note: There is no effect on investment cash flow when the operating lease method is used.

CFO - indirect method:	12/31/01	12/31/02
Sales-type lease:		
Pretax income	$ 38,198	$ 16,820
Inventory reduction	150,000	---
Cash from operations	$ 188,198	$ 16,820
Operating lease:		
Pretax income	$ 12,775	$ 12,775
Depreciation expense	7,225	7,225
Cash from operations	$ 20,000	$ 20,000

Case 11-1 Solution

Estimated time to complete this case is 2½ to 3 hrs.

This case demonstrates that, when examining a company's OBS activities, it is sometimes necessary to go beyond footnote data. When a company uses a variety of on- and off-balance sheet financing techniques, and carefully structured (generally less than 50% voting interest) investments in other entities whose operations are integral to those of the investor, the analyst must obtain as much detail as possible on those OBS activities and investments to conduct a complete analysis of the company.

Information about Texaco's affiliates was estimated in the chapter, using data from Texaco's footnotes. However, by examining the affiliates' financial statements, a more complete measure of their debt can be obtained. For example, the OBS debt of Caltex's affiliates can be added to Caltex's debt and consequently added to Texaco's share of the OBS debt of its affiliates. Measuring Texaco's debt requires examining the financial statements of its affiliates as well as its own.

1. The adjustments made to Texaco's "debt" in the chapter (see Exhibit 11-7) as a result of its OBS activities are listed in the first line of the table below. In order to calculate Texaco's ROA and interest coverage (times interest earned) ratios, adjustments must also be made to Texaco's assets and interest expense to reflect the effects of these OBS activities.

	Reported	Adjusted for					Adjusted
		Affiliates	Operating Leases	Preferred Shares	Guarantees	Throughput Agreement	
Debt	$ 7,647	$ 2,638	$ 864	$ 602	$ 336	$ 173	$ 12,260
Interest	504	171	43	34	22	11	786
Assets	28,972	7,554	864	–	336	173	37,899
EBIT	2,283	–	43	–	–	11	2,337
Equity	12,042	No Adjustment					12,042
Ratios							
Debt/equity	0.64						1.02
ROA	7.88%						6.17%
Interest coverage	4.53						2.97

Adjustments to Texaco's interest expense

Texaco's reported debt and interest expense equal $7,647 million and $504 million respectively, reflecting an interest rate of approximately 6.5%. Absent any other information we use 6.5% to calculate the interest expense on the adjusted debt for *affiliates*, *guarantees and throughput agreements*. For *operating leases*, we use 5% (as discussed on page 385 in the text.) *Dividend* payments on the preferred shares are $34 million (see Exhibit 11-6).

Adjustments to Texaco's assets

Affiliates: Currently Texaco carries its investment in affiliates on a "net asset" basis. Texaco's share of its affiliates current and noncurrent assets is shown in Exhibit 11-6 as ($3,796 + $9,321) $13,117 million. To reflect this amount, Texaco's assets must be increased by $7,554 million ($13,117 million less the net equity of $5,563 million).

Operating leases, guarantees and throughput agreements all reflect asset rights "purchased" by Texaco. Assets are increased by the present value of the debt.

Preferred shares: The adjustment to debt made for preferred shares is not strictly speaking an OBS adjustment, but a reclassification of minority interest to debt. For that reason, assets are unchanged.

Effect on ratios: The resultant effect on Texaco's ratios is significant. ROA is reduced by almost 25% from 7.88% to 6.02% and interest coverage deteriorates by 35% from 4.53 to 2.91.

Texaco's share of Caltex: Prior to proceeding, we note (for purposes of question 4) that Caltex (owned 50% by Texaco) is included as one of Texaco's affiliates. The analysis above and that carried out in the chapter implies that Texaco's share of Caltex's debt, interest expense and assets equals:[1]

Debt	=	.5 x $ 2,639	= $ 1,320
Interest expense	=	6.5% x 1,320	= 86
Assets	=	.5 x 10,309	= 5,155

---

[1] These data are based on Exhibit 11-6. For debt we use *Caltex's noncurrent liabilities* and for assets we use the sum of Caltex's *current and noncurrent assets*.

Adjustments to Texaco's EBIT

The interest portion of payments made for operating leases and throughput agreements must be added back to arrive at adjusted EBIT.[2]

2. a. and b.

Caltex Capitalization Table ($millions) and Selected Ratios

Capitalization, December 31,	1999
Current portion of debt	$ 1,588
Long-term debt & capital leases	1,054
Total debt	$ 2,642
Stockholders' equity	4,275
Total capitalization	$ 6,917
Total debt/equity	**0.62**
Total assets	$10,309
Pretax income	780
Interest expense	152
EBIT	$ 932
ROA (EBIT/assets)	**9.04%**
Times interest earned	**6.13**

Note (for purposes of question 4) that these data imply Texaco's share of Caltex's

Debt	=	.5 x $ 2,642	= $1,321
Interest expense	=	.5 x 152	= 76
Assets	=	.5 x 10,309	= 5,155

---

[2] For operating leases, the entire lease payment is an operating expense, deducted before arriving at EBIT. Our adjustment capitalizes the lease. Therefore EBIT increases by the interest component (the excess of the lease payment over depreciation; see text page 369).

3. a. The adjustments for Caltex's OBS activities are similar to those made for Texaco (in the text).
    (i) *share of affiliate debt:* We assume that "other liabilities" are primarily long-term debt requiring an adjustment of $937.
    (ii) *operating leases:* Using an assumed rate of 6%[3] the present value of Caltex's operating leases is approximately $167 million.
    (iii) *purchase commitment (similar to throughput agreement):* The present value of these payments of $700 million per year through 2007 (discounted at 6%) is $3,585 million.

b.

| | Reported | Adjusted for | | | Adjusted |
		Affiliates	Operating Leases	Purchase Commitments	
Debt	$ 2,642	$ 937	$ 167	$ 3,585	$ 7,331
Interest expense	152	56	10	215	433
Assets	10,309	2,753*	167	3,585	16,814
EBIT	932	–	10	215	1,157
Equity	4,275	No adjustment			4,275
Ratios					
Debt/equity	0.62				1.71
ROA	9.04%				6.88%
Times interest earned	6.13				2.67

*   From Exhibit 11C-1: Caltex's share of current assets plus other assets less equity in affiliates = $1,535 + $3,287 − $2,069 = $2,753

> *Note (for purposes of part 4) that these data imply Texaco's share of Caltex's*
> | | | | |
> |---|---|---|---|
> | Debt | = | .5 x $ $7,331 = | $ 3,665 |
> | Interest expense | = | .5 x   433 = | 216 |
> | Assets | = | .5 x   16,814 = | 8,407 |

---

[3] 6% approximates Caltex's average reported interest rate ($152/$2,642).

c. The adjustments to Caltex are highly significant as
    Caltex's solvency and profitability ratios deteriorate
    considerably. As a result of the adjustments,
    especially the purchase commitment, the debt to equity
    ratio almost triples, ROA decreases by almost 25% and
    interest coverage is more than halved.

4. The results accumulated throughout the solution thus far
    are summarized below:

Texaco's share of Caltex based on information from:	*Texaco's footnotes*	*50% of Caltex's reported data*	*50% of Caltex after adjusting for Caltex's OBS activities*
Source	*Question 1*	*Question 2*	*Question 3*
Debt	$1,320	$ 1,321	3,665
Interest expense	86	76	216
Assets	5,155	5,155	8,407

The estimates derived from questions 1 and 2 of Texaco's
share of Caltex's assets and debt are very close.[4] Caltex's
actual interest expense is lower, reflecting Caltex's lower
interest rate. However, when we include Caltex's OBS
activities, our measures of Caltex's debt, interest
expense, and assets increase considerably.

The following table combines the adjustments for Texaco's OBS
activities with those of Caltex to produce a more complete
measure of Texaco's leverage, ROA, and interest coverage ratios.

---

[4] The closeness of the debt estimate is worth noting as the sources for the
estimates differ considerably. For part 1, we use noncurrent liabilities as
an estimate of debt. This approximation implicitly assumes that the non-debt
portion of noncurrent liabilities equals the debt portion of current
liabilities. In the case of Caltex, this assumption is correct as the result
is equivalent to Caltex's actual current and noncurrent debt obtained in part
2.

	Texaco As Reported	Adjusted For Texaco OBS Activities (includes Caltex as reported)	Adjustment For Caltex OBS Activities	Fully Adjusted
Debt	$ 7,647	$ 12,260	$2,345	$14,605
Interest expense	504	786	130	916
Assets	28,972	37,899	3,252	41,151
EBIT	$ 2,283	$ 2,337		$ 2,337
Equity	12,042	12,042		12,042
Ratios				
Debt/equity	**0.64**	**1.02**		**1.21**
ROA	**7.88%**	**6.17%**		**5.68%**
Times interest earned	**4.53**	**2.97**		**2.51**

Columns 1 and 2 of the above table are taken directly from question 1 and reflect Texaco's reported data and the data after adjustment for Texaco's OBS activities respectively. Column 3 shows the adjustment for Caltex's OBS activities that need to be attributed to Texaco to make the data complete. This adjustment is equal to the difference between 50% of Caltex's reported data and data adjusted for its OBS activities (shown above); i.e.

```
Asset adjustment    = $ 3,665 - $1,320 = $2,345
Interest adjustment =      216 -     86 =    130
Debt adjustment     =    8,407 -  5,155 =  3,252
```

5. It would be useful to know whether Caltex's affiliates, in turn, have their own off-balance-sheet liabilities. If so, even the ratios in question 4 are incomplete.

It would also be helpful to know more about Caltex transactions with Texaco (and with the other 50% stockholder, Chevron) to obtain a better idea of the role that Caltex plays. Caltex appears to be more than an investment; how much more we can't tell from the data provided. In particular, it would be helpful to know whether Caltex's financial risks are shared equally by the two owners or whether they relate to particular operations of one of the two parent companies.

6. *Adjustment to Texaco's Debt*

Based on the table below Texaco's debt should be increased by $1,104 million ($1,053 + $51) to reflect Equilon and Motiva's respective reported and OBS debt.

	Per Exhibit 11C-2		TEXACO'S SHARE	
	EQUILON	MOTIVA	44% OF EQUILON	32.5% OF MOTIVA
Reported on Balance Sheet				
Short term debt	$ 2,157	$ 363		
Long term debt	5	1,451		
Total	$ 2,162	$ 1,814	$ 951	$ 590
OBS adjustments:				
Affiliates[1]	$ 692	$ —	$ 304	$ —
Operating leases[2]	717	439	—[4]	143
Throughput agreements[3]	297	—	131	—
Total reported and OBS	$ 3,868	$ 2,253	$ 1,386	$ 733
Amount included in Texaco's OBS debt per Texaco's footnotes[5]	$ 735	$2,095	$ 323	$ 681
Additional adjustment to Texaco debt			$1,053	$ 51

Explanations:

[1] From Exhibit 11C-2, Equilon's share of affiliate's noncurrent liabilities.

[2] Present value of operating lease payments (from Exhibit 11C-2) discounted at 5% (Equilon and Motiva's interest rate – see below).

[3] From Exhibit 11C-2

[4] No adjustment made for Equilon's operating lease as it is already included as $336 million of Texaco's Financial Guarantees (see Exhibit 11-6, P. 385)

[5] Per Exhibit 11-6, Equilon and Motiva's noncurrent liabilities.

Adjustment to Texaco's Interest Expense

The average interest rate on debt is 5% for both Equilon ($115/$2,162) and Motiva ($94/$1814). Thus, the adjustment to interest expense is $55 million (5% x $1,104).

Adjustment to Texaco's Assets

Assets must be increased by
(i) $274 million to reflect Motiva's operating leases and Equilon's throughput agreements.
(ii) Additionally an adjustment is required to reflect Equilon's affiliates. That adjustment is equal to 44% of Equilon's share (from Exhibit 11C-2) of current assets plus other assets less equity in affiliates i.e. 44% x ($750 + $1,097 - $692)= $508 million.

The total adjustment to assets, therefore, is $782 million.

The last column in the following table shows all adjustments made for the OBS activities of Texaco and all of its equity method affiliates.

	Texaco As Reported	Adjusted For Texaco OBS Activities	Adjusted For Caltex OBS Activities	Adjusted For Affiliate OBS Activities
Debt	$ 7,647	$ 12,260	$14,605	$15,709
Interest expense	504	786	916	971
Assets	28,972	37,899	41,151	41,933
EBIT	$ 2,283	$ 2,337	$ 2,337	$ 2,337
Equity	12,042	12,042	12,042	12,042
Ratios				
Debt/equity	**0.64**	**1.02**	**1.21**	**1.30**
ROA	**7.88%**	**6.17%**	**5.68%**	**5.57%**
Times interest earned	**4.53**	**2.97**	**2.51**	**2.41**

The successive adjustments results in a steady deterioration of Texaco's ratios as reflected below:

Percentage Change In Ratio	Effect of		
	All Footnotes	Texaco Footnotes Only	Affiliate Footnotes
Debt/equity	105%	60%	45%
ROA	-29%	-22%	- 7%
Times interest earned	-47%	-34%	-13%

Overall, the adjustments increased Texaco's debt-to-equity ratio by 105% from 0.64 to 1.30. Using footnote data only from Texaco's annual report resulted in a 60% increase from 0.64 to 1.02. Going the 'extra step' and examining the financial statement footnotes of Texaco's affiliates for OBS debt resulted in an additional 45% increase in the debt-to-equity ratio to 1.30.

Similarly, the ROA and the interest coverage ratios showed significant deterioration using only Texaco footnote data. Adjustments using data from the affiliates' financial statements resulted in further ratio deterioration.

Chapter 12 – Solutions

1.{S}a. The effect of an increase in the discount rate:

   (i) The projected benefit obligation (PBO) will decrease in the year of the change because the present value of a stream of cash declines when discounted at a higher rate.

   (ii) Assuming that the rate change is applied at the end of the year, it will have no effect on pension cost in the year of the change.

   (iii) The interest component of the pension cost will increase in the year following the change because a higher rate will be applied to the (lower) PBO. However, the service cost component will be lower due to the higher discount rate and this effect may overwhelm the effect on the interest cost. Note that in a mature plan, the interest cost effect may be greater than the impact on the service cost.

   b. The effect of an increase in the assumed rate of compensation growth:

   (i) The PBO will increase in the year of the change because the benefits are expected to increase.

   (ii) Assuming that the rate change is applied at the end of the year, it will have no effect on pension cost in the year of the change.

   (iii) Pension cost will increase in the year following the change because both interest cost (based on the higher PBO) and service cost will rise as PBO increases.

   c. The effect of an increase in the expected rate of return on plan assets:

   (i) The increase will have no effect on the PBO because it does not change the benefits provided by the plan.

(ii) Pension cost will decline in the year of the change because a higher return will be deducted in computing the net pension cost.

(iii) Pension cost will decline in the year following the increase for the reason cited in answer c. (ii).

2.{L}a. The most likely reason for the actuarial loss in 1998 was the decrease in the discount rate from 7.25% in 1997 to 6.75% in 1998, whereas the 1999 gain likely reflects changes in one or more actuarial assumptions because neither the discount rate nor the rate of compensation increases was changed in that year.

b. The amortization of prior service cost rose every year during the 1997-1999 period because the company has recorded plan amendments increasing the PBO in each of those years. The amortization of those annual increases generated successively higher amortization amounts each year.

c. *Note*: All amounts in the tables that follow are in $millions

Beginning balance of unrecognized net gain	$ 860.223
Amortization of net gain	(10.270)
Actuarial gain	13.833
Deferred ROA (actual - expected ROA)	153.493
Ending balance of unrecognized net gain	$1,017.279

d.

Return on Plan Assets		
At October 31	*1998*	*1999*
Plan assets (open)	$2,088.419	$2,337.713
Actual ROA	291.895	324.716
Actual % ROA	13.98%	13.89%
Expected % ROA	9.50%	8.75%

The actual return on plan assets was 13.98% in 1998 compared to the assumed 9.5% and the plan earned 13.89% in 1999 whereas the company assumed 8.75%. The actual performance was better in both years.

e. Service cost rose in 1998 despite fewer employees because the discount rate was lowered from 7.25% in 1997 to 6.75% in 1998. The lower discount rate results in a higher present value of benefits earned by the employees.

f. The expected ROA declined from 9.75% in 1997 to 9.50% in 1998 and to 8.75% in 1999. If Westvaco had continued to use the 1997 rate (9.75%), the pension credit would have been higher than reported in 1999. The reported expected ROA implies a fair value of plan assets of $1,956.83 million (Expected ROA of $171.223 at 8.75%). Had the company continued to use the 1997 expected ROA of 9.75%, expected ROA would have been $19.568 million higher (1% of $1,956.83 million) and the pension credit also higher by that amount or $101.848 million ($82.280 + $19.568). Note that Westvaco reported pension assets at October 31, 1998 of $2,088 million, nearly $132 million higher than the amount used to compute the expected return. Westvaco uses the market-related value[1] rather than actual market value to compute the expected return.

g. Westvaco reported increasing pension credits during the 1997 to 1999 period. In addition, the answer to the previous question (f) showed that had the company continued to use higher expected ROA, those credits would have been significantly higher. Westvaco may have changed the assumed ROA to deflect concerns about rising pension credits. The changes also improved the quality of earnings and created a "bank" of unamortized gains that protected the company against future actual returns below the expected returns.[2]

h. The amortization of the transition asset has consistently been $ 6.94 million a year. On October 31, 1999 Westvaco reported an unrecognized net transition asset of $ 15.966 million implying amortization for the next three years as follows:

2000	$ 6.940	
2001	6.940	
2002	2.086	(remainder)
Total	$15.966	

---

[1] See glossary on page 402 and footnote 31 on page 419.

[2] Late in 2002, MeadWestvaco (Westvaco had merged with Mead) stated that (in contrast to many companies) it expected the 2003 pension credit to be similar to the 2002 credit. Prior year gains apparently were sufficient to offset recent year negative returns.

i.   Forecast fiscal 2000 pension cost:

$ in millions Components of pension cost	Forecast 2000	Reported 2000
Service cost	$ 30.414	$ 28.638
Interest cost	75.829	74.199
Expected ROA	(228.751)	(187.501)
Amortization of transition asset	(6.940)	(6.940)
Amortization of prior service cost	5.500	5.498
Amortization of net gain	(12.385)	(22.141)
Reported pension cost (credit)	**$(136.333)**	**$(108.247)**

Service cost increased 15% in 1998 and 7.5% in 1999 despite a declining number of employees (see P. 35 of annual report). The increased discount rate was one factor is that increase. The lower assumed compensation growth rate in 1998 would have reduced service cost. We forecast service cost to increase 5% - the assumed rate of increase in compensation.

Interest cost is based on the discount rate assumption used in 1999 to calculate the PBO. Therefore, interest cost for 2000 is forecasted to be 6.75% x $1,123.389 million = $75.83 million.

Expected ROA is equal to plan assets or $2,614.295 million times 8.75% = $228.751 million. As discussed in part f, Westvaco uses the market-related value of pension assets. If that amount were obtained from management, it should be used to compute the expected ROA.

Amortization of net transition asset remains constant at $6.94 million (see answer to part h). Amortization of prior service cost is expected to increase only slightly because of the minimal addition to prior service cost in 1999.

Amortization of the net gain increased significantly in 1999 over 1998. The corridor method (footnote 21 on page 415 in text) would appear to require amortization of the excess of the opening unrecognized gain over 10% of opening assets (as assets exceed the PBO):

Fiscal year	1999	2000
Opening unrecognized gain	$ 860,223	$1,017,279
Less: 10% of opening assets	(233,771)	(261,429)
Amortizable amount	$ 628,451	$ 757,850

However fiscal 1999 amortization of $10.27 million implies an amortization period of 61.2 years, improbably long. Lacking any better information, however, we use that same amortization period to forecast 2000 amortization of $12.385 million.

The reported fiscal 2000 pension credit was $108 million, $28 million below our estimate. The two principal differences were the expected ROA and amortization of unrealized gain. With better information about these components (which management may have been willing to supply) our forecast would likely have been very accurate.

j.

At October 31	1998	1999
Service cost	$ 26.934	$ 28.966
Interest cost	71.293	71.714
Recurring cost	**$ 98.227**	**$ 100.680**
Nonrecurring costs:		
Actuarial (gain) loss	24.205	(13.833)
Plan amendments	2.469	0.380
Gross pension cost	**$ 124.901**	**$ 87.227**
Actual ROA (gain)	(291.895)	(324.716)
Nonsmoothed cost (credit)	**$(166.994)**	**$(237.489)**

k.   Pension plan cash flows:

Benefits paid	**$ 44.080**	**$ 49.797**
Employer contributions	1.479	1.663

(i)

Reported pension cost (credit)	**$ (55.337)**	**$ (82.280)**

Westvaco reported increasing pension *credits* in 1998 and 1999 in contrast to increasing recurring *costs* (sum of service and interest costs). The recurring cost shows that the company continues to generate costs of providing pension benefits. Actuarial gains and plan amendments increased the gross pension cost in 1998 but an actuarial loss and a much lower impact of amendments lowered the gross pension cost in 1999. Westvaco changed actuarial assumptions and held the line on benefits in 1999.

However, both the nonsmoothed credit and pension credit are a result of the investment performance of the pension plan.

(ii) Benefits paid to retirees increased in 1999 but by less than the increase in recurring costs. Benefits paid reflect the growth in the number of retirees, which may exceed the growth in current employees (which drives recurring costs).

Employer contributions are nearly minimal relative to both recurring and gross pension cost measures. Contributions remained low because of the overfunded plan status, helped by investment performance of the plan.

1.

Pension Plan Status At October 31	1998	1999
Plan assets	$2,337.713	$2,614.295
Projected benefit obligation	1,084.468	1,123.389
Funded status — surplus	**$1,253.245**	**$1,490.906**
Unrecognized net actuarial (gain) loss	(860.223)	(1,017.279)
Unrecognized prior service cost (credit)	52.111	47.018
Unrecognized net transition (asset) obligation	(22.906)	(15.966)
Net prepaid benefit on balance sheet	**$ 422.227**	**$ 504.679**
Difference between funded status and amount recognized on balance sheet = balance sheet adjustment	$ 831.018	$ 986.227

For a going concern, the balance sheet should reflect the economic status of the plan (plan assets at fair value less the PBO), or a surplus of $1,253.25 million in 1998 and $1,490.906 million in 1999. The difference between these amounts and those currently recognized on the balance sheet should be shown as a pension asset and added to equity. For 1998 (1999), the difference is $831.018 ($986.227) million.

m. The principal source of the difference ($155.21 million) is the unrecognized portion ($153.493 million - see part c.) of the 1999 increase in the plan assets due to the actual return on plan assets.

3.{L}a. The most likely reason for the actuarial loss of $354 million in 1998 was the decrease in the discount rate from 7.00% in 1997 to 6.80% in 1998. The lower discount rate increases the PBO, creating an actuarial loss.

b. The PBO includes both U.S. and international plans. The discount rate used for international plans decreased from 5.3% to 5.1%, increasing the PBO; the rate of compensation increase for these plans rose from 3.4% to 3.7%, also increasing the PBO. These two factors result in actuarial losses.

The increase in the U.S. discount rate from 6.8% in 1998 to 7.5% in 1999 would have lowered the PBO resulting in an actuarial gain.

c. The reconciliations of both the PBO and the plan assets include exchange rate effects because Pfizer has pension plans in its foreign operations that have currencies other than the dollar, the reporting currency of Pfizer. The direction of the change tells us whether the foreign currencies have strengthened or weakened relative to the dollar.

d. Pfizer's balance sheet reports an accrued benefit liability because the fair value of the assets of one or more of the company's pension plans is less than the benefit obligation of those plans. GAAP requires separate disclosure of the accrued obligation and any prepaid benefit on plans with a surplus. Netting of the obligation and the prepaid costs is not permitted because there is no legal right of offset, i.e., it is unlikely that the surplus in one plan can be used to offset the liability of another plan.

e. The amounts reported in accumulated other comprehensive income and the intangible pension asset represent the minimum liability adjustment or the difference between the balance sheet liability and the shortfall calculated as the accumulated benefit obligation less the fair value of plan assets.

f. *Note*: All amounts in the tables that follow are in $millions

Return on plan assets			
December 31	1997	1998	1999
Opening balance of plan assets	$2,410	$2,793	$3,194
Actual ROA	491	530	464
Actual % ROA	20.37%	18.98%	14.53%
Expected ROA	10.00%	10.00%	10.00%

g. Pfizer assumed a ROA of 10% in each of the three years while reporting higher actual returns. The assumed ROA should reflect the long-run expected ROA while the actual returns are affected by market conditions in a given year. Pfizer is using a relatively conservative assumption given the actual returns for these three years. However, those returns reflect strong equity markets; this assumed ROA may have to change to reflect future market conditions that are less favorable.

h. The lower foreign rates reflect lower actual and expected inflation in foreign countries relative to expectations and experience in the U.S.

i.

At December 31	1997	1998	1999
Service cost	$105	$151	$169
+Interest cost	145	181	192
= **Recurring cost**	**$250**	**$332**	**$361**
Nonrecurring costs:			
+Actuarial loss	240	354	87
+Plan amendments	274	15	13
= **Gross pension cost**	**$764**	**$701**	**$461**
+Actual ROA (gain)	(491)	(530)	(464)
= **Nonsmoothed cost (credit)**	**$273**	**$171**	**$ (3)**

j.

	1997	1998	1999
Reported pension cost	**$ 73**	**$139**	**$112**
Benefits paid	107	165	206
Employer contributions	50	63	76

Although nonsmoothed pension cost decreased each year, Pfizer's reported pension cost increased over the same period. This pattern was consistent with both benefits paid as well as contributions.

k.   On a going concern basis, the economic status of Pfizer's balance sheet is the difference between the plan assets and the PBO. As of December 31, 1999 that amount reflected a surplus of $117 million.

Pension Plan Status	December 31,1999
Plan assets	$3,528
Projected benefit obligation	3,411
Funded status - surplus	$ 117
Unrecognized net transition asset	(4)
Unrecognized net gains	(75)
Unrecognized prior service cost	240
Amount recognized on Balance Sheet	$ 278

However, as Pfizer was required to record a minimum liability adjustment as of December 1999, the $278 million was not reported as a net pension asset. Rather Pfizer reported the following on its balance sheet:

Prepaid pension cost	$ 537 million
Accrued pension liability	(655)
Net pension liability	$(118)
Intangible asset	79
Accumulated comprehensive income	317
	$278

Thus, the following adjustments are required
   1. Pension liability should be decreased by $235 million [$117 − (−$118)]. As a result, the balance sheet will reflect a net pension asset of $117 million to reflect the $117 million surplus.
   2. Remove the intangible asset of $79 million

The net effect of these adjustments is:
       Decrease net pension liability $ 235 million
       Decrease intangible asset $ 79 million
       Increase equity   ($235-$79) $ 156 million

1.

Components of Pension Cost	1998	1999	Forecast 2000
Service cost	$151	$169	**$177**
Interest cost	181	192	**215**
Expected ROA	(249)	(275)	**(305)**
Amortization of net transition asset	(6)	(5)	**(4)**
Amortization of prior service cost	24	19	**18**
Amortization of net gain	10	12	**-**
Curtailments and settlements	28	0	**-**
Net pension cost	$139	$112	**$ 101**

Forecasting pension data for Pfizer is complicated by the fact that data for U.S. and international plans are combined. Our computations for each component follow.

Service cost: Pfizer has been adding employees (see Financial Summary on page 62 of 1999 annual report). Salary increases also should increase service cost. Countering these effects is the effect of changes in assumptions (see part b) that reduce the service cost for 2000. We assume a 5% net increase in service cost

Interest cost: PBO x average discount rate = $3,411 X (7.5% + 5.1%)/2 = $215 million. [Using the average discount rate for 1999 produces the reported interest cost for that year.]

Expected ROA: Assets X average ROA = $3,528 X (10.0% + $7.3%)/2 = $305 million. [Using the average ROA for 1999 approximates the expected return reported for that year.]

Amortization of transition asset: as Pfizer's remaining transition asset is $4 million at year-end 1999 we assume full amortization in 2000.

Amortization of prior service cost: Pfizer appears to amortize PSC over 13 years so that 2000 amortization would equal $240/13 = $18 million.

Amortization of net gain or loss: As Pfizer has a small unrealized gain, we would expect no amortization in 2000. The 1999 loss amortization probably relates to underfunded plans. As we lack the required data, we make no assumption about 2000.

Curtailments and settlements: we assume zero absent any information that plan curtailments or settlements are expected.

4.{M}a.   The discount rate used to calculate pension expense must be the one in effect at the end of the previous year used to calculate the PBO. To calculate the PBO, Ford used a discount rate of 6.25% at the end of 1998 and 7.75% at the end of 1999 resulting in the use of the 6.25% (7.75%) rate to calculate pension expense in 1999 (2000). The discount rate of 7.50% used to compute the PBO at December 31, 2000 would be used for 2001 pension expense.

b.   The effect of the 2000 discount rate changes on 2000 and 2001:

(i)   The decrease in the PBO discount rate to 7.50% in 2000 from 7.75% used in 1999 will raise the service cost in 2001. It had no effect on 2000 service cost.

(ii)   The decrease in the 2000 PBO discount rate does not affect the 2000 interest cost because that amount is calculated as the 2000 beginning PBO times the discount rate in effect at the end of 1999. However, the 2000 decrease in discount rate will result in a higher beginning 2001 PBO and 2001 interest cost must be calculated applying the lower rate to a higher PBO increasing the reported 2001 interest cost.

(iii)   As the answers to (i) and (ii) show, there was no effect on net pension cost in 2000. As both service and interest costs will rise in 2001, net pension cost should increase. In addition the 2000 decrease in discount rate results in an actuarial loss in 2000 that will reduce the amortization of unrecognized gain in 2001. (See question 5b for our forecast of 2001 pension cost for U.S. plans.)

(iv)   The lower 2000 discount rate increased the PBO in 2000 and (assuming no further assumption change) in 2001 as well.

c.

$ millions	1999	2000
Beginning balance - PBO	$ 33,003	$ 31,846
Reported discount rate	6.25%	7.75%
Estimated interest cost	*$ 2,063*	*$ 2,468*
Reported in PBO reconciliation	2,099	2,388
Difference from reported amount	-2%	3%

Note: Because we do not have Ford's share of the PBO, we must use the gross interest cost from the second part of exhibit 12P-1.

d.

$ millions	1999	2000
Beginning plan assets	$38,417	$40,845
Actual return	4,239	979
Actual % ROA	**11.03%**	**2.40%**

e.   Effect of an increase in expected return on plan assets:

   (i)   In 2000, Ford raised its expected return on plan assets to 9.50% from 9.00% reporting an expected return of $3,281 million. Had the company continued to use the 1999 expected return of 9%, it would have reported expected return of $3,108 million [(.09/.095) x $3,281] or $173 million less. Net pension income would have been $15 million rather than the reported $188 million.

   (ii)   The change in expected return on plan assets does not change year-end plan status since that number is the difference between the year-end PBO and year-end fair value of plan assets neither of which is affected by the change in the assumed expected return on plan assets.

   (iii) Assuming that Ford's contribution is unchanged, lower net pension income (see part (i)) would result in lower accrued pension cost.

f.   Actuarial gains and losses are a function of changes in (1) actuarial assumptions (quit rates, mortality, and retirement dates) and (2) the discount and compensation increase rates. In 1999, Ford increased its discount rate for PBO to 7.75% from 6.25% in 1998 (which can be seen from the discount rates used to compute pension cost in 2000 and 1999 respectively). That increase is the most likely reason for the actuarial gain as the rate of compensation increases was held steady at 5.20%. Similarly, the 2000 actuarial loss must be due to the decrease in the discount rate to 7.5% from 7.75% as discussed in part a.

5.{M}a. *Note*: All amounts in the tables that follow are in $millions

Pension Cost Computations	December 31	
	1999	*2000*
Service cost	$ 522	$ 495
Interest cost	1,714	2,345
Recurring cost	**$2,236**	**$2,840**
Prior service cost	3,113	0
Actuarial loss (gain)	(5,298)	689
Gross pension cost	**$ 51**	**$3,529**
Actual return on plan assets (gain)	(4,239)	(979)
Nonsmoothed pension cost (credit)	**$(4,188)**	**$2,550**

Note: these calculations use pension cost components from the first part of exhibit 12P-1, as required. However the calculations of the remaining components of nonsmoothed cost require data from the second part of that exhibit. To the extent that some of the PBO and plan asset effects do not accrue to Ford, the computations of gross and nonsmoothed pension cost are misstated.

b.

Forecast Pension Cost	2001 Forecast
Service cost	$ 521
Interest cost	2,496
Expected ROA	(3,784)
Amortization of transition asset	(13)
Amortization of prior service cost	742
Amortization of (gain)/loss	(228)
Reported pension cost (credit)	**$ (266)**

2001 *service cost* is estimated to increase relative to the amount reported in 2000 at the rate of compensation increase (5.2%) assumed by the company. *Interest cost* is computed as the beginning balance of PBO $33,282 million times the year-end 2000 discount rate of 7.5%. The *expected return on plan assets* was calculated as the beginning balance of plan assets times the assumed expected ROA of 9.5%.

No changes were assumed for the *amortization of the transition asset* (no changes are expected) or *prior service cost* (there were no amendments in 2000).However the *amortization of actuarial gains* should decline because of the 2000 decline in those gains.

Using the corridor method, amortization should be based on the excess of the actuarial gains over 10% of pension assets (which exceed the PBO): $8,540 - $3,983 = $4,557. Using a 20 year period results in amortization equal to $228 million($4,557/20). The net pension credit for 2001 is estimated at $266 million. [However this forecast is subject to the same caveat noted in part a.]

c.

December 31	1999	2000	Difference
Pension Plan Status			
Pension plan assets	$40,845	$39,830	$(1,015)
Projected benefit obligation	31,846	33,282	(1,436)
Surplus (deficit)	$ 8,999	$ 6,548	$(2,451)
Less: accrued pension cost	1,474	1,903	429
Adjustment to balance sheet	**$ 7,525**	**$ 4,645**	**$(2,880)**

The economic (funded) status of Ford's pension plan is the difference between the fair value of plan assets of $40,485 million ($39,830) and the PBO of $31,846 million ($33,282), a surplus of $8,999 ($6,548) at the end of 1999 (2000). Because the balance sheet does not reflect the unamortized transition asset, prior service cost, and actuarial losses or gains, the financial statement shows a significantly different amount at the end of each year. We add the excess of the funded status over the reported balance sheet amount ($7,525 million in 1999 and $4,645 million in 2000) to the balance sheet (increase assets and equity) to report the economic status on the balance sheet. [Note: Ford's financial statements recognize a minimum liability adjustment. For simplicity we did not show those data and have ignored the minimum liability in the problem solution.]

d. The principal reasons for the difference in adjustments were:

- Ford recorded an actuarial loss of $689 million in 2000 representing the impact of a lower discount rate, which increased the PBO.

- The PBO also increased by the excess of service and interest cost over benefits paid.

- The 1999 actuarial gains were also decreased by $2,302 million because of the difference between the assumed return on plan assets of $ 3,281 million and an actual return of $979 million. Despite the decline in the plan surplus, Ford's pension asset increased in 2000 due to the reported pension income.

6.{S}a. (i)   The 1999 plan amendment added $3,113 million to the PBO at year-end 1999. This increase in PBO reduced the surplus (plan assets less PBO).

(ii) 2000 service cost was increased by the plan amendment because Ford increased benefits earned by active employees.

(iii) 2000 interest cost also increased because it must be calculated as the (now higher) beginning balance of the PBO for the year times the discount rate in effect at the end of 1999.

b.   The funded status of the plan declined because the plan amendment significantly increased the pension plan obligation. That increase results in higher service and interest costs as discussed in part a. Reported pension cost will also increase as the prior service cost is amortized over the remaining service life of the employees.

There are also broader implications. Ford's PBO calculation assumes no further pension increases. To the extent that labor contracts are likely to result in future periodic benefit increases, the PBO for these plans understates the likely obligation. While this understatement cannot be easily calculated, Ford has a significant liability that is not reported on either its balance sheet or the pension plan disclosures.

7.{L}a. The actuarial gains and losses are a function of changes in (1) undisclosed actuarial assumptions (quit rates, mortality, and retirement dates) and (2) the disclosed discount and compensation increase rates. In 2000, EDS raised its discount rate from 7.0% to 7.2%, decreasing the PBO and creating an actuarial gain. As there was an actuarial loss for 2000, it must be due to the undisclosed assumptions listed above.

In 2001, the company lowered the discount rate back to 7.0% which increased the PBO, resulting in an actuarial loss. EDS lowered the rate of compensation increase from 5.2% to 4.3%, reducing the PBO and creating an actuarial gain. The net gain for 2001 suggests that either the effect of the change in the assumed rate of compensation increase exceeded the discount rate effect or that the undisclosed assumptions generated an actuarial gain.

b. Exchange rate effects are reported in the reconciliations of both the PBO and the plan assets because EDS has pension plans in its foreign operations that have currencies other than the dollar, the reporting currency of EDS.

These effects are negative for both the PBO and plan assets for all three years. The information conveyed is that these plans are denominated in currencies that declined against the dollar over the entire three year period.

c. *Note*: All amounts in the tables that follow are in $millions

At December 31	*1999*	*2000*	*2001*
Service cost	$256	$251	$283
Interest cost	183	232	263
Recurring cost	$439	$483	$546
Nonrecurring costs:			
Actuarial (gain) loss	62	192	(98)
Plan amendments	30	(12)	(35)
Gross pension cost	$531	$663	$413
Actual ROA (gain)	(588)	(752)	421
Nonsmoothed cost (credit)	$(57)	$(89)	$834

d.

At December 31	1999	2000	2001
Reported pension cost	$160	$143	$152
Benefits paid	83	258	94
Employer contributions	141	199	176

(i) The pension costs reported by EDS for all three years are significantly lower than both the recurring cost and the gross pension cost due to the impact of the (expected) return on assets. Although the 2001 reported pension cost is lower than the 1999 amount, recurring costs have increased each year. Beneficial actuarial changes and plan amendments in 2001 enabled EDS to reverse the increase in 2000 and reduce the gross pension costs in 2001 to an amount below the 1999 amount. It may be difficult to sufficiently reduce pension costs over time. When nonsmoothed costs are considered, reported pension costs were higher in 1998 and 1999 but considerably lower in 2000 as a result of the volatility of ROA.

(ii) Benefits paid are low compared to pension costs but that may reflect the relatively low age of the firm. Contributions to the plan have been approximately equal to pension cost. The rising recurring cost and gross cost (with the exception of the likely temporary decline in 2001) combined with the underfunded status (see part i) suggest that EDS will soon have to increase contributions to the plan.

e. Termination benefits create discontinuities but we exclude them from our assessment of recurring and gross pension costs because they are nonrecurring in nature. However, we expect them to have an impact on the long-term ongoing costs of providing pension benefits.

f.

At December 31	1999	2000	2001
Benefits paid	$83	$258	$94

Benefits paid increased over the 1999-2001 period with a significant increase in 2000 which may be due to the payment of special termination benefits announced in 1999.

g.

At December 31	1999	2000	2001
Actual ROA %	**22.94%**	**23.33%**	**-10.94%**

The actual rate of return on assets is calculated as the actual return divided by the beginning balance of plan assets. For example, the 1999 rate of return is the actual return of $588 million divided by the beginning balance of $ 2,563 million or 22.94%.

h.   Forecasted 2002 pension cost:

Components of pension cost	2002
Service cost	$311
Interest cost	276
Expected ROA	(348)
Amortization of net transition liability	1
Amortization of plan amendments	(31)
Amortization of losses	14
Reported pension cost	$225

Service cost for 2002 is increased by employee additions (see Pfizer's 11 year summary for data) and salary increases. It also increases because of the reduced discount rate but decreases due to the reduced expected rate of compensation increase. We forecast service cost to increase 10.0%

Interest cost is based on the discount rate assumption used in 2001 to calculate the PBO. Therefore, interest cost for 2002 is forecasted to be 7.0% x $3,943 million (ending balance of PBO in 2001) = $276 million.

Expected ROA is equal to the 2001 ending balance of plan assets, $3,585 million times 9.7% = $348 million.

Amortization of net transition liability remains constant at $1.0 million.

Amortization of plan amendments is assumed to remain constant at the 2001 level.

Amortization of unamortized actuarial loss is assumed to increase to $14 million, calculated as ($598 - $394)/15, where $394 is 10% of plan assets (larger than the PBO) and 15 the assumed amortization period.

i. The balance sheet adjustment is the difference between the funded (economic) status and the amount recorded on EDS' balance sheet:

Pension Plan Status		
At December 31	2000	2001
Plan assets	$3,849	$3,585
Projected benefit obligation	3,538	3,943
Funded status - surplus (deficit)	$ 311	$ (358)
Net accrued benefit on balance sheet	(75)	(43)
Difference	386	(315)

For a going concern, we must incorporate the economic status of the plan or plan assets at fair value less the PBO, or a surplus of $311 million in 2000 and a deficit of $358 million in 2001. The difference between these amounts and those currently recognized on the balance sheet should be shown as a pension asset or liability and adjustment to equity. That difference is an equity increase and additional net asset of $386 million for 2000 but an equity decrease and additional liability of $315 million for 2001. *Note*: EDS has a minimum liability adjustment that we have omitted for simplicity.

j. The principal sources of the $701 million difference in the adjustment to the economic status are:
- The $405 million increase in the PBO, mainly due to benefits earned in 2001
- The $264 million decline in pension assets as the negative return and benefits paid in 2001 exceeded employer contributions and other changes.

8.{M}a. In 1999, AMR raised its discount rate from 7.0% to 8.25%, reducing the PBO; this change must have generated much of the reported actuarial gain. In 2000, the company lowered the discount rate to 7.75%, increasing the PBO and resulting in an actuarial loss.

b. *Note*: All amounts in the tables that follow are in $millions

At December 31	1998	1999	2000
Service cost	$213	$236	$ 213
Interest cost	418	433	467
Recurring cost	**$631**	**$669**	**$ 680**
Nonrecurring costs:			
Actuarial (gain) loss	300	(849)	499
Plan amendments	0	75	0
Gross pension cost	**$931**	**$(105)**	**$1,179**
Actual ROA (gain)	(850)	(7)	(735)
Nonsmoothed cost (credit)	**$ 81**	**$(112)**	**$ 444**

c.

Return on Plan Assets	December 31	
	1999	2000
Opening plan assets	$5,564	$5,282
Actual ROA	7	735
Actual % ROA	**0.13%**	**13.92%**

The actual return on pension plan assets was negligible in 1999 but nearly 14% in 2000. In a given year, the actual return on plan assets has no effect on pension cost. However, the difference between the actual and the assumed return must be accumulated in the unrecognized net gain or loss and amortized (using the corridor method) to pension cost over the remaining service life of active employees. It is this amortization expense that will affect the reported pension cost.

d.

Forecast Of Pension Cost	2001
Service cost	$236
Interest cost	499
Expected ROA	(544)
Amortization of net transition asset	(1)
Amortization of plan amendments	10
Amortization of losses	34
Forecasted pension cost (credit)	**$233**

Service cost is assumed to be equal to the 1999 amount because (1) the decline in 2000 was due to the increased discount rate and that rate was decreased at December 31, 2000, and (2) we expect it to increase by at least the assumed rate of compensation growth, assuming no change in the number of employees.

Interest cost is based on the 2000 discount rate assumption used to calculate the PBO. Therefore, interest cost for 2001 is 7.75% x $6,434 million (ending balance of PBO in 2000) = $499 million.

Expected ROA is equal to the 2000 ending balance of plan assets, $5,731 million times the assumed ROA of 9.5% = $544 million.

Amortization of net transition asset remains equal to the 2000 amount of $1.0 million.

Amortization of plan amendments is assumed to remain equal to the 2000 level; there were no 2000 amendments.

Amortization of the net loss is difficult to forecast as the unamortized amount is below 10% of plan assets. As there was amortization in 2000, it must be due to certain underfunded plans. As unamortized losses grew in 2000, we assume 2001 amortization equal to twice the 2000 amount.

e.

Pension Plan Status		
At December 31	*1999*	*2000*
Plan assets	$5,282	$5,731
Projected benefit obligation	5,628	6,434
Funded status (deficit)	$ (346)	$ (703)
Accrued pension benefit (liability) on balance sheet	74	(57)
Difference	(420)	(646)

For a going concern, we must incorporate the economic status of the plan or plan assets at fair value less the PBO, or deficits of $346 million in 1999 and $703 million in 2000. The difference between these amounts and those currently recognized on the balance sheet should be shown as a pension asset or liability and adjustment to equity. That difference is an additional liability and equity decrease of $420 million for 1999 and $646 million for 2000. *Note*: We have excluded AMR's minimum liability adjustment for simplicity.

f. The principal source of the difference in the adjustment to the economic status (an additional liability of $226 million in 2000) is that the PBO increased by more than plan assets in 2000 (despite the high actual ROA). The large PBO increase was due to recurring cost elements plus the 2000 actuarial loss of $499 million.

9.{S}a. Expected return component of 2001 pension cost = $ 4,327 million.

Given the change in assumed ROA to 8.5% for 2002, the expected ROA component will be 8.5% x $45,006 million (2001 year-end balance of pension plan assets) = $3,826 million. The lower assumed ROA and the 2000 decline in plan assets combine to reduce the expected ROA component of pension cost by $501 million ($4,327 - $3,826).

b. (i) The effect of the change in assumed ROA will increase pension cost by $450 million (1% x opening plan assets of $45,006 million).

(ii) Had GE earned its expected ROA in 2001 and all other changes to plan assets remained constant, the 2001 year-end balance would have been $7,203 million higher as shown in the table below. If the 2002 assumed ROA of 8.50% is applied to the adjusted asset amount, the 2002 ROA component of pension cost would be $612 million higher than the estimate in part a.

		December 31	
$millions		2001	2002
Actual ROA		$(2,876)	
Assumed ROA		4,327	
Difference		$ 7,203	
Reported assets at December 31		45,006	
Adjusted assets at December 31		$52,209	
ROA assumption for 2002			8.50%
Adjusted ROA component			$ 4,438
Increase ($4,438 - $3,826)			612

The total effect of the change in ROA assumption and failure to earn the assumed return in 2001 was to increase 2002 pension cost by $1,062 million, the sum of the two effects shown above.

10.{S}a. The source of the amortization of a transition asset or liability was the initial adoption of SFAS 87; at the initial adoption date firms were required to compare the projected benefit obligation to the fair value of plan assets plus accrued benefit liability or prepaid pension cost on the balance sheet. The difference between those amounts, called the unrecognized net asset or obligation, had to be amortized on a straight-line basis to pension cost over either the average remaining service period of employees or 15 years.

b. In 2001, GE did not report amortization of the transition asset; we can assume that was because the firm had fully amortized the transition asset. SFAS 87 was effective for fiscal years beginning after December 15, 1988 and earlier application was encouraged. GE either adopted early or used an amortization period of less than 15 years.

11.{S}a. A different return on assets assumption is necessary because taxable plans must pay income taxes on investment returns (dividends, interest, and capital gains or losses), reducing the after-tax returns.

b. The implied income tax rate on taxable plans must be 38.27% because an 8.1% return taxed at that rate generates a 5% return (8.1% x (1 - tax rate) = 8.1% x (1 - .3827) = 5.0%).

c. Principal may have decided to fund these plans (1) in order to retain or provide an incentive to employees in those plans, (2) because employee contracts call for funding, or (3) because supplemental pension plans for founding or key management employees may be taxable.

12.{M}a. Amounts in $millions

September 30	1998	1999	2000	2001	Total
Service cost	$ 331	$ 509	$ 478	$ 316	$ 1,634
Interest cost	1,631	1,671	1,915	1,926	7,143
(i) Recurring Cost	$1,962	$2,180	$2,393	$ 2,242	$ 8,777
Prior service cost	626	1,534	(1)	9	2,168
Actuarial loss (gain)	3,811	(2,182)	370	1,434	$ 3,433
(ii) Gross Pension Cost	$6,399	$1,532	$2,762	$ 3,685	$14,378
Actual investment return on plan assets (gain)	(1,914)	(7,114)	(9,791)	6,830	(11,989)
(iii) Nonsmoothed Pension Cost (Credit)	$4,485	$(5,582)	$(7,029)	$10,515	$ 2,389
(iv) Benefits paid	1,740	1,977	2,294	2,788	8,799
(v) Contributions	12	14	19	25	70
(vi) Reported Pension Cost (Credit)	$ (558)	$ (614)	$ (971)	$ 1,090	$(1,382)

b. The nonsmoothed pension cost of $2,389 million measures the change in Lucent's net pension obligation over the four year period resulting from benefits earned, plan changes, actuarial gains and losses, and actual investment performance. It shows that the total increase in the pension benefit obligation exceeded the return on plans assets by that amount.

Over the same period the company reported a pension credit of $1,382 million, a difference of $3,771 million from the nonsmoothed pension credit. This difference reflects the smoothing provisions of SFAS 87; over this time period the smoothing provisions did not "even out."

c. Lucent has made low or relatively insignificant contributions to the pension plans because of its high investment returns on plan assets. These returns increased plan assets, enabling Lucent to make the required benefit payments while maintaining an overfunded plan status.

d. Benefits paid have been growing rapidly. Therefore, investment performance must remain high to permit continued low contributions. The negative return for 2001 is a warning as it contributed to a significant decline in the plan surplus.

13.{S}a. One advantage of using the market-related value of plan assets is that the ROA component of pension cost (and therefore pension cost itself) is less volatile than if the actual market values were used.

The disadvantage of using the market-related value is that when investment returns are high, the ROA component of pension cost reflects those high returns only gradually, keeping pension cost higher than if actual market values were used. Companies that prefer conservative accounting methods, however, may consider this to be an advantage.

b. Returns in fiscal 1999 were very high, nearly 20%. Under the market-related method, those returns would reduce pension cost only over a five-year period. The accounting change results in immediate recognition, reducing pension cost and increasing reported earnings. Note that the ROA component of pension cost increased 24% in fiscal 1999 even though pension assets did not change in that year, suggesting that Lucent computes ROA quarterly and benefited from the accounting change in that year.

c. The accounting change makes the ROA component of reported pension cost more volatile as the effect of changes in the market value of plan assets affects that component immediately. While the ROA component rose in fiscal 2001 (the market downturn occurred late in that fiscal year) it would be expected to decline sharply in fiscal 2002 as assets fell from $45.3 billion to $35.5 billion. If Lucent had retained use of the market-related value method, it would have had a cushion of prior year returns.

d. The cumulative effect of $2,150 million should not be considered a component of 1998 operating income because it is the result of an one-time accounting change rather than the consequence of ongoing operations. In addition, it reflects changes in market values in prior years.

14.{L}a. Roche return on plan assets

(in CHF millions)	2000	2001
Plan assets (open)	10,046	10,448
Actual return on plan assets	1,175	(1,334)
Actual rate of return	11.70%	-12.77%
Expected rate of return	3% to 10%	3% to 10%

The pension plans performed better than expected in 2000. However, in 2001 the plans lost almost 13% whereas they had been expected to earn rates similar to those assumed for 2000.

b. Roche recorded actuarial gains in 2000 and losses in 2001. Because the company reports a constant range (3% to 8%) for assumed discount rates over the three-year period and a nearly constant range for compensation growth, it is not possible to determine whether the actuarial gains (losses) were due to changes in either of these rates. As discussed in part a, the investment performance of the Roche plans was above assumed rates in 2000 but below those rates in 2001. Therefore investment performance must be responsible for the actuarial gains in 2000 and losses in 2001.

c. Overall funded status of Roche benefit plans:

(in CHF millions)	1999	2000	2001
Plan assets	10,046	10,448	9,401
PBO - unfunded plans	2,648	2,423	2,440
PBO - funded plans	9,028	9,034	9,575
Total PBO	11,676	11,457	12,015
Funded status	(1,630)	(1,009)	(2,614)
Net recognized liability	(2,078)	(1,849)	(1,837)
Required adjustment	448	840	(777)

As stated in the problem, we have assumed that the recognized liability for unfunded plans represents the PBO. For funded plans, the actuarial present value gives us the PBO. We derive the funded status of the plans by deducting the total PBO from the stated fair value of plan assets. The difference between the economic or funded status of the plans and the net recognized liability constitutes the adjustment bringing the balance sheet amounts to fair value. For 1999 and 2000 the adjustment will entail a reduction in the liability (and an increase in equity). For 2001, on the other hand, the liability will have to be increased. Notice that the net recognized liability declined despite the deterioration of plan status over the period.

d. (i) Disaggregation of Roche pension plans

(in CHF millions)	1999	2000	2001
Total plan assets	10,046	10,448	9,401
Less: nonpension plan assets	576	649	530
Equals: pension plan assets	9,470	9,799	8,871
PBO - unfunded plans	2,648	2,423	2,440
PBO - funded plans	9,028	9,034	9,575
Total PBO	11,676	11,457	12,015
Less: nonpension plan PBO	703	690	737
Equals: pension plan PBO	10,973	10,767	11,278
Funded status – pension plans (deficit)	**(1,503)**	**(968)**	**(2,407)**
Net recognized liability	(2,078)	(1,849)	(1,837)
Less: net recognized liability – nonpension plans	(190)	(147)	(257)
Equals: net recognized liability – pension plans	**(1,888)**	**(1,702)**	**(1,580)**
Required adjustment - pension plans	**385**	**734**	**(827)**

(ii) Roche nonpension plans

(in CHF millions)	1999	2000	2001
Nonpension plan assets	576	649	530
PBO - nonpension plans	703	690	737
Funded status (deficit)	**(127)**	**(41)**	**(207)**
Net liability recognized	**(190)**	**(147)**	**(257)**
Required adjustment	**63**	**106**	**50**

The required adjustment equals the difference between the funded status and the net liability recognized.

e. The principal advantage of contributing Roche shares to the pension funds is the ability to make some or all of the required contribution to the pension fund without using cash. However, in economic terms, this is a misleading characterization: the contribution of shares is equivalent to the public issuance of shares and the use of the proceeds to meet the funding requirement.

One disadvantage is that large employer shareholdings link the performance of the plan to the performance of the company. If the company performs badly, the risk of an underfunded plan increases when the plan owns employer shares, increasing the possibility that additional funding will be required just when the company is suffering financial distress.

In addition, the contribution of shares results in an opportunity cost to the company because it has given up possible future increase in the value of the shares (At the appropriate time, Roche could capture that increase by issuing shares to the public).

f. 1. Unlike the single rates commonly observed in SFAS 132 disclosures, Roche reports a range of discount, compensation growth, expected return on assets, and healthcare trend rates. While this reflects worldwide operations and diverse pension plans, it makes the disclosures less useful. For example, it is not possible to determine whether actuarial gains (losses) are due to changes in discount and compensation growth rates. The range could remain constant with significant changes for certain plans.

2. IAS 19 does not require, and Roche does not provide separate data for domestic and foreign plans.

3. SFAS 132 requires a reconciliation of both the PBO and the plan assets. Roche has provided a reconciliation of the recognized liability but the company does not disclose a reconciliation of either plan assets or the PBO. As noted in the chapter (p. 431), IAS 19 does not require these reconciliations.

4. Although IAS 19 does not require it to do so, Roche provides some additional data on other postemployment benefit plans.

5. In keeping with IAS 19, Roche does not disclosure the sensitivity of the combined service cost and interest cost and the liability for other postemployment benefits to the assumed health care trend rate. Its disclosure is limited to the rate itself.

6. Finally, Roche discloses only the benefits paid for unfunded plans. There is no disclosure of payments for other postemployment benefits.

g. The analyst should ask management for the following data to facilitate analysis and comparisons with other companies:

1. Disclosure of the level and changes in the discount, compensation growth, expected return on assets, and the healthcare trend rates by geographic segment.

2. Separate data for domestic and foreign plans with emphasis on significant exchange rate effects.

3. Reconciliation of PBO and plan assets including the effects of acquisitions and divestitures.

4. Sensitivity to changes in the health care trend rate of nonpension benefit plans.

5. Disclosure of benefits paid for all pension and postemployment benefit plans.

15. {S}(i) An increase in the assumed discount rate would reduce the accumulated postretirement benefit obligation and increase the interest cost component of postretirement benefit cost. However, the higher discount rate would result in a lower service cost and that reduction would more than offset the increase in the interest cost with a net decrease in postretirement benefit costs raising reported income. This response holds for a plan with relatively young workforce – in a mature workforce, the interest rate effect could be higher than the service cost impact.

(ii) Earnings would improve if the company lowered its rate of compensation increase because that action would reduce the present value of the APBO and both the interest and service cost components would decline. *Note that rate of compensation will only have an impact on postretirement benefits if those benefits are based on compensation.*

(iii) An increase in the assumed rate of return on plan assets would increase reported earnings because the change would decrease benefit costs, since the assumed ROA offsets other components of benefit costs. This effect assumes at least partial funding for these plans.

(iv) A decrease in the estimated future health care inflation rate would reduce the APBO and both the service and interest cost components of the benefit cost increasing reported income.

16. {M}a. Service cost represents the actuarial present value of benefits earned by employees during the year. As the number of the employees declined, benefits were earned by fewer employees, reducing the service cost. Actuarial gains were reported because more employees "quit" before reaching retirement age changing the quit rates assumed in computing the benefits accrued by employees.

b. There is no expected return component because the company has not funded the postretirement plans. Note that the company does not report a fair value of plan assets and the benefits paid equal the company contribution to the postretirement plan fund. Companies may elect not to fund postretirement plans because, unlike pension plans, no tax benefits are available for postretirement plans.

c. Calculations of Postretirement Cost

At October 31 (in $thousands)	1998	1999
Service cost	$1,400	$1,200
+ Interest cost	1,500	1,200
= *Recurring postretirement cost*	$2,900	$2,400
Nonrecurring costs:		
+ Actuarial (gain) loss	1,100	(2,800)
+ Plan amendments	0	0
= *Gross postretirement cost (credit)*	$4,000	$ (400)
+ Actual ROA (gain)	0	0
= *Nonsmoothed postretirement cost (credit)*	$4,000	$ (400)

d. (i) Westvaco reported net periodic postretirement benefits costs of $ 2.1 million in 1998 and $1.3 million in 1999. The difference between these amounts and the recurring costs (sum of the service cost and interest costs) is due primarily to the amortization of actuarial gains.

Significant reported 1999 actuarial gains are responsible for converting the 1998 gross postretirement cost to a credit in 1999. The reported and computed costs will converge as the actuarial gains are amortized to reported postretirement costs. There is no difference between the gross postretirement cost and the nonsmoothed postretirement cost because there are no fund assets.

(ii) Westvaco's contribution (equal to benefits paid) was $2.9 million in 1998 and $2.5 million in 1999. These amounts are quite similar to recurring postretirement cost.

e. Forecast fiscal 2000 postretirement benefit cost:

| | Forecast 2000 | Reported 2000 |
In $thousands		
Service cost	$1,260	$1,300
Interest cost	1,343	1,300
Net amortization	(1,065)	(900)
Net postretirement benefit cost	$1,538	$1,700

Service cost declined in 1999 primarily due to the reduction in the number of employees. We assumed it would grow at the assumed rate of compensation increase.

Interest cost is calculated as the assumed discount rate of 6.75% times the 1999 ending balance of the PBO: 6.75% X $19.90 million = $ 1.34 million.

We assumed that the *amortization* rate would remain 15% of the unrecognized actuarial gains at the end of 1999. Thus, the 2000 amortization is expected to be $1.065 million (15% x $7.1).

The second column of the above table shows the actual expense reported by Westvaco. Our estimates (made without reference to the actual data) are very close except for the estimate of net amortization.

f. Adjustments to the balance sheet:

Postretirement Plan Status (in $thousands)	October 31 1998	1999
Plan assets	$ 0	$ 0
Accumulated postretirement benefit obligation	23,200	$19,900
Funded status - surplus (deficit)	**$(23,200)**	**$(19,900)**
Unrecognized net actuarial (gain) loss	(5,300)	(7,100)
Unrecognized prior service cost (credit)	(200)	(100)
Unrecognized net transition (asset) obligation	0	0
Net accrued benefit on balance sheet	**$(28,700)**	**$(27,100)**
Difference between funded status and balance sheet amounts = balance sheet adjustment	**5,500**	**7,200**

The funded status represents the economic position of the company with respect to its postretirement benefit plans. In order to adjust the balance sheet liability to this economic position, we need to reduce the reported balance sheet liability (and increase equity) by $5.5 million in 1998 and $7.2 million in 1999.

g. In both 1998 and 1999, the principal reason for the difference between the economic position and the balance sheet amounts is the amount of the unrecognized net actuarial gain.

17.{L}a. (i) The assumed health care cost trend rate is one of the most important factors determining the benefit obligation because it determines the estimated benefits earned by employees. An assumed increase in the trend rate will increase the benefit obligation at year-end 2000 because that amount is the present value of the (now, higher) postretirement benefits.

(ii) The net benefit cost for 2001 will be higher because the service cost, interest cost, and the amortization of actuarial losses will be higher. The service cost is higher because the higher trend rate implies a greater cost of benefits. Interest cost rises because the same discount rate is applied to a higher APBO. The higher health care trend rate also results in an actuarial loss which must be amortized as an element of benefit cost over time.

b. AMR increased its discount rate from 7.00% in 1998 to 8.25% in 1999 and lowered it to 7.75% in 2000. The 1999 (2000) increase (decrease) lowered (raised) the accumulated postretirement benefit obligation, generating the actuarial gain in 1999 and the loss in 2000.

c. 2000 service cost fell because of the higher 1999 discount rate. The other likely reason is that the number of employees eligible for these benefits declined, possibly due to reduced employment levels.

d. The higher discount rate was applied to the lower accumulated postretirement benefit cost (APBO). Although the APBO declines when the discount rate is increased, the higher rate offset that effect.

e.

$millions	1999	2000
Service cost	$ 56	$ 43
+ Interest cost	108	108
= *Recurring postretirement cost*	$164	$151
Nonrecurring costs:		
+ Actuarial (gain) loss	(311)	328
+ Plan amendments	0	0
= *Gross postretirement cost (credit)*	$(147)	$479
+ Actual ROA (gain)	(1)	(5)
= *Nonsmoothed postretirement cost (credit)*	$(148)	$474

f. Prior service costs represent plan amendments that change previously specified benefit formulas. Such changes must be amortized as components of benefit costs over the remaining service periods of active employees. In AMR's case, they lowered benefits. The amortization of prior service cost has remained at $5 million a year for the last three years, and is likely to remain constant if there are no future plan amendments.

In recent years, however, many companies have changed benefits, frequently lowering them. We expect AMR to change benefits as well, particularly because costs in the airline industry are substantial and profitability is under pressure. Whether the airlines can hold the line on costs will depend on negotiations with powerful unions. It is, therefore, difficult to predict the direction of the change in amortization of prior service costs. Any future benefit reductions will increase amortization, reducing net benefit cost.

g. The corridor method requires the amortization of unrecognized gains or losses in excess of 10% of the larger of the benefit obligation and plan assets. At December 31, 1999 the excess of the unrecognized gain of $395 million over 10% of the APBO (10% x 1,306 = $131 million) was $264 million. 2000 amortization of $14 million implies an amortization period of about 19 years.

At December 31, 1998 the unrecognized actuarial gain was only $89 million, well below 10% of the APBO. Thus no amortization was required in 1999.

h. 2001 forecast

Components of postretirement cost		Forecast
$millions	2000	2001
Service cost	$ 43	$ 45
Interest cost	108	132
Amortization of unrecognized net gain	(14)	0
Amortization of prior service cost	(5)	(5)
Reported postretirement cost (credit)	$132	$172

Although *service cost* declined in 2000, we assume that it will increase in 2001 because AMR has raised its assumed health care cost trend rate (see part a). However, it is difficult to estimate without additional data; we have used a 5% increase because we expect it to increase at a rate somewhat higher than the assumed rate of compensation increase (4.26%).

Interest cost has been computed as the 2000 discount rate of 7.75% times the 2001 beginning balance of APBO, $1,708 million, or $132 million.

We assume no *amortization of unrecognized gain* in 2001 given the requirements of the corridor method (see part g).

We leave the *amortization of prior service cost* unchanged (see part f).

i.

Postretirement Plan Status	December 31	
$millions	1999	2000
Plan assets	$ 72	$ 88
Accumulated postretirement benefit obligation	1,306	1,708
Funded status – surplus (deficit)	$(1,234)	$(1,620)
Unrecognized net actuarial gain	(395)	(51)
Unrecognized prior service credit	(40)	(35)
Net accrued benefit on balance sheet	$(1,669)	$(1,706)
Difference between funded status and balance sheet amounts = balance sheet adjustment	435	86

The economic position of the postretirement plan is calculated as the fair value of the plan assets less the actuarial present value of the accumulated postretirement benefit obligation. Since the accrued benefit liability on the balance sheet is higher (the unrecognized actuarial gain and prior service costs are not included), we must decrease the balance sheet amounts by the difference. For example, in 2000, the accrued liability on the balance sheet amount is lowered (and equity is increased) by $86 million to state it at $1,620 million which is the economic liability.

j. The principal reason why the 2000 adjustment in part i is much lower than the 1999 adjustment (also shown) is that the unrecognized actuarial gain has declined due to the lower discount rate and the higher health care trend rate.

k. The accrued benefit liability rose from 1998 to 2000 because AMR's contributions were less than the benefit cost for 1999 and 2000. This shortfall increased the accrued liability.

AMR Corporation	12/31/1999 Reported	12/31/2000 Reported
Service and interest cost	$ 164	$ 151
Effect of change in trend rate:		
1% increase	24	20
Percentage effect	14.63%	13.25%
1% decrease	$ (22)	$ (19)
Percentage effect	-13.41%	-12.58%
Benefit obligation	$1,306	$1,708
Effect of change in trend rate:		
1% increase	115	137
Percentage effect	8.81%	8.02%
1% decrease	$(105)	$(131)
Percentage effect	-8.04%	-7.67%

The December 31, 2000 data show that the sensitivity has *decreased* with respect to combined service and interest expense and relative to the APBO.

The decreased sensitivity with respect to service and interest cost is clear from the dollar data and confirmed by measuring sensitivity relative to the reported service and interest cost. For the APBO data, the dollar sensitivity is higher but the changes relative to the (increased) APBO confirm the reduction in sensitivity.

The increase in health care cost trend rate lowered the sensitivity of AMR's postretirement plan obligations because the higher assumed rate reduces the impact of a 1% increase. A 1% change is less significant relative to 7% than to 5%.

19.{M}a. The unrecognized prior service benefit results from plan amendments that decreased postretirement benefit obligations and, therefore, lowered the APBO. It is likely that Sears, like other companies, reduced the health benefits they offered their employees. The amount of this prior service benefit is not recognized on the balance sheet. Instead, it is amortized to expense (and reported as a component of the net benefit cost) over the remaining service period of employees expected to earn benefits.

The amortization decreases the unrecognized amount over time if there are no other plan amendments. However if the company reduces benefits further then the unrecognized prior service benefit will be increased. However, the opposite effect will be observed if the company needs to increase benefits to attract or keep employees.

b. The 1999 actuarial gain is a result of (1) the increase in the discount rate from to 8.00% in 1999 from 7.25% in 1998 and (2) any changes in one or more undisclosed actuarial assumptions. The increase in the discount rate lowered the present value of accumulated benefits, generating the reported gain. The changes in actuarial assumptions could have lowered the postretirement benefits earned by employees, reducing the APBO.

c.

	$millions Forecast
Components of postretirement cost	2000
Service cost	$ 5
Interest cost	75
Amortization of unrecognized net (gain)	(40)
Amortization of prior service cost	(102)
Reported postretirement cost (credit)	**$(62)**

We assume that the *service cost* will remain constant in 2000. The *interest cost* has been computed as the 1999 discount rate of 8% times the 1999 ending balance of the APBO or $934 million.

Because the unrecognized actuarial gain has risen relative to 1998, the amortization will increase as well. From the 1999 data it appears that Sears uses an amortization period of 12 years. The 2000 amortization is estimated at ($578 - $93)/12 = $40 million where $93 is 10% of the APBO.

Since there is no change in the prior service cost, the amortization should remain constant.

d.

	(in $millions)	1999
Postretirement Plan Status		
At December 31		
Plan assets	$	0
Accumulated postretirement benefit obligation		934
Funded status - (deficit)	**$**	**(934)**
Unrecognized net actuarial gain		(578)
Unrecognized prior service credit		(668)
Net accrued benefit liability on balance sheet		**$(2,180)**
Difference between funded status and balance sheet amounts = balance sheet adjustment		**$ 1,246**

Like many other companies, Sears does not fund its postretirement benefits. The economic position of the plans is, therefore, equal to the APBO. However, the liability on the balance sheet does not reflect the actuarial gains and the decrease in APBO due to favorable plan amendments (unrecognized prior service cost). In order to reflect the economic position of the plan, we must decrease the 1999 balance sheet liability by $1,246 million.

e. The plan contribution is exactly equal to benefits paid because the plan is unfunded and Sears makes benefit payments directly to retirees.

20.{L}a. (i) The 2000 plan amendment increased the APBO because it increased the benefits. This increase in the APBO is the principal reason for the increase in the level of underfunding (APBO – fair value of plan assets).

(ii) Service cost increased in both 2000 and 2001 because the plan amendments increased the benefits earned by employees.

(iii) Because the plan amendments must be amortized to net benefit cost over the remaining service period of employees, the annual amortization increased to reflect the higher unamortized amount.

b. An increase (decrease) in the discount rate reduces (increases) the APBO, generating actuarial gains (losses). Actuarial gains and losses also reflect changes in assumed compensation rates, and actuarial assumptions such as quit rates and mortality.

The discount rate increase in 1999 is consistent with the actuarial gain. The discount rate decreases in 2000 and 2001 are consistent with actuarial losses for those years. However the 2000 actuarial loss is far greater than the 2001 loss although the discount rate change was .25% for both years. Both losses are far greater than the 1999 gain, also based on a .25% rate change. These discrepancies suggest that other (undisclosed) actuarial assumptions had significant effects on the APBO during this period.

c. Analysis of Postretirement Plan Disclosures *Note*: All amounts in the tables that follow are in $millions

Postretirement benefit cost	*1999*	*2000*	*2001*
Service cost	$107	$ 165	$ 191
Interest cost	323	402	459
Recurring cost	**$430**	**$ 567**	**$ 650**
Nonrecurring costs:			
Plan amendments	0	948	0
Actuarial losses (gains)	(62)	534	287
Gross cost	**$368**	**$2,049**	**$ 937**
Actual ROA	(355)	85	163
Nonsmoothed cost	**$ 13**	**$2,134**	**$1,100**
Reported postretirement cost	**318**	**478**	**615**
Benefits paid	**409**	**578**	**593**
Employer contributions	**368**	**300**	**466**

GE contributions increased 27% from $368 million in 1999 to $466 million in 2001 after falling to $300 million in 2000 (that decline may reflect the favorable 1999 investment performance). Benefits paid jumped from $409 million in 1999 to $578 million in 2000 and showed a modest increase to $593 million in 2001 (a two-year increase of 45%). Thus benefits increased more rapidly than contributions.

Over the same period, reported postretirement cost increased from $318 million in 1999 to $615 million in 2001, an increase of 93% - significantly higher than the increase in benefits or contributions. In economic terms, the recurring costs (service plus interest costs) increased 51% - a lower rate of increase than reported postretirement costs because the latter includes the effect (albeit smoothed) of unfavorable plan amendments, actuarial losses, and negative investment returns on plan assets in 2000 and 2001. The same factors combined with actuarial gains and ROA gains in 1999 to present an erratic trend in nonsmoothed costs.

d. Despite a constant assumed ROA of 9.5%, the expected return increased from $165 million in 1999 to $185 million in 2001 because GE (presumably) applies the expected ROA to the market-related value (a smoothed fair value) of plan assets and high returns in the years preceding 1999 continue to increase the smoothed measure. The 2000 and 2001 decline in plan assets has not yet been reflected in expected ROA. The effect of using the market-related value of plan assets can be seen from the following table:

		1999	2000	2001
a	Expected return on plan assets	$165	$178	$185
b	Expected return on plan assets	9.50%	9.50%	9.50%
c	Implied market-related value of plan assets (a/b)	$1,737	$1,874	$1,947
	Reported market value of plan assets	$2,121	$2,369	$2,031

e.

Components of postretirement cost	Forecast 2002
Service cost	$221
Interest cost	493
Expected return on plan assets	(151)
Amortization of unrecognized net loss	71
Amortization of prior service cost	90
Reported postretirement cost	$725

Assumptions used to forecast 2002 postretirement benefit costs:

Service cost is expected to increase at the same rate as in 2001. 2000 and 2001 changes in plan amendments and actuarial assumptions imply a similar growth rate in service costs.

Interest cost is calculated as the 2001 discount rate, 7.25% times the ending 2001 APBO of $6,796 million.

The *expected ROA* of $151 million is calculated at the assumed 2002 ROA of 8.5% times the 2001 ending balance of plan assets of $1,771 million.

We assume that amortization of the unrecognized net loss increases due to the higher unrecognized amount. The 2000 amortization seems high if we assume that GE uses the corridor method. Our estimate assumes use of the corridor method and an amortization period of ten years: ($1,393 - $680)/10 = $71 million where $680 is 10% of the APBO.

We expect amortization of prior service cost to remain constant as it relates to plan amendments in 2000.

f. Assuming no change in the expected ROA from 2001 would give us an expected return of $168 or $17 million higher than the previous forecast and the net postretirement benefit cost would be reduced to $708 million.

g. and h.   *Postretirement Plan Status*

At December 31	1999	2000	2001
Plan assets	$2,369	$2,031	$1,771
Accumulated postretirement benefit obligation	4,926	6,422	6,796
Funded status - (deficit)	**$(2,557)**	**$(4,391)**	**$(5,025)**
Unrecognized net actuarial (gain) loss	61	818	1,393
Unrecognized prior service cost (credit)	100	999	909
Net accrued benefit liability on balance sheet	**$(2,396)**	**$(2,574)**	**$(2,723)**
Difference between funded status and balance sheet amounts = balance sheet adjustment	**(161)**	**(1,817)**	**(2,302)**

On December 31, 2001 (1999), the economic status (fair value of plan assets less the APBO) of the plan is a deficit of $5,025 ($2,557) million and the accrued liability on the balance sheet is $2,723 ($2,396) million. On December 31, 2001 (1999) we must, therefore, add $2,302 ($161) million to the liability (and reduce equity by the same amount) to reflect the economic status of the plan on the balance sheet.

Postretirement Plan Status			Difference between
At December 31	1999	2001	1999 & 2001
Plan assets	$2,369	$1,771	$ (598)
Accumulated postretirement benefit obligation	4,926	6,796	1,870
Funded status - (deficit)	**$(2,557)**	**$(5,025)**	**$(2,468)**
Unrecognized net actuarial loss	61	1,393	1,332
Unrecognized prior service cost	100	909	809
Net accrued benefit liability on balance sheet	**$(2,396)**	**$(2,723)**	**$ (327)**
Difference between funded status and balance sheet amounts = balance sheet adjustment	**(161)**	**(2,302)**	**(2,141)**

The actuarial loss, plan amendments, and negative asset returns are the three principal reasons for the difference between the 1999 and 2001 adjustments.

21. {M} a. The valuation of Pfizer shares should be based on the pro forma diluted earnings per share because stock-based compensation requires the use of real resources and it is an expense of conducting operations.

b. In 1998, Pfizer reduced the expected dividend yield and the risk-free interest rate. However, the effects of these changes on option value are in opposite directions. In 1999, Pfizer did not substantively change any of the four major variables used by the Black-Scholes method to value stock options. Thus, the principal reason for the increase in option values must be the higher stock price in 1998 and 1999.

c. (i) Expected dividend yield affects the fair value of the option because the dividend payment reduces the price of the stock at the ex-dividend date. Thus, the higher the dividend yield the lower the fair value of the option.

(ii) The higher the risk-free interest rate the lower the fair value of the option; the higher discount rate reduces the present value of the exercise price at the expiration of the option.

(iii) High expected stock price volatility implies higher probability of the stock price exceeding the exercise price, increasing the value of the option.

(iv) The longer the term to exercise the higher the fair value of the option since the option has a higher probability of exceeding the exercise price.

d.

```
Pfizer 12/31/1999
(in $millions except per share amounts)
                                         Weighted
                               Option     average
                               Shares    exercise
Range of                     Outstanding   price      Proceeds
Exercise prices               (millions) per share
$  0 to  $10                     85.31     $6.40     $  545.97
   10 to  15                     36.68     12.42        455.53
   15 to  20                     35.49     18.34        650.81
Total                           157.47                $1,652.31
Less shares repurchased*         50.94
Additional shares               106.53
         As reported
Book value = SE                 $8,887
Shares outstanding               3,847
Book value/share                $2.31
          Adjusted
Book value = SE                 $8,887
Adjusted shares
outstanding                      3,954
Adjusted book value/share       $2.25

* Using the treasury stock method, proceeds of $1,652.31
can be used to repurchase 50.94 million shares:
(1,652.31/$32.4375 = 50.94)
```

The adjusted book value per share is a better indicator of the resources of the firm because it includes the dilutive effect of the outstanding options whose exercise is highly likely.

e. Cash flows from tax benefits related to the exercise of stock options should be included in cash from operations because they are a consequence of stock-based compensation paid to employees. Currently, many companies do not recognize compensation expense for unqualified stock options. However, disclosures permit an adjustment (recognition of compensation expense) to reported income for those options.

Although we believe that the cash flow effects of these tax benefits should be considered as a component of cash flow from operations (when a corresponding compensation expense has been recognized for the options), analysts should note that these tax benefits are highly variable because they depend on the profitable exercise of options.

f. As noted in answer (e), the tax benefits should be considered as components of cash flow from operations if Pfizer recognizes the cost of the options in reported income. However, the caveats mentioned in (e) remain applicable.

22.{S}a. The exchange program gave employees valuable new options, replacing the nearly worthless existing options. The objective was to compensate employees and try to retain them by replacing the lost value of the existing options.

By issuing replacement options six months and a day after the cancellation, EK avoided classifying the new options as variable options. It did not have to recognize the value of the new options as compensation expense.

b. Although GAAP does not require the recognition of compensation cost for the replacement options, they do have value and the analyst must recognize their fair value as compensation expense.

Chapter 13 Solutions

Overview:
Problem Length: *Problem #s*
  {S}   4, 8, 11, 14
  {M}   1, 5, 6, 12, 15
  {L}   2, 3, 7, 9, 10, 13, 16

1.{M}a.   (i) Dividend income:

X:	$10,000 (100,000 x $.10)
Z:	0
Total	**$10,000**

Dividends are not recorded as income for Y (40% owned), but are included in "equity in income of affiliates" instead.)

(ii) Unrealized gains/losses included in stockholders' equity (all before deferred tax):

Firm	12/31/2000	2001 Change	12/31/2001
X	$(400,000)	$ 300,000	$(100,000)
Z	300,000	450,000	750,000
Total	$(100,000)	$ 750,000	$(650,000)

Y: market value changes not recognized under equity method.

(iii) Equity in income of affiliates:

Y: **.40 x $900,000 = $360,000**

b.   The investments are accounted for as follows:

Y using the equity method, as ownership exceeds 20%

X and Z at market value as "available-for-sale" securities under SFAS 115

c. | | | |
|---|---|---|
| Dividend income | $ 10,000 | part a(i) |
| Equity income | 360,000 | part a(iii) |
| **Total income** | **$370,000** | |

d. X: 100,000 x $49 = $4,900,000
    Z: 150,000 x 30 = 4,500,000

    Y: carried   at   original   cost   plus   equity   in
           undistributed earnings subsequent to acquisition.

    Carrying amount at 1/1/2001 cannot be determined but
    would be calculated as:

Carrying amount at 1/1/2000: 800,000 x $35 = $2,800,000
Plus 2000 undistributed earnings (data not available)
Plus 2001 earnings: .40 x $900,000 =   360,000
Less 2001 dividends: $.09 x 800,000 =   (72,000)

e. Mark to market returns for 2001:

Firm	Dividends	+	MV Change	=	Total Return
X	$ 10,000		$ 300,000		$ 310,000
Y	72,000		1,600,000		1,672,000
Z	0		450,000		450,000
Total	$ 82,000		$2,350,000		$2,432,000

    For firms X and Z, the total return is reported in the
    financial statements, but the market value change is
    reported as an adjustment to stockholders' equity. Bart
    does not report its mark to market return on its
    investment in Company Y. However, disclosure of the
    number of shares of Company Y held by Bart and Company
    Y's share price allows investors to calculate the
    return.

f. If consolidation were required for 40% ownership, Bart
    would consolidate firm Y. While consolidation does not
    change reported income, Bart's equity in the earnings
    of firm Y would be replaced by all revenues and
    expenses of firm Y. Similarly, Bart's investment in
    firm Y would be replaced by all of the assets and
    liabilities of firm Y. The 60% of firm Y equity (and
    income) not owned by Bart would be shown as minority
    interest.

2.{L}a. The held-to-maturity fixed maturities are measured at amortized cost. The available-for-sale fixed maturities and equity securities are measured at market value.

b. 2000 Reported ROA by Portfolio Component ($ millions)

	Total Fixed Maturities	Equity Securities	Total Portfolio
Opening balance	$14,519	$ 769	$15,288
Investment income	903	23	926
Return on assets	**6.22%**	**2.99%**	**6.06%**

Note: Opening balances from Exhibit 13-3A (p. 463). Investment income includes realized gains

All returns are below the corresponding reported 1999 returns shown in Exhibit 13-3B.

c. First, compute the mark-to-market returns, using the analysis on p. 465 as a guide.

2000 Change in MVA ($ in millions)

	Fixed Maturity Securities			
2000	Held-to-Maturity	Available for-Sale	Total	Equity Securities
Market value	$1,565	$14,068	$15,633	$ 830
Cost	1,496	13,720	15,216	840
MVA	$ 69	$ 348	$ 417	$ (10)
1999				
Market value	$1,801	$12,777	$14,578	$769
Cost	1,742	12,944	14,686	715
MVA	$ 59	$ (167)	$ (108)	$ 54

Change in MVA
Fixed maturities $417 - $(108) = $ 525
Equity securities $(10) - $ 54 =   (64)
Total portfolio $ 461

Calculation of 2000 Mark-to-Market Return

	Fixed Maturities	Equities	Total
Dividends and interest	$ 895	$ 24	$ 919
Realized gains (losses)	8	(1)	7
Reported income	$ 903	$ 23	$ 926
Change in MVA	525	(64)	461
Mark-to-market return	$1,428	$(41)	$1,387

13-3

Calculation of 2000 Mark-to-Market ROA

	Fixed Maturities	Equities	*Total Portfolio*
Opening balance	$14,578	$ 769	$15,347
Mark-to-market return	1,428	(41)	1,387
Return on assets	**9.80%**	**(5.33%)**	**9.04%**

These returns are quite different from the 2000 reported returns. The fixed maturity portfolio returns are higher whereas the equity return is lower. These results reflect the 2000 stock market decline and the rise in the debt markets as interest rates fell.

The mark-to-market returns also contrast with 1999. In 1999 equity securities showed a positive return as stock prices rose whereas fixed maturities showed a negligible return as interest income was offset by capital losses. During 1999 fixed-income securities' prices fell as interest rates rose.

These comparisons show that mark-to-market returns, while they report actual market results, are more volatile than reported returns that can be smoothed by management decisions.

d.   The mark-to-market returns clearly report the effect of market performance on Chubb's investment portfolios. To fully evaluate the performance of Chubb's portfolios, we need benchmarks. For the bond portfolio, an appropriate benchmark would be a weighted average of market returns for different fixed income portfolios, with weights equal to the weighting of Chubb's holdings (U.S. government, corporate, tax-exempt, etc.). The benchmark should also be adjusted for any differences in duration, quality, or other bond characteristics.

The equity benchmark should also reflect the composition of Chubb's portfolio, reflecting such characteristics as type of stock (preferred vs. common), capitalization (large vs. small), and any international representation.

3.{L}a.   Reported ROA by portfolio segment:

   1999
   Fixed maturities $1,429 / $20,576 =   **6.94%**
   Equity securities   135 /   2,037 =   **6.63**
   Total portfolio $1,564 / $22,613 =   6.92%

   2000
   Fixed maturities $1,426 / $19,654 =   **7.26%**
   Equity securities   94 /   2,005 =   **4.69**
   Total portfolio $1,520 / $21,659 =   7.02%

   where return equals dividend and interest income plus
   realized gains or losses.

   These data suggest that the return on the fixed income
   portfolio improved in 2000, but was partly offset by a
   reduced return on the equity portfolio.

   b.   First, compute the mark-to-market returns for 1999 and
          2000, using the analysis on p. 465 as a guide.

Change in MVA ($ in millions)

	Held-to-Maturity	Available for-Sale	Total	Equity Securities
Fixed Maturity Portfolios				
2000				
Market value	$ 0	$20,830	$20,830	$1,815
Cost	0	20,388	20,388	876
MVA	$ 0	$ 442	$ 442	$ 939
1999				
Market value	$2,772	$16,831	$19,603	$2,005
Cost	2,733	17,259	19,992	973
MVA	$ 39	$ (428)	$ (389)	$1,032
1998				
Market value	$3,259	$17,855	$21,114	$2,037
Cost	2,721	16,680	19,401	953
MVA	$ 538	$ 1,175	$ 1,713	$1,084

2000 Change in MVA
Fixed maturities $ 442 – $ (389) = $831
Equity securities $ 939 – $1,032 =   (93)
Total portfolio $738

1999 Change in MVA

Fixed maturities	$ (389)- $1,713 =	$(2,102)
Equity securities	$1,032 - $1,082 =	(50)
Total portfolio		$(2,152)

Calculation of 2000 Mark-to-Market Return

	Fixed Maturities	Equities	Total
Dividends and interest	$1,477	$ 31	$1,508
Realized gains (losses)	(51)	63	12
Reported income	$1,426	$ 94	$1,520
Change in MVA	831	(93)	738
Mark-to-market return	$2,257	$ 1	$2,258

Calculation of 2000 Mark-to-Market ROA

	Fixed Maturities	Equities	Total Portfolio
Opening balance	$21,114	$ 2,037	$23,151
Mark-to-market return	2,257	1	2,258
Return on assets	**10.69%**	**0.05%**	**9.75%**

Calculation of 1999 Mark-to-Market Return

	Fixed Maturities	Equities	Total Portfolio
Dividends and interest	$ 1,429	$ 52	$ 1,481
Realized gains (losses)	---	83	83
Reported income	$ 1,429	$135	$ 1,564
Change in MVA	(2,102)	(50)	(2,152)
Mark-to-market return	$ (673)	$ 85	$ (588)

Calculation of 1999 Mark-to-Market ROA

	Fixed Maturities	Equities	Total Portfolio
Opening balance	$19,603	$ 2,005	$21,608
Mark-to-market return	(673)	85	(588)
Return on assets	**(3.43)%**	**4.24%**	**(2.72)%**

These returns are quite different from reported returns. In 1999, both the fixed maturity and equity portfolio returns are lower. The fixed-maturity returns are negative reflecting the 1999 rise in interest rates.

The 2000 mark-to-market fixed income returns on the other hand were sharply higher than the 1999 returns (and the 2000 reported returns) as interest rates fell dramatically in 2000 and prices of debt securities rose accordingly. The mark-to-market equity returns in 2000 were negligible, reflecting the stock market decline.

These comparisons show that mark-to-market returns, while they report actual market results, are more volatile than reported returns that can be smoothed by management decisions.

c. The mark-to-market returns clearly report the effect of market performance on Safeco's investment portfolios.

d. To fully evaluate the performance of Safeco's portfolios, we need benchmarks. For the bond portfolio, a weighted average of market returns (with weights equal to the proportion of U.S. government, corporate, tax-exempt, etc. held in Safeco's portfolio) should be used. The benchmark should also be adjusted for any differences in duration, quality, or other bond characteristics.

The equity benchmark should also reflect the composition of Safeco's portfolio, reflecting such characteristics as type of stock (preferred vs. common), capitalization (large vs. small), and any international representation.

e. (i)

	1999	2000
Reported pretax	$ 332	$ 159
Less: reported return	(1,564)	(1,520)
Plus: MTM return	(588)	2,258
Equals: adjusted pretax	$(1,820)	$ 897

(ii) Managements generally oppose mark-to-market accounting because of the resulting volatility of reported income and because, when only realized gains are reported, earnings can be managed as discussed in (iii). If MTM returns were included in reported income, return volatility would be transmitted directly to the income statement as well, as illustrated in (i) above.

(iii) When only realized gains and losses are included in reported earnings, management can smooth variations in operating earnings by varying the amounts of realized gains and losses. In good years, realized losses reduce total earnings. In poor operating years, realized gains augment reported earnings. Securities sold for earnings management purposes can be replaced with other (similar) securities.

f. We disagree with Safeco management. Analysts should look at corporate profits relative to the resources available to management. In the case of marketable securities, market value is a better measure of those resources than historical cost. If those resources cannot earn an adequate return in Safeco's insurance business, that suggests that assets should be returned to stockholders for reinvestment in other businesses with higher returns. Reducing the reported asset base inflates reported ROA and ROE, suggesting that the enterprise is more profitable than it really is.

4.{S}a. Carrying amounts at December 31, 2001:

(i)   Trading: 100 x $ 37 =   **$3,700**
(ii)   Available-for-sale:(same)   **3,700**
(iii)   Equity method:
        $4,000 + 100 ($3.00 - $1.00) =   **4,200**

b. Investment income for 2001:

(i)   Trading: (100 x $1) - $300 =   **$(200)**
(ii)   Available-for-sale: 100 x $1 =   **100**
(iii)   Equity method: 100 x $3.00 =   **300**

c. Total income over holding period:

(i)   Trading: $(200)in 2001 + $200 gain in 2002 =   **0**
(ii)   AFS: $100 in 2001 - $100 loss in 2002 =   **0**
(iii)   Equity: $300 in 2001 - $300 loss in 2002 =   **0**

Over the entire holding period, all accounting methods report the same total return. The pattern of income recognition, however, differs.

5.{M}a.   2000: Cost method, unless Burry can argue that it has "significant influence" over Bowman. SFAS 115 does not apply as Bowman shares are not marketable securities.

2001: Equity method, unless Burry does not have "significant influence." If the equity method is appropriate, retroactive restatement of the Investment in Bowman account and retained earnings is required.

b.   2000:   Income and Cash from Operations both equal the dividends received during the year: $152,000 (.19 x $800,000). Cash for investment equals $(10) million.

There is no effect on the carrying amount of Burry's investment in Bowman, which remains at the acquisition cost of $10 million.

2001: Because Burry acquired an additional 1% for a total share of 20%, a retroactive restatement of the investment account and retained earnings is required:

Acquisition cost:	$10,000,000
Less:	
Share of 2000 loss (.19 x $600,000)	(114,000)
Dividends received (.19 x $800,000)	(152,000)
Restated carrying amount, 1/1/2001	$ 9,734,000

Note: The $266,000 reduction is charged to retained earnings.

2001 transactions and entries:

Restated carrying amount, 1/1/2001	$ 9,734,000
Plus: Additional acquisition cost	500,000
Share of 2001 income (.20 x $2,000,000)	400,000
Less: dividends received (.20 x $1,000,000)	(200,000)
Carrying amount, December 31, 2001	$10,434,000

Income equals Burry's proportionate interest in the earnings of Bowman: $400,000 (.2 x $2,000,000).

Cash from operations equals the amount of dividends received from Bowman: $200,000 (.2 x $1,000,000). Cash for investing equals $(500,000).

c.   2000: same as b

Income = $152,000 (.19 x $800,000)

No effect on investment

2001:   income = cash flow from dividend payments of $200,000 (.2 x 1,000,000).

The investment account at 12/31/01 would equal the total cost of $10,500,000 ($10,000,000 + $500,000).

d.   2000: Burry would recognize its proportionate share of Bowman's loss: ($114,000) = .19 x $(600,000)

Investment account would be $9,734,000 a decrease of $266,000 ($152,000 + $114,000) reflecting the share of loss and the dividends received. [See part b.]

[Alternate calculation: share of undistributed loss for 2000 = .19 x [($600,000) - $800,000] = .19 x ($1,400,000) = $(266,000)]

Cash from operations equals $152,000. Cash for investment equals $(10,000,000).

2001: Income equal to $400,000 (.2 x $2,000,000)

Cash from operations equal to $200,000 (.2 x $1,000,000). Cash for investing equals $(500,000).

Investment account equals $10,434,000, an increase of $700,000 including the $200,000 difference between income and cash flow and the additional investment of $500,000.

e.   The answer depends on the relationship between Burry and Bowman. It is unlikely that the purchase of an additional 1% interest changed that relationship. Thus B, which uses different methods for the two years, does not provide useful information. The choice is between the cost method (c) and the equity method (d).

The advantage of the cost method is that Burry's income includes only the cash flow (dividends) received. If Burry is a passive investor, the cost method provides better information. If market values were available, the total return would be the best measure.

The equity method is more appropriate when Burry is actively involved in managing Bowman and thus earning its share of the profits of Bowman. The payment of dividends may be discretionary on the part of the major shareholders.

6.{M}a. *Cost method is used for 2001:*

No effect on sales.

Income recognized = dividends received of $10 (.01 x $1,000)

Cash from operations = dividends received	$ 10
Cash for investment = cost of shares	(100)
Net cash flow	$(90)

Equity method is used for 2002:

No effect on sales

Income recognized = proportionate share of earnings
= $660 (.30 x $2,200).

Cash from operations = dividends received	$ 360
Cash for investment = cost of shares	(3,190)
Net cash flow	$(2,830)

b. 2001: December 31, 2001 (cost method) $ 100

2002: The equity method must be applied retroactively to 2001:

Initial acquisition cost	$ 100
Plus share of 2001 earnings (1% of $2,000)	20
Less dividends received	(10)
Adjusted carrying amount, January 1, 2002	$ 110

January 1, 2002 shares purchased	$3,190
Equity in 2002 earnings	660
Less: 2002 dividends received	(360)
Carrying amount, December 31, 2002	$3,600

c. The additional share purchases require that Potter consolidate San Francisco, for two reasons:

(i) It owns 100% of San Francisco's shares
(ii) It controls San Francisco.

Potter must use the purchase method of accounting (see Chapter 14) to reflect its ownership of San Francisco. The assets and liabilities of San Francisco must be consolidated with those of Potter using fair market values at January 1, 2003 (San Francisco only). Off-balance-sheet items (such as contingencies and postemployment benefits) may also be recognized. Information on fair values and off-balance-sheet items, as well as full financial statements for San Francisco, would be needed to evaluate the effect of the acquisition on Potter's 2003 financial statements.

Problems 7 through 8 should require approximately 2 hours.

7.{L}a. The market method is used for the "available-for-sale" portfolio and the equity method is used for the "affiliate on the equity method"

($ thousands)	Method	1998	1999	2000
Available for sale	Market	$164,978	$197,318	$257,973
Affiliate on equity method	Equity	35,422	41,157	46,353
Investment in marketable securities		$200,400	$238,475	$304,326

b. Disaggregate HP's earnings:

($ thousands)	1999	2000
Operating income[1]	$57,181 x .604 = $34,546	$104,790 x .578 = $60,592
Marketable securities	$ 7,757 x .604 = 4,686	$31,973 x .578 = 18,487
Affiliates	3,556	3,221
Total	$42,788	$82,300

[1] Income before taxes and equity in affiliate income less income from investments, multiplied by (1 - tax rate).

c. Disaggregate HP's assets:

($ thousands)	1998	1999	2000
Operating	$ 890,030	$ 871,224	$ 955,166
Available for sale	164,978	197,318	257,973
Affiliate	35,422	41,157	46,353
Total assets	$ 1,090,430	$ 1,109,699	$ 1,259,492

Now, compute ROA on opening asset values, for each segment:

	1999	2000
Operations	3.9%	7.0%
Available-for-sale	2.8%	9.4%
Affiliate	10.0%	7.8%
Total	3.9%	7.4%

d. The results are not very useful as the asset values are a hybrid of historical costs and market values and income amounts are not actual mark-to-market returns.

	1999	2000
e. (i) Dividends and interest	$5,210	$18,678

(Income from investments less realized gains)

	1999	2000
(ii) Realized gains and losses	2,547	13,295
(iii) Unrealized gains and losses [Change during year]	33,053	49,811

Market value adjustments (MVA)

	Market	−	Cost	=	MVA	Change
1998	$164,978		$76,770		$ 88,208	-----
1999	197,318		76,057		121,261	$33,053
2000	257,973		86,901		171,072	49,811

f. The mark-to-market return equals dividend and interest income plus realized gains plus the change in MVA (from e (iii) above):

	1999	2000
Dividends and interest	$ 5,210	$ 18,678
Realized gains and losses	2,547	13,295
Unrealized gains and losses	33,053	49,811
Pretax mark-to-market return	$ 40,810	$ 81,784
Aftertax return [pretax x (1−t)]	24,653	47,289
Opening market value	164,978	197,318
Return on assets	14.9%	24.0%

g. Since there were no sales or purchases and the affiliate paid no dividends the mark-to-market return is equivalent to the change in market price as calculated below:

		Change
1998	$ 62,437	---
1999	91,687	$ 29,250
2000	125,063	33,376

The aftertax mark-to-market ROA is the aftertax change in value as a % of the opening value:

	1999	2000
Pretax mark-to-market return	$ 29,250	$ 33,376
Aftertax return [pretax x (1−t)]	17,670	19,299
Opening market value	62,437	91,687
Return on assets	28.3%	21.0%

h. HP reported portfolio returns of 2.8% to 10% in 1999 and 7.8% to 9.4% in 2000 (part c). The mark-to-market returns (parts f and g combined) are quite different: 18.6% ($42,323/$227,415) for 1999 and 23.0% ($66,588/$289,005) for 2000.

i. The mark-to-market return is a better measure of the performance of equity-based investments over the 1998 to 2000 period. The equity method is an arbitrary accounting method. The market value measures the market's assessment of the worth of equity-based investments and is a better measure of the resources available to HP should it wish to sell its investment.

8.{S}a. Start with the carrying amounts on HP's balance sheet (see Exhibit 13P-2):

	Carrying value	Change
1998	$ 35,422	----
1999	41,157	$ 5,735
2000	46,353	5,196

Because Atwood paid no dividend, the change in carrying amount equals HP's share of the income (loss) of Atwood. As HP owns 24% of Atwood, Atwood's total pretax income must have been:

1999: $5,735 / .24 =   **$23,896**
2000:   5,196 / .24 =   **21,650**

b. The tax rate can be computed by comparing HP's pretax and after-tax equity in Atwood's income:

1999 Tax rate = [1 - (3,556/5,735)] = 38%
2000 Tax rate = [1 - (3,221/5,196)] = 38%

HP made the assumption that income from Atwood would be taxed at normal corporate tax rates. One possible reason for this assumption is that HP decided it would (eventually) sell its investment in Atwood. Had they assumed they would receive the income in the form of dividends, a lower tax rate would have been appropriate.

c. HP may have reported its equity in Atwood's income on a separate line so that HP investors could see HP's results without distortion from the highly variable results of Atwood's operations.

9. {L}a.   Exhibit 13S-1 presents the December 31, 2001 and 2002 balance sheets for Moore Motors, using the equity method to account for Moore's investment in MMF.

   b.   Exhibit 13S-2 provides Moore Motor's income statement for the year ended December 31, 2002 using the equity method for MMF.

   c.   **2002 Ratios:**

	Consolidated	Equity Method
Gross profit margin	14.27	14.27
Return on assets	5.93	5.16
Return on equity	11.68	11.68
Receivables turnover*	1.16	6.06
Times interest earned	1.73	8.03
Debt-to-equity	2.55	0.18

   *Average trade and finance receivables used in this ratio.

   d.   **Gross profit margin**: The consolidated and equity method statements report the same gross profit margin, as MMF has no operations other than financing.

   Return on assets: The ratio based on consolidated statements is more useful; the equity method reports neither the total assets used by the parent and its affiliate nor the total interest expense.

   Return on equity: Because net income and equity are the same under the equity method and consolidation, these methods report the identical ROE.

   Receivables turnover: Consolidated statements are more informative for the parent's stockholders since they include all receivables generated by the firm, unlike the equity method wherein the receivables sold to MMF are excluded from the analysis. Note the large difference in the ratio due to this exclusion.

   Times interest earned: Again, the parent's stockholders are better served by the consolidated ratio that reflects the total cost of amounts borrowed whether the debt is reported on MMF's books or those of the parent. The equity method excludes the subsidiary's interest expense as it reports only the parent's share of the net income of its subsidiary.

13-15

Debt-to-equity: The consolidated ratio is more informative; it reflects the debt of the parent as well as that of its affiliate, MMF. The equity method ratio is misleadingly low as it excludes the debt of MMF.

Exhibit 13S-1
Moore Motors-Equity Method
Balance Sheets, December 31, 2001-2002

($ thousands)	2001	2002
Cash and cash equivalents	$ 6,909	$ 7,070
Accounts receivable--trade	4,541	5,447
--subsidiary	3,515	2,898
Finance receivables	13,246	13,235
Inventories	10,020	10,065
Fixed assets (net)	30,238	32,286
Investment in finance subsidiary	7,271	7,782
Miscellaneous assets	14,908	16,092
Total assets	$ 90,648	$ 94,875
Accounts payable--trade	$ 7,897	$ 7,708
--subsidiary	14,840	14,460
Bank debt	6,255	6,557
Accrued liabilities	21,054	23,847
Accrued income tax	4,930	5,671
Total liabilities	$ 54,976	$ 58,243
Stockholders' equity	35,672	36,632
Total liabilities and equity	$ 90,648	$ 94,875

Exhibit 13S-2
Moore Motors - Equity Method
Income Statement, Year Ended December 31, 2002

Sales	$110,448
Equity in income of finance subsidiary	1,111
Interest income	1,980
Total revenues	$113,539
Cost-of-goods-sold	(94,683)
Selling and administrative expense	(6,386)
Interest expense	(849)
Depreciation and amortization	(5,664)
Total expenses	$(107,582)
Pretax income	5,957
Income tax expense	(1,733)
Net income	$ 4,224

10.{L}a. The cash flow consequences of finance or credit receivable transactions are reported as components of investment cash flows. Because MMF's credit receivables are generated by the long-term financing it provides for Moore's customers, i.e., for Moore's essential operating activities, their cash flow consequences should be reported as components of cash flow from operations.

The net cash flow impact of these transactions should be reported as operating cash flows. For the year ended December 31, 2002, the reported operating cash flow of $13,006,000 should be reduced by $5,295,000 (cash inflow of $95,394,000 from liquidation of finance receivables less cash outflow for investment in finance receivables of $100,689,000) for an adjusted operating cash flow of $7,711,000 and adjusted investing cash flow of $9,710,000.

b. Interest payments of manufacturing and retailing firms should be components of financing cash flows because they reflect firms' leverage choices. The analysis of a firm's ability to generate cash from operations should not be confused by its financing decisions. Interest payments reported by Moore's manufacturing units should therefore be reflected in its financing cash flows (see Chapter 3). However, interest incurred by MMF is an operating cost and should be considered a component of its operating cash flow.

c. Exhibit 13S-3 contains the 2002 direct method cash flows of MMF and Moore's manufacturing operations.

d. Cash flow from MMF to Moore's manufacturing operations $ thousands):

Decrease in intercompany receivables	$(380)
Dividends paid	600
Decrease in intercompany payables	617
Total	$ 837

Note that this computation does not consider the cash flow effects of transactions involving the purchase of and payments for finance receivables. Data required to evaluate these transactions has not been provided in the problem.

e. The segmentation allows the analyst to separately
determine the leverage, profitability, and cash flows
generated by the manufacturing unit and the finance
operations and to understand the impact of each segment
on the consolidated entity. Trends in these critical
performance indices can be evaluated in the light of
the industry and economic conditions that affect
manufacturing operations and those (different)
conditions that influence the financing business.

Exhibit 13S-3
Moore Motors-Equity Method
Statement of Cash Flows, Year Ended December 31, 2002
Page 1 of 2

Indirect Method:

($ thousands)	Moore Motors Finance	Moore Motors (Equity Method)
Net income	$ 1,111	$ 3,7131
Depreciation and amortization	1,504	5,664
(accounts receivable	---	(906)
(inventories	---	(45)
(accrued liabilities	(366)	2,793
(accrued income taxes	---	741
(accounts payable	---	(189)
(intercompany receivables	380	(380)
(intercompany payables	(617)	617
Miscellaneous operating cash flow	---	(414)
Cash Flow from Operations	$ 2,012	$ 11,594
Net change in fixed assets2	(1,645)	(8,065)
Net change in finance receivables2	(4,889)	(406)
Cash flow for investment	$(6,534)	$ (8,471)
Net change in bank debt2	4,993	302
Repurchase of equity	---	(1,474)
New equity issued	---	173
Dividends paid	(600)	(1,963)
Cash flow for financing	$ 4,393	$ (2,962)
Net cash flow	$ (129)	$ 161

[1] Net income less equity in earnings of finance subsidiary plus dividends
received.

[2] Only net entries possible from data provided.

Direct Method:

Sales	$ 110,448	
Δ accounts receivable	(906)	
Cash collections		$109,542
Cost-of-goods-sold	(94,683)	
Δ inventories	(45)	
Δ accounts payable	(189)	
Cash inputs		(94,917)
Selling and administrative	(6,386)	
Δ accrued liabilities	2,793	
Cash administration		(3,593)
Interest expense		(849)
Interest income		1,980
Dividend from MMF		600
Miscellaneous operating cash flow		(414)
Income tax expense	(1,733)	
Δ accrued income tax	741	
Income taxes paid		(992)
Δ intercompany receivable		(380)
Δ payables		617
Cash flow from operations		$ 11,594

Moore Motors Finance

Direct Method:

Finance revenues	$ 14,504	
Δ finance receivables	(4,889)	
Cash collections		$ 9,615
Interest expense	(7,908)	
Cash inputs		(7,908)
Net cash collections		$ 1,707
Selling and administrative	(3,540)	
Δ accrued liabilities	(366)	
Cash administration		(3,906)
Income tax expense		(441)
Δ intercompany receivable		380
Δ intercompany payables		(617)
Cash flow from operations[1]		$ (2,877)

[1] Cash flow from operations reported under the indirect method is $2,012. The difference of $4,889 [$2,012 - ($2,877)] results from reclassification of the change in finance receivables from investment to operating cash flow.

11.{S}a. Under current U.S. GAAP, the increase in ownership from 25 to 33% would have no effect; Ford would continue to use the equity method to account for its investment in Mazda.

b. Under the proposed FASB standard, it is likely that Ford would have to consolidate Mazda as it now has management control (including substantial board representation). If there is no other significant shareholder, the presumption of control would be strengthened. Possible Japanese government restriction on control of Japanese firms by foreign firms would also have to be considered.

c. (i) Proportionate consolidation would replace Ford's investment in Mazda with its proportionate share of Mazda's assets and liabilities. The resulting balance sheet would give financial statement users a more complete picture of Ford's activities. Similarly, the income statement and cash flow statement would include Ford's share of Mazda's income, expenses, and cash flows.

(ii) Unless Ford controls Mazda's operations and is fully responsible for Mazda's debt, full consolidation would overstate the importance of Mazda to Ford. It would also exaggerate reported revenues and likely misstate operating and interest coverage ratios. Without actual control, consolidated cash flow from operations would also misstate cash available to Ford.

12.{M}a. Modo Paper is described on page 22 of the Holmen annual report. The formation of Modo Paper is described on page 27 and there are references to the effect of the transaction. Footnotes 9, 10, and 11 report the effect of the deconsolidation of Modo on intangible assets, fixed assets, and financial assets (investments).

The transaction replaced the assets and liabilities of the operations contributed to Modo Paper with a net investment in Modo (Associate companies). The result is to reduce Holmen's reported assets and liabilities.

As Modo is excluded from the consolidated group as of October 1, 1999, its revenues, expenses, and cash flows are no longer included in Holmen's income and cash flow statements after that date. Instead, Holmen reports its 50% share of Modo's earnings as "interest in earnings of associate companies." The cash flow statement does not explicitly show transactions with Modo but Holmen must report transactions between itself and Modo rather than the cash flows of Modo.

b. (i) Holmen's current assets and liabilities now exclude Modo's. The effect of deconsolidation depends on the current ratios of Holmen and Modo. If the latter is higher, then consolidation reduces Holmen's current ratio.

(ii) The fixed asset turnover ratio is also affected by the deconsolidation as both revenues and fixed assets now exclude those of Modo. We can judge the effect by examining Holmen's disclosures.

The segment data on page 30 shows the effect of deconsolidation on Holmen's 1999 revenue. If we take the gross revenues (before intra-group elimination) and increase the "divested" amount by one-third (Modo is included only for nine months), we find that the divested operations accounted for more than 40% of revenues (all amounts in SKr millions):

Revenues	Reported	Adjusted	%
Group	16,404	16,404	59.6%
Divested*	8,345	11,127	40.4%
Total	24,749	27,531	100.0%
* Adjusted equals reported x 4/3			

Using the data in footnote 11, we can separate the divested fixed assets from group assets at the beginning of 1999:

Fixed assets		%
Group	20,707	75.4%
Divested	6,738	24.6%
Total	27,445	100.0%

As the divested assets accounted for a larger percentage of revenues than the percentage they represented of total (fixed) assets, asset turnover is reduced by the deconsolidation. The operations contributed to Modo were less fixed asset intensive than the remaining operations.

(iii) Return on equity is unchanged by deconsolidation. Both net income and equity remain the same. However Modo was formed by merging Holmen's contributed operations with those contributed by SCA (the joint venture partner). The combined operation is likely to have an ROE that differs from that of Holmen so that Holmen's ROE will be affected by recording its share of the joint venture earnings.

13.{L} a. and b. See Exhibits 13S-4A and 13S-4B (next two pages).

c. Exxon-Mobil's equity method affiliates have financial characteristics that are different from those of Mobil itself. Consolidation of these affiliates has the following effects:

(i)   Increase in long-term debt to equity ratio
(ii) Decrease in pretax profit margin
(iii) Lower effective tax rate
(iv) Decrease in pretax return on assets

Full consolidation has the greatest impact on these ratios. Proportionate consolidation results in ratios that are between the equity method ratios and those resulting from full consolidation.

Exhibit 13S-4A

EXXON-MOBIL CORP. CONSOLIDATION

Year Ended December 31, 2000 ($ in millions)

Balance Sheet	Exxon-Mobil	Affiliates	Eliminations	Consolidation
Current assets	$ 40,399	$ 28,784		$ 69,183
Investments	12,618	-	(6,864)	5,754
Other assets	95,983	43,209		139,192
Total assets	$ 149,000	$ 71,993	$ (6,864)	$ 214,129
Current liabilities	$ 38,191	$ 28,013		$ 66,204
Long-term debt	7,280	11,116		18,396
Other liabilities	32,772	15,539		48,311
Total liabilities	$ 78,243	$ 54,668		$ 132,911
Minority interest			10,461	10,461
Equity	70,757	17,325	(17,325)	70,757
Liabilities and equity	$ 149,000	$ 71,993	$ (6,864)	$ 214,129
Income Statement				
Sales revenues	$ 228,439	$ 81,371		$ 309,810
Other income	4,309		(2,434)	1,875
Total revenues	$ 232,748	$ 81,371		$ 314,119
Operating costs[1]	$(150,603)	$(73,739)		$ (224,342)
Operating taxes	(55,064)			(55,064)
Minority interest			3,816	3,816
Pretax income	$ 27,081	$ 7,632		$ 34,713
Income tax	(11,091)	(1,382)		(12,473)
Net income	$ 15,990	$ 6,250	$ (6,250)	$ 15,990
Ratios				
Current ratio	1.058	1.028		1.045
LT debt to equity	0.103	0.642		0.260
Pretax margin	0.119	0.094		0.112
Effective tax rate	0.410	0.181		0.359
Pretax ROA	0.182	0.106		0.162

[1] Difference between revenues and pretax income of affiliates
assumed to be operating expense.

Exhibit 13S-4B

EXXON-MOBIL CORP. PROPORTIONATE CONSOLIDATION

Year Ended December 31, 2000 ($ in millions)

Balance Sheet	Mobil	Affiliates	Eliminations	Consolidated
Current assets	$ 40,399	$ 11,479		$ 51,878
Investments	12,618	-	(2,417)	10,201
Other assets	95,983	16,712		112,695
Total assets	$ 149,000	$ 28,191	$ (2,417)	$ 174,774
Current liabilities	$ 38,191	$ 11,450		$ 49,641
Long-term debt	7,280	4,094		11,374
Other liabilities	32,772	5,783		38,555
Total liabilities	$ 78,243	$ 21,327		$ 99,570
Equity	70,757	6,864	(2,417)	75,204
Liabilities and equity	$ 149,000	$ 28,191	$ (2,417)	$ 174,774

Income Statement				
Sales revenues	$ 228,439	$ 32,452		$ 260,891
Other income	4,309		(2,434)	1,875
Total revenues	$ 232,748	$ 32,452		$ 265,200
Operating costs[1]	$(150,603)	$(29,360)		$ (179,963)
Operating taxes	(55,064)			(55,064)
Pretax income	$ 27,081	$ 3,092		$ 30,173
Income tax	(11,091)	(658)		(11,749)
Net income	$ 15,990	$ 2,434	$ (2,434)	$ 15,990

Ratios				
Current ratio	1.058	1.003		1.045
LT debt to equity	0.103	0.596		0.151
Pretax margin	0.119	0.095		0.116
Effective tax rate	0.410	0.213		0.389
Pretax ROA	0.182	0.110		0.173

[1] Difference between revenues and pretax income of affiliates
   assumed to be operating expense.

14.(S}a.   (All data in $ thousands)
         Nucor's minority interest fell by $1,525 ($280,871 –
         $282,396) in 1999. This decrease must reflect the
         minority interest in income and capital contributions
         or distributions during the year. Given distributions
         of $87,177 the minority interest in 1999 income must be
         equal to the:

Change in minority interest = 1999 income - distributions
        ($1,525)   =   ?   - $87,177

Therefore: ?   = ($1,525)+ $87,177
                                = **$ 85,652**

         This amount represents the 49% of the 1999 net income
         of the joint venture that accrues to the minority
         shareholder rather than to Nucor.

   b. Dividing the data provided by .49 results in 100% of
       the 1999 net income and 1998 - 1999 equity of the joint
       venture:

            1999 net income = $85,652/.49 = **$174,800**
            12-31-98 equity = $282,396/.49 = $576,318
            12-31-99 equity = $124,048/.49 =· $573,206

            1999 return on (average) equity equals:
              $174,800/$574,762 = 30.4%

       ROE can also be computed directly from the minority
       interest data:
              $85,652/$281,634 = 30.4%

       where $281,634 is the average minority interest.

   c. The answer mainly depends on how the joint venturers
       are responsible for the liabilities of the venture. If
       each party is responsible only for its share of joint
       venture debt, there is a strong argument for reflecting
       only that portion of the debt on Nucor's balance sheet
       (and only its share of the assets as well).

   d. (i) From the point of view of Nucor management,
            proportionate consolidation has two advantages.
            First, it can hide the profitability of the joint
            venture, as the analysis in part b would no longer
            be possible. This may be a competitive advantage.
            The second advantage is that reported debt and
            debt-based ratios decline under proportionate

consolidation. The only possible disadvantage is that reported sales and assets also decline under proportionate consolidation.

(ii) From the point of view of a financial analyst, full consolidation is better in that the analysis in part a can determine the profitability of the joint venture and thus help the analyst understand the source of Nucor earnings.

15{M}a.   See Exhibit 13S-5 (next page)

b.   *Lumex Segment:*
Modest but relatively stable operating profit margin
No trend in ROA or asset turnover
Capex rose from half of depreciation in 1992 to approximately equal for 1993/1994
Cybex Segment:
Erratic operating profit margin, declining in 1993-4
Erratic ROA; negative in 1993
Rising asset turnover but below Lumex segment
Capex relative to depreciation over 1 and rising

c.   Segment results are affected by allocation of parent overhead. Trends are affected by acquisitions and divestitures, price changes, and exchange rate changes.

Comparisons with other companies are affected by the same factors. In addition, seemingly similar segments of different firms may have different customer bases, product mixes, or production processes that limit their comparability.

d.   Improved segment analysis requires better understanding of the economic factors that affect segment sales and profitability, as well as the impact of acquisitions and divestitures, and price and exchange rate changes.

e.   Sale of the Lumex segment, with its stable profitability, left the company exposed to the volatile Cybex segment. The segment data permitted analysts to see that sale of the Lumex segment would force the firm to confront the operating difficulties of Cybex.

In early 1997, the company merged with a better managed company in the exercise equipment field, expecting that the combined firms would prove more profitable.

Exhibit 13S-5			
Lumex			
Industry Segments			
Ratio Computations, 1992 to 1994			
$ in thousands	*Years Ended December 31 ($000)*		
Lumex Segment	*1992*	*1993*	*1994*
Sales	$50,038	$54,187	$60,764
Operating profit	3,445	3,881	4,012
Identifiable assets	24,297	24,756	28,659
Capital expenditures	603	1,481	1,532
Depreciation and amortization	1,142	1,283	1,568
Operating profit margin	6.9%	7.2%	6.6%
Return on ending assets	14.2%	15.7%	14.0%
Asset turnover	2.06	2.19	2.12
Capex-to-depreciation	0.53	1.15	0.98
Cybex Segment			
Sales	$53,850	$54,781	$70,420
Operating profit	3,690	(692)	2,218
Identifiable assets	31,452	32,117	37,087
Capital expenditures	1,550	1,736	2,047
Depreciation and amortization	1,382	1,523	1,671
Operating profit margin	6.9%	-1.3%	3.1%
Return on ending assets	11.7%	-2.2%	6.0%
Asset turnover	1.71	1.71	1.90
Capex-to-depreciation	1.12	1.14	1.23

16.{L}a. See Exhibit 13S-6 on next two pages.

   b. Operating profit margin was stable overall but varied
       widely across segments. Different segments had quite
       different levels and trends. Latin America and
       Europe/Eurasia had the highest profit margins and ROAs.
       The Asia Pacific region has had declining margins and
       ROA in spite of its rapid revenue growth. Africa/Middle
       East has declined sharply since 1998 whereas the United
       States has been generally stable. Large increase in
       assets reduced the Africa ROA.

       Asset turnover has declined over the 1998-2000 period
       as asset increases have outpaced sales growth. The only
       regions that show growth in asset turnover are
       Europe/Eurasia and Asia Pacific.

       Capex is now about equivalent to depreciation. The
       ratio is highest and growing in Europe/Eurasia.

   c. & d. See Exhibit 13S-7 on last page.

   e. Geographic segment results with companies are affected
       by allocation of parent overhead. Trends are affected
       by acquisitions and divestitures, price changes, and
       especially exchange rate changes.

       Comparisons with other companies are affected by the
       same factors. In addition, geographic segments may be
       defined differently. Note, for example, that Coca Cola
       combines the Europe and Eurasia in one segment. It is
       unlikely that others firms would choose exactly the
       same combination of countries.

   f. Improved segment analysis requires better understanding
       of the economic factors that affect the sales and
       profitability of operations in different geographic
       areas. The impact of acquisitions and divestitures, and
       price and exchange rate changes must also be
       considered.

```
Exhibit 13S-6: Coca-Cola
Geographic Segments
Ratio Computations, 1998 to 2000
                    ($millions)    Years Ended December 31
```

United States	1998	1999	2000
Net operating revenues	$ 6,934	$ 7,519	$ 7,870
Operating income	1,383	1,436	1,406
Identifiable operating assets	3,467	3,591	4,271
Capital expenditures	274	269	259
Depreciation and amortization	231	263	244
Operating profit margin	19.9%	19.1%	17.9%
Return on ending assets	39.9%	40.0%	32.9%
Asset turnover	2.00	2.09	1.84
Capex-to-depreciation	1.19	1.02	1.06

Africa & Middle East	1998	1999	2000
Net operating revenues	$ 780	$ 792	$ 729
Operating income	223	67	80
Identifiable operating assets	541	672	622
Capital expenditures	22	22	11
Depreciation and amortization	40	47	54
Operating profit margin	28.6%	8.5%	11.0%
Return on ending assets	41.2%	10.0%	12.9%
Asset turnover	1.44	1.18	1.17
Capex-to-depreciation	0.55	0.47	0.20

Europe & Eurasia	1998	1999	2000
Net operating revenues	$ 4,827	$ 4,540	$ 4,377
Operating income	1,655	1,068	1,415
Identifiable operating assets	1,711	1,624	1,408
Capital expenditures	216	218	194
Depreciation and amortization	92	80	64
Operating profit margin	34.3%	23.5%	32.3%
Return on ending assets	96.7%	65.8%	100.5%
Asset turnover	2.82	2.80	3.11
Capex-to-depreciation	2.35	2.73	3.03

Exhibit 13S-6 (continued)

Latin America

Net operating revenues	$ 2,240	$ 1,961	$ 2,174
Operating income	1,056	840	916
Identifiable operating assets	1,364	1,653	1,545
Capital expenditures	72	67	16
Depreciation and amortization	93	96	96
Operating profit margin	47.1%	42.8%	42.1%
Return on ending assets	77.4%	50.8%	59.3%
Asset turnover	1.64	1.19	1.41
Capex-to-depreciation	0.77	0.70	0.17

Asia Pacific

Net operating revenues	$ 3,856	$ 4,828	$ 5,159
Operating income	1,343	1,194	956
Identifiable operating assets	1,595	2,439	1,953
Capital expenditures	104	317	132
Depreciation and amortization	101	184	211
Operating profit margin	34.8%	24.7%	18.5%
Return on ending assets	84.2%	49.0%	49.0%
Asset turnover	2.42	1.98	2.64
Capex-to-depreciation	1.03	1.72	0.63

Consolidated

Net operating revenues	$18,813	$19,805	$20,458
Operating income	4,967	3,982	3,691
Identifiable operating assets	12,459	14,831	15,069
Capital expenditures	863	1,069	733
Depreciation and amortization	645	792	773
Operating profit margin	26.4%	20.1%	18.0%
Return on ending assets	39.9%	26.8%	24.5%
Asset turnover	1.51	1.34	1.36
Capex-to-depreciation	1.34	1.35	0.95

Exhibit 13S-7

Part c.	United States		Africa & Middle East		Europe & Eurasia		Latin America		Asia Pacific	
Operating income	*1999*	*2000*	*1999*	*2000*	*1999*	*2000*	*1999*	*2000*	*1999*	*2000*
Reported	1,436	1,406	67	80	1,068	1,415	840	916	1,194	956
(a),(e)	34	131	–	64	–	174	–	63	–	524
Adjusted	**1,470**	**1,537**	**67**	**144**	**1,068**	**1,589**	**840**	**979**	**1,194**	**1,480**
Pretax income										
Reported	1,432	1,410	24	(6)	984	1,568	846	866	1,143	651
(a),(e)	34	131	–	64	–	174	–	63	–	524
(c)	–	–	–	9	–	26	–	124	–	306
(d)	–	–	–	–	–	(118)	–	–	–	–
Adjusted	**1,466**	**1,541**	**24**	**67**	**984**	**1,650**	**846**	**1,053**	**1,143**	**1,481**
Part d.										
Net revenues	$7,519	$7,870	$ 792	$ 729	$4,540	$4,377	$1,961	$2,174	$4,828	$5,159
(i) Adjusted operating margin	**19.6%**	**19.5%**	**8.5%**	**19.8%**	**23.5%**	**36.3%**	**42.8%**	**45.0%**	**24.7%**	**28.7%**
Identifiable operating assets	3,591	4,271	672	622	1,624	1,408	1,653	1,545	2,439	1,953
(ii)Adjusted ROA	**40.9%**	**36.0%**	**10.0%**	**23.2%**	**65.8%**	**112.9%**	**50.8%**	**63.4%**	**49.0%**	**75.8%**

Case 13-1 Solution

Estimated time to complete this case is 3 to 3½ hrs.

Overview:

The "punch line" for this case is Exhibit 13CS-2 (all exhibits are at the end of the case solution). Selected ratios of Coca-Cola (Coke) as reported, with Enterprises on an equity basis are compared to ratios calculated with Enterprises consolidated on a full and proportional basis.

Enterprises' operations are heavily entwined with those of Coke. Carrying the affiliate on an equity basis results in only the net assets and bottom-line income being reported for the total entity. This serves to obscure the actual liabilities of the total entity as well as the total assets and revenues required to generate the firm's income. As such, the firm's solvency and profitability ratios are distorted.

An additional consideration is the nature and *quality* of Enterprises' assets. *Approximately two-thirds of Enterprises' assets are intangible assets*, an important consideration in any credit analysis. *Moreover, these intangibles result from bottling franchises granted by Coke to Enterprises.* On a consolidated basis, as one entity, a strong argument can be made that these assets represent the *de facto* capitalization by Coke of its own brand - a practice not permitted by U.S. GAAP[1].

1. Given Coke's 38% ownership of Enterprises, representation on the board of directors, and the licenser/supplier relationship, clearly Coke is not a passive investor. The operations of Enterprises are an integral part of Coke's operations. Purchases from Coke account for approximately 40% of Enterprises' cost-of-goods-sold (Exhibit 13C-1). These close relationships suggest that either full consolidation or proportionate consolidation would be a more appropriate method of accounting, reflecting the effective control by Coke.

---

1 If one were to make the argument that brand accounting is desirable, then one would have to justify the value placed upon it by Coke and Enterprises -- it would be hard to argue that the sale was "arm's length". Furthermore, at the very least, for comparison purposes with other firms which do not practice brand accounting, such assets should be ignored.

2. The solution to this problem is presented in Exhibit 13CS-1(a)-(c). Full consolidation requires the elimination of all intercompany transactions and the addition of 100% of the assets and liabilities of Enterprises to Coke's balance sheet and 100% of the revenues and expenses of Enterprises to Coke's income statement. However, since Coke owns only 38% of Enterprises, we must also recognize that other stockholders own 62% of the assets, liabilities, revenues, and expenses. This non-Coke ownership is reported using "minority interest" accounts on the consolidated balance sheet and the income statement. On the former, the minority interest represents the 62% of the net assets of Enterprises owned by non-Coke stockholders.

While 38% of Enterprises' common equity of $2,783 (all amounts in millions) equals $1,058, Coke carries the investment at $788. The difference of $270 is deducted from intangible assets.

When preparing the consolidated income statement, we eliminate the intercompany sales from sales and COGS. Additionally, we assume that the marketing payments from Coke to Enterprises were recorded as revenues by Enterprises and adjust accordingly.

The cash flow eliminations [13CS-1(c)] are much simpler. The operating adjustments (intercompany sales and marketing payments) automatically offset as they are classified as CFO for both companies.

Consolidated net income, however, is unchanged from Coke's reported income. Thus, we must eliminate Enterprise's income of $(324). The offset is minority interest of $(201), a noncash item, and $(123), which was previously included in "Equity income, net of dividends."

Additionally, we need to adjust for the $26 of dividends paid by Enterprises to Coke. These are recorded as CFO by Coke, and CFF by Enterprises.

3. See Exhibit 13CS-2

4. Virtually all of Coke's ratios are adversely affected by the consolidation of Enterprises. Enterprises is much more leveraged, with a debt/equity ratio of 4.37 compared to Coke's ratio of .45. On a consolidated basis, Coke's debt to equity ratio increases by more than threefold, to 1.52. A similar phenomenon occurs with the debt/assets ratio. The effects are more pronounced when we consider the ratios of debt to tangible assets and to equity. Removing Enterprises' intangible assets from equity results in negative tangible equity.

   Coke reports a healthy times interest earned ratio of 20.6. This ratio, however, is biased upward as it ignores Enterprises' interest expense. On a fully consolidated basis, the ratio declines by almost 75% to 6.4.

   Enterprises' income-based ratios are also well below those of Coke. ROA and the return on sales are both negative for Enterprises. As the income of both firms is greatly affected by the "transfer price" that Coke charges Enterprises for syrup, their relative profitability may be distorted; the lower levels reported on a consolidated basis are a better measure of overall profitability. Note that ROE is not affected by consolidation, as income and equity are unchanged.

   Interestingly, receivables turnover (sales/average trade receivables) is also lower after consolidation despite Enterprises' higher ratio. The elimination of "double counting" explains this surprising result. After eliminations, sales has decreased whereas receivables have not, lowering the turnover ratio.

   Overall, the consolidated statements are less favorable to Coke than those prepared using the equity method.

5. The calculations for the proportionally consolidated statements are presented in Exhibit 13CS-3(a)-(c). The calculations are similar to those carried out on a consolidated basis except that only 38% of Enterprises' assets/liabilities and revenues/expenses are added to Coke's reported amounts. This eliminates the need for a minority interest account. Eliminations and adjustments are also reduced proportionally.

The ratio effects of proportional consolidation are also shown in Exhibit 13CS-2, where they are compared with those based on the equity method and full consolidation. Overall, the effect of proportional consolidation is similar to that of full consolidation. Leverage ratios are worse as they become larger and profitability declines. However, as only a portion of Enterprises' debt is consolidated, the decline is mitigated.

In the case of proportional consolidation, as only a portion of the intangibles are reduced, tangible equity remains positive. Debt to tangible equity increases by almost five times from .58 (equity method) to 2.79.

The proportional consolidation cash flow statement [13CS-3(c)], like the income statement, includes 38% of the cash flows of Enterprises. Adjustments are similar to those of the fully consolidated cash flow statement (see question 2); the only difference being that there is no need for a minority interest adjustment to income.

6. Data in Exhibit 13C-2 indicate the following profitability measures for Coke's other affiliates ($ in millions).

    Gross Profit $8,542/$19,955 = 43%
    Return on sales $ 735/$19,955 = 3.7%
    Return on assets $ 735/$23,892 = 3.1%

As these measures are well below Coke's (as reported or (fully or proportionally) consolidated), consolidating these other affiliates would lower Coke's profitability ratios even further. The size of the effect would depend on the degree of intercompany eliminations.

Coke's leverage ratios would also be negatively affected by consolidating these affiliates. These affiliates have total liabilities of over $12.9 billion. We do not know what portion of those liabilities is debt. However, if we assume that only 25% is debt, that would add approximately $3.2 billion to Coke's $17.3 billion consolidated debt (an 18% increase). As equity would not change, the debt to equity ratio would increase correspondingly.

7. The FASB's exposure draft would make economic or effective control the basis for consolidation policy. Such a standard would seem to require consolidation of Enterprises by Coke, given the extensive operational and managerial influence wielded by Coke.

   However, the ED would require consolidation only when an entity has a "large minority interest" in an investee and no other party has a "significant" (more than 1/3 of the largest minority interest) minority interest. The ED defines a "large minority interest" as ownership of more than 50% of the votes typically cast in an election of the Board of Directors. Coca-Cola Enterprises states that nearly 95% of its shareholders vote in such elections - in effect, KO and CCE could argue that they do not meet the control criteria in the ED.

8. As the exhibits show, in addition to whatever strategic motivations Coke may have to reduce ownership in its bottlers, it has some powerful financial motivations to do so. By keeping its ownership levels below 50%, Coke is able to keep the bottlers' debt off its own balance sheet and (given the nature of Coke and its bottlers' operations) show higher operating profitability.

9. The difference between the methods is significant. The equity method (as argued in part 1) is inappropriate and misleading. Given the interdependence of the companies one must view their activities as a unified company with a number of divisions.

   However the equity method does allow the analyst to view each portion of the Coke empire separately. In effect, it provides segment data that is superior to that required by either U.S. or IAS GAAP. When the bottler has any publicly traded securities (debt or equity) its financial statements provide better segment data than that provided under the equity method. The market valuation of publicly traded bottler securities also provides valuation data.

   Under consolidation, the financial statements of Coke include 100% of the assets, liabilities, revenues, expenses, and cash flows of its affiliates. The minority interest account shows the (net) interest in the equity and earnings held by the non-Coke stockholders of these affiliates. Proportionate consolidation, on the other hand, includes only approximately (38%-49%) of the assets, liabilities, revenues, expenses, and cash flows of the affiliates in the financial statements of Coke.

Full consolidation may, therefore, overstate the degree to which Coke is responsible for the liabilities of the affiliates. It also overstates the affiliates' contribution of revenues, expenses, and cash flows to the operations of the total entity. On the other hand, it is unlikely that Coke would allow any operationally significant affiliate to suffer financial distress that would impede its ability to effectively market Coke products.

Proportionate consolidation, on the other hand, may understate the influence of the affiliates. Like other stockholders, Coke is a residual owner. Before it can receive any return on its investment, *all* of the affiliates' liabilities must be satisfied. Coke's Statement of Cash Flows reports its proportionate share of the cash flows generated by the affiliates. However, since creditors have a senior claim on these cash flows, Coke's proportionately consolidated cash flow statement can also be misleading.

Thus, none of these three methods is fully satisfactory. Which is superior may well depend on the analyst's point of view (equity or creditor). The equity method, when supplemented by full financial statements for affiliates, enables the analyst to look at Coke from all three points of view.

Exhibit 13CS-1(a)
Coke and Enterprises – Consolidated Balance Sheet ($ millions)

	Coke	Enterprises	Adjustments Debit	Adjustments Credit	Full Consolidation
Cash and marketable securities	1,934	284			2,218
Trade accounts receivable	1,882	1,540		38	3,384
Inventories	1,055	690			1,745
Prepaid expenses and other	2,300	362		70	2,592
Current assets	**$ 7,171**	**$ 2,876**			**$ 9,939**
Equity method Investments					
Coca-Cola Enterprises	788	–		788	–
Coca-Cola Amatil Limited	432	–			432
Coca-Cola HBC S.A	791				791
Other, mainly bottling	3,117	–			3,117
Cost method investments,					–
Principally bottling companies	294	–			294
Other assets	2,792	–		510	2,282
Total investments	**8,214**	**–**			**6,916**
Property, plant and equipment	4,453	6,206			10,659
Intangible assets	2,579	14,637		270	16,946
Total assets	**$22,417**	**$23,719**			**$44,460**
Accounts payable	4,530	2,610			7,140
Accounts payable to Coca-Cola	–	38	38		–
Deferred cash payments from Coca-Cola	–	70	70		–
Notes payable and current debt	3,899	1,804			5,703
Current liabilities	**$ 8,429**	**$ 4,522**			**$12,843**
Long-term debt	1,219	10,365			11,584
Other noncurrent liabilities	961	1,166			2,127
Deferred taxes	442	4,336			4,778
Deferred cash payments from Coca-Cola	–	510	510		–
Long-term liabilities	**$ 2,622**	**$16,377**			**$18,489**
Minority interest				1,725	1,725
Preferred stock	–	37			37
Common equity	11,366	2,783	2,783		11,366
Total liabilities and equity	**$22,417**	**$23,719**			**$44,460**

Exhibit 13CS-1(b)
Coke and Enterprises – Consolidated Income Statement ($ millions)

	Coke	Enterprises	Eliminations	Full Consolidation
Net operating revenues	$20,092	$ 15,700	$(4,901)	$30,891
Cost of goods sold	(6,044)	(9,740)	4,295	(11,489)
Gross profit	**$14,048**	**$ 5,960**	**$ (606)**	**$19,402**
S G & A expense	(8,696)	(5,359)	606	(13,449)
Operating income	**$ 5,352**	**$ 601**	**–**	**$ 5,953**
Interest income	325	–		325
Interest expense, net	(289)	(753)		(1,042)
Equity income	152	–	123	275
Other income	130	2	–	132
Income before taxes	**$ 5,670**	**$ (150)**	**$ 123**	**$ 5,643**
Minority interest			201	201
Income taxes	(1,691)	131	–	(1,560)
Income before cumulative effect of accounting change	**$ 3,979**	**$ (19)**	**$ 324**	**$ 4,284**
Cumulative effect of accounting change	(10)	(302)	–	(312)
Net income	**$ 3,969**	**$ (321)**	**$ 324**	**$ 3,972**
Preferred dividends	–	(3)	–	(3)
Net income applicable to common shareowners	**$ 3,969**	**$ (324)**	**$ 324**	**$ 3,969**

Exhibit 13CS-1(c)
Coke and Enterprises – Consolidated Cash Flow Statement ($ millions)

	Coke	Enterprises	Eliminations	Full Consolidation
Net income	$ 3,969	$ (324)	$ 324	$3,969
Equity income, net of	(54)	–	(149)	(203)
Minority interest			(201)	(201)
Other adjustments	195	1,438	–	1,633
Cash flow from operations	**$ 4,110**	**$1,114**	**$ (26)**	**$5,198**
Cash flow from investing	**(1,188)**	**(2,010)**		**(3,198)**
Debt financing	(926)	946		20
Stock issuance (repurchase)	(113)	12		(101)
Dividends	(1,791)	(72)	26	(1,837)
Cash flow from financing	**$(2,830)**	**$ 886**	**$ 26**	**$(1,918)**
Effect of exchange rates	**(45)**	**–**		**(45)**
Change in cash	**$ 47**	**$ (10)**	**$ –**	**$ 37**

Exhibit 13CS-2

		As Reported	COCA COLA PART 5 Proportionate	PART 3 Full	
	Enterprises	Equity	Consolidation	Consolidation	
a) Current ratio	0.64	0.85	0.81	0.77	
b) Debt to equity	4.37	0.45	0.86	1.52	
c) Debt to tangible equity	–	0.58	2.79	–	
d) Debt to assets	0.51	0.23	0.32	0.39	
e) Debt to tangible assets	1.34	0.26	0.44	0.63	
f) Gross profit	38%	70%	66%	63%	
g) Return on sales	-2%	20%	16%	13%	
h) ROA	-1%	19%	15%	11%	
I) Return on tangible assets	-2%	21%	20%	17%	
j) ROE	-12%	35%	35%	35%	
k) Return on tangible equity	0%	93%	114%	0%	
l) Times interest earned	0.8	20.6	9.0	6.4	
m) Inventory turnover	14.1	5.7	6.2	6.6	
n) Receivables turnover	10.2	10.7	7.2	9.1	

Exhibit 13CS-3(a)
Coke and Enterprises – Proportional Consolidated Balance Sheet

	Coke	Enterprises 100%	Enterprises 38%	Adjustments Debit	Adjustments Credit	Proportional Consolidation
Cash and marketable securities	$ 1,934	$ 284	$ 108			$2,042
Trade accounts receivable	1,882	1,540	585		14	2,453
Inventories	1,055	690	262			1,317
Prepaid expenses and other	2,300	362	138		27	2,411
Current assets	**$ 7,171**	**$2,876**	**$1,093**	**$ –**	**$ 41**	**$8,223**
Equity method investments						
Coca-Cola Enterprises	788	–	–		788	–
Coca-Cola Amatil Limited	432	–	–			432
Coca-Cola HBC S.A	791	–				791
Other, mainly bottling	3,117	–	–			3,117
Cost method investments,			–			–
Mainly bottling companies	294	–	–			294
Other assets	2,792	–	–		194	2,598
Total investments	**$ 8,214**	**–**	**–**		**$ 982**	**$7,232**
Property, plant & equipment	4,453	6,206	2,358			6,811
Intangible assets	2,579	14,637	5,562		270	7,871
Total assets	**$22,417**	**$23,719**	**$9,013**		**$1,293**	**$30,137**
Current liabilities						
Accounts payable	4,530	2,610	992			5,522
Accounts payable to Coca-Cola	–	38	14	14		–
Deferred cash payments from Coca-Cola	–	70	27	27		–
Notes payable and current debt	3,899	1,804	686			4,585
Current liabilities	**$ 8,429**	**$4,522**	**$1,718**	**$ 41**		**$10,106**
Long-term debt	1,219	10,365	3,939			5,158
Other noncurrent liabilities	961	1,166	443			1,404
Deferred taxes	442	4,336	1,648			2,090
Deferred cash payments from Coca-Cola	–	510	194	194		–
Noncurrent liabilities	**$ 2,622**	**$16,377**	**$6,223**	**$ 194**		**$ 8,651**
Preferred stock	–	37	14			14
Common equity	11,366	2,783	1,058	1,058		11,366
Total liabilities and equity	**$22,417**	**$23,719**	**$9,000**	**$1,293**	**$ –**	**$30,137**

Exhibit 13CS-3(b)
Coke and Enterprises – Proportional Consolidated Income Statement

	Coke	Enterprises 100%	Enterprises 38%	Eliminations	Proportional Consolidation
Net operating revenues	$20,092	$15,700	$ 5,966	$(1,862)	$24,196
Cost of goods sold	(6,044)	—	(3,701)	1,632	(8,113)
Gross profit	$14,048	$ 5,960	$ 2,265	$ (230)	$16,083
S G & A expense	(8,696)	—	(2,036)	230	(10,502)
Operating income	**$ 5,352**	**$ 601**	**$ 228**	**–**	**$ 5,580**
Interest income	325	–	–		325
Interest expense, net	(289)		(286)		(575)
Equity income	152	–	–	123	275
Other Income	130	2	1	–	131
Income before taxes	**$5,670**	**$ (150)**	**$ (57)**	**$ 123**	**$ 5,736**
Income taxes	(1,691)	131	50	–	(1,641)
Income before cumulative effect of accounting change	**$3,979**	**$ (19)**	**$ (7)**	**$ 123**	**$ 4,095**
Cumulative effect of accounting change	(10)	(302)	(115)	–	(125)
Net income	**$3,969**	**$ (321)**	**$ (122)**	**$ 123**	**$ 3,970**
Preferred dividends	–	(3)	(1)	–	(1)
Net income applicable to common shareowners	**$3,969**	**$ (324)**	**$ (123)**	**$ 123**	**$ 3,969**

Exhibit 13CS-3(c)
Coke and Enterprises – Proportional Consolidated Cash Flow Statement

	Coke	Enterprises 100%	Enterprises 38%	Eliminations	Proportional Consolidation
Net income	$3,969	$ (324)	$(123)	$123	$ 3,969
Equity income, net of	(54)	–	–	(149)	(203)
Minority interest			–	–	–
Other adjustments	195	1,438	546	–	741
Cash flow from operations	**$4,110**	**$1,114**	**$423**	**$ (26)**	**$ 4,507**
Cash flow from investing	**(1,188)**	**(2,010)**	**(764)**		**(1,952)**
Debt financing	(926)	946	359		(567)
Stock issuance (repurchase)	(113)	12	5		(108)
Dividends	(1,791)	(72)	(27)	26	(1,792)
Cash flow from financing	**$(2,830)**	**$ 886**	**$337**	**$ 26**	**$(2,467)**
Effect of exchange rates	**(45)**				**(45)**
Change in cash	**$ 47**	**$ (10)**	**$ (4)**	**$ –**	**$ 43**

Chapter 14 - Solutions

Overview:
Problem Length   *Problem #s*
    {S}   6 - 11
    {M}   1 - 5
    {L}   12 - 13

1.{M}a.   Martin Sales (Amounts in $millions)

Method	*2000*	*2001*	*2002*
Purchase method	**$435**	**$610** ($550 + $60)	**$1,120** ($970 + $150)
Pooling method	**$525** ($435 + $90)	**$670** ($550 + $120)	**$1,120** (same)

Under the purchase method, Martin's sales include Green's sales only following the acquisition. Under the pooling method, Green's sales are included for all periods, and 2000 must be restated.

    b.   Under the purchase method (IASB GAAP):
    (i) The growth rate of reported sales is **higher** because past sales are not restated so that the addition of Green's sales following the merger increases reported sales.
    (ii) Return on equity is **lower** than under pooling. Income is reduced by higher depreciation as Green's property is recorded at its higher fair value, by higher interest expense due to amortization of the debt discount, and by amortization of any goodwill. Equity is increased by the market value of the additional Martin shares issued (under pooling, new Martin shares are added at book value). With lower income and higher equity, return on equity is reduced.
    (iii)Long-term debt-to-equity ratio is **lower** than under pooling. Debt is lower because, under the purchase method, Green's debt is recorded at its fair market value. Equity is increased by the market value of the additional Martin shares issued. With lower debt and higher equity, the ratio is reduced.

c.   Under the purchase method (US GAAP):
   (i)   The growth rate of reported sales is the **same** as reported under IASB GAAP.
   (ii) Return on year-end 2001 equity is **higher** than under IASB GAAP. Income is higher as there is no goodwill amortization. Equity is the same at the acquisition date, but slightly higher at year-end 2001 due to higher income.
   (iii) Long-term debt-to-equity ratio is the **same** as under IASB GAAP at the acquisition date.

2.{M}a. b. and d.   Acetar Combined Balance Sheet

| End of | Year 1 | | Year 2 |
	Pooling	Purchase	Purchase
Cash	$ 150	$ 150	$ 200
Inventory	1,300	1,330	1,400
Fixed assets (net)	4,000	4,050	4,145
Goodwill	0	320	304
Total assets	$5,450	$5,850	$6,049
Current liabilities	1,250	1,250	1,300
Equity	4,200	4,600	4,749
Total equities	$5,450	$5,850	$6,049

Under the pooling method, the balance sheets of Ace and Tar are combined without adjustment. When Ace acquires Tar, and the purchase method is used, the assets and liabilities of Tar (but not Ace) are restated to fair value. The excess of the purchase price ($1,500) over the fair value of the net assets acquired ($1,180) is recorded as goodwill ($1,500 - $1,180 = $320).

c.   Year 2 reported income under the purchase method is $149, calculated as follows:

Reported income under pooling	$ 200
Less: increase in COGS due to	
Tar inventory write-up	(30)
additional depreciation of Tar due	
to fixed asset write-up ($50/10)	(5)
goodwill amortization ($320/20)	(16)
Reported income under purchase method	**$ 149**

14-2

d. Balance sheet shown above. Differences between last two columns (Year 2 changes) are:
- Cash increased by change in cash
- Inventory increase of $100 from pooling method cash flow statement less $30 additional COGS under purchase method.
- Fixed assets increased by capital expenditures ($500) and reduced by depreciation ($405)
- Current liabilities increased by accounts payable increase of $50 from cash flow statement
- Equity increased by purchase method net income ($149).
- Goodwill decreased by amortization ($16).

e. Purchase Method Cash Flow Statement
Indirect Method

Net income	$ 149	
Depreciation	405	
Goodwill amortization	16	
Change in inventory	(70)	
Change in accounts payable	50	
Cash from operations		$550
Capital expenditures	(500)	
Acquisition net of cash	(1,450)	
Cash from investing		(1,950)
Shares issued for financing	1,500	
Cash from financing		$1,500
Net cash flow		$ 100

Alternatively, shares issued for financing would be shown as supplementary information and the acquisition cash flow would be shown as $50 (cash acquired), leaving the net cash flow unchanged.

f. If Acetar reported under U.S. GAAP, there would be no goodwill amortization. Assuming that goodwill is not impaired, the differences from financial statements prepared under IASB GAAP would be:
Part a: No difference
Part c: Net income for year 2 would be $16 higher due to the absence of goodwill amortization (assuming no tax effect)).

Part d: Goodwill would be $320 and equity would be $4,765, each $16 higher than under IASB GAAP due to the lack of goodwill amortization.

Part e: No difference as the absence of goodwill amortization (a non-cash expense) is offset by higher net income.

3.{M}a. For each balance sheet account, we use the difference between the sum of the 1-1-01 historical data and the 12-31-01 balance sheet amounts as well as the cash flow and additional information provided:

Accounts receivable: $550 - $500 = $50, equal to the cash flow change. Therefore fair value unchanged at $200.

Inventory: $1,600 - $1,500 = $100. As there was no cash flow change in inventory, the write-up must be $100 and fair value $400.

Goodwill: $380 increase all due to acquisition. As goodwill amortized over 20 years, original amount must have been $400 with 2001 amortization of $20 ($400/20).

Fixed assets: $6,400 - $5,500 = $900. Capital expenditures = $1,290 and depreciation $580 for a net increase of $710. Therefore write-up must be $190 and fair value $690.

Accounts payable: $1,700 - $1,500 = $200 equal to cash flow change. No write-up; fair value equals $500.

Long-term debt: $2,750 - $2,700 = $50. Debt issued was $100. The difference of $50 is due to a writedown of the debt to fair value at the time of the merger offset (partially) by amortization of that writedown. Total depreciation and amortization on the cash flow statement is $610. As depreciation is $580 and goodwill amortization is $20, the discount amortization must be $10. Thus, there must be a $60 *writedown* of the $700 debt to a fair value of $640.

Equity: $6,280 - $4,300 = $1,980 equal to stock issued of $550 + elimination of Dove equity of $(200) + net income of $1,230.

Thus, Dove's fair value balance sheet at the acquisition date must have been:

Cash	$ 0
Accounts receivable	200
Inventory	400
Fixed assets	690
Less:	
Accounts payable	(500)
Long-term debt	(640)
Net assets	$ 150

b.   As the purchase price was $550, **goodwill of $400** ($550 - $150) was recorded.

c.   If the pooling method had been used, net income would be:

Purchase method net income	$1,230
Adjustments:	
Reduced depreciation[1]	10
No goodwill amortization[2]	20
Lower interest expense[3]	10
Total adjustments	$ 40
Income tax offset[4]	(7)
Aftertax adjustment	$33
Pooling method net income	**$1,263**

[1] Average life approximately 20 years; $190/20 = approx. $10
[2] Computed in part A
[3] Debt discount of $60 under purchase method must be amortized over remaining life of 5 years. Amortization of $10 (later year amounts will be higher) increases interest expense
[4] Computed at a 35% tax rate with goodwill not tax-deductible

d.   Pooling Method Cash Flow Statement
      Indirect Method

Net income	$ 1,263	
Depreciation	570	
Increase in accounts payable	200	
Increase in accounts receivable	(50)	
Cash from operations		$1,983
Capital expenditures	(1,290)	
Cash from investing		(1,290)
Debt issued	100	
Cash from financing		100
Net cash flow		$ 793

Cash flow under the purchase method is $7 higher
because of the tax reduction resulting from the tax
deductibility of the purchase method adjustments.

e.   If Hawk used US GAAP, there would be no goodwill
      amortization.
      (i) Net income would be $10 higher
      (ii) Equity would be $10 higher due to the increase in
           net income.

4.{M}a. and b.

$ in thousands	Reported	Fair Value	US GAAP	IAS GAAP
Great Plains Software				
Balance sheet, November 30, 2000				
Cash and equivalents	$ 40,764	$ 40,764	$ 40,764	$ 40,764
Other current assets	79,794	79,794	79,794	79,794
Current assets	$ 120,558	$ 120,558	$ 120,558	$ 120,558
Property	55,814	75,814	75,814	75,814
In process R & D	234,550	200,000	–	200,000
Identifiable intangibles		100,000	100,000	100,000
Goodwill		779,596	779,596	779,596
Other assets	6,123	6,123	6,123	6,123
Total assets	$ 417,045	$1,282,091	$1,082,091	$1,282,091
Current liabilities	115,507	115,507	115,507	115,507
Long-term liabilities	11,028	11,028	11,028	11,028
Stockholders' equity	290,510	1,155,556	955,556	1,155,556
Total liabilities and equity	$ 417,045	$1,282,091	$1,082,091	$1,282,091

   a.   To complete the exhibit, we must first compute the
        value of the transaction:

        Value = # MSFT shares issued x share price

             =   1.1 x 20,226,146 x $51.938

             = $1,155,556

        The net assets of Great Plains (shown in exhibit 14P-
        2), equals $75,960, excluding all intangible assets.
        The excess amount paid ($1,155,556 - $75,960 =
        $1,079,596) must be allocated to the intangible assets
        as follows:

In process R & D (given)	$ 200,000
Identifiable intangibles (given)	100,000
Goodwill (remainder)	779,596
Total	$ 1,079,59 6

        These amounts are used to fill in the exhibit; the
        second column of the table above is the answer to part
        a.

b. The table also shows how the resulting balance sheet looks under US GAAP (third column) and IASB GAAP (fourth column). These data are used to show the effects on reported income:

	Period Years	Gross Amount	(i) US GAAP		(ii) IAS GAAP	
			F01	F02	F01	F02
In process R & D	4	$ 200,000	$(200,000)	$ -	$(12,500)	$ (50,000)
Identifiable intangibles	5	100,000	(5,000)	(20,000)	(5,000)	(20,000)
Goodwill	10	779,596	-	-	(19,490)	(77,960)
Total		$1,079,596	**$(205,000)**	**$(20,000)**	**$(36,990)**	**$(147,960)**

In process R & D is written off immediately under US GAAP, reducing income in F01. Under IAS GAAP it is amortized over 4 years, reducing income by a smaller amount in F01. In F02 there is no negative effect under US GAAP but continuing amortization under IAS GAAP.

Other identifiable intangibles have the same effect under US and IAS GAAP as they are amortized over their five year life.

Goodwill is amortized over ten years under IAS GAAP. Amortization is prohibited under US GAAP. However periodic testing for impairment is required.

c. Under the pooling method, Microsoft was not required to write off in process R & D. The goodwill and other intangibles of $234 million remained on Great Plains' balance sheet, but any required amortization would be lower than that required under purchase method accounting. As a result, MSFT reported better postacquisition operating results for Great Plains under pooling.

d. Microsoft would most likely prefer to use US GAAP. While the immediate writeoff of in process R & D would reduce earnings in the quarter following the acquisition, such charges are often reported as "nonoperating," especially when companies report "pro forma" earnings as discussed in chapter 2. In succeeding quarters, reported income is higher under US GAAP. Reported return on equity benefits from both higher income and lower equity (from the R&D writeoff).

14-8

5.{M}a.   The required calculations are presented below:

		PEP	OAT	Combined
(i)	OI/Total capital[*]	33.6%	59.0%	33.6%
(ii)	Pretax ROE	44.3%	155.2%	45.0%
(iii)	ROE	30.1%	100.3%	30.4%
(iv)	ROE ex-adjustments**			33.4%

[*] Total capital defined as common equity plus long-term debt
** Calculated as $2,539/($7,249 + $355)

b.   The data in the table above do not support the press release.[1] The management statement must be based on some other measure of "return on invested capital." However the broader issue is that any improvement is due to use of the pooling method, which suppresses the true acquisition cost of OAT. When pooling is used, the higher return ratios of Quaker Oats tend to increase the ratios for the combined company, without any real change in the operations of either company.

c.   The market value of the transaction of $13.5 billion was about 38 times Quaker's equity. Given Quaker's relatively small current and other tangible assets, most of the purchase price would have to be allocated to intangible assets, including brand names and goodwill. It is likely that at least a portion of these intangible assets would have to be amortized, reducing reported income. At a minimum, the writeup of property to fair value would increase depreciation expense.

d.   Use of the purchase method (even the US GAAP variety that does not require goodwill amortization) would reduce reported income. More important, that method would increase equity by more than $13 billion. As a result, all three return ratios computed in part a would be greatly reduced.

e.   As stated in part b, any improvement in the post-merger return ratios results from use of the pooling method as OAT's higher returns increase those of PEP. In reality, PepsiCo issued $13.5 billion of its common shares in the acquisition and received an immediate return of less than 3%; OAT's net income of $356 million is 2.64% of $13.5 billion.

---

[1] With adjustments, there is minimal improvement; without adjustment the improvement is 300 (not 200) basis points.

6.{S}a. It appears that revenues would have declined over the three year period if no acquisitions had been made. The pro forma data, which assume that the four 1998 acquisitions had occurred on January 1, 1998, indicate 1998 revenues of $177 million but actual 1999 revenues were only $149 million. Apparently 1999 revenues declined for Boron (it is possible that revenues of the acquired companies accounted for some of the decline).

The year 2000 data show a similar pattern. 1999 pro forma revenues were $170 million but actual 2000 revenues were less than $168 million.

b. The pattern discussed in part a carries over to earnings per share. The 1998 acquisitions increased EPS (the pro forma EPS exceed reported EPS) but Boron reported a loss in 1999.

The 2000 acquisitions also were accretive, as pro forma EPS exceeded reported EPS for both 1999 and 2000. But even with the boost from acquisitions, 2000 EPS was well below that reported for 1998.

In summary, the pro forma data show that Boron's acquisitions, accounted for using the purchase method, offset declining sales and earnings from its ongoing operations.

7.(S}a. (i) 20-year amortization would reduce return on equity as higher amortization expense would reduce reported income.
(ii) 20-year amortization would also reduce the interest coverage ratio, in which the numerator is earnings before interest and taxes (EBIT). Higher amortization expense would reduce EBIT.
(iii) Cash from operations would be unaffected as amortization is a noncash expense.

b. (i) After 20 years, licenses would be fully written off. Amortization would end, increasing ROE as net income is higher and equity lower (due to amortization expense in prior years).
(ii) The interest coverage ratio would also increase after 20 years as amortization ceases, increasing EBIT.
(iii) Cash from operations is still unaffected.

c. The securities prices of license holders should reflect the long-term profitability of the licenses, rather than accounting decisions that have no cash flow effects. Therefore 20-year amortization should have no impact. Securities prices should reflect the economic lives of the licenses rather than arbitrary accounting choices.

d. The SEC is charged with protecting investors, not with creating the illusion of certainty where none exists. As stated in part c, share prices should reflect long-term cash flows. Allowing companies to use optimistic accounting assumptions that "attract investment capital" does not serve the public interest, as many investors discovered when the "technology bubble" collapsed.

8.{S}a. Calculations follow (amounts in $thousands)

| | *Years ended June 30* | | |
	1998	*1999*	*2000*
Net revenues	$ 318,448	$ 376,154	$ 438,805
Cost of goods sold	(182,557)	(198,030)	(224,565)
Gross profit	$ 137,889	$ 180,123	$ 216,240
Inventory step-up	27,845	16,448	5,687
Adjusted gross profit	$ 165,734	$ 196,571	$ 221,927
Gross profit %			
Reported	43.3%	47.9%	49.3%
Adjusted	52.0%	52.3%	50.6%

b. The reported gross profit increases from 43.3% of sales in 1998 to 49.3% of sales two years later. However this increase reflects declining inventory step-up amounts rather than operating improvement. The adjusted data show little change, with the 2000 gross profit % of 50.6% slightly below the 1998 level of 52.0%.

c. Inventory step-ups result from acquisitions accounted for using the purchase method of accounting (p. 512 of text). Step-ups do not result from current operations and should be excluded from cost of goods sold when computing measures of corporate performance such as gross margin percent.

Note: We argue (in chapter 6) that replacement cost should be used to measure corporate performance. However, when replacement cost (fair value) is used for only one portion of COGS for one period only, it results in misleading comparisons with other time periods.

9. {S}a.   Under US GAAP, goodwill remains on the balance sheet until impairment or sale of the business associated with the goodwill. Under IASB GAAP, goodwill is amortized over not more than 20 years. The consequences of immediate write-off of goodwill include:

(i) Shareholders' equity is immediately reduced by the amount of goodwill. Under IASB standards, reduction takes place over time through amortization. Under both US and IASB GAAP, impairment writedown results in an equal reduction in net income and, as a result, equity.

(ii) Asset turnover is higher as the denominator is lower without goodwill on the balance sheet.

(iii) Return on equity is higher as equity is reduced by the immediate write-off. Under IASB GAAP the effect is greater, as income is also reduced by goodwill amortization.

(iv) Earnings per share is the same as under US GAAP, but higher than under IASB GAAP, where income is reduced by goodwill amortization.

(v) Cash from operations is the same under all three accounting methods; goodwill write-off or amortization does not affect cash flow, assuming that goodwill is not deductible for tax purposes.

10. {S}a.   Goodwill is more likely to be impaired (p. 527 of text) when earnings of the acquired company are depressed, reducing estimated future cash flows. When discounted cash flows are used to assess goodwill, the likelihood of impairment is increased as the discounting process results in a lower measure of value than when undiscounted cash flows are used.

b.   (i) Return on equity increases as equity is reduced by the impairment charge.

(ii) The debt-to-equity ratio increases as equity is reduced by the impairment charge.

(iii) Cash from operations is unaffected as goodwill impairment charges are noncash when taken and have no effect on future cash flows.

11. {S}a. When a company's share price declines, its value as an acquisition currency also falls. Unless the purchase price of acquisitions also declines, the amount of sales, earnings, and cash flows that can be purchased for a given number of shares is lower, making acquisitions a less desirable growth method.

b. Poor industry conditions also reduce the attractiveness of growth by acquisition because the expected contribution (sales, net income, cash flows) from acquired companies is less certain. If the acquired operations fail to produce earnings, for example, earnings per share fall due to the shares issued to make the acquisition and the acquisition will be dilutive.

12. {L}a. Derivation of Cole balance sheet at acquisition date:

	Balance Sheet Change	Cash Flow Change	Difference
Cash	$ 15,714	$ 15,714	$ 0
Marketable securities	72,981	72,476	505
Accounts receivable	43,393	39,999	3,394
Prepaid expenses	(5,696)	(7,925)	2,229
Property	43,466	30,701 [1]	12,765
Goodwill	1,033	(2,408) [2]	3,441
Total assets	$ 170,891	$148,557	$ 22,334
Accounts payable	38,865 }	–	–
Salaries	(5,013) }	34,269	2,231
Claims payable (short-term)	2,648 }	–	–
Income taxes payable	3,080	3,022	58
Dividend payable	1,139	(48,984)	50,123 [3]
Deferred income tax	(8,411) }	–	–
Future equipment repairs	2,749 }	(4,984)	4,052
Claims payable (long-term)	4,730 }	–	–
Total liabilities	$ 39,787	$(16,677)	$ 56,464
Additional capital	19,121 }	–	–
Treasury stock	14,699 }	18,693	15,127
Retained earnings	97,284	147,407	(50,123)
Total liabilities & equity	$ 170,891	$149,423	$ 21,468
Assets less liabilities & equity	0	(866)	(866)

[Footnotes on next page]

¹ Reconciliation of property account:
Net purchases $201,011   [$211,073 - $10,062]
Depreciation   (170,287)   [$172,695 - $2,408 goodwill amortization]
Loss on sale   (23)   [cash flow statement]
Net change $ 30,701

² Reconciliation of goodwill account:
Goodwill purchased $ 3,441   [Given]
Balance sheet change (1,033)
Amortization $ 2,408

³ Note that change in dividends payable = discrepancy in retained earnings.
Therefore Cole liabilities are $56,464 - $50,123 = $6,341

As the cash flow statement provides balance sheet changes that exclude the effects of the acquisition of Cole, the differences between the balance sheet changes and cash flow changes must be due to the acquisition.

The differences tell us that Roadway acquired:

Assets of Cole	$ 22,334
Liabilities of Cole (note 3 above)	(6,341)
Net assets acquired	$ 15,993

Roadway paid for Cole with:

Cash	$ 866
Roadway shares valued at	15,127
Total payment	$ 15,993

The cash paid for Cole equals the net cash flow change.

b. **Ratios**

	Cole	Roadway
Fixed asset turnover	1.49	3.73
Accounts receivable turnover	5.60	12.17
Equity to assets	0.72	0.60

c. Roadway's fixed asset and accounts receivable ratios are more than twice those of Cole. The higher ratios may be due to the advantages of size or to better management. In that case we would expect the differences to disappear as Cole in integrated into Roadway. The cash flow implications would be positive as higher turnover would reduce the investment in fixed assets and accounts receivable.

There are other possible explanations. Cole's fixed assets may be newer than Roadway's, understating the turnover ratio. Again this would imply lower future investment. The lower accounts receivable turnover might be due to the sale of receivables. This is a form of financing (see Chapter 11). If this practice were ended, the future *reported* cash flow of Roadway would be reduced.

d. If Roadway had significant foreign operations, the differences between balance sheet changes and cash flow changes could be due to changes in exchange rates. For this reason the methodology in part A could not be used to accurately derive the balance sheet of Cole.

e. Roadway purchased Cole for almost $16 million. The future earnings of Cole should be used to compute the return on this investment.

13.{L}a. Exhibit 14S-1 (final page of solutions) shows the required calculations.

b. (i)   As Agere's revenues were growing, the spinoff increased the rate of decline of Lucent's revenues from -21.6% to -28.3%.
   (ii) As Agere's comparison was better than Lucent's, the spinoff slightly increased Lucent's rate of decline.
   (iii) As Agere's cash from operations was positive for both periods, and increased in 2001, the spinoff had the effect of making Lucent's reported cash from operations even more negative. *Note*: the percentage changes are misleading. As discussed on page 113 of the text, negative numbers can distort ratio comparisons.
   (iv) As Agere's capital expenditures increased (reflecting higher revenues) the spinoff reduced the growth rate of Lucent's capital expenditures from 15.3% to 1.6%.

c. The ratios are computed in Exhibit 14S-1

d. Lucent's debt and debt-to-equity ratio following the April 2, 2001 transactions were (Lucent used the sale proceeds to reduce its debt):

Lucent total debt	$ 5,370
Less: proceeds from sale	(519)
Less: debt assumed by Agere	(2,500)
Adjusted debt	$ 2,351
Adjusted debt-to-equity ratio	0.11

e.   There was only one clear gain to Lucent from the spinoff. As shown in part d, the spinoff transactions reduced Lucent's debt-to-equity ratio from 0.24 (combined basis assuming no spinoff) to 0.11. There was also a small improvement in the current ratio from the spinoff (part c). Lucent's current ratio would have been further improved by the spinoff transactions that reduced debt (assuming that current debt was reduced). Finally, the spinoff reduced the loss from continuing operations.

The negative effects are shown in part a: lower growth rates for revenues and capital expenditures as well as more negative cash from operations.

As the most dramatic change was in Lucent's debt burden, and operating losses may have resulted in violation of debt covenants, it is most likely that Lucent's decision to spin off Agere was based on that factor.

Exhibit 14S-1	Lucent		Agere		Combined	
Amounts in $millions	2000	2001	2000	2001	2000	2001
Revenues	$ 14,320	$ 10,269	$ 2,033	$ 2,553	$ 16,353	$ 12,822
Income from continuing operations	1,441	(4,954)	159	(148)	1,600	(5,102)
Cash from operating activities	(338)	(2,825)	279	369	(59)	(2,456)
Capital expenditures	(740)	(752)	(333)	(485)	(1,073)	(1,237)
a. *Percent changes:*						
(i) **Revenue**		− 28.3%		25.6%		− 21.6%
(ii) **Income from continuing operations**		−443.8%		−193.1%		−418.9%
(iii) **Cash from operating activities**		−735.8%		32.3%		−4,062.7%
(iv) **Capital expenditures**		1.6%		45.6%		15.3%
Current assets		$ 18,819		$ 1,553		$ 20,372
Debt maturing within one year		2,314		16		2,330
Other current liabilities		7,629		1,166		8,795
Total current liabilities		**9,943**		**1,132**		**11,125**
Debt maturing within one year		2,314		16		2,330
Long-term debt		3,056		42		3,098
Total debt		**5,370**		**58**		**5,428**
Stockholders' equity		22,060		5,777		27,837
c. *Ratios (continuing operations):*						
(i) **Current ratio**		1.89		1.31		1.83
(ii) **Debt-to-equity**		0.24		0.01		0.19

14-17

Case 14-1 - Solution

Estimated time to complete this case is 5 hours.

1. Pfizer (PFE) accounted for the acquisition of Warner-Lambert (WLA) as a pooling of interests. Under that method:
    (i)   the assets and liabilities of WLA were added to those of PFE without any adjustment. Prior period balance sheets were restated to include WLA. Shareholders' equity of PFE was increased by the stated equity of WLA, regardless of the market value of the PFE shares exchanged.
    (ii) Similarly, the income statements of Pfizer include the corresponding accounts of WLA, restated as if the companies had been combined in all prior years. The income and expenses of WLA were included without any adjustment.
    (iii) The cash flow statement of WLA are added to those of PFE without adjustment, and restated for all prior years. The merger transaction is not recorded in the cash flow statement.
    (iv) Financial statement footnotes are combined and restated for prior periods.

2. Exhibit 14C1S-1 combines the financial statements of PFE and WLA at December 31, 1999. These statements are used to compute the required ratios:

		WLA	PFE	**Combined**
(i)	**Current ratio**	1.54	1.22	**1.31**
(ii)	**Total debt to equity**	0.30	0.62	**0.51**
(iii)	**Book value per share**		2.36	**2.26**
(iv)	**Gross profit margin**	0.76	0.84	**0.81**
(v)	**Pretax profit margin**	0.19	0.27	**0.24**
(vi)	**Return on (ending) equity**	32%	36%	**35%**
(vii)	**Cash from operations to debt**	158%	56%	**78%**

    Note: As neither company's income statement shows operating income, we have used pretax profit margin instead.

    Discussion: The merger with WLA improves Pfizer's current, debt/equity, and CFO/debt ratios. Profit margins are reduced, however.

Exhibit 14C1S-1

Condensed Balance Sheets at December 31, 1999

Amounts in $ millions	WLA	PFE	Combined
Cash and equivalents	$ 1,943	$ 4,642	$ 6,585
Inventories	979	1,654	2,633
Other current assets	2,768	4,895	7,663
Current assets	$ 5,690	$11,191	$16,881
Property (net)	3,342	5,343	8,685
Investments and other assets	793	3,277	4,070
Intangible assets	1,616	763	2,379
Total assets	$11,441	$20,574	$32,015
Short-term debt	$ 297	$ 5,001	$ 5,298
Other current liabilities	3,391	4,184	7,575
Current liabilities	$ 3,688	$ 9,185	$12,873
Long-term debt	1,250	525	1,775
Deferred income tax	463	301	764
Other long-term liabilities	942	1,676	2,618
Stockholders' equity	5,098	8,887	13,985
Total liabilities and equity	$11,441	$20,574	$32,015
Million shares outstanding		3,758	6,198

Condensed 1999 Income Statements	WLA	PFE	Combined
Sales	$12,929	$16,204	$29,133
Cost of goods sold	(3,042)	(2,528)	(5,570)
Selling, general, administrative	(5,959)	(6,351)	(12,310)
Research and development	(1,259)	(2,776)	(4,035)
Other expense, net	(228)	(101)	(329)
Pretax income	$ 2,441	$ 4,448	$ 6,889
Income tax expense	(798)	(1,244)	(2,042)
Minority interest		(5)	(5)
Income from continuing operations	$ 1,643	$ 3,199	$ 4,842
Discontinued operations		(20)	(20)
Net income	$ 1,643	$ 3,179	$ 4,822

```
┌─────────────────────────────────────────────────────────────────────┐
│ Exhibit 14C1S-1 (continued)                                           │
│ Condensed 1999 Cash Flow Statements                                   │
│           Amounts in $ millions    WLA        PFE      Combined       │
│ Operating activities             $ 2,437    $ 3,076    $ 5,513        │
│ Investing activities             (1,234)    (2,768)    (4,002)        │
│ Financing activities               (500)    (1,127)    (1,627)        │
│ Exchange rate effects               (15)         26         11        │
│ Discontinued operations                        (20)       (20)        │
│ Change in cash                   $   688    $  (813)   $  (125)       │
└─────────────────────────────────────────────────────────────────────┘
```

3. If PFE had accounted for the acquisition as a purchase, the financial statement effects would have been very different:

    a. The value of the transaction (market value on the merger date of PFE shares exchanged) must be recorded in Pfizer's financial statements as the acquisition amount.

    b. All identifiable tangible and intangible assets and liabilities (including any not previously recognized) of WLA must be added to those of PFE at their fair values on the merger date. Any excess of the acquisition amount over the net fair value of WLA assets must be allocated to goodwill.

    c. Post-merger income and expenses of WLA must reflect the purchase method adjustments to assets and liabilities. For example, depreciation expense is based on the fair value of WLA fixed assets on the merger date rather than their historical cost.

    These effects can be seen from the pro forma statements in Exhibit 14C1S-2, located after the solution text.

    Starting with the balance sheet, the first step is to compute the value of the Pfizer shares used to acquire Warner-Lambert:

    $32.44 x 2,400 million shares = $ 79,154 million

    The second step is to restate the assets and liabilities of WLA to fair value using the information provided in question 3 and Exhibit 14C1-2. Most of the adjustments are relatively simple, and are footnoted in exhibit 14C1S-2. However several adjustments are complex, and are explained in the following paragraphs.

The most complex adjustment relates to WLA's employee benefit plans. As shown in the following table, we must replace the accruals required by SFAS 87 and 106 with the actual plan status on December 31, 1999.

$ millions	Pensions	OPEB	Combined	Required	Adjustment
Actual plan status					
Net benefit assets	$ 10		$ 10		
Net benefit (obligation)		$ (277)	(277)		
Reported plan status					
Prepaid benefit cost	219		219	$ 10	$ (209)
Accrued benefit liability	(161)	(169)	(330)	(277)	53

The required column is the actual plan status. The adjustment column shows the adjustments to the balance sheet accruals required to replace the historic accruals with that actual plan status. Prepaid pension cost is assumed to be included in investments and other assets; accrued benefit liability is assumed to be included in other long-term obligations. Note that the intangible pension asset and comprehensive income component are effectively removed by the elimination of all intangibles and the replacement of historical equity with the value of the shares issued.

The next step is to compare the amount paid for Warner-Lambert with the fair value of the net assets acquired:

Value of transaction	$	79,154
Fair value of assets acquired		9,525
Fair value of liabilities		(5,815)
Net fair value	$	3,710
Excess	$	75,444

This excess is the goodwill. [Note that the in-process R & D is included among the acquired assets even though it will be written off immediately.]

Discussion: The pro forma balance sheet is substantially changed from the combined balance sheet resulting from use of the pooling method. The most significant differences result from the recognition of the value of transaction, as it greatly increases post-merger equity and requires recognition of more than $75 billion of goodwill. The ratio effects of these differences are discussed in question 5.

4. Exhibit 14C1S-3, located after the solution text, contains the pro forma income statement for 1999 assuming that Pfizer used the purchase method to account for its acquisition of Warner-Lambert. The footnotes explain the calculations and the assumptions made.

No income statement adjustments have been made for the following balance sheet adjustments due to complexity and/or the lack of information:
- Elimination of WLA deferred tax assets and liabilities
- Elimination of WLA intangible assets
- Restatement of benefit plan assets and liabilities

Discussion: The purchase method adjustments reduce the 1999 earnings of WLA by half. The major factor is the immediate writeoff of IPRD; the effect of inventory revaluation is an additional factor. Note that, under US GAAP, no amortization of goodwill is permitted.

5. Ratios based on the purchase method are shown in the following table:

		WLA Reported	WLA Adjusted	PFE	Combined
(i)	Current ratio	1.54	1.45	1.22	**1.29**
(ii)	Total debt to equity	0.30	0.02	0.62	**0.08**
(iii)	Book value per share			$ 2.36	**$14.04**
(iv)	Gross profit margin	0.76	0.74	0.84	**0.80**
(v)	Pretax profit margin	0.19	0.09	0.27	**0.19**
(vi)	Return on (ending) equity	32%	1%	36%	**5%**
(vii)	Cash from operations to debt	158%	160%	56%	**78%**

Comparison with unadjusted ratios (question 2): While there is little change in the current ratio, the debt-to-equity ratio is much lower due to the higher equity. Book value per share is much higher for the same reasons. [However, if calculated, debt-to-tangible equity and tangible book value per share would be little different from the ratios under the pooling method, as both exclude acquisition goodwill.]

Profit margins are reduced by the purchase method adjustments, especially the pretax margin that reflects the writeoff of IPRD. Return on equity declines significantly due to the combined effect of lower net income and higher equity.

6. (i) Pfizer's income statement for 2000 would report the income and expenses of WLA starting with the acquisition date. It would reflect the purchase method adjustments, with the effects of the inventory writeup and the writeoff of IPRD depressing reported income. Year 2000 ratios would be similar to those computed in question 5, depending on the actual operating results for that year compared with 1999.

(ii) Income statements for years following 2000 would report all WLA income and expenses and would continue to reflect the purchase method adjustments for fixed assets, the amortization of debt discount, and any of the longer lived effects (such as deferred taxes) for which no adjustments were computed due to complexity or lack of information.

(iii) The cash flow statement for 2000 would report the cash flows of WLA starting with the acquisition date. The acquisition itself would not be reported, as shares were issued; however the cash acquired would be reported in investing cash flow.

(iv) Cash flow statements for years following 2000 will report all of the cash flows of WLA.

7. Pfizer preferred using the pooling method for the following reasons:

a. Reported income was higher due to the absence of the effect of purchase method adjustments.

b. Return on equity (and return on assets) remained high as income was higher and equity lower than if the purchase method were used.

c. The restatement of prior year balance sheets and income and cash flow statements presented smoother trends.

d. Use of the purchase method would have required additional costs for appraisals of assets and liabilities and the accounting adjustments required.

8. Advantages of pooling method for financial analysts:

1. Comparability due to restatement of prior year financial statements.
2. Earnings forecasting facilitated by restatement and lack of purchase method adjustments.

Disadvantages of pooling method for financial analysts:

1. Does not reflect the economic effects of management's decision to make acquisition.
2. Keeps acquired assets and liabilities at historic cost, allowing management to realize "gains" by selling selected assets or settling liabilities.
3. The advantages cited above are offset by the fact that the two companies will not be operated as they were prior to the merger, making forecasts based on restated data hazardous.

9. The balance sheet effects are the same under US and IAS GAAP except that under US GAAP, the value of in-process research and development must be expensed on the acquisition date. Under IAS GAAP that value is capitalized and amortized over its estimated useful life. We have assumed a ten-year life. The resulting balance sheet is shown in Exhibit 14C1S-4.

The income statement under IAS GAAP, Exhibit 14C1S-5, differs in two respects from the US GAAP statement (Exhibit 14C1S-3):
1. The capitalized IPRD must be amortized over its ten-year life.
2. Goodwill must be amortized over not more than 20 years (the assumption used in Exhibit 14C1S-5).

The net effect of these two adjustments is that pretax income from WLA is now negative as goodwill amortization exceeds the restoration of the IPRD writeoff.

The ratios under IAS GAAP follow:

		WLA			Purchase
		Reported	Adjusted	PFE	Method
(i)	Current ratio	1.54	1.45	1.22	1.29
(ii)	Total debt to equity	0.30	0.02	0.62	0.08
(iii)	Book value per share			$ 2.36	$ 14.20
(iv)	Gross profit margin	0.76	0.74	0.84	0.80
(v)	Pretax profit margin	0.19	(0.14)	0.27	0.09
(vi)	Return on (ending) equity	32%	-1%	36%	2%
(vii)	Cash from operations to debt	158%	160%	56%	78%

Comparison with purchase method ratios under US GAAP: The only significant difference is that the amortization of goodwill turns the pretax income of WLA negative, reducing the pretax profit margin and return on equity even further than under US GAAP.

10. Pfizer would prefer US GAAP because it does not require the amortization of goodwill. That amortization would reduce reported income each year for twenty years, unless impaired sooner.

11. The payment to American Home Products and the transaction costs are clearly nonoperating (and nonrecurring) and should be excluded from net income for valuation purposes.

The "restructuring" and "integration" costs are both operating and recurring (companies frequently close or reconfigure operating entities). For that reason those charges should be included in net income for valuation. However they should be segregated to facilitate earnings forecasts.

Exhibit 14C1S-2
Pro Forma Balance Sheets at December 31, 1999
Amounts in $ millions

| | Warner-Lambert (WLA) | | | PFE | Purchase |
	Reported	Adjustments	Adjusted	Reported	Method
Cash and equivalents	$ 1,943		$ 1,943	$ 4,642	$ 6,585
Inventories[1]	979	271	1,250	1,654	2,904
Other current assets[2]	2,768	(595)	2,173	4,895	7,068
Current assets	$ 5,690	$ (324)	$ 5,366	$11,191	$ 16,557
Property (net)[1]	3,342	658	4,000	5,343	9,343
Investments and other assets[2]	793	(634)	159	3,277	3,436
Intangible assets[3]	1,616	(1,616)	-	763	763
In-process R & D[4]		1,000	1,000		
Total assets ex-goodwill[5]	$11,441	$ (1,916)	$ 9,525	$20,574	$ 29,099
Acquisition goodwill[5]		75,444	75,444	-	75,444
Total assets		$ 73,528	$84,969	$20,574	$104,543
Short-term debt	$ 297		$ 297	$ 5,001	$ 5,298
Other current liabilities	3,391		3,391	4,184	7,575
Current liabilities	$ 3,688	$ -	$ 3,688	$ 9,185	$ 12,873
Long-term debt[6]	1,250	(28)	1,222	525	1,747
Deferred income tax[7]	463	(463)	-	301	301
Other long-term liabilities[8]	942	(37)	889	1,676	2,565
Total liabilities	$ 6,343	$ (544)	$ 5,799	$11,687	$ 17,486
Stockholders' equity[9]	5,098	74,056	79,154	8,887	87,041
Total liabilities and equity	$11,441	$ 73,528	$84,969	$20,574	$104,543
Million shares outstanding				3,758	6,198

Footnotes on next page

14C1-9

Footnotes for Exhibit 14C1S-2

1 Replace cost of inventories and property with fair value given in question 3(ii).

2 Net pension asset of $209 and deferred tax assets of $1,020 (Exhibit 14C1-2) are deducted from other current assets and investments and other assets. Investments and other assets are reduced to the value of investment securities and net pension assets (both in Exhibit 14C1-2) with $634 adjustment. Balance of $595 is removed from other current assets.

3 Reduce to zero as required by purchase method.

4 IPRD valued given in question 3(ii) written off immediately.

5 Goodwill computed in solution text.

6 Replace carrying amount with fair value (Exhibit 14C1-2).

7 Deferred tax liabilities (Exhibit 14C1-2) eliminated under purchase method.

8 Benefit plan adjustment (see discussion) plus foreign exchange contract liability (Exhibit 14C1-2).

9 Replace historical equity of WLA with value of transaction (see discussion), reduced by writeoff of IPRD.

Exhibit 14C1S-3
Pro Forma Income Statement, Year Ended December 31, 1999

Amounts in $ millions	WLA Reported	Adjustments	Adjusted	PFE Reported	Purchase Method
Sales	$12,929	$ -	$12,929	$16,204	$29,133
Cost of goods sold[1]	(3,042)	(271)	(3,313)	(2,528)	(5,841)
Selling, general, administrative[2]	(5,959)	(44)	(6,003)	(6,351)	(12,354)
Research and development[3]	(1,259)	(1,000)	(2,259)	(2,776)	(5,035)
Other expense, net[4]	(228)	(3)	(231)	(101)	(332)
Pretax income	$ 2,441	$ (1,318)	$ 1,123	$ 4,448	$ 5,571
Income tax expense[5]	(798)	461	(337)	(1,244)	(1,581)
Minority interest				(5)	(5)
Income from continuing operations	$ 1,643	$ (856)	$ 787	$ 3,199	$ 3,986
Discontinued operations				(20)	(20)
Net income	$ 1,643	$ (856)	$ 787	$ 3,179	$ 3,966

[1] Expense inventory writeup

[2] Additional depreciation expense (assumes 15 year life)

[3] Writeoff of IPRD

[4] Amortization of debt discount over 10 years

[5] Assumes 35% tax rate

Exhibit 14C1S-4
Pro Forma Balance Sheets at December 31, 1999 Under IAS GAAP

Amounts in $ millions	WLA Reported	Adjustments	Adjusted	PFE Reported	Purchase Method
Cash and equivalents	$ 1,943		$ 1,943	$ 4,642	$ 6,585
Inventories[1]	979	271	1,250	1,654	2,904
Other current assets[2]	2,768	(595)	2,173	4,895	7,068
Current assets	$ 5,690	$ (324)	$ 5,366	$11,191	$ 16,557
Property (net)[1]	3,342	658	4,000	5,343	9,343
Investments and other assets[2]	793	(634)	159	3,277	3,436
Intangible assets[3]	1,616	(1,616)	–	763	763
In-process R & D[4]		1,000	1,000		1,000
Total assets ex-goodwill	$11,441	$ (1,916)	$ 9,525	$20,574	$ 30,099
Acquisition goodwill[5]		75,444	75,444	–	75,444
Total assets		$ 73,528	$84,969	$20,574	$105,543
Short-term debt	$ 297		$ 297	$ 5,001	$ 5,298
Other current liabilities	3,391		3,391	4,184	7,575
Current liabilities	$ 3,688	$ –	$ 3,688	$ 9,185	$ 12,873
Long-term debt[6]	1,250	(28)	1,222	525	1,747
Deferred income tax[7]	463	(463)	–	301	301
Other long-term liabilities[8]	942	(37)	905	1,676	2,581
Total liabilities	$ 6,343	$ (528)	$ 5,815	$11,687	$ 17,502
Stockholders' equity[9]	5,098	74,056	79,154	8,887	88,041
Total liabilities and equity	$11,441	$ 73,528	$84,969	$20,574	$105,543

Footnotes on next page

Footnotes for Exhibit 14C1S-4

[1] Replace cost of inventories and property with fair value given in question 3(ii).

[2] Net pension asset of $209 and deferred tax assets of $1,020 (Exhibit 14C1-2) are deducted from other current assets and investments and other assets. Investments and other assets are reduced to value of investment securities and net pension assets (both in Exhibit 14C1-2) with $634 adjustment. Balance of $595) is removed from other current assets.

[3] Reduce to zero as required by purchase method.

[4] Replace carrying amount with fair value (Exhibit 14C1-2).

[5] Goodwill computed in solution text.

[6] Replace carrying amount with fair value (Exhibit 14C1-2).

[7] Deferred tax liabilities (Exhibit 14C1-2) eliminated under purchase method.

[8] Benefit plan adjustment (see discussion) plus foreign exchange contract liability (Exhibit 14C1-2).

[9] Replace historical equity of WLA with value of transaction (see discussion).

Exhibit 14C1S-5

Pro Forma Income Statement, Year Ended December 31, 1999 Under IAS GAAP

Amounts in $ millions	WLA Reported	Adjustments	Adjusted	PFE Reported	Purchase Method
Sales	$12,929	$ -	$12,929	$16,204	$29,133
Cost of goods sold[1]	(3,042)	(271)	(3,313)	(2,528)	(5,841)
Selling, general, administrative[2]	(5,959)	(44)	(6,003)	(6,351)	(12,354)
Research and development[3]	(1,259)	(100)	(1,359)	(2,776)	(4,135)
Other expense, net[4]	(228)	(3)	(231)	(101)	(332)
Goodwill amortization[5]		(3,772)	(3,772)		3,772
Pretax income	$ 2,441	$(4,190)	$(1,749)	$ 4,448	$ 2,699
Income tax expense[6]	(798)	1,466	668	(1,244)	(576)
Minority interest				(5)	(5)
Income from continuing operations	$ 1,643	$(2,723)	$(1,080)	$ 3,199	$ 2,125
Discontinued operations				(20)	(20)
Net income	$ 1,643	$(2,723)	$(1,080)	$ 3,179	$ 2,099

1 Expense inventory writeup
2 Additional depreciation expense (assumes 15 year life)
3 IPRD assumed to have 10 year life
4 Amortization of debt discount over 10 years
5 Assumes 20 year life
6 Assumes 35% tax rate

Case 14-2 - Solution

Estimated time to complete this case is 3 hours.

1. The merger was accounted for the acquisition of Mead (MEA) by Westvaco, using the purchase method. The financial statement effects are:
    (i)   The post-acquisition balance sheet includes the assets and liabilities of Mead stated at their fair values on the date of acquisition (January 29, 2002). The excess of the purchase price over the fair value of net assets acquired is shown as acquisition goodwill.
    (ii) The income statement includes Mead's revenues and expenses only after the acquisition date. In addition, the income and expense amounts are affected by the fair value adjustments to MEA's assets and liabilities. However, under SFAS 141, no amortization of acquisition goodwill is permitted.
    (iii) The cash flow statement includes MEA cash flows only after the acquisition date. The amounts would be affected by any tax consequences of the acquisition.
    (iv) Financial statement footnotes for periods following the acquisition would include the relevant amounts for Mead.

2. The following table shows the required ratios for each company (as reported) and the pro forma combined companies:

	Ratio	Westvaco	Mead	Pro forma
(i)	Current ratio	1.45	1.26	1.24
(ii)	Total debt to equity	1.21	0.67	0.83
(iii)	Book value per share	$22.86	$23.38	$ 27.27
(iv)	Gross profit margin	17.6%	13.9%	15.2%
(v)	Operating profit margin	8.3%	1.4%	4.1%
(vi)	Interest coverage ratio	1.57	0.54	1.04
(vii)	Return on ending equity	3.76%	-0.73%	0.70%

Discussion: The *pro forma* (post-acquisition) ratios are very different from Westvaco's ratios, for two reasons.

First, the ratios for Mead are quite different; most significant are Mead's lower debt burden and lower profitability.

Second, the purchase method adjustments also affect some ratios. For example, replacing Mead's reported equity with the value of the shares used to acquire the company raises

Westvaco's' book value per share and lowers the debt-equity ratio, but further reduces the interest coverage ratio and return on equity.

3. (i) Reported revenue will increase over the 2001 – 2003 period as the revenues of Mead are included in part of 2002 and all of 2003.
   (ii) Reported income will also tend to increase as Mead's income is included following the January 29, 2002 acquisition date. However the cyclicality of paper company earnings may offset the addition of Mead's earnings.
   (iii) Cash from operations will also increase as Mead's CFO is included for 2002 only following January 29 but for all of 2003.
   (iv) Balance sheet ratios for 2002 will reflect the combination of the two companies and the purchase method adjustments, as illustrated in the answer to question 2. Thus they will not be comparable to the Westvaco ratios for fiscal 2001. The 2003 ratios will be comparable to the 2002 ratios as any differences will reflect real changes during 2003.

4. The advantage of the *pro forma* data is that they provide a "baseline" against which future financial statements can be measured. For example, subsequent reported revenues can be compared with *pro forma* revenues to determine whether revenue changes are due to operating increases or just to the inclusion of Mead. [MeadWestvaco, in its earnings releases in 2002, provided those comparisons to facilitate analysis of their results.]

5. Restructuring charges are often part of normal operations as companies continually refine their operations to reflect changing business conditions. Therefore normal restructuring charges should be included in pro forma net income for analysis purposes. However transaction costs and restructuring costs that are due solely to the merger should be excluded. Earnings forecasts, however, should consider the expected change in charges that are included in pro forma net income.

6. If Westvaco's acquisition of Mead were accounted for under the IAS purchase method:

    (i)   The pro forma balance sheet (Exhibit 14C2-1) would be unchanged as the differences between US and IAS GAAP do not affect Mead.
    (ii)   The pro forma income statement (Exhibit 14C2-2) would change as goodwill must be amortized under IAS GAAP. The $314 million of goodwill would have to be amortized over not more than 20 years, reducing reported income.

7. Assuming that the merger had been accounted for as the acquisition of Westvaco by Mead, the accounting process would be reversed. Mead's assets and liabilities would remain at their historical cost but Westvaco's assets and liabilities would be adjusted to their fair values. Exhibit 14C2S-1 (next page) shows the pro forma balance sheet under that assumption, using the fair value adjustments provided.

    The process used to prepare that balance sheet is similar to that used to prepare Exhibit 14C2-1. First, we must compare the value of the transaction with the net fair value of Westvaco's assets and liabilities (amounts in $millions):

Value of transaction[1]		$ 3,078
Transaction costs		35
Total purchase price		$ 3,113
Fair value of assets acquired[2]	$ 6,963	
Fair value of liabilities assumed[3]	(3,684)	
Net fair value		3,279
Excess fair value		$ (166)

1. Number of Westvaco shares times share price = 102.4 million X $30.06
2. Total assets + fair value adjustments – historical goodwill = $6,787 + $135 + $145 + $461 – $565 million.
3. Total liabilities + fair value adjustments = $4,446 + $100 + 145 – $1,007 million.

Notice that the net fair value of Westvaco's net assets *exceeds* the transaction value. Not only is there no acquisition goodwill, but this excess must reduce the adjustment to net property. The remaining adjustments are explained in Exhibit 14C2S-1.

Exhibit 14C2S-1. MeadWestvaco
Pro Forma Condensed Balance Sheet
Acquisition of Westvaco by Mead

October 31, 2001

Amounts in $ millions	Westvaco	Adjustments Amount	#	Mead	Combined
Assets					
Cash and equivalents	$ 81			$ 51	$ 132
Accounts receivable	415			471	886
Inventories	426	$ 135	1	540	1,101
Other current assets	94	–		107	201
Total current assets	$ 1,016	$ 135		$ 1,169	$ 2,320
Property (net)	4,227	440	2	3,129	7,796
Prepaid pension asset	780	–		317	1,097
Goodwill	565	(565)	3	257	257
Other assets	199	–		587	786
Total assets	$ 6,787	$ 10		$ 5,459	$12,256
Liabilities and equity					
Current debt	173	–		227	400
Other current liabilities	528	154	4	698	1,380
Total current liabilities	$ 701	$ 154		$ 925	$ 1,780
Long-term debt	2,660	245	5	1,315	4,220
Deferred income tax	1,008	(1,007)	6	591	592
Other liabilities	77	–		311	388
Total liabilities	$ 4,446	$ (608)		$ 3,142	$ 6,980
Stockholders' equity	2,341	618	7	2,317	5,276
Liabilities and equity	$ 6,787	$ 10		$ 5,459	$12,256
Millions of shares	102.4			99.1	198.5

Adjustment #

1. Fair value adjustment to inventories given
2. Fair value adjustment to timberland + capitalized operating
   leases - excess of fair values over purchase price
3. Elimination of Westvaco goodwill
4. Debt incurred for payments to Mead shareholders ($119) and
   transaction costs ($35)
5. Fair value adjustment to long-term debt (given) + capitalized
   operating leases
6. Elimination of deferred income tax (given)
7. Replace Westvaco equity with value of MWV shares issued;
   subtract $119 paid to MEA shareholders (similar to dividend)

8. Changing the acquirer from Westvaco to Mead results in significant changes the financial statements:

(i) While use of the purchase method still results in rising reported revenues, the amounts will differ. Reported 2001 revenues equal those of Mead (rather than Westvaco). 2002 revenues include Mead for the entire year but Westvaco only for the period following the acquisition date (January 29). 2003 revenues, however, will be same under both assumptions as it includes the revenues of both Mead and Westvaco for the entire year.

(ii) The shift in acquirer also affects the trend of reported income. As for revenues, 2001 income would be that of Mead alone. 2002 income includes Mead for the entire year, Westvaco for the period following the acquisition date, and the effect of purchase method acquisitions on Westvaco's income (rather than Mead). The 2003 income includes both companies for the entire year. However it will still differ from income under the original assumption as it reflects the purchase method adjustments for Westvaco rather than Mead.

(iii) The trend of CFO is similar to that of revenues. 2001 CFO is that of Mead alone; 2002 includes the CFO of Westvaco for the period following January 29. 2003 CFO should be the same under both methods (unless the change in acquirer has cash income tax effects).

(iv) Balance sheet ratios for 2001 are those for Mead alone (see solution to question 2). The 2002 ratios are based on the combined balance sheet and income statement for that year, which differ from those resulting when Westvaco is the acquirer. The 2003 ratios will reflect the balance sheet and income statement of the combined companies. However, they will still differ from those under the initial assumption as the purchase method adjustments to both the balance sheet and income statement for Westvaco (rather than Mead) persist for many years.

9. If the merger were accounted for using the pooling method under IAS GAAP, then there would be no purchase method adjustments; the historical data for both companies would be combined without any adjustment (except for the transaction costs). The resulting balance sheet and income statement are shown in Exhibits 14C2S-2 and 14C2S-3 respectively (next two pages). The only adjustments are for the transaction costs.

Exhibit 14C2S-2. MeadWestvaco
Pro Forma Condensed Balance Sheet
Pooling Method   October 31, 2001

Amounts in $ millions	Westvaco	Mead	Adjustments		Combined
Assets			Amount	#	
Cash and equivalents	$ 81	$ 51			$ 132
Accounts receivable	415	471			886
Inventories	426	540			966
Other current assets	94	107			201
Total current assets	$ 1,016	$ 1,169			$ 2,185
Property (net)	4,227	3,129			7,356
Prepaid pension asset	780	317			1,097
Goodwill	565	257			822
Other assets	199	587			786
Total assets	$ 6,787	$ 5,459			$12,246
Liabilities and equity					
Current debt	173	227			400
Other current liabilities	528	698	154	1	1,380
Total current liabilities	$ 701	$ 925	$ 154		$ 1,780
Long-term debt	2,660	1,315			3,975
Deferred income tax	1,008	591			1,599
Other liabilities	77	311			388
Total liabilities	$ 4,446	$ 3,142	$ 154		$ 7,742
Stockholders' equity	2,341	2,317	(154)	2	4,504
Liabilities and equity	$ 6,787	$ 5,459	$ -		$12,246
Millions of shares outstanding	102.4	99.1			198.5

Adjustment #
1. Debt incurred for payments to Mead shareholders and other costs
2. Same as # 1 (see solution text).

14C2-6

```
Exhibit 14C2S-3. MeadWestvaco
Pro Forma Condensed Income Statement
Pooling Method                        Year ended October 31, 2001
                              Westvaco    Mead    Adjustments  Combined
Amounts in $ millions                           Amount    #
Sales                         $ 3,935   $ 4,176                $ 8,111
Cost of goods sold             (3,241)   (3,597)               (6,838)
Gross margin                  $   694   $   579              $ 1,273
Selling and administrative       (364)     (494)                (858)
Restructuring charges             (52)      (45)                 (97)
Other revenues                     48        19                   67
EBIT                          $   326   $    59              $   385
Interest expense                 (208)     (110)      (9)   1     (326)
Pretax income                 $   118   $   (51)  $ (9)      $     58
Income tax expense                (30)       34        3    2       12
Net income                    $    88   $   (17)  $ (6)      $     65

Earnings per share              0.87      (0.18)                 0.33
Average shares (millions)      101.5       99.1                 197.6

        Adjustment #
1. Interest on new debt and transaction costs (see solution text).
2. Income tax effect of added interest expense
```

10.1 (i)   The combined balance sheet reflects the historical
            costs of the assets and liabilities of both
            companies. The fair values are ignored for both
            companies. Total assets are more than $1.3 billion
            lower than in Exhibit 14C2-1; liabilities are more
            than $400 million lower. Because stockholders' equity
            equals the historical amounts combined rather than
            the market value of shares issued, it is $900 million
            lower.

    (ii)   The income statements for both 2001 and 2002 are
            restated as if the companies were combined for both
            years. Revenues in Exhibit 14C2S-3 are higher than in
            Exhibit 14C2-2 as Mead is included for the entire
            year; net income is higher for the same reason and
            because there are no purchase method adjustments to
            reduce income.

    (iii)   The cash flow statement for 2001 would be restated to
            include both firms. The 2002 cash flow statement

would also include both firms for the entire year. Thus reported CFO will be higher for both years under the pooling method, assuming that both Westvaco and Mead have positive CFO.

(iv) Financial statement footnotes for fiscal 2001 will be restated to include the relevant information for both companies. Under the purchase method the 2001 footnotes will remain those of the acquirer.

10.2   The ratios under the pooling method are:

	Ratio	Westvaco	Mead	Combined
(i)	Current ratio	1.45	1.26	1.23
(ii)	Total debt to equity	1.21	0.67	0.97
(iii)	Book value per share	$22.86	$23.38	$22.69
(iv)	Gross profit margin	17.6%	13.9%	15.7%
(v)	Operating profit margin	8.3%	1.4%	4.7%
(vi)	Interest coverage ratio	1.57	0.54	1.18
(vii)	Return on ending equity	3.76%	-0.73%	1.44%

When the pooling method is used, the financial statement ratios are weighted averages of the ratios of the two combining companies. There are no purchase method adjustments. Comparison with the ratios computed in question 2 shows some significant differences:

	Ratio	Purchase	Pooling
(i)	Current ratio	1.24	1.23
(ii)	Total debt to equity	0.83	0.97
(iii)	Book value per share	$ 27.27	$22.69
(iv)	Gross profit margin	15.2%	15.7%
(v)	Operating profit margin	4.1%	4.7%
(vi)	Interest coverage ratio	1.04	1.18
(vii)	Return on ending equity	0.70%	1.44%

The debt-to-equity ratio is higher, mainly because equity is lower (although debt is slightly higher as well). We can see the equity difference in the book value per share. As the price of Westvaco shares at January 29, 2002 exceeded the stated book value, the purchase method increases reported equity.

Profitability ratios are higher under the pooling method because there are no purchase method adjustments reducing income. Interest coverage is higher for the same reason.

Return on equity is higher as higher income more than offsets lower equity.

10.3 (i)   Under the pooling method, the trend of reported revenue will mirror the actual revenue trend of the combined companies (see answer to 10.1 (ii)).

(ii)   Under the pooling method, the income statements are combined for all periods presented (including prior periods). Therefore the trend in reported revenues for 2001 – 2003 will reflect operating changes alone.

(iii) Reported CFO is also combined for all periods presented so that reported changes reflect only operating changes.

(iv)   As both balance sheets and income statement are combined for all periods, changes in balance sheet ratios will reflect only real changes.

11.   In this case, the balance sheet and income statement effects of the two methods (question 10.2) are opposite; the balance sheet looks better under the purchase method but the income statement looks better under pooling.

The balance sheet ratios under pooling were probably acceptable as the companies are not overly leveraged. Therefore the higher profitability under the pooling method would most likely result in a preference for that method.

For some companies, however, the better balance sheet ratios (especially debt/equity) might result in a preference for the purchase method. An additional incentive for the purchase method is the "illusion of growth" (see text pages 512-3) that results, especially for companies that make many acquisitions.

Chapter 15 - Solutions

Overview:
Problem Length   *Problem #'s*
    {S}   4, 5, 7, 12
    {M}   1 - 3, 6, 9, 10, 13 -15
    {L}   8, 11

1.{M}a.   Because the functional currency of Nippon MT is the yen, the *current rate* method should be used to translate the yen financial statements into US dollars, the reporting currency.

     b.   See Exhibit 15S-1 (page 2) for income statement and balance sheet translation.

     c.   The lower value of the yen relative to the US dollar reduced the earnings of Nippon MT after translation into dollars as the (average) current exchange rate is used to translate all income statement components.

     d.   The alternative method is the temporal method, which would be required if Nippon MT
- Operated in a highly inflationary economy, or
- Was highly integrated with Master Toy, requiring the use of the US dollar as its functional currency

     e.   Under the temporal method, nonmonetary assets and liabilities (such as inventories and fixed assets) are translated at the historical rate. Monetary assets and liabilities are translated at the current rate. Income statement items related to nonmonetary assets and liabilities (such as COGS and depreciation expense) are translated using historical rates while those related to monetary assets and liabilities are translated at the average rate for the period.

        The temporal and current rate methods also differ in the definition of the currency exposure: the net monetary position of the foreign unit is the measure of risk under the temporal method whereas the net assets (that is, the stockholders' equity) delineate the exposure when the current rate method is used.

The different definition of exposure and the dissimilar exchange rates used to translate various assets and liabilities generate disparate amounts of translation gain or loss. These amounts are also displayed in different financial statements; the temporal method reports translation gain or loss in the income statement whereas the current rate method reports the gain or loss is a component of other comprehensive income.

Exhibit 15S-1. Nippon MT	(thousands)		Exchange rate	
Statement of Income and Retained Earnings	Yen	Dollars	Rate	Explanation
Sales	700,000	$ 5,000	140	Average rate
Expenses				
Cost of sales	280,000	2,000	140	Average rate
Depreciation	126,000	900	140	Average rate
Selling, general, and administrative	77,000	550	140	Average rate
Total expenses	483,000	$ 3,450		
Income before taxes	217,000	$ 1,550		
Income taxes	(98,000)	(700)	140	Average rate
Net income	119,000	$ 850		
Retained earnings December 31, 1997	250,000	2,000		Given
	369,000	$ 2,850		
Dividends	(58,000)	(400)	145	Rate when paid
Retained earnings December 31, 1998	311,000	$ 2,450		
Balance Sheet				
Assets				
Cash and receivables	60,000	$ 400	150	Year-end rate
Inventory	180,000	1,200	150	Year-end rate
Land	200,000	1,333	150	Year-end rate
Fixed assets	346,000	2,307	150	Year-end rate
Total assets	786,000	$ 5,240	150	Year-end rate
Liabilities and stockholders equity				
Liabilities	300,000	2,000	150	Year-end rate
Capital stock	175,000	1,750	100	Given
Retained earnings	311,000	2,450		Computed above
Cumulative translation adjustment		(960)		Plug[1]
Total liabilities and stockholders' equity	786,000	$ 5,240		

---

[1] Assets - liabilities - capital stock - retained earnings.

2.{M}a.

Fuente, Ltd.

Balance Sheet, December 31, 1999

	LC	Dollars	Rate	Exchange rate Explanation
Cash	15.2	$ 17.5	0.87	Year-end rate
Accounts receivable	3.8	4.4	0.87	Year-end rate
Inventories	7.7	8.9	0.87	Year-end rate
Fixed assets (net)	35.6	40.9	0.87	Year-end rate
Other	12.1	13.9	0.87	Year-end rate
Total assets	74.4	$ 85.5		
Current liabilities	13.3	15.3	0.87	Year-end rate
Long term debt	19.6	22.5	0.87	Year-end rate
Total liabilities	32.9	$ 37.8		
Stockholders' equity	41.5	47.7	0.87	Year-end rate
Total liabilities and equity	74.4	$ 85.5		

Income Statement, Year Ended December 31, 1999

	LC	Dollars	Rate	Exchange rate Explanation
Revenue	47.1	$ 49.6	0.95	Average rate
Cost of goods sold	(16.9)	(17.8)	0.95	Average rate
Depreciation	(3.2)	(3.4)	0.95	Average rate
Other operating costs	(14.8)	(15.6)	0.95	Average rate
Operating profit	12.2	$ 12.8		
Interest expense	(3.4)	(3.6)	0.95	Average rate
Pretax income	8.8	$ 9.3		
Income tax expense	(3.2)	(3.4)	0.95	Average rate
Net income	5.6	$ 5.9		

b. Under the all-current method, the income statement is translated at the average rate while the balance sheet is translated at the year-end exchange rate. Therefore ratios that use only income statement data or only balance sheet data are unchanged; ratios that mix income statement and balance sheet data are different, assuming that the average and year-end rates differ.

   (i)   Different: earnings at the average rate, equity at the closing rate.
   (ii) Same: debt and assets both at the closing rate.
   (iii) Same: net income and revenues both at the average rate.
   (iv) Different: receivables at the closing rate, revenue at the average rate.

c. Under the temporal method, monetary assets and liabilities are translated at the current rate; other assets (mainly inventories and fixed assets) and liabilities are translated at the historical rate. In the income statement, COGS and depreciation are translated at the historical rate. These differences from the all-current method affect ratios as follows:

   (i)   Different: both net income and assets are different under the temporal method.
   (ii) Different: debt is the same but assets different.
   (iii) Different: revenue is the same but net income is different.
   (iv) Same: both accounts receivable and revenue are the same under the two methods.
   (v)   Same: as the quick ratio compares cash and accounts receivable to current liabilities, it is the same under both methods.

3.{M}a. With dollar as the functional currency, FI is translated using the temporal method.

Year ended December 31, 2001	Ponts (Millions)	Exchange Rate (Ponts/$)	Dollars (Millions)
Balance Sheet:			
Cash	82	4.0	$ 20.50
Accounts receivable	700	4.0	175.00
Inventory	455	4.0	113.75
Fixed assets (net)	360	4.0	90.00
Total assets	1,597		$ 399.25
Accounts payable	532	4.0	$ 133.00
Capital stock	600	3.0	200.00
Retained earnings	465		132.86
Translation adjustment	---		(66.61)
Total liabilities and equities	1,597		$ 399.25
Income Statement:			
Sales	3,500	3.5	$1,000.00
Cost of sales	(2,345)	3.5	(670.00)
Depreciation expense	(60)	3.5	(17.14)
Selling expense	(630)	3.5	180.00)
Net income	465		$ 132.86

*Translation Adjustment $= 600 \left\{ \dfrac{1}{3} - \dfrac{1}{4} \right\} = 600\ (1/12) = \$(50.00)$

$$+ 465 \left\{ \frac{1}{3.5} - \frac{1}{4} \right\} = 465\ (1/28) = \underline{(16.61)}$$
$$\$(66.61)$$

b. (i) **Dollar:** Inventory and fixed assets translated at historical rates.

Pont: All assets and liabilities translated at current exchange rates.

Dollar: Translation gain (loss) computed on the basis of net monetary assets.

Pont: Translation gain (loss) computed on the basis of net investment (all assets and liabilities).

(ii) **Dollar:** All revenues and other expenses are translated at the average rate for the period; cost of sales and depreciation expense translated at historical rate.

Pont: All revenues and expenses translated at average rates for the period.

Dollar: Translation gain(loss) included in net income (volatility increased).

Pont: Translation gain(loss) reported in separate component of stockholders, equity. Net income is less volatile.

(iii) **Dollar:** Financial statement ratios skewed by translation effects.

Pont: Ratios in dollars are similar to ratios in ponts.

4.{S}a. Functional currency = hib means that local financial statements are prepared in hib and then translated into dollars.

First-in-First-Out	Last-in-First-Out
Cost of goods sold: Opening inventory of hib 6,000 becomes COGS; translate at rate when sold ($1 = 6 hib) makes COGS $1,000	Purchases during the year of hib 7,500 becomes COGS; translate at rate when sold ($1 = 6 hib) makes COGS $1,250
Ending inventory: Purchases during the year of hib 7,500 translated at closing rate of $1 = 6 hib makes inventory $1,250	Opening inventory of hib 6,000 remains in inventory; when translated at the closing rate makes inventory $1,000

Note: COGS and ending inventory must total hib 13,500, the sum of opening inventory and purchases, regardless of inventory method.

b. Functional currency = dollar means that calculations are made using dollars; temporal method rules apply.

First-in-First-Out	*Last-in-First-Out*
Cost of goods sold: Opening inventory of $1,500 (hib 6,000/4) becomes COGS	Purchases during the year of $1,500 (hib 7,500/5) become COGS
Ending inventory: Purchases during the year of $1,500 remain in inventory	Opening inventory of $1,500 remains in inventory

Note: COGS and ending inventory must total $3,000, the sum of opening inventory and purchases.

c. The essence of LIFO is that (with rising prices) higher priced purchases become COGS, whereas lower priced goods remain in inventory; FIFO is the reverse, resulting in higher income (lower COGS) and higher inventory valuation.

The choice of functional currency interacts with the choice of inventory method. When the functional currency is the hib (local currency), the normal LIFO/FIFO effects are directly transmitted to the parent company financial statements. This accords with the objective of SFAS 52 of having parent results replicate subsidiary results.

However, the temporal method applies when the dollar (the parent or reporting currency) is used as the functional currency. Price changes are measured in dollars rather than hibs. In this case, the unit price in dollars has not changed. Purchases are at $15 (hib 75/5), which is unchanged from the cost of opening inventory (hib 60/4). Thus, in dollars there is no price change and LIFO = FIFO.

Generalizing, the choice of functional currency determines whether the effects of changing prices are determined in the local currency or the reporting currency. Depending on the interplay between price changes and currency exchange rates, the impact of LIFO versus FIFO can be quite different depending on the choice of functional currency.

5.{S}a. As shown below, the higher value of the yen reduced the growth rate (in yen) of sales to North America.

	Years ended		
	1998	1999	% change
Sales (Yen millions)	53,753	82,717	54%
Exchange rate	128.53	123.61	
Sales ($ millions)	$ 418	$ 669	60%

b. As Takeda's operating expenses are incurred in yen, the higher value of the yen reduces revenues but not expense, reducing the operating profit margin on export sales to North America.

6.{M}a. As shown below, in Skr, the sales decline in Great Britain and France was:

	Sales in Skr millions		
	1998	1999	Change
Great Britain	2,622	2,066	-21.2%
France	2,284	1,839	-19.5%

b. In local currencies the sales (rounded) were:

	1998	1999	% Change
Great Britain	2,622	2,066	
Skr/Sterling	13.24	13.39	
Great Britain (£)	**198**	**154**	**-22.1%**
France (Skr)	2,284	1,839	
Skr/French franc	1.36	1.35	
France (Ffr)	**1,679**	**1,362**	**-18.9%**

c. As shown in parts a and b, the local currency sales decline was slightly greater in Britain but lower in France. The currency changes made the sales declines closer that they really were.

d. For commodity products that are easily transported, prices tend to equalize (assuming no trade barriers). Thus local currency sales changes, which are a mix of volume and price changes, may not accurately reflect real sales levels as currency rate changes effect local currency prices.

e. The decline in the Swedish krona will (all other things being equal) increase the krona amount of sales made in British pounds. Conversely, sales denominated in Euros translate to fewer krona when the krona rises against the Euro. For forecasting purposes, the analyst should forecast in local currencies, then apply the expected exchange rate to predict sales in the parent currency.

f. The translation differences are negative for both classes of fixed assets and the related depreciation balances. The negative differences mean that currency changes reduced the carrying value in Swedish krona of fixed assets denominated in other currencies, indicating that the krona rose in value against these currencies during 1999.

7.{S}a. The currency translation adjustment, which results from the all-current method, means that Lucent must use local currencies as functional currencies for some non-US operations. However, there are also translation gains and losses, suggesting that either Lucent uses the US dollar as the functional currency for some non-US operations or that there are transaction gains and losses that result from remeasurement from local to functional currencies.

b. The change in the currency translation adjustment was negative in all three years, indicating that the currencies to which Lucent was exposed declined in value (in the aggregate) relative to the US dollar.

c. If Lucent has operations in countries whose currencies declined against the dollar, cash balances in those currencies should decline when translated into dollars. Thus the positive effect on cash for all three years is surprising. The most obvious explanation is that Lucent's cash balances were held mainly in currencies that appreciated against the dollar.

d. As stated in the answer to part a, there are two
    possible sources of the foreign currency exchange
    losses. One is that Lucent used the dollar as the
    functional currency for some foreign operations (such
    as foreign sales branches or in hyperinflationary
    economies), resulting in remeasurement losses when
    local currency financial statements are translated into
    US dollars.

    The second possible source is remeasurement losses when
    local currency transactions are translated into non-
    dollar functional currencies. For example, a French
    subsidiary (using the Euro as functional currency) may
    have transactions in British pounds.

8.{L}a. The following table shows the percent change in the
    Swiss franc against each of the three currencies. Note
    that we have reversed the ¥/SFR relationship to
    facilitate the discussion in the remainder of the
    question.

	Exchange rates		% *change*
	1999	*2000*	*1999 - 2000*
(i) Average rates			
SFR/$	1.50	1.69	**13%**
SFR/€	1.60	1.56	**- 3%**
SFR/¥	0.0075	0.0064	**-15%**
(ii) Year-end rates			
SFR/$	1.60	1.64	**2%**
SFR/€	1.61	1.52	**-6%**
SFR/¥	0.0064	0.0070	**10%**

b. The yen had the greatest decline against the Swiss
    franc in 2000, using the average rate; measured by the
    year-end rate, the Yen had the largest percent gain.
    The dollar rose against the Swiss franc by either
    measure. *Note*: the yen exchange rates illustrate the
    importance of distinguishing between rate effects based
    on the average rate versus those based on the closing
    rate.

c.   The changes in the value of the Yen versus the Swiss franc had the following effects on the Swiss franc amounts of yen-denominated amounts:

(i)   Revenues decline in Swiss francs due to the lower average rate for 2000 versus 1999.
(ii)   Operating income also declines due to the lower average rate for 2000 versus 1999.
(iii) Operating margin should be unchanged in percent (average rate used to translate both revenue and operating income).
(iv)   Assets rise in Swiss francs as the year-end exchange rate has risen from 1999 to 2000.
(v)   Capital expenditures decline in Swiss francs (assuming that they occur evenly throughout the year) due to the lower average rate.

d. and e.

| | Amounts in millions | | % change |
	1999	2000	1999-2000
d. Revenues (SFR)			
(i) European Union	9,326	9,012	-3%
(ii) North America	10,130	10,636	5%
e. Revenues (LC)			
(i) European Union (€)	5,829	5,777	-1%
(ii) North America ($)	6,753	6,293	-7%
d. Segment assets (SFR)			
(iii) European Union	14,107	15,157	7%
(iv) North America	18,922	17,296	-9%
e. Segment assets (LC)			
(iii) European Union (€)	8,762	9,972	14%
(iv) North America ($)	11,826	10,546	-11%

Explanation: SFR data obtained from p. 71 of Roche's annual report. The local currency data are calculated by dividing by the respective local currency exchange rates (SFR/€ and SFR/$). For revenues (assets) the average (year-end) rate is used.

As shown in the table (prior page), the trend of revenues and segment assets in local currencies is significantly different from the trend in Swiss francs.

Currency changes distort the trend in revenue. Segment revenues declined in both the European Union and North America in local currencies; in Swiss francs, however, North American revenues increased. Using Swiss francs, it appears that revenues in North America grew 5% but that European Union revenues fell 3%. However, in local currencies, revenues in both segments fell, but the European Union decline was smaller (-1%) as compared to North America (-7%).

The currency effect also distorts the change in segment assets. The 6% decline in the Euro reduces the growth rate of European Union segment assets from 14% to 7%. The 2% rise in the dollar partly offsets the large decline in North American segment assets.

f. Roche reported currency translation gains of €274 million for 1999 and losses of €374 million for 2000, suggesting that the Swiss franc declined in 1999 and rose in 2000. The table on p. 54 of Roche's annual report shows that the franc declined (year-end rates) versus the dollar and Euro in 1999 (more francs per foreign currency unit) but rose versus the Japanese yen, confirming the net translation gain as the exposure to Japan is relatively small (geographical segment data is in Roche footnote 4).

In 2000 the Swiss franc rose against the Euro but declined versus the dollar and yen. Large European Union segment assets and the relatively greater gain against the Euro could have produced a net translation loss. If we assume that non-Euro European currencies also fell against the Swiss franc, the effect of translating the large European segment assets would have also contributed to the translation loss for 2000.

g.   For 2000, property shows a translation loss, which accords with the overall translation loss discussed in part f. However intangible assets show a translation gain, despite the overall loss. The footnote 13 detail shows that the translation gain on goodwill more than offset the translation loss on other intangible assets. It appears (see footnote 3) that Roche's goodwill largely resulted from the Genentech acquisition in 1999, and is therefore denominated in dollars. As the dollar rose against the Swiss franc in 2000 (see part a) there would be a translation gain for 2000.

h.   If Roche used the Swiss franc as its functional currency worldwide, the financial statement effects would be widespread:
(i)   Inventories, fixed assets, and any other nonmonetary assets would be recorded in Swiss francs at their historical rates, rather than translated at current rates at each balance sheet date.
(ii)   There would be no currency translation adjustment; all currency gains and losses would flow through net income (see (vi) below).
(iii) Revenues would be unaffected as local currency revenues would continue to be translated into Swiss francs using the average exchange rate.
(iv)   Cost-of-goods-sold would be computed (under the temporal method) using historical exchange rates.
(v)   Depreciation expense would also be computed (under the temporal method) using historical exchange rates.
(vi)   The amount of foreign currency translation gains and losses would differ because those gains and losses would be based on net monetary assets (temporal method) rather than all net assets (current rate method). In addition, all gains and losses would be included in net income, rather than the currency translation adjustment.

9.{M}a.

$ in millions	Fiscal years ended October 31		
	1997	1998	1999
(i) Sales	$ 220.5	$ 184.0	$ 140.8
% change		-17%	-23%
(ii) Operating profit	47.9	35.2	25.2
% change		-27%	-28%
Operating profit margin	22%	19%	18%
(iii) Capital expenditures	30.7	41.1	31.0
% change		34%	-25%
(iv) Segment assets	301.4	322.4	257.4
% change		7%	-20%

b. and c.

BRL in millions	Fiscal years ended October 31		
	1997	1998	1999
(i) Sales	233.7	211.6	239.4
% change		-9%	13%
(ii) Operating profit	50.8	40.5	42.8
% change		-20%	6%
Operating profit margin	22%	19%	18%
(iii) Capital expenditures	32.5	47.3	52.7
% change		45%	11%
(iv) Segment assets	331.5	383.7	501.9
% change		16%	31%

d. The depreciation of the real over the two year period results in U.S. dollar growth rates that are far lower than the underlying growth rates. 1999 sales, for example, are 2% higher than the 1997 level in reai but 36% lower in US dollars. Segment assets are, similarly, 51% higher in reai but 15% lower in dollars.

e. The percent changes computed in part a report the operating performance of Rigesa in its local market. As Rigesa is not a major importer or exporter, exchange rate changes do not greatly affect its operations in Brazil. Thus its performance is best measure in its local currency. From Westvaco's perspective, however, the US dollar changes are more reflective of the benefits of its investment.

f. The operating margins are shown in the tables in parts a and c. The operating profit margin is identical in both currencies as both revenues and operating expenses are translated at the average rate for each period.

g. (i) As the 2000 average rate of 1.90 is lower (in $US) than the 1999 average rate of 1.70, the growth rate of sales in dollars will be lower than the growth rate in reai.
   (ii) Same as part (i).
   (iii) As discussed in part f, the operating profit margin is not affected by exchange rate changes.
   (iv) As the 2000 closing rate of 1.83 is higher (in $US) than the 1999 closing rate of 1.95, the growth rate of segment assets in dollars will be higher than the growth rate in reai.

10.{M}a. Subtracting U.S. income of E&O, Erzi's income statement in dollars follows:

($ millions)	2000	2001	2002
Revenues	$ 50.0	$ 60.0	$ 70.0
Operating expenses	25.0	27.0	29.0
Income taxes	7.0	9.4	11.8
Net income	$ 18.0	$ 23.6	$ 29.2
% Change: Sales		20%	17%
Net income		31%	24%

To remove the impact of exchange rate changes we convert the income statement to LC's (using the *average* exchange rate for each year):

	2000	2001	2002
Exchange rate	1	1.5	0.75
Revenues	LC50.0	LC40.0	LC93.3
Operating expenses	25.0	18.0	38.7
Income taxes	7.0	6.3	15.7
Net income	LC18.0	LC15.7	LC38.9
% Change from operations:			
Sales		(20%)	133%
Net income		(13%)	147%

These data give the operating results of Erzi; 2001 operating performance declined whereas 2002 was a "boom" year.

Looking at the consolidated results of E&O, we can now disaggregate the effect of Erzi's operations and that of exchange rate changes for the 2000 - 2002 period:

	Sales	Net income
Erzi's operations[1]	$ 43.3	$ 20.9
Exchange rate effects[2]	(23.3)	(9.7)
Net change	$ 20.0	$ 11.2

[1] The dollar change in sales and income assuming that the exchange rate remained at the 2000 level of 1.0.
[2] The effect of the decline in the LC on reported sales and net income (2002 amounts x .25).

b. Sales were unaffected by the choice of functional currency as they were translated at the average rate for the year regardless of that choice.

Net income was affected by the functional currency choice. If the LC was the functional currency, translation adjustments did not affect net income; if the dollar was the functional currency, translation gains and losses were included in the determination of net income.

11.{L}a. The Swiss Franc (or another non-dollar currency) must have been the functional currency for the Swiss subsidiary. Use of the dollar as the functional currency for that unit would have reported translation adjustments as part of income, rather than accumulating them in the stockholders' equity account.

b. The deferred translation gains of $3,213,000 reflect appreciation of the functional currency of the Swiss subsidiary against the dollar; net assets of that subsidiary were translated into an increased dollar amount.

c. (i) The gain on liquidation did not result from operating activities but from the recognition of previously deferred exchange rate effects.

(ii) The gain should not be considered 1991 income as it was generated over the life of the subsidiary and recognized in 1991 only because management chose to liquidate in that year.

d. Change in cumulative translation adjustment:

1991 $ (6,405,000) [The $3,213,000 reduction in the CTA due to the liquidation must be excluded.]
1990   13,246,000
1989   (3,607,000)

Because the liquidation of the inactive subsidiary was completed in the first quarter of 1991, the effect of exchange rate changes is captured by the decline of $6,405,000 on foreign net assets of $96,933,000 (net assets on October 31, 1990 of $100,146,000 less the $3,213,000 of deferred gains relating to the Swiss subsidiary):

$$\frac{\$(6,405,000)}{\$96,933,000} = (6.61\%)$$

Thus, the functional currencies used by the firm declined by 6.61% against the dollar in 1991. The actual decline may be higher since the net assets of the Swiss unit should be deducted from the net assets, resulting in a lower denominator. However, that information is not available.

e. The cash flow statement reports that the 1991 effect of exchange rate changes on cash was $(2,075) million. Using the result of part D, the estimated cash balance in nondollar functional currencies at October 31, 1990 was:

$$\$(2.075)/.0661 = \$31.392 \text{ million.}$$

Note: This calculation ignores the effect of exchange rate changes on the increase in cash balances during 1991.

Commercial Intertech's total balance of cash and cash equivalents at October 31, 1990 was $12,049 million, making the estimate clearly wrong. We can conclude that the company kept cash balances in foreign currencies that depreciated by more than the functional currency average computed in part D. Given the size of the loss, an analyst might have questioned management about it.

f. First we must estimate inventories in nondollar functional currencies. One estimate would compare 1991 foreign sales to total sales (in $ millions):

$$\$229/\$437 = 52.4\%$$

The comparison of total foreign assets at October 31, 1990 to total assets would result in a 44.6% estimate.

Either of these percentages can be applied to total inventories at October 31, 1990 of $59,762 million to estimate foreign inventories. The result is then multiplied by the adjustment factor computed in part D to obtain the estimated effect of exchange rates on inventories in nondollar functional currencies:

$$.524 \times \$59,972 \times .0661 = \$2.07 \text{ million}$$
$$\textbf{or} \quad .446 \times \$59,972 \times .0661 = \$1.77 \text{ million}$$

The actual effect can be estimated by comparing the balance sheet change in inventories with the cash flow change (data not provided in problem). This method, which assumes no acquisition or divestiture activity for the year, results in an estimate of $2.76 million.

As this estimate is somewhat higher than that arrived at by using the geographic segment data, it appears that the company has higher inventories relative to sales (lower inventory turnover) in its foreign subsidiaries. An alternative explanation would be higher inventories in weaker currencies (similar to part E).

g. Reported foreign net assets:

1991	$ 94,709,000
1990	100,146,000
Decrease	$ 5,479,000

The net decrease of $5,479,000 was reported after a total decline in the CTA of $9,618,000 of which $6,405,000 was due to exchange rate changes and $3,213,000 stemmed from the liquidation of the Swiss subsidiary. Thus, the firm must have *increased* its local currency investments in its foreign subsidiaries.

h. (i) The percentage decline in foreign sales is significantly below the decline factor computed in part D. However the part D factor is based on comparison of exchange rates at fiscal year-ends. The effect on sales is based on average rates for the fiscal years, which might be quite different.

Therefore, while the sales decline probably reflects weak foreign currencies, and should not surprise us, more data is needed to estimate the exchange rate impact on reported sales.

(ii) The data needed would be average exchange rates for the fiscal year, preferably weighted by Commercial Intertech's sales in each foreign currency.

(iii) Year to year sales comparisons are also affected by volume changes, price changes (in local currencies), and acquisition and divestiture activities. Removing exchange rate changes from the sales trend may permit better focus on these other effects.

12.{S}a. When the dollar was the functional currency, nonmonetary assets such as fixed assets were translated using the historical rate, as required by the temporal method. The devaluation of the Real did not reduce the carrying value of fixed assets from earlier years.

With the real as the functional currency, all fixed assets are translated at the current rate, reducing the US dollar carrying amount of fixed assets from earlier years. This reduction also reduced stockholders' equity (Alcoa's share of Aluminio's net assets) and minority interest (the portion of Aluminio's net assets owned by other shareholders).

b. (i) Sales are unaffected as they continue to be translated using the average rate for each period.
   (ii) Cost of goods sold are translated using the current average rate, rather than the historical rate under the temporal method (real as functional currency). Exchange rate changes will directly affect translated COGS after the change.
   (iii) Depreciation expense will also be translated at the average rate for the period after adoption of the real as the functional currency, rather than the historical rate under the temporal method.

13.{M}a. The first step is to convert equity in income of affiliates from dollars to LC

	Base	Year 1	Year 2
Income in $	$ 100	$ 140	$ 225
Exchange Rate LC 1 =	$1.00	$1.40	$1.50
Income in LC	LC 100	LC 100	LC 150

Year 1 : No change in operations as LC income remained at LC 100. The full increase of $40 is a result of exchange rate change.

Year 2 : Operations increased by 50%. Therefore, in *base year* dollars,[2] the transaction effect is $150-$100 = $50 and the exchange rate effect is $225-$150 = $75.

---

[2] Note that the answer for year 2 will differ depending on whether the year 2 change is measured relative to the base year (as we do) or whether the change is measured relative to year 1.

b.

	(i) *LC*		(ii) *Dollars*	
	Year 1	Year 2	Year 1	Year 2
Opening value	1,000	1,200	1,000	1,680
Close value	1,200	1,300	1,680	1,950
Capital gain	200	100	680	270
Dividend	20	100	28	150
Return	220	200	708	420
Rate	22.0%	16.7%	70.8%	25.%

c. (i)

	Year 1	Year 2
Opening balance	$1,000	$1,512
Equity income	140	225
Dividends	(28)	(150)
Subtotal	$1,112	$1,587
Exchange rate gain	400	108
Closing balance	$1,512	$1,695

Calculation of exchange rate gain =
    Change in exchange rate x opening balance

Year 1	(1.4/1.0 - 1)	x	$1,000	= $400
Year 2	(1.5/1.4 - 1)	x	$1,512	= $108

(ii) The CTA at the end of year 1 is $400, the exchange rate gain for the year. At the end of year 2, the CTA is $508 ($400 + $108).

(iii) Given the equity income and investment in affiliates and dividends received, one could calculate the change in the CTA. That change divided by the opening balance in the investment account would yield the percentage change in the exchange rate.

Year 1: Δ in CTA=($1,512-$140+$28-$1,000)=$400
    % Δ in exchange rate = $400/$1,000 = 40%

Year 2: Δ in CTA=($1,695-$225+$150-$1,512)=$108
    % Δ in exchange rate = $108/$1,512 = 7.14%

14.{M}a. FX book value is $1,750 (LC 3,500/2) at time of merger. Since the amount paid was $2,000, the excess of $250 increases net fixed assets.

	AMREK	FX	Merged
Cash	$ 2,000	$ 250	$ 2,250
Accounts receivable	3,000	1,000	4,000
Inventory	1,500	250	1,750
Net fixed assets	5,500	750	6,250
	$12,000	$2,250	$14,250
LTD	7,000	250	7,250
Equity	5,000	2,000	7,000
	$12,000	$2,250	14,250

b. Since the acquisition was effected by the issue of shares and the only cash was the $250 FX held at the time of the merger, the cash flow statement would report

Acquisition net of cash acquired = $250 as an inflow.[3]

c. Under pooling, the net assets would not be revalued upwards. Therefore depreciation would be lower and income higher.

d. Change in CTA =$ 200
Net assets of FX at acquisition = $2,000
Exchange rate change = $200/$2,000 = 10%, or from $0.50 on January 1, 2000 to $0.55 on December 31, 2000.

The exchange rate at December 31, 2002 must be:
$1.00/.55 = **LC 1.82**

e.

	A/R	Inventory
Opening balance	$3,000	$1,500
Acquisition	1,000	250
Exchange rate effect (10% of above)	100	25
Change on cash flow statement (plug)	**400**	**(275)**
Closing balance	$4,500	$1,500

---

[3] An alternative method (not recommended by GAAP but perhaps more informative from an analytic point of view) would be to recognize the implicit cash flows as:

  CFI: Acquisition net of cash acquired   ($1,750)
   CFF: Issue of shares   2,000

15.{M}a. The exact amount of the equity *cannot be* determined. It will, however, be $500 less on a pooling basis as compared to purchase. In pooling the *book value* of COL's equity or net assets ($3,000) will be used rather than the amount used under purchase accounting; i.e. the price paid for COL's net assets ($3,500).

b. (i) Since Δ in CTA = $300 and for pooling, net assets are $3000, the Δ in exchange rate is $300/$3,000 = 10%

Therefore since the effect on cash is also 10%, cash acquired should be $20/.10 = **$200**.

(ii) At acquisition there will be no effect as in pooling, the acquisition is not reflected in the SoCF. For 2000, the cash flows of COL will be added to those of ASU.

c. (i) Under purchase the net assets are $3,500. Since the Δ in CTA = $300, the percent change in the exchange rate is $300/$3,500 = 8.6%.

Therefore cash acquired = $20/.086 = **$233**

(ii) At acquisition:[4]
CFI:
Acquisition (net of cash acquired) 233 (inflow)

The issuance of shares for the acquisition would be reported in the section "significant noncash investing and financing activities." Cash flows for 2000 would be similar to those reported under the pooling method. The only difference would be any tax consequences of the purchase method adjustments.

---

[4] An alternative method (not recommended by GAAP but perhaps more informative from an analytic point of view) would be to recognize the implicit cash flows as

    CFI: Acquisition net of cash acquired   ($3,267)
    CFF: Issue of shares   3,500

d. Under the pooling assumptions, the change in exchange rate was 10% resulting in an exchange rate of LC 1 = $1.10. Therefore foreign sales were $33,000/1.10 = LC 30,000.

Estimates of future sales are:

	2000	2001	2002
Foreign sales in LC	LC30,000	LC20,000	LC25,000
Exchange rate	1.10	1.65	1.32
Foreign sales in $	$ 33,000	$ 33,000	$ 33,000
Domestic sales	567,000	567,000	567,000
Total sales	$600,000	$600,000	$600,000

Where LC sales decline by one third in 2001 and then increase 25% in 2002.

Under the purchase assumptions, the change in exchange rate was 8.6% resulting in an exchange rate of LC 1 = $1.086. Therefore foreign sales were $33,000/1.086 = LC 30,387.

Estimates of future sales are:

	2000	2001	2002
Foreign sales in LC	LC30,387	LC20,258	LC25,323
Exchange rate	1.086	1.65	1.32
Foreign sales in $	$ 33,000	$ 33,426	$ 33,426
Domestic sales	567,000	567,000	567,000
Total sales	$600,000	$600,426	$600,426

Where LC sales decline by one third in 2001 and then increase 25% in 2002.

Case 15-1 Solution

Estimated solution time is 1 to 1 1/2 hours.

Case Overview: the objective of this case is to show the effect of exchange rate changes by examining a company with significant foreign operations in a single currency. Case 15-3 examines a multicurrency case, using IBM.

Note: the answers to the questions posed are supplemented by actual data from AFLAC's 1996 financial statements, shown in [square brackets].

1. (a) The decline in the yen against the dollar should reduce revenue growth as Japanese revenues are translated into fewer dollars.

    [The average exchange rate for the yen versus the dollar was 107.67 for the second quarter of 1996, 21.6% below the 90.39 rate for the 1995 quarter. While yen revenues rose 9.7%, that growth was more than offset by the lower value of the yen.

    Corporate revenues declined 9.9% for the second quarter of 1996. This decline was caused by the lower yen and should not have surprised anyone.]

    (b) Pretax income is also affected by the yen/dollar exchange rate and would be expected to decline.

    [While AFLAC Japan's pretax income rose 9.8% (in yen), it fell in dollars. AFLAC's total pretax earnings declined 9.8%.]

    (c) When examining the change in the CTA for the first six months of 1996, we must consider the exchange rate change for the first half only. The rate was 110 at June 30, 1996 as compared with 102.95 at December 31, 1995. This 6.8% decline in the yen would be expected to produce a negative CTA, given AFLAC's yen exposure.

    [AFLAC's second quarter report, however, shows that the CTA rose to $221.3 million at June 30, 1996 from $213.3 million at December 31, 1995. The second quarter report does not provide an explanation for this surprising result.]

(d) Asset growth for the first six months of 1996 should also be affected by the decline in the value of the yen, as assets at December 31, 1995 will be translated into fewer dollars at June 30, 1996.

[Total reported assets at June 30, 1996 were $24,671 million, slightly below the $25,022 million at December 31, 1995. Actual asset increases during the period were more than offset by the effect of yen weakness.]

2. Shifting investments from yen to dollars increases the investment income of AFLAC Japan. Because dollar interest rates are higher, the same investments earn higher income when invested in dollar investments.

This effect is compounded when the yen declines against the dollar. Dollar investment income translates into more yen, increasing investment income for AFLAC Japan even further.

Both of these effects increase pretax income of AFLAC Japan (in yen).

[AFLAC's 1996 annual report states that AFLAC Japan's investment income grew 12.5% in yen even though interest rates in Japan declined, reducing the income on yen investments.]

For the consolidated enterprise, the shift from yen investments to dollar investments again increases reported investment income. This shift also mitigates the effect of the weak yen on translated investment income (which is lower as the yen falls).

This translation effect, however, disappears in consolidation, as exchange rate changes do not affect the investment income derived from dollar investments.

The increase in investment income, therefore, offsets to some extent the effect of the 1996 decline in the yen.

[AFLAC's investment income fell slightly in 1996, after a large 1995 gain. Increased yen investment income and increased investment income from U.S. operations were more than offset by the effect of the weak yen on the translation of yen investment income to dollars. The average exchange rate for 1996 was 108.84, 13.5% below 1995. Consolidated pretax income also declined excluding nonrecurring income.]

3. If the U.S. dollar investments of AFLAC Japan were remeasured into yen, exchange rate changes would result in translation gains and losses that are included in reported income. [The yen is the functional currency for AFLAC Japan.]

These translation gains and losses would be included in the net income of AFLAC Japan, and therefore would be included in the consolidated net income of AFLAC.

Thus, the 1995 yen rise would have resulted in translation losses (as dollar investments are remeasured into fewer yen) that would have reduced the reported income of both the Japanese subsidiary (AFLAC Japan) and the parent (AFLAC). In 1996, both would have reported translation gains as dollar assets were remeasured into more yen as that currency declined.

Note: the FASB Emerging Issues Task Force (EITF) considered this issue in 1996 (Issue No. 96-15), indicating a difference of opinion among auditors as to the correct accounting treatment. The EITF reached a consensus that:

> *the entire change in the fair value of foreign-currency denominated AFS [available-for-sale] debt securities should be reported in stockholders' equity.[1]*

The EITF also agreed that gains and losses on hedges of such investments should be reported in the SFAS 115 component of equity [rather than with foreign currency gains and losses].

This consensus was nullified by SFAS 133 – the gain or loss on hedges of AFS securities must now be reported in earnings as well as the foreign currency component of the gain or loss on the AFS investment. Because AFLAC adopted SFAS 133 in 2001, the accounting change does not affect the years in the case. Like other companies, AFLAC now reports the gains and losses in other income.

These conclusions would not apply to foreign-currency denominated debt securities designated as held-to-maturity.

---

[1] November 14, 1996 EITF Meeting Minutes, p. 35

Case 15-2 - Solution

Estimated time to complete this case is 5 hours.

1. Exhibit 15C2S-1 contains the balance sheet for 1998 - 2000, following the format of Exhibit 15C2-1.

Exhibit 15C2S-1
Aracruz Balance Sheet by Currency
$ in thousands

		December 31		
		1998	1999	2000
Cash and equivalents	$US	$ 123,464	$ 298,656	$ 17,387
	R	29,607	13,934	704
	Total	$ 153,071	$ 312,590	$ 18,091
Investment in debt securities	$US	696,404	189,480	323,032
Accounts receivable:	$US	52,519	71,074	80,887
	R	21,518	12,903	13,179
	Total	$ 74,037	$ 83,977	$ 94,066
Inventories	$US	82,942	69,639	80,976
Other current assets	$US	23,864	37,273	86,773
Current assets		$1,030,318	$ 692,959	$ 602,938
Property, plant, equipment	$US	1,892,451	1,702,747	1,664,322
Other long-term assets	R	277,720	205,297	187,198
Total assets		$3,200,489	$2,601,003	$2,454,458
Non-debt current liabilities	R	65,515	57,842	64,098
Total debt	$US	1,262,876	686,008	424,388
	R	259,879	162,330	117,464
	Total	$1,522,755	$ 848,338	$ 541,852
Other long-term liabilities	R	44,619	41,138	75,025
Total liabilities		$1,632,889	$ 947,318	$ 680,975
Minority interest	R	436	373	362
Stockholders' equity		1,567,164	1,653,312	1,773,121
Total liabilities and equity		$3,200,489	$2,601,003	$2,454,458

2. ARA's net debt by currency (total debt less cash and equivalents and investment in debt securities) is computed in the following table:

$ in thousands		December 31		
		1998	1999	2000
Cash and equivalents	$US	$ 123,464	$ 298,656	$ 17,387
	R	29,607	13,934	704
	Total	$ 153,071	$ 312,590	$ 18,091
Investment in debt securities	$US	696,404	189,480	323,032
Total debt	$US	$1,262,876	$ 686,008	$ 424,388
	R	259,879	162,330	117,464
	Total	$1,522,755	$ 848,338	$ 541,852
Net debt by currency	**$US**	**(443,008)**	**(197,872)**	**(83,969)**
	R	**(230,272)**	**(148,396)**	**(116,760)**
	Total	**$ (673,280)**	**$(346,268)**	**$(200,729)**

3. The net debt by currency, converted to reais, is shown in the following table.

Reai in thousands		December 31		
		1998	1999	2000
Net debt by currency	$US	(536,040)	(354,191)	(164,579)
	R	(278,629)	(265,629)	(228,850)
	Total	(814,669)	(619,820)	(393,429)

The net debt in the prior table has been translated into reais using the year-end exchange rates provided. For example, the 1998 $US debt is $443,008 X 1.21 = 536,040 reais.

4. As Aracruz maintains its accounts in $US, the exchange rate has no effect on its $US dollar debt. To answer this question we must compare the change in net reai debt in reais with the change in $US:

in thousands	1998	December 31 1999	2000
Net reai debt in $US	$(230,272)	$ (148,396)	$(116,760)
Change from prior year		(81,876)	(31,636)
% change		(35.6)%	(21.3)%
Net reai debt in reais	(278,629)	(265,629)	(228,850)
Change from prior year		(13,000)	(36,779)
% change		(4.7%)	(13.8%)

The percentage reduction in reai debt is much greater in dollars than in reais. In addition the year 2000 percent decline increases in reai but declines in dollars. The explanation is that the declining value of the reai reduced the $US equivalent of the reai debt. To see this effect, we must separate the change in debt into operating and exchange rate effects.

In 1999, debt in reai was reduced by 13,000. Measured in dollars (using the average rate) that amount translates into an *operating* effect of $7,182 [(13,000)/1.81]. The balance of the change $74,694 ($81,876 - $7,182) is the *exchange* rate effect.[1]

The results are summarized below

$in thousands	1999	2000
Exchange rate effect	$ (74,694)	$ (11,538)
Reduction in reai debt	(7,182)	(20,098)
Total change	$ (81,876)	$ (31,636)

The table shows that in 1999, most of the reduction is reai debt was due to the exchange rate effect. In 2000 most of the decline was due to reduction in the reai debt itself.

---

[1] For 1999, the exchange rate effect can be determined as:
Effect on opening balance 278,629 x (1/1.79 - 1/1.21) = (74,614)
Effect on change (13,000) x (1/1.79 - 1/1.81) = (80)
(74,694)

5. Because ARA's accounts are measured in $US, monetary assets and liabilities in non-dollar currencies must be translated into dollars at each balance sheet date. As we see from question 4, exchange rate effects can obscure operating changes in these non-dollar monetary amounts.

6. Exhibit 15C2S-2 contains the income statements for 1998 to 2000, following the format of Exhibit 15C2-2.

Exhibit 15C2S-2

Aracruz Income Statement by Currency

		Years Ended December 31		
$ in thousands		1998	1999	2000
Revenues: Domestic	R $	38,449	$ 33,796	$ 43,601
Export $US		462,163	550,729	751,900
Total revenue		$ 500,612	$ 584,525	$ 795,501
Sales taxes	R	(39,490)	(43,459)	(63,240)
Cost of sales	R	(349,621)	(311,190)	(344,515)
Other expenses	R	(109,657)	(95,535)	(74,988)
Total operating cost		$ (498,768)	$ (450,184)	$ (482,743)
Operating income		1,844	134,341	312,758
Equity in affiliate				(1,313)
Financial income		104,840	100,692	64,849
Financial expense		(120,955)	(120,336)	(101,461)
Translation gain (loss)		(7,780)	(7,454)	8,812
Other expense (income)		(65)	146	120
Pretax income		$ (22,116)	$ 107,389	$ 283,765
Income tax expense		25,306	(16,679)	(82,065)
Minority interest in loss		257	63	11
Net income		$ 3,447	$ 90,773	$ 201,711

7. To answer this question we must compute the net assets by currency. Using the $US amounts in Exhibit 15C2-1:

| $millions | | December 31 | |
Currency	1998	1999	2000
$US	$ 1,608,768	$ 1,682,861	$ 1,828,989
R	(41,604)	(29,549)	(55,868)
Equity	$ 1,567,164	$ 1,653,312	$ 1,773,121

Aracruz has net reai-denominated liabilities each year, and as we have assumed that all nonmonetary assets and liabilities are denominated in $US, we would expect the decline in the reai versus the dollar to result in translation gains on the net reai monetary liability for each year. The translation loss for 1999 must be due to other factors.[2]

8. If Aracruz used the Brazilian reai as its functional currency, the financial statements would differ from those provided in the case exhibits. One significant differences are that non-monetary assets and liabilities (primarily inventories and property) would be translated into $US at the historical exchange rate rather than the current rate. In addition, the effect of exchange rate changes on reai-denominated monetary assets would be accumulated in stockholders' equity (cumulative translation adjustment) rather than being included in net income.

    (i)   Total assets would be higher as inventories and property are translated at the (higher) historic rate.

    (ii) Stockholders' equity would be higher due to the translation effect just discussed and the effect of higher income, discussed in (iii).

    (iii) Because Aracruz had net (monetary) assets in dollars, the depreciation of the reai would have resulted in translation gains that would have been included in net income with the reai as the functional currency. This effect is likely to offset higher depreciation expense that would have resulted from use of the historical exchange rate for property.

---

[2] One possibility is that some assets and liabilities are denominated in Euros, which we combined with $US amounts in the case exhibits. Fluctuation in the $/Euro exchange rate could result in remeasurement losses in 1999 that offset gains on the reai. Another possibility is that our assumption that all nonmonetary assets and liabilities are denominated in $US is not correct. [The point of this question is that financial statement effects that differ from expectations can be used to question management and obtain better insight into a company.]

9. Aracruz provides sufficient data for several different computations of the average sales price per tonne, as shown in Exhibit 15C2S-3 (on the next page). The domestic average price is well above the export price, perhaps due to trade barriers; both prices fluctuate. The export price is determined by world market prices. Perhaps the most useful measure is the net revenue (sales less sales taxes) per tonne for all production ($399.66 per tonne in 1998).[3] This appears to be the measure that the company highlights in its report.

10. Using the average exchange rate for the year, exhibit 15C2S-3 also shows the average sales price per tonne in reais for each year. This price measure shows rapid increases from 1998 to 2000 as the higher dollar price is compounded by the lower value of the reai.

11. Exhibit 15C2S-3 computes an average selling price of $573.07 per tonne for 2000, compared with $427.23 for 1999, an increase of $145.84 per tonne.

    If we multiply that price difference by year 2000 sales of 1,272.7 tonnes, the result is just over $188 million, slightly more than the $186 million stated in the annual report.[4]

12. Exhibit 15C2S-3 shows the operating cost (cost of sales plus other expenses) per tonne in both dollars and reais. The per/tonne cost rises steadily in reais; in dollars it declines in 1999, but rises slightly in 2000.

    As operating costs are incurred in reais (see Exhibit 15C2-2), the reai measure is more useful for forecasting. Annual changes reflect inflation in Brazil and are not (directly) affected by the exchange rate.

---

[3] We believe that showing sales tax as a deduction from sales rather than an operating expense provides better data for analysis.

[4] The $186 million is apparently based on a price differential of $145.84 per tonne, which can be obtained from the average prices reported by the company (which differ slightly from our computations).

Exhibit 15C2S-3
Components of Operating Income

	Years Ended December 31		
Revenues ($ in thousands)	*1998*	*1999*	*2000*
Domestic	$ 38,449	$ 33,796	$ 43,601
Export	462,163	550,729	751,900
Total	$ 500,612	$ 584,525	$ 795,501
Sales taxes	(39,490)	(43,459)	(63,240)
Cost of sales	(349,621)	(311,190)	(344,515)
Other expenses	(109,657)	(95,535)	(74,988)
Total operating cost	$ (498,768)	$ (450,184)	$ (482,743)
Operating income	1,844	134,341	312,758
Exchange rate (R/$US)	*1.16*	*1.81*	*1.83*
Sales volume (000 tonnes):			
Brazil	68.8	59.4	54.7
Export	1,085.0	1,205.9	1,218.0
Total	1,153.8	1,265.3	1,272.7
9. Computed revenues ($US/tonne):			
Domestic	$ 558.85	$ 568.96	$ 797.09
Export	425.96	456.70	617.32
Total	433.88	461.97	625.05
Net of sales tax	399.66	427.62	575.36
10. Computed revenues (R/tonne):			
Domestic	648.27	1,029.81	1,458.68
Export	494.11	826.62	1,129.70
Total	503.30	836.16	1,143.84
Net of sales tax	463.60	773.99	1,052.91
12. Computed operating cost:			
$US/tonne	$ 398.06	$ 321.45	$ 329.62
R/tonne	461.75	581.82	603.20
13. Operating margin			
$US/tonne	$ 1.60	$ 106.17	$ 245.74
R/tonne	1.85	192.17	449.71

13. Exhibit 15C2S-3 also shows the operating profit (revenues less operating cost) per tonne in both dollars and reais. Operating margins rose sharply from 1998 to 2000 in both currencies. However both measures are affected by the exchange rate changes.

Measuring in dollars, operating costs per tonne are reduced by the depreciation of the reai, increasing the operating margin (aided by higher prices).

Measuring in reais, revenues per tonne are increased by the depreciation of the reai, again increasing the operating margin, despite higher operating costs.

14. The preceding questions have set the stage for an exercise in forecasting by isolating the factors that contribute to Aracruz' profitability. The forecast is shown in exhibit 15C2S-4 (on the next page).

Exhibit 15C2S-4 is a reduced version of Exhibits 15C2S-2 and 15C2S-3. It starts with sales and revenue per tonne ($US), both assumed to be unchanged. 2001 revenue in $US is therefore unchanged. Reai revenue is either unchanged (case I) or 20% higher (case II), depending on the exchange rate assumption.

Operating costs in reai are assumed to increase either 10% (case I) or 15% (case II). Those operating costs are then translated into dollars at the exchange rate assumed for each case.

The operating margin per tonne in $US is then multiplied by sales (in tonnes) to produce an estimate of operating income. Case I results in a 13.4% decline in operating profit due to higher (reai) operating costs. In case II, operating costs in reais increase more, but the further depreciation of the reai reduces the dollar cost per tonne, increasing operating profit by 5.6%.

Exhibit 15C2S-4
Forecasts of Operating Income
$ in thousands

| | Years Ended December 31 | | 2001 Forecast | |
	1998	1999 Reported	2000	Case I	Case II
Sales volume (000 tonnes):					
Brazil	68.8	59.4	54.7	54.7	54.7
Export	1,085.0	1,205.9	1,218.0	1,218.0	1,218.0
Total	1,153.8	1,265.3	1,272.7	1,272.7	1,272.7
Exchange rate (R/$US)	1.16	1.81	1.83	1.830	2.196
Computed revenues ($US/tonne):					
Total	$433.88	$461.97	$625.05	$625.05	$625.05
Net of sales tax	399.66	427.62	575.36	575.36	575.36
Computed revenues (R/tonne):					
Total	503.30	836.16	1,143.84	1,143.84	1,372.61
Net of sales tax	463.60	773.99	1,052.91	1,052.91	1,263.49
Computed operating cost:					
$US/tonne	$398.06	$321.45	$329.62	$362.58	$315.88
R/tonne	461.75	581.82	603.20	663.52	693.68
Operating margin per tonne ($US)	$1.60	$106.17	$245.74	$212.78	$259.48
Operating margin per tonne (R)	1.85	192.17	449.71	389.39	569.81
Forecast operating income ($US millions)				$ 270,808	$ 330,237
% change from 2000				-13.4%	5.6%

15C2-9

15. Clearly any forecast of Aracruz earnings is highly sensitive to both the assumed exchange rate and the change in real costs (inflation in Brazil). Whether looked at from a dollar perspective or a reai perspective, depreciation of reai increases operating profits while inflation decreases them.

Changes in these variables are, however, connected. Depreciation of the reai tends to increase prices in Brazil, albeit with some lag.

Before moving on, we should also note that the earnings forecast is also highly sensitive to assumptions about export prices, production levels, and productivity. In this case we held these factors constant to highlight the impact of the exchange rate and local inflation. However a financial analyst would have to make assumptions in these areas to produce a reasonable forecast.

16. (i) Depreciation of the reai can be expected to widen profit margins and increase reported income (all measured in reais). Higher reported income should result in a higher reai stock price.
    (ii) The stock price in dollars, however, is also impacted by the exchange rate. If the depreciation of the reai is rapid, that effect may offset the higher expected earnings. However, for a company like Aracruz whose output is exported, the effect of higher earnings should result in a higher stock price in dollars.

17. Aracruz's functional currency ought to be the US dollar for two reasons. First, virtually all of its output is exported, and the export price is set in dollars. Thus revenues are almost completely dollar denominated. Second, most of the company's financing is dollar denominated. While the fact that most operating costs are in reais is an argument for using the reai as the functional currency, the revenue and financing factors dominate the decision. Moreover, operating decisions are swamped by exchange rate considerations; the pulp price in dollars combined with operating costs in reais determine the operating margin, and how much to produce.

18. If Aracruz were a subsidiary of a U.S. company that accounted for its investment using the dollar as functional currency, then the following would result:

(i) The parent's investment in Aracruz would be steadily reduced as the value of the reai declined. The net assets would be translated into fewer dollars at the lower exchange rate. [That conclusion assumes that the exchange rate effects exceed the earnings of Aracruz, as in the years shown here.]

(ii) The resulting loss would appear in the cumulative translation adjustment section of the parent's stockholders' equity.

(iii) If the positive effect of higher earnings (resulting from reai depreciation) exceeds the effect of the lower reai, then (in question 16) we argued that the dollar stock price should rise. This conclusion contradicts the lower equity described in part (i).

19. If the functional currency were the reai:

(i) The translation gain or loss would depend on the net dollar monetary assets, rather than Aracruz' entire net assets. It appears (see Exhibit 15C2S-1) that Aracruz has net monetary assets in dollars as the total of inventories and property is still well below net assets in dollars. Therefore, depreciation of the reai would result in a translation gain (remeasurement into reai) as the dollar monetary assets translate into more reai. However the reai net assets would then be translated into fewer dollars. While the computations are complex, the likely result is still lower equity at the parent level.

(ii) While the translation loss would still go through equity, the large remeasurement gain would be reported in income, distorting that measure. While Aracruz had some translation gains and losses using the dollar as functional currency (see question 7) those gains and losses averaged about 1% of revenue (see exhibit 15C2S-2).

(iii) Assuming that equity is still reduced when the reai depreciates, then the answer given to 18(iii) still applies.

Case 15-3 Solution

Estimated solution time is 3 to 4 hours.

Case Overview: the objective of this case is to illustrate the effect of exchange rate changes on a multinational company. While this is mostly a teaching case (most issues are considered within the case itself), the required questions extend the case to cash flow analysis.

For exchange rate information use the data provided in Exhibit 15C3-4:

	1989	1990
Year-end rate	.937	.837
Average rate	.986	.891

1. (a) Balance sheet translated at *year-end rate*
   (millions of $US and LC)

	12/31/89		12/31/90	
	$US	LC	$US	LC
Cash (5% of CA)	$ 1,018	LC 954	$ 1,217	LC 1,019
Other current assets	19,343	18,124	23,120	19,351
Current liabilities	(12,124)	(11,360)	(15,917)	(13,323)
Net working capital	$ 8,237	LC 7,718	$ 8,420	LC 7,047
Net property	9,879	9,257	11,628	9,733
Investments	6,822	6,392	9,077	7,597
Total assets	$24,938	LC 23,367	$29,125	LC 24,377
Long-term debt	$ 3,358	LC 3,146	$ 5,060	LC 4,235
Other liabilities	2,607	2,443	2,699	2,259
Deferred taxes	1,814	1,700	2,381	1,993
Total liabilities	$ 7,779	LC 7,289	$10,140	LC 8,487
Net assets (equity)	17,159	16,078	18,985	15,890
Total equities	$24,938	LC 23,367	$29,125	LC 24,377

(b) Income statement translated at *average rate* for year
   (millions of $US and LC)

	$US	LC
Revenues	$ 41,886	LC 37,320
Earnings before tax	7,844	6,989
Income tax expense	(3,270)	(2,914)
Net income	$ 4,754	LC 4,075

(c) Net assets at December 31, 1989   LC 16,078
     Net income for 1990   4,075
     Subtotal   LC 20,153
     Net assets at December 31, 1990   (15,890)
     Discrepancy   LC 4,263

There must be dividends paid and/or share redemptions by IBM's foreign subsidiaries during 1990. It is possible that a small portion of the discrepancy is the result of valuation allowances included in equity.

2. Investments translated at *average rate* for the year.

	$US	LC
Investment in property	$ 3,020	LC 2,691
Net property at December 31, 1989		LC 9,257
Investment for 1990		2,691
Subtotal		LC 11,948
Net property at December 31, 1990		(9,733)
Difference		LC 2,215

This difference reflects depreciation expense for the year. We assume (lacking data) that there were no acquisitions or divestitures and there were no property dispositions during the year.

3. (a) Exhibit 15C3S-1 uses the transactional analysis method to produce a summarized cash flow statement in LC units. Note that:

• Depreciation must be reclassified from CFO to CFI to properly compute those two components.

• Net cash flow should equal the change in cash to check our calculations.

• Net income equals the sum of all income statement components to ensure that none were omitted or incorrectly copied.

Exhibit 15C3S-1
1990 Cash Flow Statement
IBM Non-U.S. Operations
Millions of LC

	Income Statement	Balance Sheet 12/31/89	Balance Sheet 12/31/90	Change	Cash Effect +	Cash Effect −
Pretax income	6,989				6,989	
Other current assets		18,124	19,351	1,227		1,227
Current liabilities		11,360	13,323	1,963	1,963	
Other liabilities		2,443	2,259	(184)		184
Depreciation expense	2,215				2,215	
Income tax expense	(2,914)					2,914
Deferred tax		1,700	1,993	293	293	–
Cash from operations						**7,135**
Depreciation expense	(2,215)					2,215
Net property		9,257	9,733	476		476
Investments		6,392	7,597	1,205		1,205
Cash for investment						**(3,896)**
Long-term debt		3,146	4,235	1,089	1,089	
Dividends paid [1 (d)]						4,263
Cash from financing						**(3,174)**
Net cash flow						**65**

[Net income]   4,075

(b) Translation of LC cash flow components to $US at the *average rate* for 1990 of .891 (data in millions):

	LC	$US
Cash from operations	7,135	8,008
Cash for investment	(3,896)	(4,373)
Cash for financing	(3,174)	(3,562)
Net cash flow	65	73

(c) Percentage of consolidated cash flow obtained from non-U.S. operations ($ millions):

		Total	Non-US	Percent
i.	Cash from operations	$7,472	$8,008	107%
ii.	Cash from debt financing	2,958	1,222	41
iii.	Cash for investment	(7,144)	(4,373)	61

iv. It appears that IBM's 1990 operating cash flow was derived *entirely* from its non-U.S. operations. These operations accounted for 61% of investment cash flow, similar to their proportion of operations (measured by revenues or assets). This suggests that IBM's U.S. operations had significant liquidity problems.

IBM's foreign operations were able to pay more than $4 billion in cash dividends to the parent company (part 1c).

The debt financing ratio (ii.) may not be meaningful. Much of IBM's debt is short-term and the short-term debt of the non-U.S. operations is not broken out. This problem also affects the computation of CFO. If the short-term debt (included in current liabilities) of IBM's non-U.S. operations rose, CFO has been overstated.

More analysis would be needed to understand whether these conditions were temporary or reflected longer term trends.

It must also be remembered that these conclusions are based on summarized data and simplifying assumptions. It is possible that more detailed data would modify these conclusions.

In sum, the data derived suggest that IBM's non-U.S. operations in 1990 were much healthier that domestic operations. The data could have been used to question management about these conditions.

(d) The effect of exchange rates on cash and cash equivalents:

	LC	Multiplier*	$ Effect
Beginning cash balance	LC 954	.1275	$122
Effects on:			
Cash from operations	7,136	.0724	517
Cash for investment	(3,896)	.0724	(282)
Cash for financing	(3,174)	.0724	(230)
Net effect			$ 127
Actual effect(Exhibit 15C3-2)			$ 131

* The beginning cash balance was translated at the rate of .937 at December 31, 1989 but is now translated at the rate of .837. The effect on LC cash is [(1/.937)-(1/.837)] = .1275.
Cash flows during 1990 are assumed to have originated at the average rate of .891 but are now translated at the year-end rate of .837. The effect on 1990 cash flows is therefore [(1/.837)-(1/.891)] = .0724.

Alternative method:
Cash balance at December 31, 1989: LC954/.937		$ 1,018
1990 increase in cash (net cash flow): LC65/.891		73
Subtotal		$ 1,091
Cash balance at December 31, 1990: LC1019/.837		(1,217)
Effect of exchange rates on cash		$ (126)

The difference between the computed and the actual effect is quite small, suggesting that our assumption that non-U.S. cash is 5% of current assets was approximately correct. Even if it were exactly correct, differences in the distribution by currency would introduce an element of error. Another possible source of error is the assumption that 100% of IBM's foreign operations uses local functional currencies.

The point of this exercise is that non-U.S. cash and cash equivalents can be estimated by estimating cash flows and reversing this process. Subtracting the effect of rate changes on cash flows from the total effect provides the impact on the beginning cash balance. As we know the exchange rate, we can estimate the beginning cash balance. Thus the actual effect, provided in the consolidated cash flow statement, provides the answer; the question is the amount of non-U.S. cash and cash equivalents.

Chapter 16 - Solutions

1.{S}a.   Because their stated interest rate remained constant at 6.5% on both 12/31/00 and 12/31/01, the Notes due 8/12/02 must be the fixed rate notes. The stated interest rate on the Notes due 5/01/02 was 6.81% at 12/31/00, but it declined to 1.88% at 12/31/01 - those must be the variable rate obligations.

b.   The difference between the stated and the effective rate on a variable rate obligation may result from an interest rate swap based on different indices. AXP must have swapped the variable rate obligation based on one underlying, e.g., LIBOR, for a rate based on a different index, e.g., the Federal Funds rate.

c.

Amounts in $millions			*Effective*	
Years Ended	*Notes due*	*Balance Outstanding*	*Interest Rate*	*Interest Expense*
	a	*B*	*c*	*b x c*
12/31/2000	8/12/2002	$400	6.83%	$27.32
	5/01/2002	400	6.90%	27.60
	Total			$54.92
12/31/2001	8/12/2002	411	6.43%	26.43
	5/01/2002	400	1.88%	7.52
	Total			$33.95

The interest expense for each note for each year is computed by multiplying the principal amount of the note by the effective interest rate.

Interest expense based on the stated rates (assuming no swaps) is computed in the table on the following page.

Amounts in $millions Years Ended	Notes due	Balance Outstanding	Stated Interest Rate	Interest Expense
	a	b	c	b x c
12/31/00	8/12/02	$400	6.50%	$26.00
	5/01/02	400	6.81%	27.24
Total				$53.24
12/31/01	8/12/02	411	6.50%	26.72
	5/01/02	400	1.88%	7.52
Total				$34.24

Comparing interest expense from these two tables for both years, we compute the effect of the swaps on interest expense for both years:

Effect of Swap		
Year	$ millions	% Δ
2000	$ 1.68	3.2%
2001	(0.29)	-0.8%

The effect of the swaps was to increase 2000 interest expense by $1.68 million or 3.2%. In 2001, the swaps decreased interest expense by $.29 million or less than 1%. While the swaps may have provided AXP with protection against some possible interest rate changes, they had an immaterial effect on interest expense in 2000 and 2001.

d.   Both swaps were most likely intended to lower the exposure to changing interest rates. Because AXP expected lower rates, the fixed rate notes were swapped into variable rates; the swap increased 2000 interest expense (the effective rate was higher than the stated rate) but reduced interest expense in 2001 (the effective rate was lower than the stated rate).

The underlying (index on which the effective rates were calculated) was changed on the variable rate obligations; AXP must have expected a decline in rates based on the new underlying index. However, the swap increase 2000 interest expense as the company paid 6.90% on obligations with a stated rate of 6.81%. There was no difference in rates at 12/31/01.

2.{S}a.   PepsiCo likely wanted to reduce financing costs by replacing fixed rate debt with variable rate debt with lower interest rates.

b.   The notional amounts of the swaps must have declined because the amount of the fixed rate debt declined. Another possible reason for the lower notional amounts of the swaps is a decline in the duration of PepsiCo debt.

c.   The fair value of an interest rate swap is measured as the present value of the expected net payments on the swap, based on interest rates in effect at each measurement date (see box 10-1 on text pages 334-5).

On December 31 2000, the company reported that it received an average rate of 4.4% on its swaps compared to an average pay rate of 4.9%. Despite the negative spread, the swaps had a net positive fair value, equal to the present value of the net amounts expected by PepsiCo.

On December 31 2001, the company reported an average receive rate of 5.6% on its swaps compared to an average pay rate of 1.7%. The reported positive fair value reflects the decline in variable rates from December 31, 2000, increasing the present value of the net amounts expected by PepsiCo.

d.

PepsiCo	(Amounts in $millions)				Effect on Interest Expense
		Weighted Average			
	Notional Amounts	Receive Rate	Pay Rate	Difference	
Date	a	b	c	d = c − b	e = a X d
12/31/2000	$1,335	4.40%	4.90%	0.50%	$ 6.68
12/31/2001	1,077	5.60%	1.70%	-3.90%	(42.00)

The swaps increased 2000 interest expense by $6.68 million but decreased 2001 expense by $42.00 million.

e. Interest rate swaps that hedge fixed-rate obligations are fair value hedges under SFAS 133 (see text page 600). Therefore the swaps (as well as the underlying debt) must be marked to market quarterly and the noneffective portion of the hedge reported as income. The fair value of the swaps must be reported as an asset or liability on the balance sheet. [Note that these examples predate the adoption of SFAS 133. However on December 31 2000 (2001), PepsiCo reported the fair value of the interest rate swaps in the amount of $12 ($32) million as a component of prepaid expenses and other current assets. The fair value of the swaps (the present value of the expected net receipts) is reported as a prepaid expense because it represents the expected reduction in future interest payments.]

f. The swaps allowed PepsiCo to achieve its goal of lower borrowing costs in 2001 as shown in answer e. The 2000 impact was slightly adverse.

3.{S}a. PepsiCo uses fixed-price purchase orders, futures, swaps, and options to manage commodity price risk. Generally, these types of derivative contracts should be treated as cash flow hedges. At inception and on each financial statement date, these hedges must be marked to market and recorded as assets or liabilities. The effective portion of any gain or loss is reported as a component of other comprehensive income. When the underlying commodities are purchased, the realized gain or loss must be reported as a component of cost of goods sold.

b. Forward commitments to purchase goods and services used in the production of its products must be reported in the footnotes only when they are take-or-pay contracts that meet the requirement of SFAS 47 (see text page 377). They would be neither recognized in the financial statements nor marked to market because such contracts qualify for the normal purchases and normal sales exemption (see Box 16-2, text page 598).[1]

When the underlying goods and services are purchased, the contract price is reported on the income statement as a component of cost of goods sold or selling, general, and administrative expenses. Any gain or loss on goods (services) is implicitly reported as part of gross margin (operating margin) at the time output is sold.

c. To evaluate potential gains and losses on firm commitments and purchase contracts, we would need the following:
   i. Fair values of the commitments or contracts, if available.
   ii. The terms of PepsiCo contracts (quantities, prices, and dates) and the price at which it would be able to purchase the contracted amounts in the market place (i.e., the spot price of the contract). The difference between spot and contract prices would enable the analyst to establish whether the contracts will increase or decrease COGS (and therefore gross margin) when the related outputs are sold.
   iii. For services, the difference between contract price and the cost of the same services (e.g. transportation) at current prices would enable the analyst to determine the effect of the contracts on operating margins. It would also help determine whether changes in selling, general, and administrative expenses have been affected by those contracts.

4.{S}a. Kemet was exposed to increasing prices from a limited number of suppliers. The company must have used the purchase contract to fix the price it would pay and

---

[1] If the forward commitments do not qualify for the normal sales and normal purchases exemption, they would meet the definition of a derivative and therefore, have to be marked to market.

ensure availability of the amount of tantalum required to meet operating needs.

b. Although the purchase contract is a derivative, it is not treated as such for financial reporting purposes because it qualifies for the normal purchases and normal sales exemption (see Box 16-2, text page 598). U.S. GAAP permits this exception under the rebuttable presumption that the purchase contract applies to commodities that will be used in the production process and the company will take physical delivery of the commodity.

c. Kemet discloses the purchase contract as a commitment, stating the gross amounts it has contracted to pay ($2 billion) and the term over which the payments will be made (5 years). There is no financial statement recognition when the contract is entered into.

d. We need the fair value of these contracts to determine the unrealized gain or loss on these contracts. This gain or loss should be added or deducted from reported earnings to measure the performance of the management.

Alternatively, we need the contract amounts and price, and the spot price of tantalum for 2002 to determine the effect of the contract on reported COGS, gross margin, and net income. For 2003 we need the contract amounts and prices, as well as market prices to estimate those same effects in 2003.

To the extent that Kemet exercises the commitment to purchase tantalum in 2003, the realized gain or loss would be reported as a component of cost of goods sold when the goods containing the tantalum are sold. Separate disclosure of that amount would facilitate evaluation of management performance.

e. Alternatively, Kemet could have purchased options to purchase the required amount of tantalum. The advantage is that Kemet would not have committed to purchase a specified amount of tantalum given adverse price changes and would have remained free to exercise the option only if a gain could be realized. In effect, options require significantly lower investments relative to firm purchase commitments.

One disadvantage is that Kemet would have paid a premium for the option. In addition, there may be counterparty risk if there were no exchange-traded options on tantalum.

f.   Purchases contracts that are treated as derivatives or embedded derivatives must be marked to fair value on each reporting date and the related gain or loss recognized in earnings if the derivatives qualify as fair value hedges. If the derivatives meet the criteria for cash flow hedges, the unrealized gain or loss is reported as a component of other comprehensive income. Given changing prices, balance sheets and income statements (for fair value hedges) would reflect the volatility of those prices providing the investor useful information regarding operating trends and profitability.

In contrast, when purchase contracts qualify for the normal sales and normal purchases exemption, changing prices are not reflected in either the balance sheet or the income statement. It is likely that the resulting financial statements will be misleading in that they reflect older rather than current prices for critical inputs to the production process.

5.{S}a. It appears that Aracruz uses hedges to protect its € receivables against changes in the €/$ exchange rate. The volume of foreign exchange contracts rose sharply in 1999, but fell in 2000, mirroring the change in € receivables. The 2001 increase in the volume of foreign exchange contracts exceeds the small increase in € receivables. However it is possible that a large increase in receivables was expected in early January 2002. Similarly, the high level of forwards relative to receivables at December 31, 1998 may reflect an expected increase in receivables during the first quarter of 1999.

b. Under SFAS 133, which Aracruz adopted in 2001, these contracts are accounted for as cash flow hedges and marked to market at each balance sheet date. The effective portion of the hedge should be reported in other comprehensive income and included in net income in the period when the receivables are collected.

c. As the Euro declined against the dollar over most of the four-year period, it is surprising that hedges against a Euro decline should result in losses. The most likely explanation is that the year-end exchange rates were above the rates at which the company hedged its exposures.

6.{s}a. Tokio Marine has exchanged a portion of its Japanese earthquake and typhoon risks for a portion of Swiss Re's California earthquake, Florida hurricane, and French storm exposures. Assuming that the Japanese risks are uncorrelated with the California, Florida, and French risks, Tokio has diversified its risk portfolio. As it has reduced its exposure to Japanese earthquake and typhoon losses, it is an economic hedge.

Swiss Re has also diversified its risk exposure by taking on Japanese earthquake and typhoon risk in exchange for a reduction in its exposure to California earthquakes, Florida hurricanes, and French storms.

b. As these contracts are not considered to be derivatives,[2] there would be no accounting recognition

---

[2] Both SFAS 133 and IAS 39 exclude insurance contracts (see Box 16-2 on page 598, except for contracts that contain embedded derivatives.

at inception. Each company would recognize its losses on the assumed risks and would reduce its losses from the exchanged risks[3] as such losses can be estimated.

7.{S}a. 1. Foreign currency (FC) forward sales are used to convert expected FC denominated cash flows from operations to fixed U.S. dollar amounts. These derivatives allow the company to fix the dollar cash flows of foreign units and fix or manage the dollar amount of operating profitability.

2. The interest rate swaps, caps, and floors enable the company to lock in a specific net interest income or margin on the investment certificates and fixed annuities. The margin or spread is the primary determinant of profitability for such products.

3. AXP limits its exposure to volatile equity markets using the options and futures with payoffs that offset the changes in the equity market indices used to determine payments to holders of the investment and certificate products. If it did not hedge, large changes in the equity markets would affect the profitability of equity-linked products, making it more volatile.

b. 1. AXP is exposed to the fluctuations in the U.S. dollar to foreign currency exchange rates on foreign currency receipts generated by its non-U.S. operations. The FC forward contracts are economic hedges of those exposures because they allow AXP to fix the dollar amount received for a specified amount of FC denominated cash flows eliminating the effect of exchange rate changes on that foreign currency exposure.

2. The company invests the proceeds from sales of investment certificates and fixed annuities in order to generate income required to pay promised returns on those products. The interest rate caps, swaps, and floors provide an economic hedge in that they offset the effect on interest rate changes on net interest income.

---

[3] Insurance companies refer to the exchanged risk as "reinsurance assumed" and "reinsurance ceded."

16-9

3. The options and futures used to manage the equity risk on its investment and certificate products that promise returns tied to equity markets are economic hedges because their payoffs will offset the effects of changes in the equity market indices on AXP's liabilities for those products.

c. All three hedges would qualify as accounting hedges if the company designated them as such, identified the exposures hedged, and established the methods to be used to measure effectiveness.

8.{S}a. Under SFAS 133 and IAS 39, Holmen would be required to segregate and separately report the debt (the host contract) and the conversion option (the embedded derivative) because all of the following conditions would be met:

1. The economic characteristics and risks of the conversion feature are not related to those of the host contract, debt. This condition is satisfied because the debt is convertible into Holmen shares; the economic characteristics of an equity option differ from those of a fixed rate bond.
2. Other applicable GAAP does not require the hybrid instrument (the convertible bond) to be reported at fair value with changes in the fair value reported in earnings. Since Holmen has issued this convertible bond, this criterion is satisfied as well; both U.S. and IAS GAAP require the use of historical cost accounting for debt.
3. A separate instrument with the same terms as the embedded derivative would meet the definition of a derivative; the conversion feature is in essence a call option and qualifies as a derivative.

Because the convertible bond meets all three criteria, the debt and conversion feature would be reported separately. Because the conversion feature is a derivative, it would be reported at fair value on each balance sheet date and the change in fair value would be reported in earnings.

The proceeds from the bond issue would be allocated to the debt and derivative components based on their relative fair values.

b. When the conversion feature is ignored, the effective interest rate and interest expense on the bond issue are based on the total proceeds received. Under SFAS 133 and IAS 39, a portion of the proceeds would be allocated to the embedded derivative (that is, to equity) resulting in a lower carrying amount for the debt component and therefore a higher effective interest rate.

The higher effective interest rate would result in higher periodic interest expense and lower earnings in the years following the bond issuance. In addition, the conversion option would be marked to market and the change in fair value included in net income for each period (see Alliant Energy example on text page 604).

9. {S}a.   (i) With the exception of dividends received (reported as components of cash flows from operations), SFAS 95 reports the cash flow consequences of nonoperating changes in the net investment in all subsidiaries as a component of cash flows from investing activities. From a financial reporting perspective, Black & Decker has correctly classified the cash flows from hedges of net investments in foreign subsidiaries as cash flows from investing activities.

   (ii) To the extent that the company's foreign currency hedges relate to its operating activities, the company has made the appropriate classification decision. Because SFAS 95 classifies interest payments as components of cash flows from operations, BDK has correctly classified the cash flow consequences of its hedges of interest rate exposures.

   b.   The classification of cash flows from hedging activities related to net investments in foreign subsidiaries should be based on the degree of operational integration between the reporting entity and its foreign subsidiaries. When the operations of the foreign unit are integral to the operations of the reporting entity (for example, the foreign unit manufactures a critical component for product(s) sold by the U.S. parent), the cash flow consequences of hedging activities related to that net investment should be treated as components of cash flows from operations.

   When the investment in a foreign unit involves an investment with no implications for operating activities, the cash flow effects of hedging activities related to those entities belong in the cash flow from investment category.

10.{M}a. Delta Airlines (DAL) limited its hedging to the next year's fuel needs; American Airlines (AMR) took a longer and view and hedged forward (albeit a low 7% (5%) for the second year out in 2000 (2001)) as many as two years beyond the next year (following the reporting year).

Although the difference between amounts hedged declined over the three years, AMR hedged a much smaller portion of its anticipated fuel needs for the next year. However, on a combined basis (three years), AMR hedged more than DAL and AMR was more consistent (67% in 1999 and 66% in 2001) than DAL (down to 46% hedged in 2001 compared to 80% in 1999).
However Delta discloses a higher proportion of fuel needs hedged during the year; the year-end disclosures may have understated DAL's hedging activities compared with those of AMR (which does not make a similar disclosure).

	Delta			*American*		
	1999	*2000*	*2001*	*1999*	*2000*	*2001*
% of fuel needs hedged during the year	75%	67%	58%	ND	ND	ND
% of expected fuel needs hedged:						
Next year	80%	51%	46%	48%	40%	40%
Following year	0	0	0	19%	15%	21%
Following year	0	0	0	0%	7%	5%
Total	80%	51%	46%	67%	62%	66%

ND = not disclosed

b. DAL discloses the % of fuel needs hedged each year whereas AMR does not provide those data. This information would allow analysts to question management about significant changes in the % of fuel needs actually hedged during the year compared to amounts reported at the end of the previous year. The analysts could also evaluate the change in strategy (actual % hedged versus % hedged at the beginning of the year) given market prices of fuel and operations during the year.

AMR discloses the cost of ineffective hedges but DAL does not. The cost and reason(s) for the ineffectiveness would improve our understanding of management's strategy and permit a better informed evaluation of management and company performance.

Delta reports (2001 only) the average hedge price at year-end. This information should improve 2002 earnings forecasts as the analyst is better able to predict the effect of fuel price changes on operating expenses.

c. The following table shows the effect of hedging gains on reported fuel expense, operating income, and income before accounting change. The left-hand column labels the rows and shows the computations.

	Delta Airlines	*Years ended December 31*		
	Analysis of Fuel Price Hedging Activities	*1999*	*2000*	*2001*
	Amounts in $millions			
	Reported data			
a	Hedge gains	$ 79	$ 684	$ 299
b	Operating income (loss)	1,318	1,637	(1,602)
c	Net income before accounting change	1,262	928	(1,216)
	Aircraft fuel expense			
d	As reported	(1,421)	(1,969)	(1,817)
e = d − a	Excluding hedge gains	(1,500)	(2,653)	(2,116)
f = b − a	Operating income (loss) excluding hedge gains	1,239	953	(1,901)
g =.65 x a	Hedge gains net of 35% tax	51	445	194
h = c − g	Net income excluding hedging gains	1,211	483	(1,410)
	Hedging gains as a % of reported			
a/d	**(i) Fuel expense**	5.56%	34.74%	16.46%
a/b	**(ii) Operating income**	5.99%	41.78%	-18.66%
g/c	**(iii) Net income before accounting change**	4.07%	47.91%	-15.98%

d. The following table continues the row labels from part c and shows the effect of Delta's fuel hedging activities on year-to-year income comparisons.

	Delta Airlines	Years ended December 31		
	Amounts in $millions	*1999*	*2000*	*2001*
c	*Net income before accounting change*	$1,262	$928	$(1,216)
	(i) % change from prior year	**N.A.**	**-26.5%**	**-231.0%**
h = c - g	*Net income excluding hedging gains*	$1,211	$483	$(1,410)
	(ii) % change from prior year	**N.A.**	**-60.1%**	**-391.9%**

e. The following table shows the effect of Delta's hedging activities on Delta's per gallon fuel cost. The row labels continue from previous tables.

	Delta Airlines	Years ended December 31		
		1999	*2000*	*2001*
i	Fuel consumed (millions of gallons)	2,779	2,922	2,649
	Average fuel price in cents per gallon			
d/i	**(i) As reported**	**51.13**	**67.39**	**68.59**
e/i	**(ii) Excluding hedge gains**	**53.98**	**90.79**	**79.88**
	% improvement	5.3%	25.8%	14.1%

f. The following table compares fuel expense as a percent of operating revenues for Delta and American, both including and excluding hedging gains. The left hand column continues the row labeling for Delta.

		Delta			American		
		1999	*2000*	*2001*	*1999*	*2000*	*2001*
i	Operating revenue	$14,883	$16,741	$13,879	$17,730	$19,703	$18,963
	Fuel expense as a % of						
d/i	Operating revenues	9.5%	11.8%	13.1%	9.6%	12.7%	15.2%
e/i	Excluding hedging gains	10.1%	15.8%	15.2%	10.2%	15.4%	15.4%

DAL appears to be more successful because hedging has allowed it to lower fuel costs more than AMR. While fuel expense as a percent of operating revenues was similar for the two companies excluding gains (see table above), Delta had significantly lower fuel costs (including hedging gains) relative to operating revenues for both 2000 and 2001.

While the pre-hedging fuel cost data suggest that the two airlines have similar fuel needs and face similar costs, it would be helpful to know American's:

- Fuel use in gallons
- Fuel costs per gallon before hedging.

These data would allow the analyst to understand any differences in fuel requirements or costs due to differing aircraft or route structure.

g. Delta hedged forward a lower amount of fuel needs every year; from 80% in 1999 to 46% in 2001. However, note that the actual % of fuel needs hedged during the year is very different from the percentage held at the beginning of the year (In 2000 (2001), 80% (51%) was hedged at the beginning of the year but 67% (58%) was hedged during the year). Also, note that Delta does not hedge forward beyond the year following the reporting year.

There are several possible explanations for this trend:

- higher volatility or spreads in the futures markets for oil commodities that are used to hedge jet fuel, raising hedging costs
- the increased difficulty of predicting trends in travel (and therefore, fuel needs) due to political and economic factors
- Delta's view of the likely trend of fuel prices compared with current prices

11.{M}a. Amerada Hess engages in hedging activities to fix the selling prices of its products and reduce or eliminate the effect of volatile oil and gas prices on its revenues and income.

b. Amerada likely reduced its crude oil hedges because it expected higher prices in 2002 and did not want to limit the price at which it could sell its output. The company may have increased the amount of natural gas hedged for the opposite reason: it expected lower gas prices in 2002 and 2003.

c. Additional information necessary for an evaluation of hedging activities on earnings:

- The effect of hedging activities on revenues and operating income
- Amounts and timing of hedge maturities (for example, how many million barrels of crude oil must be delivered each quarter and at what price),
- The fair value of the derivative contracts by maturities for each type of derivative used including realized and unrealized gain and loss on derivative contracts, and
- The ineffective component of the derivative contracts and where that amount is reported on the income statement.

This information allows us to better understand the impact of hedging activities on revenues reported by the company. Changes in the amount and types of derivatives used should be evaluated with reference to the analysts' understanding of the economics of the facilitate forecasts of earnings for the company.

d. (i) If oil and gas prices increased in 2002, Amerada would have lost the opportunity to sell hedged output at these higher prices. If the price increases fell short of the hedge prices at which Amerada had the right to sell hedged crude oil and gas quantities, Amerada would have realized above market prices and reported higher income.

(ii) Hedges protected Amerada against decreases in oil and gas prices. To the extent that it hedged,

2002 reported income was higher than if all output had been sold in the spot market.

e. Additional information needed to evaluate the success of Amerada's hedging activities:

- Realized and unrealized gains and losses on the different types of derivatives used by the company, for each period

- Methods used to estimate fair value including identification of any critical assumptions and the impact of unfavorable changes in prices or underlying indices, and

- In the event the company has computed fair values of the derivatives using option pricing or present value methods rather than market prices or quotes from unrelated financial institutions, why management believes that its methods provide more reliable information. Management should do its best to quantify the distinction between its methodology and that used in the marketplace.

The gains and losses would allow us to quantify the contribution of hedging activities on revenues. The disclosures on measurement methods will permit an evaluation of the quality of (1) revenue recognized and (2) management.

12. {S}a   Because the net monetary liabilities of Amerada's North Sea Operations are likely denominated in pounds sterling, and Amerada would like to fix the dollar amounts paid to settle the obligations, the company must have purchased sterling for future delivery at specified exchange rates. The company must be long pound sterling and short the dollar.

b.   Because Amerada uses the $U.S. as the functional currency for its North Sea operations, all non-dollar denominated assets and liabilities must be translated (remeasured) to $U.S. on all financial statement dates and the gain or loss reported in the income statement. The company's hedging activities must be designed to reduce or eliminate the income variability that is a consequence of the remeasurement process.

Alternatively, if Amerada could designate the pound sterling as the functional currency, the application of U.S. GAAP would require the recognition of translation gains or losses in the cumulative translation adjustment account, a component of stockholders' equity. Little or no volatility due to the pound sterling would have to be reported in the income statement, reducing the incentive to hedge the foreign currency accounting exposure (although the economic incentives would remain).

c.   One reason for the reduction in the notional value of the foreign exchange contracts may be that management expected sterling to decline against the dollar. However, a more likely reason is that the company reduced its exposure to the pound sterling by settling sterling denominated obligations or effectively reducing its net monetary liabilities.

13.{S}a. Holmen hedges its foreign currency exposures to reduce the impact of exchange rate fluctuations on its revenues and its income from operations.

b. At December 31, 2001, Holmen had increased its hedge amounts to nearly 80% of its annual euro cash flows (86% of pound sterling) compared to far lower amounts at the end of 1999 and 2000. Panel B shows a declining Swedish krona (relative to both euros and pounds) through 6-30-01. There was marginal improvement against both currencies as of 12-31-01. The lower value of the krona increased revenues and operating income of non-Swedish operations when measured in krona.

Holmen most likely increased amounts hedged to lock in the higher revenue and operating income, protecting them against possible strengthening of the Swedish krona relative to the euro and the pound.

c. The decline of the SEK relative to both the euro and the pound limited the benefit (increase in revenues and earnings) that Holmen was able to recognize. The company's hedges would have capped the krona received for euros and pounds whereas the foreign currencies would have translated into higher krona amounts as that currency declined.

14.{M}   *Note*: The purpose of this question is to illustrate the financial statement effects of management's accounting choices regarding derivatives.

a. Resh faces two types of risks; market value risk on its fixed-rate investments and cash flow risk on its variable rate debt. The effects of interest rate changes on Resh for both these instruments are similar – interest rate increases adversely effect Resh whereas interest decreases are beneficial ; i.e.

(i) An increase in interest rates would increase Resh's borrowing costs on its variable rate debt and lower the market value of its investments

(ii) A decrease in interest rates would decrease Resh's borrowing costs on its variable rate debt and increase the market value of its investments.

Note that only the change in borrowing costs would be reflected in earnings, as the mortgages would be carried at cost.[4]

b. By entering the swap, *to the extent the swap is an effective hedge,*[5] Resh has neutralized the risks described above.

(i) When interest rates increase, receipts from the variable portion of the swap will increase and the value of the hedge will increase as the value of the fixed rate portion of the swap declines. These effects are opposite to the effects (described in a(i)) on Resh's fixed rate investments and variable rate debt. Given the positive fair value of the hedge, Resh would now have increased counterparty risk – the risk that the other party to the swap cannot pay.

---

[4] If Resh held securities (such as mortgage-backed bonds) the answer would differ. We also ignore any prepayment feature, which would be accounted for as an embedded derivative.

[5] Resh may have "basis" risk, the risk that the index underlying the company's original debt issue differs from the prime rate. The solution assumes that there is no basis risk in this case.

(ii) When interest rates decrease, receipts from the variable portion of the swap will decrease and the value of the hedge will decrease as the value of the fixed rate portion of the swap increases. Again, these are opposite to the effects (described in part a(ii)) on Resh's fixed rate investments and variable rate debt.

The remainder of the problem discusses the accounting impact of the swap.

c. If Resh does not designate the swap as a hedge, the swap is reported by itself on a mark to market basis and the fixed rate investments are reported on a historical cost basis.

(i) 2000 income would be increased by the higher variable rate receipts (offsetting the higher interest payments on its variable rate debt).[6] Income would also be increased by the mark-to-market gain on the derivative.

(ii) 2001 income would be reduced by the lower variable rate receipts (but this effect would be offset by lower interest payments on the variable rate debt). Income would also be reduced by the mark-to-market loss on the derivative.

(iii) and (iv) Resh would treat the swap as a derivative held for trading and mark it to market on each balance sheet date. The gain (in 2000) and loss (2001) would be recognized on the balance sheet as part of retained earnings.

---

[6] The difference between the amounts received and amounts paid would be recognized by the company but would not necessarily offset on the interest expense line.

d. The effects of designating the swap as a "cash flow" hedge of its variable rate debt are similar to the above except for the impact of the mark to market gains on the swap. They are not reported in income but are included in other comprehensive income.

(i) 2000 income would by increased by the higher variable rate receipts (offsetting the higher interest payments on its variable rate debt).[7]

(ii) 2001 income would be reduced by the lower variable rate receipts (but this effect would be offset by the lower interest payments on the variable rate debt).

(iii) and (iv) Resh would report the swap at fair value (mark to market) on each balance sheet date because it has designated the swap as a hedge of the variable rate debt. Assuming that the swap is completely effective, the 2000 gain and 2001 loss would be included in other comprehensive income.

e. If Resh designates the swap as a "fair value" hedge of its fixed rate investments, then the hedged item (the fixed rate investment) is also reported on a mark to market basis.

(i) 2000 income would be increased by the receipt of 7% (offset against the required variable rate payment) and payment of 6%. The difference would be reported as lower interest expense. Income would also include any increase in fair value of the swap *and* any change in market value of the investments. If the hedge were fully effective, the fair value adjustments would offset each other.

---

[7] The difference between the amounts received and amounts paid would be recognized by the company as an offset on the interest expense line.

(ii) 2001 income would be lower because Resh would receive 5% (offset against the required variable rate payment) and pay 6%. The difference between the amounts received and amounts paid would be recognized as higher interest expense. Income would also include any change in fair value of the swap *and* any change in market value of the investments. If the hedge were fully effective, the fair value adjustments would offset each other.

(iii) and (iv) Resh must report both the swap and the fixed income investments (the hedged item) at their fair value on the balance sheet.

f. The purpose of the swap was to eliminate the possible effect of changing interest rates on the fair value of Resh's investments and on the interest expense cash flows on its variable rate debt. However, as the table below indicates, the accounting consequences differ considerably from the economic consequences, depending on whether the swap is designated as a hedge of the investments, the debt, or neither.

Summary of Economic and Accounting Effects of Interest Rate Changes (assumes hedge is 100% effective)

Effect of Interest Rate	On	Economic			Accounting Swap Designation		
		Without hedge (a)	Effect on swap	Net effect of swap (b)	Not designated as hedge (c)	Cash flow hedge (d)	Fair value hedge (e)
Increase	Net assets	D	I	N	I	I	N
	Income	D	I	N	N	N	N
Decrease	Net assets	I	D	N	D	D	N
	Income	I	D	N	N	N	N

I = Increase
D = Decrease
N = No effect or Neutral if hedge is effective

Chapter 18 - Solutions

Overview: Problem Length   Problem #'s
        {S}   3,7
        {M}   1, 2, 4 - 6, 8 - 10

Problems 1-3 deal with the takeover of Kraft by Philip Morris. If assigned together, they would require approximately 1 1/2 hrs of work.

1.{M}a.	**Before Kraft**	**Consolidated**
Pretax interest coverage[1]	10.64X	3.76X
Long-term debt/total capital[2]	28.11%	61.99%
Cash flow/total debt[3]	71.14%	23.14%

[1]   ($4,820+$500)/$500 $4,420+$1,600)/$1,600

[2] $3,883/($3,883+$9,931) $15,778/($15,778+$9,675)

[3] $$\frac{(\$2,820+\$750+\$100-\$125)}{(\$3,883 + \$1,100)} \quad \frac{(\$2,564+\$1,235+\$390-\$125)}{(\$15,778 + \$ 1,783)}$$

b.   Pretax interest coverage moves from the AA range to the BBB range. Long-term debt/total capital shifts from A to less than B. Cash flow/total debt declines from between A and AA to BB.

c.   Prior to the merger, Philip Morris debt would have a strong A rating based on these criteria. After the Kraft merger, BB would be appropriate based on these same criteria.

2.{M}*Note:* *The answers given below concern the effect of the merger on the probability of bankruptcy as predicted by Altman's models. It is not clear that ratio changes caused by external events (such as an acquisition) have the same predictive ability as those resulting from normal operations.*

The variables used in Altman's two models are listed below by category:

	1977 model	**1968 model**
Activity		Sales to total assets
Liquidity	Current ratio	Working capital to total assets
Leverage and Solvency	Equity (market) to debt Times interest earned	Equity (market) to capital
Profitability	Return on assets Retained earnings to total assets	Return on assets Retained earnings to total assets
Earnings Variability	Standard error of ROA	
Size	Total assets	

Activity

(1968 model) Sales to total assets

Sales increased by $11,610 (approximately 33%) from $33,080 to $44,690 as a result of the merger. Although Exhibit 18P-1 does not provide the data directly, we can infer from the data available that the increase in assets would be greater.

Debt plus equity increased[1] by $12,322. When we consider that current operating liabilities and other (nondebt) liabilities also increased as a result of the merger, we can infer that total assets grew by *at least* $12,322.

---

[1] Total debt + equity (post merger) = $1,783 + $15,778 + $9,675 = $27,236
(pre merger) = $1,100 + $3,883 + $9,931 = 14,914
Increase = $12,322

If, prior to the merger, the asset turnover ratio was greater than 1, then adding a given amount ($11,610) to the numerator and a larger amount to the denominator would reduce the ratio, increasing the likelihood of bankruptcy.

If, on the other hand, the asset turnover ratio was less than 1 prior to the merger, then more information about actual asset levels is needed to determine the effect on this ratio.

Liquidity

(1977 model) Current ratio
(1968 model) Working capital to total assets

The information in Exhibit 18P-1 is insufficient to assess the impact of the merger on working capital and the current ratio.

Leverage and Solvency

(1977 model) Market value of equity to debt
(1968 model) Market value of equity to capital

Before the merger, Philip Morris' total debt was $4,983 billion ($1,100 + $3,883). As a result of the merger, total debt increased more than threefold to $17,561 million ($1,783 + $15,778). Unless the market value of equity increased by the same proportion [Philip Morris' market value actually *decreased* following the merger announcement] the equity to debt (capital) ratio would be reduced considerably, increasing the likelihood of bankruptcy.

(1977 model) Times interest earned

From problem 1, we have

	Before Kraft	**Consolidated**
Pretax interest coverage	10.64X	3.76X

Based on the (1977) model, the reduction in the coverage ratio would increase the likelihood of bankruptcy.

Profitability

(Both models)   Return on assets

Philip Morris' EBIT rose from $5,320 million ($4,820 + $500) to $6,020 million ($4,420 + $1,600). EBIT decreased from 16% of sales ($5,320/$33,080) to 13.5% ($6,020/$44,690). The impact on ROA depends on the asset turnover (discussed earlier). However, unless asset turnover increased by (at least) 18.5%, the net effect would be a reduction in ROA.

(Both models)   Retained earnings to total assets

Since the merger is accounted for under the purchase method, Kraft's retained earnings are eliminated. As total assets increase, this ratio would be greatly reduced. The reduced ratio results in prediction by the model of a greater likelihood of bankruptcy.

Earnings Variability

(1977 model) Standard deviation of ROA

Similar to portfolio diversification, the variance of return measures such as ROA should decline following the merger, reducing the likelihood of bankruptcy.

Size

(1977 model) Total assets

As total assets increase as a result of the merger, the model predicts a smaller likelihood of bankruptcy.

3. {S} The theoretical as well as empirical models (Exhibit 18-3), indicate that beta risk is a function of both the operating (unleveraged beta) and financial (leveraged) risk of the company. As Philip Morris' debt increased by approximately $12 billion as a result of the merger without a commensurate increase in equity the firm's financial leverage increased. *Ceteris paribus*, this should result in an increase in financial risk and beta.

   The effect on operating risk depends on how Kraft's cost structure compares with that of Philip Morris, that is, on the mix between fixed and variable costs. The impact on beta would depend on the answer to this question.

4.{M}a.

	Coca-Cola Company (KO)	Coca-Cola Enterprises (CCE)
(i) Short-term liquidity		
Current ratio	0.85	0.64
Quick ratio	0.45	0.40
Inventory turnover	5.7	14.1
Receivables turnover	10.7	10.2
(ii) Capital structure & long-term solvency		
Debt to equity	0.45	4.37
Times interest earned	20.6	0.8
(iii) Asset utilization		
Inventory turnover	5.7	14.1
Receivables turnover	10.7	10.2
PP&E turnover	4.5	2.5
Total asset turnover	0.9	0.7
(iv) Operating profitability		
Gross profit	70%	38%
Return on sales	20%	(2)%
ROA	19%	(1)%
ROE	35%	(12)%

(i) KO has better short-term liquidity as its current and quick ratios are higher. Its accounts receivable turnover is also higher. CCE, on the other hand, has a significantly higher inventory turnover ratio.

(ii) KO's ratio of long-term debt to equity is far lower than CCE's. Despite KO's substantial short-term debt, its total debt to equity ratio is still much lower. CCE's higher debt burden and lower profitability result in an interest coverage ratio that is far below that of KO.

(iii) As noted in (i), CCE's inventory turnover is far above KO's whereas its receivables turnover ratio is slightly lower. As CCE is more capital intensive than KO, its property and total asset turnover ratios are well below those of CCE.

(iv) KO is more profitable than CCE by all measures. Higher gross margins are carried down to net income. Given its lower capital requirements, KO's return ratios are far higher.

b. & c.

1. The adjustment of KO investments from carrying amount to market value increases both assets and equity. The effect is to reduce leverage but also asset turnover and return ratios.

2. KO and CCE's debt should be increased by the OBS debt. For KO, the adjustment equals the contingent guarantee of $451 million. In CCE's case the adjustment is considerably larger, equal to the present value of the future payments to suppliers. Recognition of these obligations increases the leverage of CCE by a greater amount than KO, thus increasing the differences noted above.

3. Additionally, as an offset to the debt, the companies' assets should be increased. The effect will be to decrease return and turnover ratios. Again, the effect is larger for CCE given the relatively large amount of OBS debt.

4. KO's income should be reduced by the option costs. The effect will be to lower profitability and interest coverage ratios for KO. However, given the magnitude of these costs (relative to KO's income), the effects are not significant and will only minimally impact the KO-CCE comparison. *Note: KO started expensing employee stock options in 2003*

5. Increase CCE debt to its market value. The adjustment raises its leverage even more. For comparison purposes, the fair value of KO's debt should also be obtained.

6. Increase CCE's liabilities by $361 million, lower its assets by $1 million, and reduce equity by $362 million to replace the pension asset with the economic liability for the underfunded pension plan. The effect will be to increase CCE's leverage - again widening the difference between itself and KO.

5.{M}a. & b. The ratios and bond rating categories based on reported data follow. Comparing the ratios with those in Exhibit 18-4, we find the implied rating to be "all over the place" ranging (depending on the category) from CCC to A and all points in between. Overall a rating of between BB and BBB would seem to be implied.

Exhibit 18-4 Ratio	Ratio	Implied Rating	Calculations	
			Numerator	Denominator
EBIT/interest	2.19	BB	$ 272	$ 124
EBITDA/interest	4.45	BB-BBB	$ 552	$ 124
Free CFO/Total debt	0.12	A-BBB	$ 183	$ 1,477
Return on capital	0.07	B	$ 272	$ 3,648
EBIT/Sales	0.10	<CCC	$ 272	$ 2,802
Long-term debt/capital	0.40	BBB	$1,427	$ 3,598
Total debt/capital (includes STD)	0.40	A	$1,477	$ 3,648

Source: Westvaco financial statements (debt and capital per Chapter 17)

c. The ratios and corresponding Z"-score for Altman's Z"-score model are computed below. The Z"-score of 5.95 implies a rating of BBB (see Exhibit 18-5), similar to that implied by the analysis in parts a. and b.

	Numerator	Denominator	Ratio	Weight	Ratio X Weight
Working capital/total assets	$ 313	$4,897	0.06	6.56	0.42
Retained earnings/total assets	$1,608	$4,897	0.33	3.26	1.07
EBIT/total assets	$ 272	$4,897	0.06	6.72	0.37
Book value of equity/total liabilities	$2,171	$2,726	0.80	1.05	0.84
Intercept					3.25
Z" Score					**5.95**

Source: Westvaco financial statements (debt and capital as per Chapter 17)

d. Westvaco's actual rating of A- was higher than the BBB rating implied by the results of parts a through c.

S&P reduced Westvaco's rating to BBB+ in May 2000 and to BBB in June 2001 (see Box 10-3 on page 344). This action supports the opinion of many observers that rating agency actions tend to lag economic changes. Rating agencies have also been accused of being reluctant to make adverse ratings changes because their fees are paid by the corporations whose debt they rate.

6.{M}a.& b.   The ratios and bond rating categories based on adjusted data follow. Comparing the ratios with those in Exhibit 18-4, we find the implied rating to be higher than for the reported data. EBIT (and EBITDA) were improved by removal of restructuring costs. Debt was increased slightly but not as much as capital. As a result, solvency ratios (interest coverage and debt to capital) improved. Similarly, return on sales increased as EBIT went up but sales remained the same. The only ratio that deteriorated was return on capital as capital was increased more than EBIT. Overall, the adjusted data imply a rating of BBB+.

Exhibit 18-4 Ratio	Ratio	Implied Rating	Calculations	
			Numerator	Denominator
EBIT/interest	2.70	BB-BBB	$ 335	$ 124
EBITDA/interest	4.96	BB-BBB	$ 615	$ 124
Free CFO/Total Debt	0.17	A	$ 262	$ 1,577
Return on capital	0.06	B	$ 335	$ 6,081
EBIT/Sales	0.12	B	$ 335	$ 2,802
Long-term debt/capital	0.25	AA	$ 1,527	$ 6,031
Total debt/capital (incl. STD)	0.26	AAA	$ 1,577	$ 6,081

Source: Chapter 17 analysis of Westvaco – see Exhibits 17-1, 17-2, 17-3 and 17-4. For EBIT, added (pretax) restructuring charges and asset sales (Exhibit 17-3) to reported EBIT.

c.   The data in Exhibit 18-4 are based on reported, not adjusted data. Similar adjustments for all companies comprising the sample in Exhibit 18-4 and average ratios based on the revised data may yield the same relative ratings for Westvaco if the positive effect on Westvaco is no greater than for the average company.

d.   The adjusted data result in a Z″ score of 7.46:

	Numerator	Denominator	Ratio	Weight	Ratio X Weight
Working capital/total assets	$ 389	$6,500	0.06	6.56	0.39
Retained earnings/total assets	$ 2,203	$6,500	0.34	3.26	1.10
EBIT/total assets	$ 335	$6,500	0.05	6.72	0.35
Book value of equity/Total liabilities	$ 4,504	$1,996	2.26	1.05	2.37
Intercept					3.25
Z″ SCORE					7.46

Exhibit 18-5 on page 664 equates this score to a bond rating between AA and AA+ compared with the BB rating implied by the unadjusted data (see question 5c).

While the cautions about relative ratios discussed in part c also apply to the Z'' scores, the higher absolute values of the ratios based on adjusted data do suggest that Westvaco's default risk is lower than it appears from the unadjusted data.

e. For the same reasons discussed in part D, the adjusted data suggest that Westvaco is a stronger company financially than it appears from the unadjusted data with less bankruptcy risk.

7.{S}a. The following table lists the implied ratings from Exhibit 18-4 for the ratios provided.

| Company Actual Rating In Parentheses () | Implied Rating | | | |
| | Total Debt To Capital | | Interest Coverage | |
	1999	2000	1999	2000
Westvaco (A-)	A	BBB - BB	BB	BBB
International Paper (BBB+)	A	BBB - BB	BB	BB
Georgia-Pacific (BBB-)	BB	B	BBB	BB

The data in Exhibit 18P-3 imply ratings that confirm the *relative* rankings of the three companies; i.e. Westvaco is stronger than International Paper (IP) and both are superior to Georgia-Pacific (GP). However, the actual ratings themselves were above those implied by reference to Exhibit 18-4.

b. The data in Exhibit 18P-3 show an increase in the debt to capital ratio for all three companies and, as a result, a potential ratings downgrade. The interest coverage ratio declined for both IP and GP, but rose for Westvaco. Based on these two ratios, all three companies are candidates for downgrades based on 2000 data.

c. If 1999 and 2000 are cyclical peaks, then ratios over an entire business cycle would be expected to be lower. Ratings based only on peak data are likely to be too high.

The fact that 1999 and 2000 were prosperous years may at first seem anomalous given the deterioration described in part b, and may strengthen the argument for the downgrade. More data with respect to changes in sales, profitability, and cash flows would be required to better address this issue.

8.{M}a.   The solution to this problem is based on the ratios calculated below. The "implied ratings" are based on the data provided in Exhibit 18-4.

Exhibit 18-4 Ratios	2000		2001	
	Calculations	Implied Rating	Calculations	Implied Rating
Interest coverage	$322/$18 = 17.89	AAA	$19/$21 = 0.90	B
Free CFO/total debt	$(50)/$537=(9.3)%	CCC	$172/$594 = 29.0%	AA
Return on capital	$322/$2,174=14.8%	BBB	$19/$2,150 =0.9%	CCC
Operating income/sales	$322/$4,049 = 8.0%	<CCC	$19/$3,090 = 0.6%	<CCC
Total debt to capital	$537/$2,174=24.7%	AAA	$594/$2,150=27.6%	AA-AAA

Steelcase's 2000 ratios ranged from AAA to less than CCC. The overall A- rating seems to have been a compromise between these extremes. The decision to revise its outlook may come from the deterioration in the profitability ratios and the resultant decline in the interest coverage (solvency) ratio, despite the improved free CFO to debt ratio.

b.   The following information would be helpful:
   i.   The factors that led to the 2002 sales decline. Temporary factors (e.g. a strike) would suggest that the sales decline is temporary and would argue against a downgrade.
   ii.   The reason for the decline in EBIT. If was due to a nonoperating item, for example, that amount should be excluded and the ratios recalculated.
   iii. Accounting policies on revenue and expense recognition; these would cast light on the company's quality of earnings. Lower quality earnings would support a downgrade.
   iv.   Footnote data on retirement plans and off-balance-sheet obligations. Adjusted ratios (interest coverage, free CFO/debt, and total debt to capital) should be a better indicator of the appropriate rating.

c. The decision to reaffirm may have due to two factors.
    i. The strong solvency ratios (CFO/total debt and debt/capital) which implied ratings of AA - AAA. Free CFO to debt improved from the 2000 level.
    ii. The company's strong cash flow and free cash flows – both increased considerably in 2000.

d. The data in Exhibit 18-4 are based on averages taken over the whole economy. Different criteria and or different weightings may be appropriate for certain industries and/or certain companies.

The comparison also ignores differing accounting methods and use of off-balance-sheet financing techniques by different companies.

9.{M}a. *EBIT/interest expense*, the interest coverage ratio, is an indicator of the degree of protection available to creditors with respect to receiving interest payments. The ratio measures the firm's ability to meet interest payments out of current earnings. The higher the ratio, the less risky the firm.

Long-term debt/total capitalization measures the proportion of a firm's financing provided by debt. The higher that proportion, the higher the firm's financial leverage as the higher debt requires higher interest payments. The firm is riskier as the probability of insolvency increases as the firm may find it difficult to meet interest and principal payments.

Debt, ultimately, is repaid by internally generated cash flows. Funds from operations act as a surrogate for CFO and *funds from operations/total debt* measures the extent to which internally generated funds (operating cash flows excluding working capital changes) are available for debt service. The ratio indicates the proportion of debt a firm can pay off from annually generated funds.

A firm's long-term solvency depends on its ability to generate profits. *Operating income/sales* provides a measure of a firm's profitability. As that measure excludes the effects of capital structure and tax position, it makes all firms comparable.

b. *EBIT/interest* expense rose from 3.46 to 5.65 from 1999 to 2003. Exhibit 18-4 shows median ratios of 6.1 for an A rating and 3.7 for a BBB rating. Thus, based on this ratio, Alpine would now receive an A rating.

Exhibit 18-4 shows a 33.9% *long-term debt/capital* ratio for the A rating and 42.5% for the BBB rating. Alpine's ratio rose from 28% in 1999 to 44% in 2003, implying a BBB rating.

Funds from operations/total debt declined considerably from 1999. However, the current level of more than 50% approximate the 55.4 ratio required for an AA rating.

Operating income/sales in the 12-14% range falls between the BB and B ratings that show ratios of 15.9% and 11.9% respectively.

The four ratios together (A, BBB, AA, and BB/B) suggest an appropriate rating of slightly better than BBB. While two ratios are higher, operating income/sales is very low. As profitability is the ultimate determinant of financing health, that ratio should probably received greater weight.

c. Alpine is paying 100 basis points more than US Treasury Notes, equivalent to what a BBB-rated firm is paying. As Alpine's ratings are slightly better than BBB, the Alpine bond should trade at a smaller spread. O'Flaherty should recommend the Alpine Chemical bond for purchase. Before doing so, however, O'Flaherty should examine the reasons for the low ratio of operating income to sales and ensure that the low ratio does not indicate operating weakness that is likely to impair Alpine's ability to pay future bond interest and principal.

10.{M}a. **Interest Coverage** = EBIT/interest = $4,450/$942 = **4.72**

Leverage = Long-term debt/equity = $10,000/$33,460=**0.30**

Current ratio = Current assets/current liabilities
= $4,735/$4,500 = **1.05**

b. The ratios imply an A rating. Interest coverage and the current ratio are within the A rating ranges whereas Leverage is at the border of A and AA. The 55 bps premium is slightly higher than the 50 bps implied by the A rating.

c. The effect of the three items on the ratio components is presented below.

$thousands	Reported	Adjusted for			Adjusted
		Affiliate guarantee	A/R sale	Lease	
Current assets	$4,735		$500		**$5,235**
Current liabilities	4,500		500	$ 386[1]	**5,386**
Long-term debt	10,000	$995		5,758[2]	**16,753**
Interest expense	942		40[3]	614[1]	**1,596**
EBIT	4,450		40[3]	0[4]	**4,490**

1 Interest expense = 10% x $6,144 = $614. The current portion of the capitalized lease is $386, equal to the $1,000 payment less the portion that is the interest expense.

2 Effect on long-term debt equals total debt less current portion = $6,144 - $386.

3   Assumes that Montrose recognized $40 million discount as loss on sale of receivables.

4 Because the lease is new, fiscal 2001 expense does not include the lease payment. Therefore EBIT is unchanged.

The adjusted ratios are:

Interest coverage = EBIT/interest = $4,490/$1,596 = **2.81**

Leverage = Long-term debt/equity = $16,753/$33,460 = **0.50**

Current ratio = Current assets/current liabilities
= $5,235/$5,386 = **0.97**

d. The adjusted ratios fall into the following ratings categories:
Interest coverage: BB
Long term debt/equity: BBB/BB
Current ratio   BBB

The overall rating should be between BB and BBB.

Smith is not being compensated for its credit risk as the adjusted ratios imply a rating of BBB/BB and a risk premium of 100 - 125 basis points.

Chapter 19 - Solutions

Overview:

Problem Length	*Problem #'s*
{S}	1, 2, 15,16,17
{M}	3,4,5, 7, 10,11,12, 14
{L}	6, 8, 9, 13

1.{S}The models should give identical results. Using 2003 expected dividends of $4.50, a discount rate r of 20%, and growth rate g of 15%, we find that:

$$P = \frac{D}{r-g} = \frac{\$4.50}{.20-.15} = \$90$$

The dividend payout ratio for both 2002 ($4.05/$10.03 = 40.4%) and 2003 ($4.50/$11.40 = 39.5%) is approximately 40%. The long term growth rates for earnings and dividends differ. This is possible only if the payout rate will change over time. Thus, in an earnings-based model using the earnings growth rate of 14%, we must use another (higher than 40%) estimate for the payout ratio. A payout ratio of 47.5% would result in the same valuation:

$$P = \frac{kE}{r-g} = \frac{(.475)(\$11.40)}{.20-.14} = \$90$$

Based on these models, Emfil shares are not attractive at a price of $115, and should not be added to the portfolio.

2.{S}a.

$$P = \frac{E}{r}$$

$$\frac{P}{E} = \frac{1}{r}$$

$$r = \frac{1}{P/E}$$

For a firm with a P/E ratio of 12

$r = 8.25\%$

b. (i) The increase of $3 is transitory. The market is saying that the price/earnings ratio should reflect only the "normal" earnings of $10 per share.

(ii) The increase of $3 is permanent and earnings in the future are expected to remain at $13. The market value is based on $13 per share of normal earnings.

(iii) The increase of $3 implies not only permanence but growth as future earnings are expected to increase above the present level of $13.

3.{M}a.   The P/E ratio with a dividend payout of k, discount
           rate of r and growth rate equal to g can be derived as:

$$P = \frac{kE(1+g)}{r-g} \quad and \quad \frac{P}{E} = \frac{k(1+g)}{r-g}$$

           For the Lo Company:

$$\frac{P}{E} = \frac{.2(\$1+.04)}{.10-.04} = 3.467$$

   b.   Hi's P/E ratio must be identical to that of Lo (3.467)
          as both firms have the same market value and earnings.

   c.   Lo Company

		2001	2002	2003	2004	2005
1)	Earnings/share	$ 1.00	$ 1.04	$ 1.08	$ 1.12	$ 1.17
2)	Number of shares	1,000	1,000	1,000	1,000	1,000
3)	Net income	$1,000	$1,040	$1,082	$1,125	$1,170
4)	Dividends paid	200	208	216	225	234
5)	New investment	800	832	865	900	936
6)	Firm value at period end	3,467	3,605	3,750	3,900	4,056
7)	Price per share	3.47	3.61	3.75	3.90	4.06
8)	P/E ratio	3.467	3.467	3.467	3.467	3.467

Calculations:
1)   Given
2)   Since no new financing and no stock dividends or splits,
      shares must remain constant over time.
3)   Earnings per share x number of shares
4)   Dividends per share (given) x number of shares
5)   Net income - dividends paid
6)   (.2 x next year's income)/(.10-.04); 2005 value assumes
      that net income continues to grow at 4% rate.
7)   Firm value/number of shares
8)   Firm value/current year net income

Hi Company

	2001	2002	2003	2004	2005
1) Earnings/share	$ 1.00	$ 0.80	$ 0.64	$ 0.51	$ 0.41
2) Number of shares	1,000	1,300	1,690	2,197	2,856
3) Net income	$1,000	$1,040	$1,082	$1,125	$1,170
4) Dividends paid	1,000	1,040	1,082	1,125	1,170
5) New investment	800	832	865	900	936
6) New financing	800	832	865	900	936
7) Firm value at period end	3,467	3,605	3,750	3,900	4,056
8) Price/share before new issue	3.47	2.77	2.22	1.77	1.42
9) P/E ratio	3.467	3.467	3.467	3.467	3.467
10) Shares issued	300	390	507	659	857
11) Price/share at new issue	$ 2.67	$ 2.13	$ 1.71	$ 1.37	$ 1.09

Calculations based on issuance of shares at end of year:
1) Given
2) 2001 given; From 2001 on, previous year shares plus new shares issued
3) Earnings per share x number of shares
4) Dividends per share (given) x number of shares
5) Identical in amount to that computed for Lo Company
6) Equal to (5)
7) Identical to Lo Company [(.2 x next year's income)/(.10-.04)]; 2001 value assumes that net income continues to grow at 4% rate.
8) Firm value/number of shares
9) Firm value/current year net income

Since (number of shares + shares issued) x price per share at new issue = firm value; and
Shares issued x price per share at new issue = new financing, therefore:
10) shares issued = new financing/price per share at new issue
11) price per share at new issue = (firm value - new financing)/number of shares (item 2)

d.   The growth rate is 4% for net income, dividends, and firm value. For the Lo Company, EPS also grows at 4% since the number of shares is constant. The Hi Company, on the other hand, keeps issuing new shares. Therefore, although net income is growing, earnings per share declines. This problem demonstrates the effect of dividend policy on reported growth rates.

e.   The company's return on new investments is 5%.

Using the formula for growth,
        $g = (1-k)$ x ROE,

with k = 20% and g =4%, ROE = 5%.

Alternatively, using 2002 as an example, on the additional investment of $800 the company's income increases by $40 or 5%.

This return is lower than the required rate of return of 10%. Hence, the low P/E ratio. Both companies would be better off paying out all earnings as dividends and not making any new investments.

Firm value would then equal $1,000/.10 = $10,000

4.{M}a.   The EBO model defines value =

current book value + present value of abnormal earnings

To compare the situation of all dividends being paid
out versus one of only some dividends paid out we need
only compare the present value of abnormal earnings
since opening book value is identical.

If all income is paid out as dividends, then book value
will remain constant at $10,000 and income will stay at
$1000/year. With a dividend payout of 20% as in problem
3, income will grow at 4%.

	Dividends = 100%; no growth			Dividend payout=20%; Growth = 4%			
Year	Open Book Value	Income	**Abnormal Earnings**	Open Book Value	Income	Dividends	**Abnormal Earnings**
2000	$10,000	$1,000	**$0**	$10,000	$1,000	$200	**$0**
2001	10,000	1,000	**0**	10,800	1,040	208	**(40)**
2002	10,000	1,000	**0**	11,632	1,082	216	**(82)**
2003	10,000	1,000	**0**	12,497	1,125	225	**(125)**
2004	10,000	1,000	**0**	13,397	1,170	234	**(170)**
2005	10,000	1,000	**0**	14,333	1,217	243	**(217)**

Reinvesting some income results in negative abnormal
earnings whereas 100% dividend payout results in
abnormal earnings = 0. Thus, it is clearly preferable
to pay out all earnings as dividends.

When all income is paid out as dividends, the value of
the firm will equal the opening book value of $10,000
(the same as in problem 3) since the present value of
the abnormal earnings is zero.

b. The pattern of income and dividends will be identical as these are independent of book value. Abnormal earnings, however, will differ.

(i) Open Book Value = $9,000

Dividends = 100%; no growth   *Dividend payout=20%; Growth = 4%*

Year	Open Book Value	Income	**Abnormal Earnings**	Open Book Value	Income	Dividends	**Abnormal Earnings**
2000	$9,000	$1,000	**$100**	$9,000	$1,000	$200	**$100**
2001	9,000	1,000	**100**	9,800	1,040	208	**60**
2002	9,000	1,000	**100**	10,632	1,082	216	**18**
2003	9,000	1,000	**100**	11,497	1,125	225	**(25)**
2004	9,000	1,000	**100**	12,397	1,170	234	**(70)**
2005	9,000	1,000	**100**	13,333	1,217	243	**(117)**

Here again, abnormal earnings for the 100% payout is greater (or equal) to abnormal earnings for the 20% payout. Hence, all income should be paid out as dividends. Note that for 100% payout, abnormal earnings are a perpetuity of $100. Therefore their present value is $100/.1 = $1,000 and

value =   current book value + present value of abnormal earnings
      = $9,000 + $1,000 = $10,000 as before

(ii) Open Book Value = $11,000

Dividends = 100%; no Growth   *Dividend payout=20%; Growth = 4%*

Year	Open Book Value	Income	**Abnormal Earnings**	Open Book Value	Income	Dividends	**Abnormal Earnings**
2000	$11,000	$1,000	**$(100)**	$11,000	$1,000	$200	**$(100)**
2001	11,000	1,000	**(100)**	11,800	1,040	208	**(140)**
2002	11,000	1,000	**(100)**	12,632	1,082	216	**(182)**
2003	11,000	1,000	**(100)**	13,497	1,125	225	**(225)**
2004	11,000	1,000	**(100)**	14,397	1,170	234	**(270)**
2005	11,000	1,000	**(100)**	15,333	1,217	243	**(317)**

Once again, abnormal earnings for the 100% payout is greater (or equal) to abnormal earnings for the 20% payout. Hence, all income should be paid out as dividends. Note that for 100% payout, abnormal earnings are a perpetuity of ($100). Therefore their present value is ($100)/.1 = ($1000) and

value =   current book value + present value of abnormal earnings
      = $11,000 - $1,000   = $10,000 as before

5.{M}a. Cash flow before interest payments (i.e., free cash flow to the firm) is the same regardless of which bond is issued:

(in $ millions)	Conventional		Zero Coupon	
	2003	2004	2003	2004
EBIT	$ 20	$ 20	$ 20	$ 20
Taxes	(6)	(6)	(6)	(6)
Free cash flow	$ 14	$ 14	$ 14	$ 14

However cash flows reported in accordance with SFAS 95 differ:

(in $ million)	Conventional		Zero Coupon	
	2003	2004	2003	2004
Cash flow pre interest	$14.0	$14.0	$14.0	$14.00
Interest paid	(1.0)	(1.0)	---	---
Tax benefit	0.3	0.3	0.3	0.33
	$13.3	$13.3	$14.3	$14.33

The venture receives a tax benefit of 30% of interest expense in both cases because of the deductibility of interest expense.

b. For the conventional bond, bondholders will receive $1 million annually. The zero coupon bondholders will receive no cash interest. The after-tax interest paid by the firm is $0.7 million for the conventional bond, but a $0.3 million *inflow* for the zero coupon bond.

c. and d.

> The answers to parts a and b imply that the amount available for dividends is based on reported cash flows that depend on the form of the bond. This implication is incorrect. The "fallacy" is that, on January 1, 2005 the conventional bond will require a debt repayment of $10 million. The zero coupon bond, however, will require payment of $12.1 million. The extra $2.1 million[1] precludes the use of the "extra" cash flow for dividends. Focusing on the free cash flows, however, indicates that firm values are identical as long as their WACCs are equivalent.[2]

6.{L}a. g = (1 – dividend payout) x ROE

12% = (1 – k) x 20%

1 – k = .6

k = .4

Dividend payout ratio is 40%

b.   With a dividend payout ratio of 40 %, new investment (from equity) must be .6 x $30,000 = $18,000

Current interest expense of $5,000 at an interest rate of 10% implies debt of $50,000. At a growth rate of 12%; new investment from debt will equal .12 x $50,000 = $6,000. [Alternate calculation: interest expense used to calculate debt level; $5,600/.10 = $56,000.]

Total investment:
Replacement (depreciation) = $ 8,000
New investment =   24,000   ($18,000 + $6,000)
Total $32,000

---

[1]
$1 million for two years	=	$ 2.0 million
10% interest on first year's $1 million	=	.1
Total accrued interest at 1-1-2005		$ 2.1 million

[2] The relative WACCs are also a consideration as, after 2003, the zero coupon bond will result in higher debt. In most cases, the debt/equity ratio will rise.

c. *Cash Flow Statement*

	Current	Forecast
Net income	$30,000	$33,600
Depreciation	8,000	8,960
Cash from operations	$38,000	$42,560
Cash for investment	(32,000)	(35,840)
Cash for financing:		
New debt	6,000	6,720
Dividends paid	(12,000)	(13,440)
	$(6,000)	$(6,720)
Change in cash	0	0

Note: *this cash flow statement assumes no change in working capital accounts.*

d. *Free Cash Flow Calculation*

	Current	Forecast
Operating income	$ 35,000	$ 39,200
Depreciation	8,000	8,960
	$ 43,000	$ 48,160
Investment	(32,000)	(35,840)
Free cash flow	**$ 11,000**	**$ 12,320**
Financing cash flows:		
New debt	6,000	6,720
Interest paid	(5,000)	(5,600)
	$ 1,000	$ 1,120
Dividends paid	(12,000)	(13,440)
Financing cash flow*	**$(11,000)**	**$(12,320)**

*Remember that interest paid must be reclassified from operating to financing cash flow for purposes of valuation.

e. The value of the debt is:

($50,000 + $6,000) = $ 56,000

The value of the equity is:

$$\frac{\$12,000 \times (1.12)}{.15 - .12} = \frac{\$13,440}{.03} = \underline{448,000}$$

Value of the firm is: $\underline{\$504,000}$

Check: WACC=($56,000/$504,000)(.10) + ($448,000/$504,000)(.15) = .14444

[FCF(1+g)]/(WACC−g)=[$11,000(1.12)]/(.14444−.12)=$12,320/.02444=$504,000

7.{M}(i) When the opening book value is $168,000, then forecasted net income of $33,600 yields an ROE of 20%. This amount is equal to the return assumed for new investment opportunities and the ROE in any year (see table below) is consistent with that long term rate of return.

Year	Open Book Value	Net Income grows by 12%	.15 x Open Book Value	Abnormal Earnings	ROE = Net Income / Open Book Value
1	$168,000	$33,600	$25,200	$ 8,400	20%
2	188,160	37,632	28,224	9,408	20%
3	210,739	42,148	31,611	10,537	20%
4	236,028	47,206	35,404	11,801	20%
5	264,351	52,870	39,653	13,218	20%

In this case all factors, net income, book value and abnormal earnings grow by 12%. Therefore in an EBO framework the valuation is straightforward and equal to

$$EBO \text{ Valuation} = B_0 + \frac{(ROE - r)}{r - g} B_0 = \$168,000 + \frac{.20 - .15}{.15 - .12} \$168,000 = \$448,000$$

identical to the amount obtained in problem 6.

(ii) When the opening book value is $212,000 then the (accounting) ROE will not immediately equal 20% but will converge towards that amount over time as the table below indicates. Were we to extend this table and apply the EBO valuation we would obtain the $448,000 as above.

Year	Open Book Value	Net Income grows by 12%	.15 x Open Book Value	Abnormal Earnings	ROE = Net Income / Open Book Value
1	$212,000	$33,600	$31,800	$ 1,800	15.8%
2	232,160	37,632	34,824	2,808	16.2%
3	254,739	42,148	38,211	3,937	16.5%
4	280,028	47,206	42,004	5,201	16.9%
5	308,351	52,870	46,253	6,618	17.1%
6	340,073	59,215	51,011	8,204	17.4%
7	375,602	66,320	56,340	9,980	17.7%
8	415,394	74,279	62,309	11,970	17.9%
9	459,962	83,192	68,994	14,198	18.1%
10	509,877	93,175	76,482	16,694	18.3%

As extending the table indefinitely is not feasible (or desirable),[3] we make use of the following formula (presented in Appendix 19-B on the CD and website) to estimate value.

$$P_0 = B_0 + \sum_{j=1}^{T} \frac{\left(ROE_j - r\right)B_{j-1}}{\left(1+r\right)^j} + \left\{ \frac{B_{T-1}}{\left(1+r\right)^T} \left[\frac{\left(ROE_T - \overline{ROE}\right)c}{1+r-c(1+g)} + \frac{\left(\overline{ROE}-r\right)}{r-g} \right] \right\}$$

The formula makes explicit forecasts of abnormal earnings for a number of years (in our case we use 5 years) and then estimates (discounted aggregate) abnormal earnings after that based on the rate of convergence of ROE_t to the long-run rate of return. The rate of convergence c, is based on the following relationship (see text page 1103)

$$ROE_t = \overline{ROE} + c(ROE_{t-1} - \overline{ROE})$$

where $\overline{ROE}$ is the long-run ROE and equals 20% in our case. After 5 periods ROE_T = 17.1% and ROE_{T-1} = 16.9%; B_{T-1} = \$308,351

Therefore ROE_6 = 20% + c(ROE_5 - 20%)

                  17.1% = 20% + c(16.9% - 20%)

Thus, c is approximately equal to .9. Substituting in the valuation formula yields.

$$P_0 = 212000 + \frac{1800}{1.15} + \frac{2808}{1.15^2} + \frac{3937}{1.15^3} + \frac{5201}{1.15^4} + \frac{6618}{1.15^5} + \left\{ \frac{308351}{\left(1.15\right)^5} \left[\frac{(.171-.20).9}{1.15-.9(1+.12)} + \frac{\left(.20-.15\right)}{.15-.12} \right] \right\}$$

P_0 = **\$451,021**

This amount differs from the \$448,000 computed in part (i) by approximately one-half percent.

---

[3] This does not mean that the EBO model does not work as well as the DCF models. First, we picked a "poor" starting point for book value. In part (i) the EBO model was as efficient as the DCF models. More important, in this example we assume that abnormal earnings opportunities are available indefinitely (to infinity). The advantages of the EBO model are in those (more realistic) situations where equilibrium conditions result in abnormal earnings dissipating and convergence to steady-state is quicker.

8.{L}a. From problem 6 we have $6,000 of new investment financed by debt. The present value factor for 5 years at 10% is 3.79 yielding lease payments of:

$$\frac{\$6,000}{3.79} = \$1,583 \text{ per year}$$

b. The difference between the two forecast statements is in the selling and interest expense categories. We begin by disaggregating these items from the current and forecast income statements of problem 5:

Selling Expense:

	Current	12% Increase	Forecast
Depreciation	$ 8,000	$ 960	$ 8,960
Other	17,000	2,040	19,040
Total	$25,000	$ 3,000	$28,000

Interest Expense	$ 5,000	$ 600	$ 5,600

The new investment of $24,000 increases depreciation by $960. With $6,000 of the new investment as a lease, the additional depreciation (on the remaining $18,000) is only $720.

Reconciliation for operating lease:

Selling Expense:

	Current	Increase	Forecast
Depreciation	$ 8,000	$ 720	$ 8,720
Other	17,000	2,040	19,040
Rent expense			1,583
Total			$29,343

The difference of $1,343 ($29,343 - $28,000) between selling expense for the operating lease method and that for Problem 6 is due to $1,583 rent expense replacing $240 of depreciation.

Interest Expense: The $600 difference between the two methods represents the interest expense on the leased asset. Under the operating expense all payments are included in selling expense.

Reconciliation for capital lease:

Selling Expense:

	Current	Increase	Forecast
Depreciation	$ 8,000	$ 720	$ 8,720
Other	17,000	2,040	19,040
Amortization of leased asset			1,200
Total			$28,960

The $1,200 amortization of leased assets replaces $240 of depreciation, increasing selling expense by $960 ($28,960 - $28,000) as compared with the problem 6 forecast. Note that amortization is not equal to depreciation because the leased assets must be amortized over the (5 year) lease term unless there is a bargain purchase option.

Interest Expense: is the same as interest on the capital lease equals interest on the debt that it replaces.

c. Before presenting the cash flow statements, we discuss the cash flow consequences of the lease.

Increased cash outflow to lessors: The lease requires annual outlays of $1583, all charged to cash from operations for the operating lease. [$600 is interest and the remaining $983 is principal repayment for the capital lease]. In the problem 5 scenario, only $600 in interest is paid.

Decrease in replacement cost: Our example assumes that depreciation equals replacement cost for acquired assets. When some assets are leased, this equality no longer holds as depreciation is reduced by $240. However, leased assets "used up" must still be replaced. We assume that such replacement is effected through additional leases.

To maintain similar levels of debt and equity the company must obtain additional cash of $743 ($983 - $240) each year by borrowing.

Cash Flow Statement, Operating Lease:

	Current	Forecast
Net income	$30,000	$32,857
Depreciation	8,000	8,720
Cash from operations	$38,000	$41,577
Cash for investment	(26,000)	(28,880)
Cash for financing:		
Dividends paid	(12,000)	(13,440)
New debt	---	743
Total	(12,000)	(12,697)
Change in cash	0	0

Lease payments are included in cash from operations. The "acquisition" of the leased asset, however, is ignored in the statement of cash flows.

d. *Cash Flow Statement, Capital Lease:*

	Current	Forecast
Net income	$ 30,000	$ 32,640
Depreciation/amortization	8,000	9,920
Cash from operations	$ 38,000	$ 42,560
Cash for investment	(26,000)	(28,880)
Cash for financing:		
Dividends paid	(12,000)	(13,440)
Debt repayment (lease)		(983)
New debt	---	743
Total	$(12,000)	$(13,680)
Change in cash	0	0

Principal payments for the leased assets are included in cash for financing but the interest payment is part of cash from operations. The actual acquisition of the leased assets is not shown directly in the cash flow statement. Rather, it is disclosed as a "significant noncash investment and financing activity."

e.   *Free Cash Flow Calculation*

Based on reported cash flows alone, free cash flow (after removing interest) appears to be:

	Current	Forecast Year Operating	Forecast Year Capital
Operating income	$35,000	$37,857	$38,240
Depreciation	8,000	8,720	9,920
Cash from operations	$43,000	$46,577	$48,160
Cash for investment	(26,000)	(28,880)	(28,880)
Reported free cash flow	$17,000	$17,697	$19,280

However, economically, these cases are identical to the problem 6 case, where free cash flow is $12,320 (6-D). The only difference from that case is that the LZ company has leased assets rather than purchasing them, and two different accounting methods are used to account for the lease.

To obtain this result, we must adjust reported free cash flow by treating leases as investment and financing activities:

	Current	Forecast Year Operating	Forecast Year Capital
Reported free cash flow	$17,000	$17,697	$19,280
Rent expense	---	1,583	---
Acquisition of leased assets	(6,000)	(6,960)	(6,960)
Free cash flow	$11,000	$12,320	$12,320

For the forecast year, leased assets acquired = $6720 + $240. The first component is 12% above the current year amount, reflecting the assumed 12% growth rate. The second component is required to replace "used up" assets (see Part c).

Free cash flows are identical to those of problem 6.

f.   The solutions will be identical to problem 5e as the leases are another form of investment and debt and should be so treated in any valuation model.

g.   Leases should not affect a valuation model as long as appropriate analytic adjustments are made. Leases are a form of investment and debt and their substitution should not affect valuation.

9.{L}a.

Common Size Statements for 1999-2001

	1999	2000	2001
Sales	100.0%	100.0%	100.0%
Cost of goods sold	-40.0%	-42.0%	-38.0%
Gross margin	60.0%	58.0%	62.0%
Selling and administrative	-15.0%	-14.7%	-18.2%
Depreciation expense	-11.3%	-12.2%	-16.8%
Operating income	33.8%	31.1%	27.0%
Interest expense	-10.0%	-10.4%	-13.2%
Pretax income	23.8%	20.7%	13.8%
Income tax expense	-8.3%	-7.2%	-4.8%
Net income	15.4%	13.5%	9.0%

b. The forecasted financial statements are presented in Exhibits 19S-1(a)-(c). The discussion below outlines the procedure used in generating these forecasts. It should be noted that the forecasting procedure, by definition, requires certain assumptions. The ones we make are not the only ones possible; other (reasonable) assumptions will result in different forecasts.

▪ **We begin with the income statement [Exhibit 19S-1(a)]**

Sales, COGS, and *selling & administrative expenses* have been "given" in problem as:

- *Sales* **= $404.8 (15% growth)**
- *COGS* **= $161.9 (40% of sales)**
- *Selling & administrative* **expense = $66.0 (3% growth)**

Forecasting depreciation and interest expense requires forecasts of (gross) fixed assets and long-term debt, respectively. As discussed below (re balance sheet), gross fixed assets are determined to be $1,297. Since the firm depreciates its assets over 23 years, we arrive at

Depreciation expense = $1,297/23 = $56

Similarly, as we assume an additional $10 of borrowings (see discussion below re cash flow statement), *interest expense* increases to $47.6 (8% of $595).

Income tax expense is equal to 35% of pretax income, thus completing the income statement.

Exhibit 19S-1(a) Forecasted Income Statement 2002

	1999	2000	2001	Forecast 2002	Forecast Comments
Sales	$400.0	$440.0	$352.0	$404.8	15% growth
Cost of goods sold	(160.0)	(184.8)	(133.8)	(161.9)	40% of sales
Gross margin	$240.0	$255.2	$218.2	$242.9	
Selling & administrative	(60.0)	(64.7)	(64.0)	(66.0)	3% growth
Depreciation expense	(45.0)	(53.8)	(59.3)	(56.0)	23 year life
Operating income	$135.0	$136.7	$ 94.9	$120.9	
Interest expense	(40.0)	(45.6)	(46.4)	(47.6)	8% of debt
Pretax income	$ 95.0	$ 91.1	$ 48.5	$ 73.3	
Income tax expense	(33.3)	(31.9)	(17.0)	(25.7)	35% tax rate
Net income	$ 61.8	$ 59.2	$ 31.5	$ 47.6	

Exhibit 19S-1(b) Forecasted Balance Sheet 2002

	1999	2000	2001	Forecast 2002	Forecast Comments
Assets					
Cash	$ 33.4	$ 26.3	$ 31.3	$ 32.9	See SoCF
Accounts receivable	66.7	73.3	73.3	84.3	T/O = 4.8
Inventories	26.7	30.8	27.9	33.7	T/O = 4.8
Fixed assets	900.0	1,000.0	1,020.0	1,040.0	T/O =.4
Total assets	$1,026.7	$1,130.4	$1,152.5	$1,190.9	
Liabilities and equity					
Accounts payable	$ 20.0	$ 23.1	$ 16.7	$ 20.2	T/O = 8
Accrued liabilities	6.7	7.7	5.6	6.7	T/O = 24
Long-term debt	500.0	570.0	585.0	595.0	See SoCF
Stockholders' equity	500.0	529.6	545.2	569.0	
Liabilities & equity	$1,026.7	$1,130.4	$1,152.5	$1,190.9	

Exhibit 19S-1(c) Forecasted Statement of Cash Flows 2002

	1999	2000	2001	Forecast 2002	Forecast Comments
Net income	$ 61.8	$ 59.2	$31.3	$ 47.6	from I/S
Depreciation expense	45.0	53.8	59.3	56.0	from I/S
Δ Accounts receivable	(7.0)	(6.7)	--	(11.0)	from B/S
Δ Inventories	(6.0)	(4.1)	2.9	(5.8)	from B/S
Δ Accounts payable	5.0	3.1	(6.4)	3.5	from B/S
Δ Accrued liabilities	2.0	1.0	(2.1)	1.1	from B/S
Cash from operations	$100.8	$106.3	$85.0	$ 91.4	
Capital expenditures	(100.0)	(153.8)	(79.3)	(76.0)	see discussion
Cash for investment	$(100.0)	$(153.8)	$(79.3)	$(76.0)	
Δ Long-term debt	30.0	70.0	15.0	10.0	see discussion
Dividends	(30.9)	(29.6)	(15.8)	(23.8)	50% payout
Cash for financing	$ (0.9)	$ 40.4	$(0.6)	$(13.8)	
Change in cash	(0.1)	(5.9)	5.1	1.6	
Free cash flow	0.8	(47.5)	5.7	15.4	

- **We turn now to the balance sheet [Exhibit 19S-1(b)]**

The problem states that "other financial statement relationships (ratios) are unchanged from 2001". This requirement is not as straightforward as it sounds given the cyclical nature of the Beta company as we shall see when we discuss fixed assets.

Accounts receivable and inventory: For 2001, the company had turnover ratios of 4.8. The 2002 forecast is therefore

> **Accounts receivable = $404.8/4.8 = $84.3 and**
> **Inventory   = $161.9/4.8 = $33.7**

Similarly, *accounts payable* and *accrued liabilities* are respectively 1/8 and 1/24 of cost of goods sold for both 2000 and 2001. The 2002 forecasts are therefore

> **Accounts payable   = $161.9/8 = $20.2 and**
> **Accrued liabilities = $161.9/24 = $ 6.7**

Turning to fixed assets, the sales to net fixed assets ratio has been .44, .44 and .35 in the years 1999 – 2001. Given the nature of fixed assets, the company could not reduce its investment in these assets during the cyclical downturn (in 2001), as the company requires those assets to maintain its operating capacity. It did, however, cut its capital expenditures by approximately 50% -- (most of the expenditures ($51 out of $71) were to maintain current capacity, if we assume depreciation is a rough approximation of economic depreciation).

For 2002, as the company is coming out of the cyclical downturn, we forecast a similar pattern of behavior. Setting a sales to net fixed assets ratio equal to .39 (between the low of .35 and the "normal" ratio of .44) results in

***Net fixed assets* = $404.8/.39 = $1,040 (rounded).**

Having determined net assets we can now determine gross fixed assets by solving the following equation.

Net fixed assets =
        Gross fixed assets – accumulated depreciation

Since *accumulated depreciation =*
                $201 + (gross fixed assets/23)

and *net fixed assets = $1,040*

***Gross fixed assets* = $1,297; *depreciation* = $56 and *accumulated depreciation* = $257**

Since the company has a 50% dividend payout ratio, *stockholders' equity* increases by 50% of net income.

***Stockholders' equity* = $545.2 + (½ x $47.6) = $569.0**

That leaves *long-term debt* and *cash*; forecasting one determines the other. As discussed below, we assume $10 of new borrowings bringing long-term debt to $595. *Cash*, per the statement of cash flows, increased by $1.6 from $31.3 to $32.9.

- ## Statement of cash flows [Exhibit 19S-1(c)]

The statement of cash flows is straightforward. *Net income* and *depreciation* are taken from the forecasted income statement (Exhibit 19S-1(a)). The *changes in the working capital accounts* reflect the balance sheet changes (Exhibit 19S-1(b)) for these items.

Capital expenditures equals the change in gross fixed assets; i.e. $1,297 - $1,221 = $76.

Dividends equal ½ of income = ½ x $47.6 = $23.8

Without any additional borrowings the change in cash would be $(8.4) and the cash balance $23, considerably lower than for any of the prior years. **Borrowings** are assumed to be $10 to bring the cash balance to levels of previous years. Thus, having set borrowings to $10 the resultant change in cash is $1.6.

c. (i) and (ii)
In the discussion to follow, for both parts (i) and (ii), we assume that the change in sales only affects sales, gross margin, and the working capital accounts related to sales and COGS. That is, we assume that selling expenses will still show an increase of 3% over the previous year. PP&E and capital expenditures will remain unchanged from our assumption in parts a. and b.

As a result of the 5% increase/decrease in sales, gross margins will increase/decrease by 3% (60% x 5%) from amounts calculated in parts a. and b. The effect on pretax income however, will be larger than 5% due to operating and financial leverage (see Chapter 4) as a substantial portion of Beta's expenses are fixed in nature (selling and administrative, depreciation and interest costs).

Cash from operations will increase/decrease in similar fashion to income. The changes, however, will be somewhat mitigated by changes in the working capital accounts; e.g. increased sales will increase CFO, but increased sales will require increased investment in working capital thus offsetting some of the increase in CFO.

At present, debt has been set at $10. An increase (decrease) in sales will increase (decrease) in equity and at the same time require less (more) borrowing The result will be an improvement (deterioration) in the debt/equity ratio.

10.{L}a.   *Statement of Cash Flows*
Net income $19,200
Depreciation   8,500
                                                 $27,700

Changes in operating accounts:
Accounts receivable   (500)
Accounts payable   500
   Cash from operations $27,700

Cash for investment:
  Fixed assets   (9,000)
Cash for financing:
  Dividends paid   (16,700)

Change in cash $ 2,000

To estimate free cash flow we assume that the increase
in cash of $2,000 is needed for operations, not held as
"excess" cash by the firm. After reclassifying interest
expense (after tax) from cash from operations to cash
for financing:

Operating income (net of tax) $ 21,000
Depreciation   8,500
   Funds from operations $ 29,500

Changes in operating accounts:
  Cash $ (2000)
  Accounts receivable   (500)
  Accounts payable   500
                                              (2,000)
Adjusted cash from operations $ 27,500

Cash for investment: (9,000)
   Free cash flow   **$ 18,500**

Cash for financing:
  Interest (net of tax)   (1,800)
  Dividends paid   (16,700)
  Total $(18,500)

b.   Begin by estimating the fixed and variable cost
      components of the income statement. We use the method
      shown in Appendix 4-A and the equation:

Fixed costs = total costs - (variable cost % x sales)

COGS: Increase in cost of $3,000 for sales increase of
$10,000 implies variable cost percentage of 30% and
fixed costs of $20,000.

Selling and General: Increase of $2,000 for sales
increase of $10,000 implies variable cost percentage of
20% and fixed selling and general costs of 0.

If fixed selling costs are 0, $8,500 of depreciation
must be included in cost of goods sold. To complete the
forecast of operating income we must forecast
depreciation expense.

Estimating Fixed Asset Investments and Depreciation:

Average fixed asset turnover ratio for 2001 and 2002 is
     Using gross assets   1.06
     Using net assets   1.70

Our forecast should maintain these ratios and also be
consistent with depreciation expense of 8%-9% of gross
fixed assets (implying an average life of about 12
years). That forecast is:

	2003	*2004*	*2005*
Sales	$150,000	$180,000	$200,000
Fixed assets (gross)	140,000	170,000	190,000
Accumulated depreciation	(52,500)	(66,500)	(81,500)
Fixed assets (net)	$ 87,500	$103,500	$108,500

As 2002 accumulated depreciation was $(41,000), we can
derive depreciation expense from the annual change in
accumulated depreciation (assuming no retirement of
fixed assets):

	2003	*2004*	*2005*
Depreciation expense	$ 11,500	$ 14,000	$ 15,000

These estimates yield the following turnover ratios
(consistent with the historical pattern):

	2003	2004	2005
Fixed assets (gross)	1.07	1.06	1.05
Fixed assets (net)	1.71	1.74	1.84
and depreciation rates of	8.2%	8.2%	7.9%

These estimates allow us to forecast (pre- and
posttax) operating income:

	2003	2004	2005
Sales	$150,000	$180,000	$200,000
Cost of goods sold	(68,000)	(79,500)	(86,500)
Selling and general	(30,000)	(36,000)	(40,000)
Operating income	$ 52,000	$ 64,500	$ 73,500
Operating income (after 40% tax)	$ 31,200	$ 38,700	$ 44,100

To complete the income statement we need to estimate the
firm's interest expense.

Forecast of borrowing needs and interest expense:

Turnover ratios for current operating accounts are:

        Cash   10
        Accounts receivable   12
        Inventory   8.5
        Accounts payable   6

These turnover ratios imply the following working
capital accounts, based on the sales and cost of goods
sold figures determined earlier:

	2003	2004	2005
Cash	$ 15,000	$18,000	$ 20,000
Accounts receivable	12,500	14,500	16,500
Inventory	7,500	9,000	10,000
Accounts payable	(11,500)	(13,500)	(14,500)
Operating working capital	$ 23,500	$28,000	$32,000

To estimate the company's borrowing needs, we
need the following additional assumptions:

(1) The present level of dividends ($16,700) will be maintained as funds are needed to finance expansion.

(2) Any cash needed will be borrowed. Excess cash will be used to repay debt.

(3) Although borrowing would most likely be done throughout the year, for simplification we assume that borrowings occur at year end.(This will also be relevant for valuation purposes.)

	2003	2004	2005
Opening balance of debt	$ 30,000	$ 49,300	$ 50,758
Interest expense (10%)	3,000	4,930	5,076
Net of tax (60%)	1,800	2,958	3,046
Operating income after tax	31,200	38,700	44,100
Depreciation expense	11,500	14,000	15,000
Change in operating w.c.	(6,500)	(4,500)	(4,000)
Cash from operations [before interest exp.]	$ 36,200	$ 48,200	$ 55,100
*Cash for investment and financing:			
Increased fixed assets (gross)	(37,000)	(30,000)	(20,000)
Dividends paid	(16,700)	(16,700)	(16,700)
Interest (net of tax)	(1,800)	(2,958)	(3,046)
Subtotal	$(55,500)	$(49,658)	$(39,746)
Borrowing (repayment) [Cash from operations less cash for investment and financing]	19,300	1,458	(15,354)
Closing balance of debt [Opening balance plus borrowing (less repayment)]	$ 49,300	$ 50,758	$ 35,404

Income statements and balance sheets follow:

	2003	2004	2005
Income Statement:			
Sales	$150,000	$180,000	$200,000
Cost of goods sold	(68,000)	(79,500)	(86,500)
Selling and general	(30,000)	(36,000)	(40,000)
Operating income	$ 52,000	$ 64,500	$ 73,500
Interest expense	(3,000)	(4,930)	(5,076)
Pretax income	$ 49,000	$ 59,570	$ 68,424
Tax expense	(19,600)	(23,828)	(27,370)
Net income	$ 29,400	$ 35,742	$ 41,054
Balance Sheet:			
Cash	$ 15,000	$ 18,000	$ 20,000
Accounts receivable	12,500	14,500	16,500
Inventory	7,500	9,000	10,000
Current assets	$ 35,000	$ 41,500	$ 46,500
Fixed assets (gross)	$140,000	$170,000	$190,000
Accumulated depreciation	(52,500)	(66,500)	(81,500)
Fixed assets (net)	$ 87,500	$103,500	$108,500
Total assets	$122,500	$145,000	$155,000
Accounts payable	$ 11,500	$ 13,500	$ 14,500
Debt	49,300	50,758	35,404
Stockholders' equity	61,700	80,742	105,096
Total liabilities & equity	$122,500	$145,000	$155,000

c.   Estimate of free cash flow:

	2003	2004	2005
Operating income after tax	$ 31,200	$ 38,700	$ 44,100
Depreciation	11,500	14,000	15,000
Change in operating w.c.	(6,500)	(4,500)	(4,000)
	$ 36,200	$ 48,200	$ 55,100
Increased fixed assets	(37,000)	(30,000)	(20,000)
Free cash flow	$ (800)	$ 18,200	$ 35,100
Cash for financing:			
Interest (net of tax)	(1,800)	(2,958)	(3,046)
Borrowing (repayment)	19,300	1,458	(15,354)
Dividends paid	(16,700)	(16,700)	(16,700)
Total	$ 800	$(18,200)	$(35,100)

d.   After 2005, the company will reach "steady state" and
maintain operations equal to that year. At that point,
it will not need new investments in fixed assets or
working capital. Cash for investments will be required
only for replacement. If we assume that depreciation
approximates replacement of assets we have the
following forecast:

	2006 and later
Operating income after tax	$44,100
Depreciation	15,000
Change in operating working capital	0
Cash from operations	$59,100
Increase in fixed assets	(15,000)
Free cash flow	$44,100

If we assume that all free cash flows are used to pay
interest and dividends:

	2006 and later
Cash for financing:	
Interest (net of tax)	$ (2,025)
Dividends paid	(42,075)
Total	$(44,100)

Dividends to equity shareholders are ($ thousands):

	2003	*2004*	*2005*	*2006 and later*
Dividends	16.7	16.7	16.7	42.1

Value of equity at end of 2005 = $\dfrac{\$42.1}{.15}$ = \$280.7

Value at end of 2002 = $\dfrac{\$16.7}{(1.15)}$ + $\dfrac{\$16.7}{(1.15)^2}$ + $\dfrac{\$16.7 + \$280.7}{(1.15)^3}$

$\qquad\qquad\qquad$ = \$222.7

As value of equity $\quad$ = \$222.7
and value of debt $\quad$ = $\underline{\quad 30.0}$
Value of firm $\qquad\quad$ \$252.7

Alternatively, the value of the firm can be determined using free cash flows:

($ thousands)	*2003*	*2004*	*2005*	*2006 and later*
Free cash flows	(.8)	18.2	35.1	44.1

We must first estimate WACC.
As the after tax cost of debt = .06:

$$WACC = \frac{\$222}{\$252} \, x\,.15 + \frac{\$30}{\$252} \, x\,.06 = .139$$

Value of firm at end of 2005 $\quad$ = $\dfrac{\$44.1}{.139}$ = \$316.6

Value at end of 2002 $\qquad$ = $\dfrac{\$(.8)}{(1.139)}$ + $\dfrac{\$18.2}{(1.139)^2}$ + $\dfrac{\$35.1 + \$316.6}{(1.139)^3}$

$\qquad\qquad\qquad$ = \$251.3

The slight discrepancy between the two answers (\$252.2 and \$251.3) is due mainly to rounding. In addition, since the amount of debt (relative to the value of equity) changes from period to period, the WACC changes also. We have ignored this refinement and used a constant WACC as the changes from period to period are slight.

11.{M}

$300 Charge Taken in 2000

	Open Book Value	Income Before Restruct.	Restruct. Charge	Net Income	.10xOpen Book Value	Abnormal Earnings
2001	$5,700	$1,050	0	$1,050	$570	$480
2002	6,750	1,100	0	1,100	675	425
2003	7,850	1,150	0	1,150	785	365

Book Value at end of 2003: $7,850 + $1,150 = $9,000

EBO Valuation =

B_{2000}	+ PV of Abnormal Earnings in Year 2001, 2002 and 2003
$5,700	+ $480/(1.1) + $425/(1.1)^2 + $365/(1.1)^3
$5,700	+ $1,062 **= $6,762**

$$B_{2000}$$
$$\$5{,}700 + \$480/(1.1) + \$425/(1.1)^2 + \$365/(1.1)^3$$
$$\$5{,}700 + \$1{,}062 = \mathbf{\$6{,}762}$$

Restructuring Charge Recognized Over Three Years

	Open Book Value	Income Before Restruct.	Restruct. Charge	Net Income	.10xOpen Book Value	Abnormal Earnings
2001	$6,000	$1,050	150	$ 900	$600	$300
2002	6,900	1,100	100	1,000	690	310
2003	7,900	1,150	50	1,100	790	310

Book Value at end of 2003: $7,900 + $1,100 = $9,000

EBO Valuation =

$$B_{2000} \quad + \text{PV of Abnormal Earnings in Year 2001, 2002 and 2003}$$
$$\$6{,}000 + \$300/(1.1) + \$310/(1.1)^2 + \$310/(1.1)^3$$
$$\$6{,}000 + \$762 = \mathbf{\$6{,}762}$$

This exercise shows that the EBO valuation is indifferent to accounting methods. Both yield a valuation of $6,762 at the end of 2000. The differences in open book value are offset by the differences in abnormal earnings.

b. (i) and (ii)
   When the valuation is done as at the beginning of 2000, the result is similar[4]. The EBO valuations are identical at $6,147.1. Abnormal earnings in years 2001-2003 are identical to those calculated in a; abnormal earnings for 2000, however, must be included in the calculations.

$300 Charge Taken in 2000

	Open Book Value	Income Before Restructuring	Restructuring Charge	Net Income	.10xOpen Book Value	Abnormal Earnings
2000	$5,000	$1,000	$300	$ 700	$500	$200
2001	5,700	1,050	0	1,050	570	480
2002	6,750	1,100	0	1,100	675	425
2003	7,850	1,150	0	1,150	785	365

EBO Valuation =
Open Book Value + PV of Abnormal Earnings in Year 2000 to 2003

$$= \text{Open Book Value} + \frac{\$200}{1.1} + \frac{\$480}{1.1^2} + \frac{\$425}{1.1^3} + \frac{\$365}{1.1^4}$$

$$= \$5,000 \quad + \$181.8 + \$396.7 + \$319.3 + \$249.3 = \mathbf{\$6,147.1}$$

---

[4] Note that the valuation calculated at the end of 2000 is 10% (the required rate of return) higher than the valuation calculated at the beginning of 2000; i.e. $6,761.8 = 1.1 x $6,147.1. An alternative way of viewing the problem is presented below:
   Choice 1 - **Immediate Writeoff**
      PV of abnormal earnings (2001 - 2003) = 1,062
      Discounted to beginning of year 2000 = 1062/1.1 = $ 965
      2000 abnormal earnings = 700 - 500 = 200
      Discounted to beginning of year 2000 = 200/1.1   =   182
      PV of abnormal earnings (2000 - 2003) $1,147
      Opening Book Value   5,000
                                                     $6,147
   Choice 2 - **Charge over 3 years**
      PV of abnormal earnings (2001 - 2003) = 762
      Discounted to beginning of year 2000 = 762/1.1 =   693
      2000 abnormal earnings = 1000 - 500 = 500
      Discounted to beginning of year 2000 = 500/1.1   =   454
      PV of abnormal earnings (2000 - 2003) $1,147
      Opening Book Value   5,000
                                                     $6,147

Restructuring Charge Recognized Over Three Years

	Open Book Value	Income Before Restructur.	Restructur. Charge	Net Income	.10xOpen Book Value	Abnormal Earnings
2000	$5,000	$1,000	0	$1,000	$500	$500
2001	6,000	1,050	150	900	600	300
2002	6,900	1,100	100	1,000	690	310
2003	7,900	1,150	50	1,100	790	310

EBO Valuation =
Open Book Value + PV of Abnormal Earnings in Year 2000 to 2003

$$= \text{Open Book Value} + \frac{\$500}{1.1} + \frac{\$300}{1.1^2} + \frac{\$310}{1.1^3} + \frac{\$310}{1.1^4}$$

$$= \quad \$5,000 \quad + \$454.5 + \$247.9 + \$232.9 + \$211.7 = \mathbf{\$6,147.1}$$

12.{S}a. Assuming that the market value of Kraft prior to the merger was "appropriate" the amount by which Philip Morris "overpaid" can be calculated (in $ millions) as:

Market value of Kraft prior to merger ($65 x 120)	$ 7,800
Amount paid for acquisition of Kraft ($90 x 12)	(10,800)
"Overpayment"	$(3,000)

On a per share basis, the overpayment should have decreased the market price of Philip Morris shares by:

$$\frac{\$3,000}{234} = \$12.80 \text{ per share}$$

The actual market price decrease of $4.50 was considerably less than the amount determined by the asset based approach.

b. The smaller decline in the price of Philip Morris shares suggests that the market expected synergistic effects from the merger that partly offset the "overpayment". Investors in Philip Morris may have believed that Kraft was "undermanaged" and that its profitability would be improved by Philip Morris management.

c. The problem in using any of the DCF models is predicting the effect of the acquisition on the parameters of the model.

(i) For example, the acquisition of Kraft would be expected to have no immediate effect on dividends paid to Philip Morris shareholders. The need to service the debt incurred to buy Kraft, however, might reduce the future growth rate of dividend payments, reducing their present value. The higher leverage of Philip Morris following the merger would also increase the required discount rate, further decreasing the stock price.

(ii) For an earnings-based model, the effect on current earnings (dilution) as well as the effect on the growth rate and discount rate, must be considered.

(iii) The Kraft acquisition reduces the free cash flow of Philip Morris initially. After tax interest expense of $770 million [11% x $10,800 x (1 - .35) exceeds the free cash flow of Kraft (estimated as CFO + interest - capital expenditures = $607 + $81 - $260). As in the other cases, the effect on the growth rate and discount rate must also be considered.

The advantage of the dividend model is that there is no effect on the current level of dividends; thus only the growth rate and discount rate effects must be estimated.

13.{S}
a.(i) From a theoretical perspective there are a number of problems with the price to cash flow ratio suggested by the article. The measure used, net income + depreciation + amortization, is equal to funds from operations (FFO), an incomplete measure of cash flow. It does not reflect changes in operating working capital accounts or other adjustments required to calculate CFO as defined by SFAS 95. FFO has been shown to have little or no explanatory power beyond that provided by net income.

The theoretical basis for a price to cash flow ratio is based on a free cash flow model. As noted in the chapter, free cash flow is considerably different from CFO, and is even more distant from FFO.

(ii) Notwithstanding the discussion above, the price to cash flow ratio may be a useful "filter," similar to the price to earnings ratio (PER). As noted in the chapter, the PER itself is predicated on the assumption that earnings is a useful surrogate for or predictor of cash flows to investors. Thus, the efficacy of both ratios depends to some extent on how well they can predict relevant variables of interest.

b. Although CFO as well as earnings can be effected by choice of accounting method, nevertheless CFO may be more useful than earnings as it is less subject to manipulation by the selection of accounting principles. On the other hand, CFO suffers from a conceptual limitation relevant to valuation in that it does not reflect the cost of asset replacement (whereas the depreciation component of earnings may approximate this cost). This limitation may be overcome if replacement cost is a constant proportion of cash flow. In this case, it will be imbedded in the price to cash flow ratio. Ultimately, however, the usefulness of the ratio should be tested empirically.

c. Norris' article provides two examples of how CFO can be manipulated. In one case (Enron), a *financing* cash inflow is treated as operations; in the other (Global Crossing) an operating outflow is classified as *investments*. Using free cash flows will only solve the problem associated with the "second" form of manipulation as free cash flows = operating less investment cash flows. Thus, it is irrelevant whether the cash flow is treated as operating or investing. However, the problems associated with the first form of manipulation is not solved with the price-to-free-cash-flow as (mis)classifying an operating (or investing) cash flow as financing will bias reported free cash flows.

14.{S}a. "Core earnings" attempts to take on some of the characteristics of each of the four definitions of income. However, ultimately it is not identical to any of them.

Although core earnings as defined by S&P excludes items such as asset sales, it differs from operating income as it includes interest income/expense. By including items that are abnormal in nature and size, such as restructuring charges, "core earnings" differs from both permanent and sustainable income. Finally, it is not equivalent to economic income as it excludes capital items and valuation adjustments that are part of economic earnings.

b. While no single amount can measure the performance of a complex organization, valuation models require precise inputs. The outputs (values) of such models are only as good as those inputs. Therefore users of valuation models must decide on a definition of earnings that is most likely to provide valuations that are useful for making investment decisions.

c. Reported earnings includes both permanent and transitory components. Permanent components are expected to persist, and help the analyst estimate the "earnings power" of the company, and ultimate the value of its securities. Transitory components have only dollar-for-dollar effects on valuation. Ideally, a core earnings measure should include all permanent earnings components, but exclude transitory ones.

d. To Whom It May Concern:

My major concern is related to the purpose and definition of core earnings. Whereas it may be true that analysts and investors are confused and frustrated by reported earnings, it is not clear that the Standard & Poor's definition of core earnings will produce better corporate ratings.

I believe that, if S&P ratings are to be useful measures of the risk of fixed income investments, they need to be based on an earnings measures that includes all operating components but excludes components that are transitory in nature.

The definition does not seem to have an underlying
and/or consistent definition of what should be included
and excluded from core earnings. For example, if the
objective is to exclude one time nonoperating items,
why are asset sales excluded whereas restructurings are
included? Similarly, what is the rationale for
including pension costs but not gains? Finally, why are
hedging gains and losses, which are sometimes critical
indicators of corporate risk management, excluded?

In conclusion, I urge you to reconsider your definition
of core earnings, based on a sound conceptual basis for
determining the adjustments to reported earnings.